BACK FROM THE FUTURE

BACK FROM THE FUTURE

CUBA UNDER CASTRO

SUSAN EVA ECKSTEIN

PRINCETON UNIVERSITY PRESS

PRINCETON, NEW JERSEY

Copyright © 1994 by Princeton University Press
Published by Princeton University Press, 41 William Street,
Princeton, New Jersey 08540
In the United Kingdom: Princeton University Press,
Chichester, West Sussex
All Rights Reserved

Library of Congress Cataloging-in-Publication Data

Eckstein, Susan, 1942–
Back from the future : Cuba under Castro /
Susan Eva Eckstein.
p.   cm.
Includes bibliographical references (p.   ) and index.

ISBN 0-691-03445-1 (cloth)
ISBN 0-691-02987-3 (paperback)
1. Communism—Cuba.   2. Cuba—Social policy.   3. Cuba—Economic
policy.   4. Cuba—Politics and government—1959–.   I. Title.
HX158.5.E35   1994
338.97291—dc20   93-45884   CIP

This book has been composed in Adobe Sabon

Princeton University Press books are printed
on acid-free paper and meet the guidelines for
permanence and durability of the Committee on
Production Guidelines for Book Longevity
of the Council on Library Resources

Second printing, and first paperback printing, 1995

Printed in the United States of America by Princeton Academic Press

10   9   8   7   6   5   4   3   2

To Michelle, Rachel, and Paul

WITH LOVE

CONTENTS

LIST OF TABLES

PREFACE

CUBA, A SMALL COUNTRY with a trade-dependent economy, withstood the domino collapse of Soviet Communist bloc states between 1989 and 1991, though not without tremendous economic, social, and political costs, and not without giving up much of what the Cuban revolution had stood for. But Fidel Castro's need to modify the country's course of development to external as well as domestic circumstances reflects the history of the revolution. After an initial period of radicalization, when Fidel Castro tried to create, from a Marxist perspective, a utopian communist society, he "retreated" and accommodated to conditions far short of that ideal. *Back from the Future*, as the title suggests, describes how and explains why the "retreat" occurred.

This book is a study of economic and social policy under Castro: not specifically of who makes policy and the personal motivations of policymakers but of contextual factors influencing policy choices and, above all, policy outcomes. Castro has learned all too well the limits to his ability to remake society as he would have liked, his charisma and centralized control of the economy and polity notwithstanding. Even policies inspired by the best of intentions, by lofty ideals, met up with obstacles.

Studies of Communism have presumed ideology to be a major policy determinant. Official discourse suggests this to be so. I will show, however, that even in the most seemingly ideologically inspired and driven periods, policy was grounded in governmental economic and political considerations as well. Policies accordingly have not been as irrational as critics claim. I also take issue with the view that Communist regimes are strong behemoth states. Castro and Cuban Communism have been circumscribed by global political and economic dynamics, by formal and informal state dynamics, and by forces in civil society. My work thus contributes to a revisionist interpretation of Cuban history under Castro and, implicitly, a revisionist view of state socialist dynamics elsewhere.

For three decades developments under Castro were shaped by Cold War politics. The Soviet Union, and to a lesser extent the former Communist countries of Eastern Europe, influenced island options. But so too did Western countries and global market conditions, even though Cold War politics typically blinded analysts from recognizing their importance.

Domestically, formal and informal state dynamics influenced policy choices and outcomes. Castro's personalistic style of rule and his consolidation of an oligarchically structured "vanguard party" and state apparatus did not free him from institutional considerations and institutional constraints. Over the years he had to address political, administrative, and economic concerns—as all governments must. As new problems arose and old problems were not resolved, Castro shifted his policy emphasis, sometimes dramatically, and often in ways that will be shown to be concealed at the ideological level.

Underestimated in Communist studies in general, including of Cuba, has been the role of ordinary people. Even though citizens were never entirely free to organize on their own or to express their points of view in any Communist Party–run regime, in none did they simply march to state orders. They have influenced policy implementation, if not policy formation, informally and indirectly: through, for example, foot-dragging, pilferage, desertion, black-market and sideline activity, absenteeism, and hoarding. They have done so in patterned ways shaped by their traditions and everyday experiences.

How the contextual factors have shaped policy-making and outcomes has varied over time. Neither society nor the state, or the global arena itself, are static entities. For this reason policies and their effects must be examined historically, which they are in the chapters that follow.

Totalitarian models of politics erred in incorrectly portraying Communist regimes as all-powerful and internally cohesive. They attributed too much importance to the role of Leninist parties and their leadership, and to the influence of the Marxist-Leninist ideology propagated.[1] They viewed formal politics too much as a force sui generis and took the political structures and ruling ideology at face value, to an extent that folk in those societies did not.

Interest-group analyses of Communist political systems corrected the monolithic view of Soviet-style states.[2] Such analyses highlighted how institutions under the "vanguard party" regimes developed and promoted their own corporate interests. Yet they too erred in presuming political forces to operate sui generis and in assuming ordinary people in civil society to be passive subjects of elite-determined decisions.

At the other extreme have been Marxist and non-Marxist studies of communism that ascribed too much weight to the role of societal forces. According to the "convergence school of thought," exigencies of industrialization and modern society propelled bureaucratism under capitalism and socialism alike, to the point that socialism and capitalism evolved similarly.[3]

Marxists, by contrast, have argued that class dynamics and distinctive dominant modes of production set socialist and capitalist societies apart.[4] While different class configurations influence policy options and responses to policies, governments are constrained, as argued above and illustrated in the book, by international and domestic political dynamics that are not reducible to "underlying" class relations. Moreover, societies actually combine features attributed, theoretically, to capitalism and socialism. For structurally explicable reasons, Castro drew on diverse mixes, at different times, of state and market features associated with what Max Weber would call ideal-typical socialist and capitalist societies, respectively—in both the externally and the domestically oriented economy.[5] With the crisis that followed the collapse of the Soviet bloc Castro even emphasized precapitalist practices.

Immanuel Wallerstein takes the analysis of capitalism to the global level.[6] Although post-World War II geopolitics led to the formation of two political, ideological, and trade blocs, he argues that the Soviet bloc was never self-contained. The weaker of the two blocs, it was subject to global capitalist dynamics. State influence over global and domestic relations depends, in his view, on the "position" of countries within, and mode of integration into, the world economy. The larger, more diverse, and more complex an economy, and the less dependent it is on trade in a commodity commanding weak earnings in international markets, the greater its strength and effectiveness. Yet his systemic global analysis belittles the importance of domestically rooted political dynamics on the one hand, and geopolitical and political forces not reducible to "underlying" economic forces at the international level on the other.

In Eastern Europe a revisionist perspective evolved in the 1980s that addressed deficiencies of the aforementioned approaches. Above all, in Hungary scholars began to examine specific institutional processes of state socialism before the collapse of Communist Party rule there.[7] They highlighted in different domains how institutional arrangements differed in market and state-centered economies, and they offered theoretical explanations for the differences. Some of their work also revealed spheres of social action operating semi-independently of the Communist Party and government, and the importance of informal along with formal organizational dynamics. These "institutionalists" pointed to the relative autonomy of society and to the capacity of social institutions to limit state power and action, while never losing sight of how institutions were shaped by the political-economic context in which they were embedded. My work shares this theoretical perspective. However, I assign greater weight to the global context in which institutions, including the state itself, are embedded.

To "tease out" as much as possible the impact that policies associated with the Cuban revolution have had, I compare, where possible, developments in Castro's Cuba both with prerevolutionary trends and with contemporary developments in other Latin American countries, countries that have shared somewhat similar historical and cultural experiences with Cuba. In domains where Cuba developed in distinctive ways under Castro, the revolution can be presumed to be of consequence.

In writing this book I relied mainly on primary and secondary source materials available in the United States. I also benefited from four visits to Cuba: one in the mid-1970s, and in 1991, 1992, and 1993. On these visits I had the opportunity to meet with a range of social scientists, government functionaries, and ordinary people. I tried to talk to a broad range of people, but I interviewed no representative sample of the population and my contacts, except on two visits, were confined to Havana. In Cuba I attained some materials unavailable in the States, and I gained a feeling for how Cubans experienced their country's revolution. The visits in the 1990s also familiarized me all too well with the devastating impact that the abrupt termination of "Communist solidarity" had on people's lives, and with how the government on the one hand, and the populace on the other, tried to deal with the crisis.

Available source materials are far from ideal. Cuba is not a politically open country, and only limited statistical and other documentary materials are made public (if they exist at all). And because the print media are state-owned and controlled, they tend to present an *oficialista*, officially approved, view of Cuba; even when information is accurate, coverage is selective. The situation, moreover, is made worse by the questionable reliability of certain data, and shifts over time in bases of data compilation.[8] Some statistics may be exaggerated because the bureaucrats who report information convey what they think their superiors want conveyed.[9] And problems are compounded by my effort to use data that allow for comparative as well as historical assessment. For these reasons the statistical data I cite should be viewed as rough estimates, not "hard facts."

Information became especially sparse with the crisis of the 1990s. Not only did the government then deliberately conceal information that it had made public for years, but employees of the state planning commission and statistical institutes were reassigned to other jobs to limit data collection. It is noteworthy that the government in the 1990s continued to release health statistics while it released hardly any economic data. Access to new materials might call for some modifications in my findings. However, I believe my analysis, in the main, will stand the test of time.

An understanding of Cuba (or any other country, for that matter) rests not merely on access to plentiful data, and data of high quality. Differences in opinion about the revolution's performance, and the rationale and rationality of state policy, are not the result of paltry data alone.[10] They reflect differences in interpretations of data as well. I remember a conference I attended where a Cuban and a Cuban-American presented papers on island demographic trends, a topic on which there *is* statistical information. The two speakers agreed on the "facts," on demographic trends, but had entirely contrasting explanations of these trends. The

Cuban attributed the island's low fertility rate, for example, to the government's family-planning facilities and to other accomplishments of the revolution; the Cuban-American to the failures of the revolution and to people's desire to reduce family size under the circumstances.

If contrasting views were reducible to data deficiencies, it would imply empirical reductionism and relieve scholars of interpretative responsibilities. But disagreements about developments in Castro's Cuba often derive from the a priori assumptions on which scholarly (and some not-so-scholarly) analyses have been based.

Differences in interpretations are often traceable to the conceptual lenses through which scholars have viewed Cuba: in particular, to the "level of anlaysis" whereby Cuban policies and trends have been examined. The Cuban economy is perceived differently from a macro- and microeconomic perspective, for example, as I will document.

Some differences in "levels of analyses" are tied to scholars' personal politics. Economic analyses by persons critical of the revolution tend to draw on neoclassical economic assumptions, while analyses by more sympathetic folk often are based on macro-level assumptions. To attribute different analyses to scholars' personal politics, however, would suggest political-ideological reductionism, as inadequate as empirical reductionism. (It would also, of course, anger many academics who believe themselves to be objective, value-free, and "above" politics!)

In recognizing the potential autonomy of forces operating at both the macro and micro levels, I am able to explain policies that otherwise seem irrational. What is good, for example, for enterprises and the populace (as income earners or spenders) is not necessarily good for the state. A government can implement policies that, in principle, are rational from its own vantage point, but not from that of enterprises (including state-owned enterprises) and individuals. And differences in the concerns and priorities of the three may undermine policy implementation. By way of illustration, market openings under socialism may enhance production that serves enterprise and individual interests while undermining the government's ability to control what is produced and the revenue thereby generated. Prohibition of private economic activity may accordingly make sense, in principle, from the vantage point of the state's "narrow" economic interests, even if output is sacrificed in the process.

This book covers the Castro era through 1993, but the main emphasis is on the latter 1970s through the early 1990s. In the first chapter, my thesis about the forces shaping policy-making and, above all, policy implementation is elaborated both in the abstract and with specific reference to Cuba. Given the importance of the state to policy initiatives, the evolution of the state under Castro is delineated, in turn. The chapter also includes a brief description of prerevolutionary Cuba and the movement that brought the Old Regime to its heels. To the extent that policy choices and outcomes are affected by historically grounded contextual factors, then prerevolutionary conditions can be expected to set parameters to the revolutionary transformation.

Chapters 2 through 4 address the different economic strategies Castro's government pursued between 1959 and 1993. They show how shifts in strategies were rooted in economic and political problems that policies in effect failed to resolve, because they generated unanticipated consequences. The rationale for the shifts will be shown, however, often to be concealed at the ideological level, for political reasons. Chapter 2 accounts for the official push for Marx's utopian communist state of societal development, where people would work for the collective good, not individual gain, and for the official "retreat" to socialism after 1970, a "retreat" involving the gradual reintroduction of contained market features and increased economic dealings with the West. Chapter 3 focuses on the so-called campaign to rectify errors and negative tendencies: the government's effort, in the latter 1980s, to clamp down on the private market activity it had come to tolerate and to reemphasize voluntary labor and "moral incentives" associated with the late 1960s' "push for communism," policies it had reined in for economic and political reasons. The seeming irrational policy shift, identified with a reemphasis on Marxism-Leninism and principles Ernesto "Ché" Guevara had stood for, moreover, defied Communist regime "liberalization" trends at the time. The government's renewed moral campaign will be shown to be partially rooted, ironic as it seems, in a growing hard currency crisis. The shift in state strategy will be shown to be rooted only secondarily in the ideology legitimating and officially inspiring the policy shift.

Chapter 4 describes the transition from "Communist solidarity" to Communist solitary: the crisis brought about by the collapse of the Soviet bloc and state efforts to respond to it. The so-called Special Period, designed to "save the revolution" and fend for "Socialism or Death," will be shown even more than in years past to incorporate initiatives more characteristic of, in Max Weber's sense, an ideal-typical capitalist than an ideal-typical socialist society. It even led, as noted, to a "retreat" to policies reminiscent of precapitalism. The chapter will also highlight how Castro's efforts to preserve the "best of socialism"—social welfare guarantees and planned development—have been sabotaged by state bureaucrats and ordinary people and not merely by the "new world order." Global and domestic forces combined contributed to a de facto withering away of the state, but not because Marx's utopian communist stage was reached.

Chapters 5 and 6 focus on social policies: on policies addressing health welfare and rural/urban inequities. Here Castro more effectively remade society. Yet the very social successes of the revolution will be shown to have compounded government problems.

In chapter 7, Cuba's overseas assistance programs are described. The widely held view in the United States that Cuba "went international" at the behest of the Soviet superpower proves to be misleading, as is the official reason given in Cuba—that internationalism was morally driven by a commitment to "socialist solidarity." Castro and his global ambitions are central to any understanding of Cuban internationalism, but both the success and the limitations of the overseas endeavors have been affected by global geopolitical and domestic economic and political conditions.

The final chapter puts the Cuban revolution and the Cuban experience under Communism in historical and comparative perspective. Empirical findings are summarized, and theoretical implications of the Cuban experience are delineated.

Back from the Future is the culmination of more than a decade and a half of (intermittent) work on Cuba. During this period I wrote numerous articles on Cuba, and I benefited both from discussions with informed people about Cuba and from critical readings of my work by colleagues. It is impossible to acknowledge all those who have heightened my understanding of the island's revolution. As best I can remember, the following people generously critiqued earlier articles that have directly or indirectly influenced this final product: Robert Alford, Claes Brundenius, Daniel Chirot, Carmen Diana Deere, Sergio Díaz-Briquéts, Jorge Domínguez, George Eckstein, Peter Evans, Julie Feinsilver, Lois Wolf Goodman, Walter Goldrank, Frances Hagopian, Shane Hunt, Terry Karl, James Kurth, Saul Landau, Daniel Levine, Kristen Luker, Carmelo Mesa-Lago, S. M. Miller, Pedro Monreal, James O'Connor, Alfred Padula, Jorge Pérez-López, Merifeli Pérez-Stable, Joseph Potter, Arthur MacEwan, James Malloy, James Scott, Theda Skocpol, Rosemary Taylor, Lois Wasserspring, and Peter Winn.

Walter Epstein, in his own special way, deserves mention. He was my summer conscience. Every August on Martha's Vineyard he would politely inquire about my work and point out to me that I repeatedly mentioned I was writing a book on Cuba. By the summer of 1993 I could finally tell him that my work would become his: he would soon have my book to read.

Certain people directly helped in the writing of the book. José Luis Rodríguez, through mid-1993 associate director of Cuba's Centro de Investigaciones de la Economía Mundial (and subsequently Minister of Finance), is one such person. CIEM graciously hosted my second trip to Cuba, and José Luis provided me with materials and detailed comments on my work over the years, far beyond the call of duty. José Luis, along with Elena Alvarez, Miguel Figueras, and Gerardo Trueba of Cuba, plus Andrew Zimbalist, Manuel Pastor, Eliana Cardoso, Ann Helwege, and I, together participated in a "working group" on the Cuban economy, financed by the Ford Foundation under the auspices of the Latin American Studies Association. The group met several times, both in Cuba and the States, in 1991 and 1992. The other Cuban participants as well as José Luis deepened my understanding of the revolution. Andrew Zimbalist has been helpful in other ways as well. I have benefited from the collaboration that went into a jointly authored article and from his comments on some other works of mine on Cuba, including an earlier draft of this book.

The book is the better for very detailed readings of earlier drafts also by Jeffery Paige, Frances Piven, John Walton, and Maurice Zeitlin. I am most appreciative of their time, their criticisms, their insights, their suggestions. They have been wonderful friends and colleagues. I have benefited from comments by some anonymous readers as well.

The book is the better thanks also to Roy Thomas's superb editing of my manuscript. It was a pleasure to work with him as well as with Mary Murrell at Princeton University Press.

In addition, I appreciate the many Cubans and foreigners living in Cuba who talked with me and shared their views of island developments over the years. Since I regard these conversations as confidential, the people must remain nameless. In writing the book I also benefited from discussions with Cuban-Americans.

In doing the work that culminated in this book I benefited, in turn, from many funding sources. My 1992 trip, which involved participation in a conference on inter-American relations, was financed by the John D. and Catherine T. MacArthur Foundation and organized by the Institute of Latin American and Iberian Studies at Columbia University; Douglas Chalmers and Marc Chernick very kindly involved me in the scholarly exchange. Radcliffe College's Bunting Institute, the Joint Committee on Latin American Studies of the Social Science Research Council and the American Council of Learned Societies, the Rockefeller Foundation, Boston University, Harvard University (the NOMOS program), the Tinker Foundation, and the World Policy Institute, in addition, all provided me with research, travel, and salary funds to work on my study of Cuba as well as other Latin American revolutions. And the Center for Cuban Studies, in turn, financed my first visit to the island, a trip that contributed to my decision to study Cuba. I alone, of course, bear responsibility for the content of this book.

Last but certainly not least I have my family to thank. They have tolerated my trips to Cuba, more conversations about Cuba than they would have liked, and the time it took to produce the book. My husband, Paul Osterman, has raised many an issue over the years that has sharpened my thinking about Cuba. He has kindly also become more of an expert on Cuba than he would choose, and reluctantly shared his computer expertise with me.

ABBREVIATIONS

ANAP	National Small Peasants Association
CANF	Cuban-American National Foundation
CDR	Committees for the Defense of the Revolution
CECE	State Committee for Economic Collaboration
CIS	Commonwealth of Independent States
COMECON	Council for Mutual Economic Assistance
CTC	Cuban Labor Confederation
FMC	Cuban Women's Federation
INDER	National Institute of Sports, Physical Education, and Recreation
INTUR	National Tourism Institute
ISO	International Sugar Organization
JUCEPLAN	Central Planning Board (state planning agency)
MININT	Ministry of the Interior
OPP	Organs of Popular Power
ORI	Integrated Revolutionary Organizations
PCC	Cuban Communist Party
PSP	People's Socialist Party
PURS	United Party of the Socialist Revolution
SDPE	System of Economic Management and Planning
UJC	Union of Young Communists

BACK FROM THE FUTURE

Chapter One

THE LIMITS AND POSSIBILITIES OF SOCIALISM

CUBA IS AN ISLAND of some ten million people, only ninety miles from the United States. Despite its small size, its revolution shook the world. Marching triumphantly into Havana in January 1959, Fidel Castro led a nationalist and then socialist movement that defied the "Colossus of the North," in a region considered the United States' sphere of influence. And Castro succeeded even though Cuba was heavily dependent on its northern neighbor for trade and investment.

The Cuban revolution is Fidel's revolution. Without his charisma modern Cuban history would be different. Yet to see developments in Cuba as the act of a single individual assigns an importance to Fidel he does not deserve. He reshaped Cuba, and even influenced other Third World countries, but under circumstances not of his choosing. Castro had to come to terms with the limits of his personal power over the years. There are historical and structural limits to leadership. Fidel is no exception.

Historical and structural factors that will be shown in the chapters that follow to shape Castro's ability to make and remake society are rooted, as noted in the preface, in the global political economy and, domestically, in dynamics rooted in the state apparatus itself and in civil society.[1] After discussing how and why these factors are of consequence, a brief history of prerevolutionary Cuba and the conditions giving rise to the revolution appear. And because the state is so central to this study of economic and social policy-making, the chapter ends with a brief description of the evolution of the state and of state–civil society relations under Castro.

CONTEXTUAL FACTORS AFFECTING STATE POLICY OPTIONS

The Weight of the Past

The seizure of power is an event. But any government, including one born of revolution, is limited in what it can do by the productive capacity of the "inherited" economy. In Third World countries where resources are meager and poorly developed, this constraint is especially great.

Castro very quickly had to come to terms with the peculiarities of the island's economy, above all the key role sugar played. His efforts to develop a balanced nationally oriented economy were shaped by this vestige of the past. Cuba was historically integrated into the world economy as a sugar producer.

People, moreover, do not easily break with the values, beliefs, and attitudes they have long had, passed on for generations by families. Culture is embedded in national as well as class and race-specific experiences. Spanish colonialism brought with it slavery and associated racism, plus a Catholic world order premised on hierarchy and elitism. The abolition of slavery and independence never entirely wiped out the colonial heritage, although nationalism in the course of the independence struggle became an additional cultural force, and postcolonial subjugation to U.S. influence added a materialist strand to Cuban culture that was felt strongest in Havana.

Slavery, in turn, never entirely obliterated the beliefs and traditions of the subjugated population. Slaves brought from Africa for the developing sugar economy retained, in modified form, certain tribal customs and values. Since many slaves came as late as the mid-nineteenth century, their African past was only a generation old at the time of independence. Newly formed Afro-Cuban religions functioned as "cultures of resistance," not only to white elite–imposed Catholicism but also to slavery and Colonialism. They were important in the independence movement and have remained so since.

After taking power Castro sought to socialize the populace to new values and new loyalties. He sought to create what Ernesto "Ché" Guevara, the Argentine-born doctor turned revolutionary who collaborated closely with Castro, defined as the "new man" (and woman): egalitarian, selfless, cooperative, nonmaterialistic, hardworking (at both manual and nonmanual tasks), and morally pure. Even when people outwardly appeared to take on these new values, they privately retained old sentiments and passed them on to their children. Sometimes the new beliefs were fused with the old. Reflecting fusion, it became not uncommon to find among the laboring classes statues of Santa Barbara, a syncretic, brown Virgin, alongside glasses of water for the spirits and pictures of Fidel, Ché, and other revolutionary heroes.[2]

The revolutionary government was not merely haunted and "held back" by traditions rooted in the past. Castro also astutely *used* history, historical symbols, and national passions. Even after a generation of Communist rule he still identified the revolution with the island's main national heroes, heroes of Cuba's struggle for independence, and with the major battles of the independence movement. He portrayed the revolution less as a break with the past than as a fulfillment of the revered heroes' mission, all the more so after the delegitimation of world Communism.

Global Geopolitical, Political, and Economic Dynamics

Were the past the determinant of the present, little could or would change. Leadership's ability to remake society is also influenced by global political and economic forces at hand. No country, especially in the Third World, can operate in an international vacuum.

Developments in the less industrial world, since the close of World War II until the collapse of the Soviet Union, were shaped by Cold War politics, along with longer standing but constantly changing world market structures. Third World governments have had to come to terms with these externally rooted factors. Cold War politics pressured Third World countries to ally with one of the two superpowers: the United States or the Soviet Union. Each superpower influenced countries within its bloc economically, politically, and ideologically. The United States appropriated Latin America into its "sphere of influence," to the point that Latin American countries became heavily dependent on their northern neighbor for aid and trade, and they allied with the United States internationally. The United States, in turn, felt it could intervene directly or indirectly in the internal affairs of bloc-affiliated countries.

The evolution of the Cuban revolution is a by-product of the Cold War. Hostile to a nationalist movement in its backyard that jeopardized its own businessmen's interests, Washington first tried to contain and then to subvert the revolution, only to contribute to its radicalization and to Cuba's alliance with the Soviet Union. While the movement's radicalization illustrates how Washington mistakingly overestimated its ability to shape developments in its claimed "sphere of influence," superpower rivalries help explain why the Soviets were willing to provide Cuba with aid and trade and why Castro embraced the Soviets. When the Soviet Union ceased to be a superpower, much less exist, Cuba was hard hit by the costs of its former Soviet alliance, with few remaining benefits.

Shaped by the Cold War, Castro never became a complete pawn of Moscow. As will be documented, he on occasion implemented policies at odds with Moscow's and he manipulated Cold War politics to his country's advantage.

Moreover, at the global level capitalist-market dynamics had a bearing on socialist Cuba, much more so than Cold War politics led observers to recognize. Analysts who perceived a "Sovietization of Cuba," a common theme in the literature of the revolution through the mid-1980s, tended to assume, analytically and, in the main, empirically, that the Soviet and Western blocs were competing, mutually exclusive systems, and that the revolution served mainly to shift island dependency on the United States to the Soviet Union.[3] But the Soviet bloc never was self-contained. Soviet policies toward bloc-member countries were, in part, adapted to global market conditions. And member countries on their own were directly affected by world market dynamics and policies of capitalist countries. World systems theory, discussed in the preface, helps account for why governments ideologically committed to socialism that "socialized" ownership of most of their economy might be concerned with external market-oriented trade and financing, and other foreign exchange–linked activity.

But Third World options have also been shaped by international politics, independently both of Cold War and world market dynamics. Governments have certain discretionary power that may affect their foreign dealings. U.S. policy toward Cuba, for example, will be shown not to be explained merely in terms either of trade-based market considerations or superpower politics. Washington remained hostile to Cuba while being conciliatory to Communist China and the Soviet Union, even after Castro encouraged foreign investment and even after Castro had the country's constitution revised to strengthen foreign investment guarantees. Washington's stance toward Cuba is partly a function of the island's proximity to the United States and continued enforcement of the nineteenth-century Monroe Doctrine. It also was influenced by administration ties, especially under Presidents Ronald Reagan and George Bush (1980 to 1992), to the Florida-based Cuban-American exile community. Washington's strategy toward Cuba became a domestic and not merely a foreign policy matter,[4] especially with the growth of the Cuban-American voting bloc (with successive waves of emigration) and the increased economic and political power of conservative Cuban-American lobbyists.

Third World governments, if skillful, can mediate the impact of global geopolitical and economic forces. A master tactician, Castro will be shown not only to have extracted more concessions from Moscow than other Third World Communist-bloc members did but also to have influenced world politics disproportionate to the country's global economic importance. His strengths, however, ultimately became his weakness. In the post–Cold War, Castro's Cuba became exceptionally isolated and economically vulnerable.

Formal and Informal State Dynamics

Fidel might wish that he could say *l'état c'est moi*. However, the Cuban state is much more than his institutional personification.[5] He has been circumscribed in what he has been able to do even by state economic, political, and administraive exigencies, and by state bureaucratic and organizational dynamics.

Indeed, the government's efforts to address simultaneously economic, political, and administrative matters may create problems. In expanding the productive capacity of an economy, for example, governments typically can count on the political loyalty of those whose living standards improve. But in stimulating investment governments may cut into their own revenue base and weaken their political support, especially in the short run—their economic base to the extent that they allow enterprises, including state-owned enterprises, to retain profits, and their political base to the extent that they tax economic activity and emphasize investment over consumption. Governments may also sacrifice domestic consumption for export, to finance imports and repay foreign loans (and accumulated interest on loans) contracted to complement meager domestic sources of capital; these sacrifices may also be politically costly.

Ideological antipathy to capitalism did not keep Communist governments during the Cold War from seeking the products of capitalism and capitalist financing to attain them. While Western funds expanded state socialist economic opportunities, they also came to drain fiscal resources when Western bank interest rates soared in the latter 1970s and when governments faced difficulties generating hard currency earnings for repaying accumulated debts.

In capitalist economies governments have depended heavily on creating conditions that induce private investment.[6] By contrast, when economic ownership is largely nationalized a government need not face the risk that enterprises will divest should revenue-absorbing policies that cut into enterprise profits be implemented; in general, their investment decisions need not be driven as much by profit considerations at the micro, or enterprise, level. But they are faced with other constraints that limit their economic effectiveness.

Under state socialism ownership of the "means of production" eliminated private business resistance to prolabor policies, but as János Kornai has persuasively argued, budgetary problems have arisen because of the politicization of state allocations: firms have not been pressured to balance expenditures with earnings,[7] because the state absorbs excess expenditures. When subsidies, taxation rules, credit repayment conditions, and pricing are all negotiable, they make for what he calls "soft" budgetary constraints. Demand for inputs and investments tend to be unconstrained and to induce shortages in turn. Under the circumstances, politics may undermine the most efficient allocation of resources and pressure the state to overspend and spend wastefully.

Economic problems of state socialist regimes have been further compounded by low labor productivity. Removing the threat of unemployment, the governments have sought to motivate workers out of a commitment to the collective good. Sometimes state managers have also encouraged labor's commitment by involving workers in enterprise decision-making and by making workers *feel*—through consultations—that they are so involved. But workers in state socialist regimes have not, for reasons discussed below, necessarily identified and collaborated fully with management.

Faced with problems of chronic shortages and low productivity and distortions in the allocation of resources, state socialist governments have tried a diverse range of corrective measures over the years.[8] Reformers in state-planned economies have argued that the introduction of certain market features would help correct for inefficiencies of central planning and allow for the "best of both worlds." However, partial reforms never resolved old problems adequately, and they generated new distortions and imbalances. The history of state socialist economies has been punctuated by cycles of decentralization and centralization, expanding markets and restoration of bureaucracy. Oscillation between market and plan each set off political and economic pressures for the alternative coordinating mechanism, to correct emergent imbalances. However, even when reforms raised production and productivity and improved consumer satisfaction, they typically did not resolve state fiscal exigencies. Budgetary constraints remained soft while the reforms reduced state control over the economy and society.[9] Market reforms reduce the *share* of the surplus directly appropriated by the state, in allowing enterprises to retain some of the profits they generate and in allowing small-scale private (or cooperative) activity that is difficult to monitor (and tax). Unless production expands substantially, state revenues may diminish while individuals and firms prosper.

Tension between central government and enterprise economic priorities thus are embedded in market forces. Production and productivity may be maximized when market features operate, and enteprise interests may thereby best be served. Yet when market forces are kept at bay, the government can maximize its control over what gets produced and the revenue generated, in accordance with economic plans. Therefore, official policies that may appear economically irrational at the microeconomic enterprise level (because of their adverse effect on firm productivity and profits) may be rational from the state's vantage point. The socialist state may opt, for its own institutional reasons, for maximizing its own revenue over productivity.

Specific policies promoted by the Soviet Union compounded problems for Marxist-Leninist regimes, problems not inherent to state socialism but to the historical form it took in the once superpower. The Soviet Union, both at home and in bloc-affiliated countries, stressed large-scale state enterprises. Large-scale units of production were to allow for economies of scale, but they contributed to organizational inflexibility and bottle-necks. Wrong investment decisions, under the circumstances, had big rip-ple effects. Economic problems were also exacerbated by Soviet technol-ogy, inferior to that available in the West. Moreover, the Soviet Union gave priority to basic and intermediate industries. The industries were to stimulate "upstream" consumer manufacturing in turn, but people's de-sires for material goods, both in quantity and quality, went unsatisfied for decades. This stymied worker motivation.

Informal dynamics rooted in formal state structures and processes may further circumscribe leadership initiatives. Interest-group and institu-tional analyses of state socialism, as well as the sociological literature on organizations, for different reasons help explain how and why this is so. Interest-group analyses, as noted in the preface, stressed that bureaucra-cies, though state-affiliated, develop their own institutional interests which they are likely to defend and promote. High-level bureaucrats have also been said to be well-positioned to use their offices not only for insti-tutional but also for private ends. In the context specifically of Commu-nist Party states, Milovan Djilas elaborated on how bureaucratic dynam-ics contributed to the emergence of a "new class."[10] The class used its position to extract benefits from the state.

Sociological literature gives added reason to anticipate possible leader-ship subversion of organizational objectives. The desire of leaders to maintain their positions of influence and the tendency of large-scale or-ganizations to give officers a near-monopoly of power may contain rank-and-file participation in organizational decision-making and result in abuse of organizational resources for leadership-defined ends.[11] Com-pounding problems, managers of state socialist enterprises typically are evaluated by political and not merely or mainly by economic criteria, even when, as in Cuba, they have become professionalized and increas-ingly technically skilled.[12] And their enterprise performance has tended to depend at least as much on their political influence as their technical ex-pertise, their political influence affecting access to resources.

Accordingly, formal state structures and concerns can be expected to constrain leadership policy options and policy implementation. So too can informal sociopolitical dynamics rooted in the very formal state structures.

Pressures from Civil Society

Forces encumbering fulfillment of organizational goals may emanate from people in subordinate positions and not merely from those in au-thority. Even though people have not been entirely free to organize and articulate their interests in any Communist Party–dominated regime, overall they have affected, to varying degrees at different times, what states have been able to do.

People's views on matters are shaped by their positions in institutional hierarchies and by their cultural heritages. If their concerns are not tended to through formal institutional channels, they may well turn to informal, covert, and possibly illegal means to see that they are. Folk in civil society, no matter how humble they are, may accordingly limit what leadership can accomplish.

Potentially conflicting points of view and interests are rooted in positions of domination and subordination, even when all members of an institution or organization share certain common concerns and commitments. Persons in positions of dominance may deliberately try to obscure disparities of interests through ideology and other means and accordingly inculcate a sense of "false consciousness" serving the perpetrators' interests. Subordinates do not, however, necessarily believe what they are told, even if they are outwardly submissive.

Power relations influence how people in subordinate positions respond to conditions not to their liking. People in subordinate positions may not directly express their grievances if they fear reprisal. The institutional setting and the broader society in which the institutions are embedded influence how they respond. Discontent is rarely expressed in overt well-coordinated ways where opposition is illegal or personally risky. Under the circumstances it typically is "expressed" in covert, seemingly uncoordinated ways, such as through foot-dragging, arson, sabotage, hoarding, tax evasion, absenteeism, desertion, pilferage, black-market and sideline activity, mockery, joking, and gossip.[13] And if an electorate is dissatisfied with candidate choices, ballot destruction may become commonplace.

Such "everyday forms of resistance," as James Scott calls them, can be veiled behind outward loyalty and deference, certain cooperation and compliance. They may be legal or illegal, depending on the political-economic system and specific government regulations. Under state socialism black-market activity, for instance, is a mode of defiance against bureaucratic allocative mechanisms that falls outside the law; the same private activity at other times may be legal, including under such regimes. But foot-dragging typically is not illegal in the same sense; and labor's opting for sideline activity has been legal at some times but not at others under state socialism. Similarly, emigration, when people opt to "exit," to defy the system altogether rather than tolerate or protest conditions they dislike, has often been illegal under state socialism but not under democratic-capitalist regimes.

Options people have, or consider themselves to have, influence responses to experiences in any one setting. The greater the diversity of options, the less dissatisfaction with conditions in any one setting is apt to evoke rage. The Cuban government, however, will be shown to have experienced the complex consequences that increasing worker options may have. In diversifying labor's economic options, to improve productivity and consumer and producer satisfaction, the government created new bases for quiet worker defiance of state regulations. When it permitted private sideline activity, workers manipulated the reforms to their own advantage. Aggregate output improved, but the state's ability to regulate what was produced and the revenue thereby generated suffered. State and individual interests conflicted.

Whether legal or not, such covert activity can undermine what states and enterprises can accomplish. Crackdowns on perpetrators of illegal activity do not necessarily result in "law and order." Unless the risks of law evasion come to be perceived as far exceeding possible gains, the law will continue to be violated, even if the perpetrators change. Evasion of the law will persist as long as the conditions that initially gave rise to the law's evasion remain.

Persons in positions of domination are most apt to feel the need to respond to pressures "from below" when resistance is massive and sudden, especially if it is overt but even if it is covert. Employers, including the state when it owns the "means of production," can accordingly be expected to respond to worker resistance that results in sudden decreases in productivity—especially when there are no alternative sources of labor on which to draw (owing to labor regulations, skill requirements, or full employment). Rarely in Latin America has labor, for example, had as great an impact on state policy and rarely has it won as substantial economic and political concessions as the seemingly uncoordinated acts and publicly unarticulated complaints of Cuban workers in the late 1960s.[14] At the time, as detailed in chapter 2, workers were called upon to work more and receive less in the name of the "rapid transition to communism." They absented themselves from work in record numbers and their on-the-job performance deteriorated. The government responded to the ensuing economic and political crisis by both increasing worker material rewards and by granting labor greater participatory rights in enterprise, union, and government decision-making.

Some two decades later, states in Eastern Europe responded neither with reform nor with repression to political crises caused by sudden mass civil disobedience; instead, they allowed for their own transformation. The Cuban government, by contrast, sought to preempt likely anti-Communist "contagion" by a combination of stepped-up reform and repression. The different government responses reflect the range of variability in state socialist responses to actual and potential pressures from civil society.

Covert nonsanctioned forms of resistance may challenge authority less than outward opposition, but that is not necessarily so. At the time of writing (in 1993), nominally nonpolitical forms of resistance, including large-scale black-market activity, foot-dragging, corruption, and crime, did more to erode government legitimacy and effectiveness than the work of formal dissident groups.

Informal forms of defiance and resistance have received little attention in studies of Communism because political analysts typically focused on formal political institutions, formal political behavior, and official ideology. They have taken the political system at face value. The activity has received little attention also because information about informal, non-sanctioned activity is difficult to come by and often must be inferred. Not only do the perpetrators of covert activity not want to draw attention to themselves for fear of reprisal, but the government does not want to publicize how ineffective its authority is and how unpopular its policies are.[15]

Castro has tolerated revelations of corruption, disobedience, and illegality mainly when he has sought to legitimate policy shifts and when he has sought to legitimate the removal of leaders from political office. The launching of both the campaign to "rectify errors and negative tendencies" in the mid-1980s and the Special Period at the beginning of the 1990s, as described in chapters 3 and 4, were associated with such revelations. And the very public handling of arrests, imprisonments, and executions of top-ranking officials in 1989 (also described in chapter 3), allegedly for corruption, drug dealings, and other illegal activity, was undoubtedly in no small part designed to justify the purging of leaders whom the populace had been told to entrust for decades and to warn people in positions of authority that they best comply with the "rules of the game." Punishment, as Emile Durkheim long ago pointed out, is designed to reinforce the moral and legal order, and not merely to penalize individuals who violate the law.[16]

IDEOLOGY AS A FORCE SUI GENERIS UNDER STATE SOCIALISM?

State socialist regimes appear ideologically driven. They have based their claims to legitimacy on Marxist-Leninist moral principles. To the extent that such regimes are ideologically driven, the beliefs should inspire and influence policy choices, and policy initiatives should be consistent with the ideology the governments espouse.[17]

Even if policies are consistent with the moral principles elites advance to justify them, however, the basis for policy selection is not necessarily rooted merely or mainly in those principles. Elites may have their own individual or institutional reasons for policy initiatives. And if policies are not ideologically determined, the possibility exists that they are designed to address concerns other than the principles propagated to justify them.

Meanwhile, subordinates may not internalize the beliefs, values, and ideology propagated by the ruling elite. Their views are likely to be mediated by their positions and experiences in institutional settings and by long-standing traditions. The previously discussed ways that ordinary citizens may subvert state plans and initiatives imply that ideological domination may be far less than public debate reveals. Culture is an arena over which the politically and economically weak may have some control.[18]

At the elite level, moreover, ideology is not necessarily fixed. At the same time that one-party states have restricted public ideological debate, much effort may go into the manipulation and interpretation of the ideological heritage.[19] Party cadre have differed in their interpretation of Marxism-Leninism, their differences depending partly on their institutional vantage points, partly on different philosophical bents; this has been true in all Communist regimes, and within each over time. Which interpretation of the ideological heritage has received voice has often varied with government priorities and efforts to correct unintended consequences of previous policies.

Although leadership is not bound in its action by the principles it espouses, those principles may affect the range of options considered. The principles, in turn, may generate their own contradictions or problems. Moral commitments may, for example, induce persons in authority to implement policies, such as social programs, that conflict with their fiscal concerns. The moral principles elites advance may also generate expectations they do not or cannot fulfill. The failure of leadership to practice what it preaches may make folk cynical, angry, and disobedient. And publicly proclaimed principles may be interpreted in ways the propagators did not intend. Abroad, for example, the anti-Communist world has responded more to the rhetoric than to the reality of Marxist-Leninist states. With respect to Cuba this became particularly apparent in the latter 1980s. The U.S. government, and the U.S. media in turn, took (or chose to take) at face value the stepped-up ideological orthodoxy associated with the official campaign to "rectify errors and negative tendencies"; this stood in the way of any "normalization" of U.S.-Cuban relations, even though Castro at the time was making increased concessions to foreign capital and initiating market reforms.

The complex possible relationships between ideology and social structure give reason to believe that Marxist-Leninist–legitimated regimes may have been less ideologically driven over the years than portrayed in studies of Communism. In the chapters that follow, ideological rationales for economic and social policies will be described, but their policy-determining role will not be assumed a priori.

THE HISTORICAL ROOTS OF THE CUBAN REVOLUTION

If Castro's use of power is circumscribed by history and if Castro himself is a by-product of the country's historical heritage, prerevolutionary conditions help explain revolutionary dynamics. Castro's triumphal rise to power, on January 1, 1959, followed decades of political conflicts, violence, and instability.

Cuba's political independence, which came only at the end of the nineteenth century, involved a struggle that took on a radical and anti-imperialist character. José Martí is considered the hero of the nationalist struggle. After independence Cuba's upper classes were unable to maintain political order. No political party or group of parties held on to power for a sustained period of time. Although the island briefly experienced constitutional democracy in the immediate post–World War II period, *caudillos* typically were the most authoritative force.

The working class grew in size and strength during the first half of the twentieth century. It played a particularly decisive role, along with students, in bringing down an initially popular president who in power turned dictator—Gerardo Machado, in 1933. Urban workers went on strike and sugar workers took over mills. By the mid-1950s over half the labor force, including in the sugar sector, was unionized.[20] The proportion of the island's labor force in the organized labor movement was one of the largest in the world.[21] Yet by the 1950s the labor movement had become largely economistic, typically more concerned with wage increases than with broad political change.[22]

The Moscow-linked People's Socialist Party (PSP) also grew in size in the decades preceding the revolution. However, government repression led to a decline in the Party's influence after World War II. Under attack, subservient to Moscow's advocacy then of peaceful coexistence, and internally divided, the party became increasingly accommodationist. It played little direct role in the struggle that led up to Castro's seizure of political power in 1959.

Fidel, the son of a well-to-do cane grower, was trained as a lawyer. He became a member of the non-Marxist Ortodoxo Party's national assembly and a congressional candidate in an election Fulgencio Batista annulled after seizing power in 1952.[23] The young lawyer had petitioned Cuba's Supreme Court to declare the Batista government unconstitutional, but his petition was denied. With the electoral road to power closed by Batista and the Supreme Court, Castro turned to armed struggle.

The armed struggle that was critical to Castro's victorious overthrow of Batista began on July 26, 1953. Castro led an armed group of fewer than two hundred in an attack on the Moncada barracks that day. The barracks, the island's second most important military establishment, were located in Santiago de Cuba, the island's second most important city. Castro proclaimed Martí the instigator of the rebellion and noted that 1953 marked the centenary of Martí's birth.[24]

Castro used the law to legitimate his rebellion. As he argued in his famous trial for the attack on the Moncada, Batista ruled dictatorially, not with constitutional power. Castro claimed that he had tried in vain to punish the power-hungry men who had violated the law, to overthrow the illegal regime, and to restore the legitimate constitution.[25]

Objectively, the Moncada attack was a failure. Most of the rebels were tortured when captured. Half were killed, the rest imprisoned. Even the Moscow-aligned PSP repudiated the Moncada attack. Symbolically, though, the attack was important to the revolution. The movement associated with Fidel that five and a half years later destroyed Batista's regime came to be known as the Twenty-sixth of July Movement (from the date of the Moncada attack). July 26 also became the day that Castro annually commemorated the revolution once he was in power (except in 1992). Moreover, the attack on the barracks and the political trial that followed made Castro's name a household word in Cuba. His self-defense captured the popular imagination. In the speech he outlined a program for social justice and national integrity. Had his rebel forces seized power, he noted, they would have restored the 1940 Constitution, implemented agrarian reform in the countryside and profit-sharing in industry, and confiscated misappropriated wealth. He argued that the people had the right to resist oppression and injustice, and that the right to rebellion had its roots in Cuba's very existence as a nation. He ended his five-hour self-defense with words that came to reverberate around the world: *"Sentence me,"* he cried. *"I don't mind. History will absolve me"* (italics in the original).

Castro's impressive defense did not suffice to keep him from imprisonment. Upon release in 1955 his popularity grew. With his party, the Ortodoxos, torn apart by factional struggles and personal rivalries, and electoral politics under Batista a mockery, Castro decided once again to abandon conventional politics. His tactic, however, changed. This time it would involve a rural-based guerrilla movement. He went into exile in Mexico, where he befriended "Ché" Guevara. In December 1956, Castro, Ché, and guerrilla allies sailed to Cuba on the boat *Granma*. The boat, like the Moncada attack, took on symbolic significance. Once in power Castro named the official newspaper in honor of the boat.

The fate of the guerrillas who accompanied Castro's return was no better than that of the participants in the Moncada attack three years earlier. However, the few survivors—among them Fidel's brother Raúl and Ché—established a base of operations in Oriente Province, from where Castro's Rebel Army cadre of two thousand successfully launched the movement that ultimately drove Batista from office in January 1959.

Peasants formed the critical social base of Castro's guerrilla movement.[26] They were moved less by ideology than by the prospect of improving their life situation. The Rebel Army established a few peasant schools and implemented a limited land reform in the eastern region, policies consistent with ideas presented in Castro's Moncada defense trial. The numerically larger rural proletariat, centered at the sugar plantations, was not active, in the main, in the anti-Batista struggle, though they supported the revolution.[27] After the abolition of slavery in 1886, former slaves had been transformed into wage laborers. And as the sugar economy expanded after slavery, plantations continued to appropriate remaining small-peasant holdings. Land-deprived peasants were pressed to join the ranks of the rural proletariat, minimally on a seasonal part-time basis.[28]

Critical as the Oriente mobilization was to the revolution, simultaneous struggles in the city helped make the overthrow of Batista possible. Urban challenges to the regime's authority were especially important because Cuba by the 1950s was, by Third World standards, an exceptionally citified society. The urban populace increasingly allied with Castro's Twenty-sixth of July Movement. The movement built on nationalist and populist concerns dating back to the independence movement.

Students, workers, businessmen, and professionals turned against Batista. A student attack on the presidential palace in 1957, public demonstrations by women, and general strikes both in 1957 and the following year, along with clandestine antigovernment labor activity, contributed to the erosion of the political order. Meanwhile, some well-to-do individuals helped finance the anti-Batista struggle. The prerevolutionary Moscow-aligned PSP, however, did not actively and openly support the movement until some four months before Fidel triumphed.

Castro even enjoyed the support of *santeros*, priests of *santería*, a popular Afro-Cuban syncretic religion. Many of the rebels carried with them both rosaries and *santería* bead collars. *Santeros* placed "protections" in Castro's path, and Castro came to be known as "El Caballo" (the Horse). The horse had mysterious qualities to believers, the *santería* priest being known as the "horse" of the saints.[29] The syncretic religion helped nurture a "culture of resistance" to the established political order, a role it had similarly played in the independence movement.

Castro's success rested, in turn, on Batista's inability to muster support from his presumed allies. Even after the revolution became radicalized, many of the well-to-do preferred to leave rather than resist and fight at home.[30] Castro, moreover, benefited from defections of military cadre. Resistance to the rebels, in essence, was minimal.

By the time Castro, at age thirty-three, marched triumphantly into Havana on New Year's Day 1959, his support was broad-based and multiclass. As the photojournalist Lee Lockwood, who happened to be in Cuba at the time, noted, the city erupted in joy.[31] Hope permeated the island. Cubans from all walks of life exuberantly embraced the bearded guerrilla. The central highway became a 500-mile-long parade route lined with Cubans waiting to catch a glimpse of the charismatic hero as he passed. In each provincial capital the new leader made a speech that lasted four to six hours, at times in the middle of the night.

Islanders had diverse reasons for supporting Fidel. Hostile to the corrupt and repressive Batista regime, many found the new *caudillo*'s nationalism, populism, and morality appealing. Castro promised to "purify" the country. The country had become subservient to the United States economically, politically, and culturally, and Havana had become the "brothel and Las Vegas of the Caribbean," patronized primarily by U.S. tourists. Casinos, controlled by the mafia, symbolized the vice and corruption of Batista's cronies as well as the corrupting U.S. influence.

The influence of the United States had increased in the course of the twentieth century. As Cuba's struggle for independence from Spain neared victory, the United States intervened and occupied the country in 1899. As a condition for ending the occupation, Washington imposed the infamous Platt Amendment (abrogated only in 1934), which gave it authority to intervene militarily at its own discretion, to establish a naval base at Guantanamo, and to restrict Cuba's ability to enjoin treaties with other countries. By the time the Platt Amendment was superseded by Washington's so-called Good Neighbor Policy, U.S. political authority over Cuban affairs was entrenched. When Cubans, for example, rebelled against the Machado dictatorship in 1933 and ushered into office Ramón Grau San Martín, the U.S. government withheld recognition of the new government; the U.S. stance contributed to the quick downfall of the government and the return, more or less, of the status quo ante. Two decades later the United States provided Batista with military support that brought Cuban constitutional democracy to an abrupt halt. However, it subsequently withdrew that support when Batista's civilian support dissipated as Castro's popularity spread. Castro at the time appeared to be no threat to U.S. business and political interests.

U.S. influence was perhaps more pervasive in Cuba than elsewhere in Latin America in the 1950s, economically and culturally as well as politically. Various twentieth-century trade agreements had facilitated U.S. business access to the Cuban market. The Reciprocal Trade Agreement, in particular, lowered Cuban tariffs on certain U.S. imports and specified that duties on many U.S. imports were not to be raised. In return, Cuba was guaranteed a share of the U.S. sugar market, with the United States agreeing to pay above the going world-market price for the island sweet. Since considerable U.S. capital was invested in the sugar sector, U.S. and not merely Cuban business benefited from the quota system.

The agreements served to reinforce and strengthen both the importance of sugar in the economy and Cuban-U.S. economic ties. In the 1950s Cuba was the world's largest producer and exporter of sugar. The nation produced about 17 percent of all sugar in the world, more than one-third of the sugar consumed in the United States, and over half the sugar that entered the international market.[32] As a result, Cuba had one of the most monoproduct export and trade-dependent economies in Latin America (see Appendix, Table 1.1), and most investment in industry was concentrated in sugar-related activity.[33] The trade agreements the United States had successfully negotiated made imports typically too competitive with domestic industry (outside the sugar sector) to attract domestic investors. The wealthy, under the circumstances, sent much of their money abroad and spent it on luxury consumption rather than investing it in non–sugar-related productive ventures at home.[34]

Though Cuba had an agricultural economy, large areas of good land were kept idle, and cultivated land was not used efficiently. The larger the landholding, the lower the land-utilization rate. A study found that Cuba, in the 1950s, ranked seventeenth of the eighteen principal sugar-producing nations in sugarcane yields per hectare.[35]

An inequitable distribution of land, the seasonal nature of sugar employment, and an urban if not industrial governmental investment bias, in turn, kept much of the rural population poor. When Batista was deposed, over 40 percent of the rural population was illiterate, less than 10 percent of rural homes had electricity, and less than 3 percent of rural households had indoor plumbing. Malnutrition was widespread, and there were only three general hospitals in the countryside.[36]

Neither the island's trade vulnerability and dependence on the U.S. nor the social and economic injustices, in themselves, however, explain the revolution. Other countries in Latin America shared many of these characteristics with Cuba, without ever stirring a state-class transformation comparable to Cuba's. Indeed, on some measures Cuba fared well relative to other countries in the region: it had—according to available data— the third lowest (tied with two other countries) Gini Index value of land concentration,[37] the lowest infant mortality rate, and one of the highest life-expectancy rates in the region (see Appendix, Table 5.2).[38] It also ranked tenth in per capita income, the median in the region (see Appendix, Table 2.1). If poor social and economic conditions alone prompt rebellion, many other Latin American countries should have undergone political upheavals before Cuba.

Insecurities distinctive to a labor-intensive sugar economy more than abject poverty help explain why Cubans rebelled. In the latter 1950s about 20 percent of the national labor force was unemployed during the so-called *tiempo muerto* ("idle season"), and 9 percent were without jobs during the peak period of employment.[39] Some 14 percent were also said to be underemployed. The seasonal nature of employment was disconcerting to laborers and their families. Workers who experienced job and income insecurity were more inclined than workers with stable employment and earnings to support the revolution.[40] Even in agriculture Castro's support was concentrated among the economically insecure. It was the squatters, those without legal land title, who were vital to the guerrilla movement in Oriente.

Social and economic problems provided necessary conditions for the national revolt, but Castro sparked the flame. It was Castro's astute manipulation of a potentially "revolutionary situation" and his charismatic appeal that explain his mass support, first for overthrowing Batista and then for the sociopolitical transformation.

STATE TRANSFORMATION UNDER CASTRO

The state was radically transformed after 1959. Castro was central to the transformation, but he alone did not determine its form and its evolution over the years.

Charisma and the Party of Disciples

Castro, a brilliant orator, ranks among the twentieth century's most charismatic rulers. As an unsympathetic foreign journalist once acknowledged, Castro had a mystical and magical influence, a commanding spell, with a tremendous power to convince people.[41] Some thirty years after the fall of Batista, she found that Castro still "cajoled, even joked, even flirted with *las masas*. They loved it. He loved it too."[42]

Max Weber, the most perceptive writer on the subject of charisma, noted that the charismatically qualified leader is obeyed by virtue of personal trust in him, his heroism, and his exemplary qualities. He is set apart from ordinary people and treated as endowed with superhuman or at least exceptional powers.[43] A pure, charismatic leader stands outside routine obligations of family life and routine ties to this world in order to do justice to his mission. In its pure form charismatic authority knows no limits except territorial, though it is never a source of private gain.[44] The charismatic leader, the German authority added, subscribes to the proposition "It is written . . . but I say unto you."[45] Charisma, in turn, has the capacity to transform the society in which it is embedded. Yet it is an inherently unstable source of authority. It depends not merely on a leader's extraordinary personal qualities but even more importantly on his subjects' belief in his mission and on his performance of that mission. To remain charismatic a leader must constantly prove his worth.

In many respects a textbook case of a Weberian ideal-typical charismatic leader, Castro in power came to be seen as an ascetic, devoted to the revolutionary cause. He flaunted no wealth and appeared morally pure, while seeming, in the words of one observer, "head of everything."[46] His mother's funeral in 1963 marks the last mention of his private life in the Cuban press.[47] The media was instructed not to comment on his personal doings.

His charisma, in turn, rested on an electric and messianic link with the masses. He made ordinary people feel a sense of dignity and importance. Indicative of how he appealed to them, Castro noted that "You all know very well that we are not capable of imagining that this phenomenon [charisma] is the mere consequence of personal magnetism. . . . A revolution is not the work of a man . . . or a group of men. Revolutions are the work of an entire people."[48]

Obviously recognizing charisma to be an inherently unstable basis of rule, in power Fidel turned to traditional and especially to rational-legal bureaucratic forms of legitimation and authority as well, the two other and more stable bases of rule in Weber's view. Castro, from his Moncada attack to his 1990s defense of "Socialism or Death," very publicly identified with Martí and Cuba's independence movement: traditional sources of legitimation. And less explicitly though no less effectively, Castro drew on the *caudillo* style of rule so common before the revolution.

Yet Castro immediately also brought together organizationally the groups involved in "making the revolution" and then transformed that organization. While the prerevolutionary PSP initially dominated his newly formed Integrated Revolutionary Organizations (ORI), most PSP influentials were removed from office within a few years and the ORI was restructured as the United Party of the Cuban Socialist Revolution (PURS).[49]

In 1965 PURS, in turn, was transformed into the Cuban Communist Party (PCC). Unlike the prerevolutionary PSP, the PCC was relegated the role of a "vanguard" Leninist party, following the Soviet example—albeit under Fidel's tutelage. It became the only legal party, with membership in it being highly selective. The proportion of the population belonging to it ranged from less than 1 percent to a high of about 6 percent—with an additional 8 percent in the Party's youth division, the Communist Youth Union (UJC).[50] Workers could propose candidates, but they were outnumbered by white-collar folk at the base as well as at higher levels.[51] This is partly because the Union of Young Communists, a main channel of Party recruitment, operated largely at the universities.

The PCC was topped by a Political Bureau and Secretariat, then by a broader-based Central Committee comprised of individuals holding important posts in industry, government, and the military. A prerequisite for top posts in all three Party organs was loyalty to Fidel. Fidel and his brother Raúl held, respectively, the two top Party posts.

The Party can best be understood as an organization of disciples.[52] Since an organization of disciples is essential for charismatic rule not to be strictly personal and transitory, the marriage between Castro and Communism was well suited to the problem of routinizing charisma. Yet this aspect of routinization tends to generate its own set of problems, for as Weber recognized, only a small group is likely to be sufficiently idealistic after the initial stages to devote their lives purely to their call. Disciples and followers come to make their living, materially, out of their calling. In the process they are prone to appropriate power, control, and economic advantages for themselves;[53] faced with this problem, Castro saw to it that the Party was periodically purged of individuals failing in their duty.

While avowed disciples used their Party affiliation for their own aggrandizement, selective purges notwithstanding, PCC members did not as a collectivity enjoy the same institutionalized prerogatives that their Eastern European comrades did, if for no other reason than fewer opportunities. Cuba had no Party stores, for example, in contrast to other Soviet-bloc countries.[54] Party privileges of significance were reserved for high-ranking cadre.[55] Top officials had access to cars, foreign travel, and coveted housing, which some used to build up their own informal followings, a practice known as *sociolismo*, or "buddy socialism."

Select rank-and-file Party members who held valued jobs and jobs that allowed for travel and dealings with foreigners also enjoyed privileges denied ordinary Cubans. Their privileges derived not from their Party status per se but from the opportunities that Party loyalty made possible. Abroad they could purchase fashionable clothing, videocassette recorders, and other state-of-the-art consumer goods, purchases revealing the value they placed on Western material culture. But at home, with the crisis of the 1990s, perks enjoyed by the select disciples became as meager as petrol for cars, rights to use air-conditioning, and pastries for parties.[56]

Efforts to routinize rule did not stop with the formation of a "vanguard party." In conjunction with an official campaign to "institutionalize the revolution" in the mid-1970s, the first of what subsequently became routine Party congresses was held; at the time, a new system of governance and a new socialist constitution were also instituted, both of which recognized the Party's "leading role." Then in the early 1990s, the Party was restructured: membership eligibility was broadened, access to internal Party leadership posts was democratized, and an amended constitution redefined the Party as a "people's," not a "proletariat party" (see chapter 4).

The formation and subsequent reorganization of the Party, and the formalization of Party rule notwithstanding, dynamics operating both within and outside the "vanguard" institution will be shown to have circumscribed over the years policy options and outcomes. And Castro will also be shown to have made Communism in Cuba—in practice, if not in outward form—distinctive from other Soviet-bloc countries.

State-Society Relations

Castro soon after assuming power also created new mass organizations and subordinated old ones to his political control. Through the mass organizations he captured and channeled a participatory impulse unleashed with the revolutionary process, and he undermined competing bases of political loyalty.

Membership in the mass organizations was not selective, in contrast to the Party. However, the top leadership of the organizations served at Castro's discretion, and they were drawn from the same select pool of loyalists as the leadership of Party and government organs. Meanwhile, the concerns of the organizations were determined more by Castro and his close associates than by people at the base.

The mass organizations grouped forces in civil society on a territorial and functional interest-group basis. Four mass organizations targeted the adult population: the Committees for the Defense of the Revolution (CDR), the National Small Peasants Association (ANAP), the Cuban Women's Federation (FMC), and the Cuban Labor Confederation (CTC). Nearly all citizens belonged to the respective organizations. While each organization involved somewhat different constituencies and focused on somewhat distinctive concerns, their memberships and involvements overlapped.

Formed initially to defend the revolution against counterrevolutionaries, including against the U.S.-backed 1961 Bay of Pigs invasion by Cuban exiles, the CDRs subsequently expanded their activity.[57] Portrayed by regime critics as a spy organization, the CDRs at the local level coordinated nightly neighborhood safety watch and community-support work. They sponsored campaigns to improve health standards (e.g., blood donation and immunization drives), to enroll students in school, and to encourage people to work. They also were active in recycling and in encouraging voluntary labor. CDR's success varied by neighborhood.

The most common citizen complaint was that committee members were busybodies.

The FMC, in turn, initially provided opportunities for women to learn work skills, and it encouraged women both to do voluntary and paid labor-force work. When formed it helped integrate women who had been economically and politically marginal into the revolution.[58] While not a feminist organization, it did address women's concerns.

ANAP grouped small private farmers whose land was never collectivized, while the CTC grouped together members of sixteen industry-based unions. Subject to state repression prior to the revolution, at the national level labor lost whatever autonomy it previously had as Castro consolidated power. Both organizations came to serve as channels through which government directives affecting the respective constituencies were disseminated and support for those directives attained, even when antithetical to rank-and-file interests. At the base levels, though, the organizations were somewhat responsive to membership concerns, in some periods more than in others.[59]

Youth were organized by educational level.[60] The organizations, though formally autonomous of the Party, in practice were closely tied to the UJC, the youth division of the Party. The Cuban Pioneers' Union grouped nearly all primary school students. Besides serving a recreational function, the Pioneers helped socialize children into the norms of the new society. The Pioneer scarves that schoolchildren were asked to wear symbolized political loyalty or at least conformity among the young. The Federation of Secondary School Students promoted school attendance, athletics, study groups, regime loyalty, and an honor code against cheating. University students had their own organization, the University Students' Federation (FEU); its history was the most checkered. Largely because the university organization failed to quell or contain student discontent in the 1960s, it was dissolved for a few years.[61] University students, it will be remembered, had a history of political involvement prior to the revolution.

By the latter 1980s the organizations that had captured the revolution's initial participatory impulse became largely empty shells, still there in form but minimally in substance. Society had changed since the early 1960s while the organizations and their leadership had not. Reflecting the dwindling importance of the organizations at the grass-roots level, a study of six thousand demands made in four municipalities in the latter 1980s found that only 6 percent of the issues raised were by local CDR, FMC, or youth group chapters.[62] The early 1990s witnessed public discussions of disbanding the FMC and of Castro's inability to count any longer on the CDRs to maintain "law and order."

State efforts to control civil society extended to leisure-time activity as well. Sports activities were organized on a national scale, under the aegis of Party appointees who served, like the heads of the mass organizations, at Fidel's and his close associates' discretion.[63] Castro here capitalized on Cubans' love of athletics, as participant and spectator. He even brilliantly took advantage of the 1991 Pan American Games, which took place in Cuba in the midst of the government's worst crisis. His presence at the various events was highly visible, so much so that a foreign correspondent commented that the esteemed president seemed "like a department store Santa . . . handing out the golds."[64] Castro also joined his fellow countrymen in doing "the wave," reminding them of his magical ability to be "at one" with them.

Castro relied, in turn, on athletes to be powerful role models. They were encouraged through the political indoctrination accompanying their subsidized training to "serve the revolution" and be self-sacrificing. The internationally renowned boxer, Teofilo Stevenson, accordingly, refused a million dollar award for a professional boxing match to "retain the love of his countrymen." Similarly, Alberto Cuba Carrero dedicated the gold medal he won for the marathon at the 1991 Pan American Games to the people who built housing for the attending athletes. And he announced that he would give the medal to Fidel.[65] With star athletes turning over their awards, international competitions prevented a select group with exceptional skills from accumulating wealth based on the reward system of the capitalist world. But the importance of their refusal to accept material rewards was also symbolic. Gifts represent a voluntary type of support for a "calling," typical under charismatic rule.[66]

Cultural institutions, in turn, served both as instruments of sociopolitical control[67] and of socialization to the New Order. Through these institutions Castro and the Party articulated their ideological, moral, and political points of view as well as any changes in interpretations over the years. Yet the institutions operated with a modicum of administrative and cultural autonomy—least during periods of political and economic crisis, and most during periods of major policy transition.[68]

Radio and television were more important than newsprint to Cubans, and Castro made good use of them. He was the first revolutionary leader in the world to use television in a big way. In his early years of rule he appeared on national radio and television nearly daily, to explain revolutionary goals and encourage popular participation. Broadcasting was tightly controlled, though its programming was not monolithic. Channels showed foreign feature films, from Western as well as Eastern-bloc countries. Through the films Cubans were exposed to Western material culture.

After the U.S. government began, in 1985, to beam from Florida the anti-Castro Radio Martí, the media competition led Cuban stations to air more diverse and informative programs than in years past. Call-in shows were established where people could voice complaints. The government's success in blocking the beaming of Florida-based Television Martí later in the decade, though, kept television more politically controlled.

The arts, in turn, enjoyed certain autonomy of expression, although explicit criticism of the regime was never tolerated and even allegorical criticism was not during crisis periods, such as in the Special Period of the early 1990s. Castro set official guidelines early on in a famous speech in which he pronounced "within the revolution everything, against it nothing." The maxim, designed to contain diversity within political parameters, served as a catch-all phrase that the national leadership trumped up when self-serving. It was used in 1971 to imprison the poet Herberto Padilla. The Padilla affair turned such international literati as Jean-Paul Sartre and Susan Sontag, initial supporters of Castro, against the revolution, and Padilla, upon release from prison, went into exile. The maxim was even used to justify prohibition of the Beatles and long hair, said to represent degenerate Western culture.[69] In its effort to regulate the published word, the government relied on the writers' union to reprimand writers critical of the revolution and to press for "unity." The top union leadership here too were Party people of political stature.

Although the government clamped down on a black cultural movement that encouraged black separatism,[70] different cultural mediums drew on Afro-Cuban and Yoruba culture, with official support (through, for example, the National Folklore Group and the African and Caribbean Studies Centers). In so doing the government strengthened prerevolutionary identities and customs. Afro-Cuban culture has remained important because of and not merely despite the Marxist-Leninist state, and its articulation reflected Castro's appeal, in part, to tradition as a basis of legitimation.

Castro's stance toward religion similarly combined tolerance with selective repression and control. Recognizing Marx's famous dictum that "religion is the opiate of the people" and the early anti-Communist stance of the island's Catholic hierarchy, Castro restricted but never outlawed religious activity. While the government and Party became professedly atheistic institutions, in the 1980s church-state relations improved. The publication of *Fidel and Religion* in 1985 signaled the state's changed stance. Indicative of this change, beginning in 1990 the government allowed the broadcasting of Christmas and Easter services, in 1991 Party membership was officially extended to believers, and in 1993 two religious leaders (as detailed in chapter 4) were allowed to run in the National Assembly elections. The new tolerance was both a response and stimulus to a surge of religiosity, above all of syncretic religions but even of evangelical Protestantism, and it may reflect an attempt by the national leadership to co-opt a domain of growing importance where state influence had previously been minimal.[71]

In sum, state permeation of civil society became extensive under Castro. Interorganizational leadership linkages enhanced Castro's and the Party's ability to regulate social and cultural life. However, state-linked groups enjoyed certain autonomy over their internal affairs, above all at the grass-roots level, and the diminution of active involvement in the mass organizations by the 1990s was symptomatic of the limits of state control and the covert ways islanders resisted conditions not to their liking.

Formal Organs of Government and Informal Dynamics of Governance

Castro's government, officially operating under Party guidance, combined controlling with decentralizing and oligarchic with democratizing tendencies over the years. In contrast to the Soviet model on which it was molded, it allowed both for a greater concentration of power and for a greater participatory impulse.

Executive power was formally vested, at the highest level, in the Council of Ministers and, above all, in its Executive Committee. The committee comprised Fidel (the President), his brother Raúl (the First Vice President), and the vice presidents of the Council of Ministers. The 31-member Council of State, made up of persons elected by the National Assembly, had legislative responsibilities, except when the Assembly met; the National Assembly, as detailed below, consisted of deputies who typically attended three-day sessions twice a year. In 1986 members of the Council of State were put in direct charge of ministries, whereas before then they generally had no specific portfolios. As of the early 1990s the organs of central government also included JUCEPLAN (the central planning board), seven state committees, five national institutes, the Academy of Sciences, and the National Bank.[72]

Governance at one level, as noted, was highly centralized, oligarchic, and autocratic. Fidel used his exceptional powers to formalize what has been dubbed "dynastic Communism."[73] In addition to arranging for top posts in the Party and government to be reserved for himself, he saw to it that his younger brother Raúl, was Minister of the Armed Forces, Second Secretary of the Party, First Vice President of the Council of State and Government, and next in line. Succession under charismatic rule is often addressed by such designation by the charismatic individual. Leadership dynamics here reflect dynamics characteristic of charismatic and not merely or mainly of Communist rule.[74] Filial loyalty spared Raúl his job, imprisonment, and possibly his life in 1989 when other influential functionaries were not so spared (as detailed in chapter 3). Non-kin recruited to leadership, moreover, drew, in the main, from a select pool of disciples.

At the same time, though, there was considerable leadership renewal, especially since the 1980s, and Castro sanctioned several efforts over the years to decentralize and, to a certain extent, to democratize the administrative apparatus and system of governance. The first effort at decentralization, known as Poder Local (Local Power), occurred in the latter 1960s, in conjunction with a campaign to thwart "parasitic bureaucratism." Poder Local was supposed to undermine the power base of bureaucrats who viewed their positions as sinecures, and to unleash "unnecessary" bureaucrats for productive work. Bureaucrats were accused of obstructing effective governance and productive activity. Never effectively implemented on a national scale, Poder Local withered away as the government centralized control of the economy, the polity, and society to press for the 1970 goal to produce ten million tons of sugar (as described in chapter 2).

The successor to Poder Local, the Organs of Popular Power (OPP), was introduced nationally in 1976. At its base have been 169 municipal assemblies, which functioned as local government bodies. Citizens in the respective districts chose their local Municipal Assembly delegates by secret ballot in, by law, multicandidate elections. These locally elected officials had to "render accounts" of their activities to people in their districts several times a year and hear citizen complaints. They were subject to recall if deemed irresponsible by their constituents. Meanwhile, elected delegates retained their regular employment, designed to prevent them from becoming yet another bureaucratic stratum. They were to earn what Marx called a working man's wage—essential, in Marx's view, for democratic socialism.[75]

At the municipal level the OPP operated democratically in practice and not merely theory. Elections, for one, resulted in considerable municipal delegate turnover. Between 1976 and 1984, for example, about half the delegates voted into office changed hands each election, and over a tenth of elected delegates were recalled for failing at their job.[76] Second, electoral turnout was high.[77] Third, municipal meetings during these years were filled, in some instances, with intense discussions of constituent concerns, which contributed to policy reforms.[78]

At the national level Popular Power, the "supreme organ of state power," was responsible for passing annual and five-year plans (until five-year plans were disbanded with the crisis of the early 1990s), approving the national budget, and making laws; it also officially exercised control over governmental bodies and appointed members to the Council of State. But there was little effective democratization of governance at this or the provincial level up until 1992. OPP representatives to the provincial and national assemblies until then were indirectly elected, by the "lower" level assemblies (by the municipal and provincial assemblies, respectively), and about half of the National Assembly delegates were appointed by the country's top leadership. National delegates were in the main Party members, and many held top Party posts. Castro and his brother Raúl, moreover, held the two top positions in the Council of State of the National Assembly of People's Power, as well as the top positions in both the Executive Committee of the Council of Ministers and the PCC, thereby preventing any institutionally based leadership autonomy.

Meaningful democratization will be shown to be encumbered not merely by oligarchic tendencies at the higher levels of the Popular Power system. It was encumbered also by bureaucratic resistance and unfavorable macro conditions, and at the municipal level by countervailing centralizing tendencies inherent in an economy premised on planning. Yet autocratic rule in some respects promoted democratic principles more at the national than the local level. "Social minorities"—namely women and dark-skinned Cubans, for example—were better represented at the higher than the lower levels of Popular Power. In 1976 and 1981 women accounted, respectively, for about three and two times the percentage of National than Municipal Assembly representatives.[79] Castro had explicitly called for the election of women after seeing how few of them had been elected in Matanzas Province, where Popular Power had first been introduced on an experimental basis in 1974. Similarly, in 1976 blacks and mestizos accounted for about 28 percent of Municipal Assembly delegates but made up 38 percent of National Assembly representatives.[80]

Growing disillusion with Popular Power led to reforms, beginning in Havana in 1989. New People's Councils with full-time administrators to tend to local concerns were introduced; the councils became closely linked to Popular Power. Then the revised Constitution of 1992 granted the electorate the right to elect directly Provincial Assembly delegates and National Assembly deputies, as well as municipal delegates (see chapters 4 and 6).

Castro, in turn, built up and transformed the military. His Rebel Army after 1959 took control of administration and nationalized industries, mobilized support for the new government, and provided the organizational core of the new society. As Castro consolidated power the army assumed more traditional military functions, though never to the exclusion of civic involvements.[81] The military, together with paramilitary militia, quelled counterrevolutionary movements, and in the 1970s they became more heavily involved in overseas missions than any other Third World country (see chapter 7). Links with the Party were strong. There were Party cells within units of the armed forces, and officers with rare exception were Party men. Moreover, active officers accounted for a substantial proportion of the Party's Central Committee, and Raúl Castro served both as Minister of the Armed Forces and the second highest-ranking Party official.[82]

Under Castro the country became heavily militarized, and not merely because of overseas involvements. Compared to other Latin American countries, as of the mid- to latter 1980s Cuba imported more arms, it had a larger armed forces (relative to the size of its population), and it devoted a larger portion of its national income to military expenditures (except for Nicaragua under the Sandinistas).[83] Castro's government, moreover, acquired offensive weapons capable of carrying nuclear bombs, and it developed its own limited "military-industrial complex" that centered on the manufacturing of light weapons (including for export). As of mid-1990 the armed forces numbered 180,000, some half of whom were conscripts. At the time, the country also had a 100,000 strong Youth Labor Army, a civil defense force of 50,000, and a Territorial Militia that involved 1.3 million islanders.[84]

The military buildup was a by-product of Cold War politics. Castro felt the need to have a strong defense apparatus in light of continued U.S. hostility, and the Soviets, for their own strategic interests, helped train and arm Cuba militarily. The island received an estimated $1.5 billion in Soviet military aid before Moscow cut it off in 1992,[85] and as many as 40,000 Soviet soldiers are believed to have been stationed in Cuba at their peak (after the Bay of Pigs invasion).[86]

Following the cutoff of Soviet assistance Castro's government had to finance all its military expenditures. In the face of continued U.S. hostility, defense needs could not be ignored. Also working against a demilitarization in the post–Cold War was the very defense establishment created over three decades. The armed forces, above all the officer corps, became a force unto themselves, able to pressure the government for their own institutional advantage. Because of their clout they enjoyed better social security and salary benefits than civilians, and they ran their own factories, farms, tourist facilities, and other economic enterprises.[87] Interest-group politics and informal social dynamics help explain their privileges. Problems of "insubordination," rooted in informal dynamics, became transparent in 1989 when one of the country's most esteemed officers, Gen. Arnaldo Ochoa Sánchez, was executed for crimes against the state (see chapter 3).

Yet, as described in chapter 4, the crisis that shook the economy in the early 1990s dealt a blow to the military. Top-ranking officers remained influential, but the armed forces establishment was downsized and recruits had to give beans priority over bullets, that is, grow food for their own subsistence rather than tend to conventional military matters. And the shift came just when the country was left to its own means of defense.

To maintain domestic order the government relied also on Ministry of the Interior (MININT) police. With the crisis of the 1990s they became especially visible. Politically powerful, MININT had the highest percentage of PCC and UJC membership of any state organ, and its top leadership, not surprisingly, served at Fidel's discretion. But MININT employees, at all levels, will be shown to have used their positions for their own advantage, just as other state functionaries did; this too became apparent in the 1989 trials that sent Ochoa to death row.

Thus, despite centralization of formal power and the development of an elaborate repressive apparatus, Castro's government was limited in its ability to rule as it so chose by informal social forces that asserted themselves within the state apparatus itself. How Castro used the powers of the state and with what success are the subjects of the remainder of the book.

Chapter Two

THE "PUSH FOR COMMUNISM" AND
THE "RETREAT TO SOCIALISM"

1959 TO 1985

CUBA'S MAIN PROBLEMS, Castro noted in his "History Will Absolve Me" defense for his Moncada attack, were land, industrialization, housing, unemployment, education, and health. He also expressed concern with the plight of the unemployed and only seasonally employed, the exploited industrial worker, the underpaid teacher, and the debt-ridden small businessman. He said he would have taken immediate steps to combat these issues and to assure everyone a decent livelihood, plus restore public liberties and political democracy, had he taken power.[1]

When Castro actually took over the government in 1959, he had no more of an economic blueprint than that outlined in his Moncada defense speech.[2] But island developments quickly took on a dynamic of their own, influenced by Old Regime heritages, international politics and economics, and forces "unleashed" by the revolution. In the process the class structure and the role of the state were transformed.

Castro quickly set out to diversify the island's economy away from sugar. He promoted "inwardly" oriented import-substitution development then in vogue in Latin America. Island underdevelopment was attributed in good part to dependence on sugar and the fluctuations in world market prices that this entailed. Castro differed from mainstream import-substitution strategists mainly in his simultaneous emphasis on the common man.

Redistributive and other economic measures put idle resources to work and stimulated demand-based growth. Measures included price controls, tax and rent reductions, guaranteed employment, a raise in the minimum wage, and an agrarian reform that gave sharecroppers, tenant farmers, and squatters rights to land and the full product of their labor.

Meanwhile, Castro sought better trade deals. When the Soviets, with whom Cuba had traded on a small scale before the revolution (on a hard currency basis), agreed to sell Cuba oil cheaper than Western companies, U.S.-owned island refineries refused to process the crude. Castro responded by nationalizing the refineries.[3] Relations between Havana and

Washington thereby soured, leading up to the United States's refusal to honor prerevolutionary sugar-export accords and ultimately to a trade embargo. While expecting the economic sanctions to contain Castro's economic nationalism, the United States inadvertently contributed to the complete appropriation of U.S.-and foreign-owned businesses and to Cuba's alliance, at the height of the Cold War, with the Soviet Union; the new alliance followed the Soviet's willingness to purchase sugar that the United States refused. By November 1961, Castro's pro–"popular" sector bias and the logic of events led him to announce that he was a Marxist-Leninist: words that resounded around the world. Most businessmen and other middle- and upper-class people opposed to his reforms, to his new ideological identity, and to his new foreign alliance, left the country, preferring to "exit" rather than defy domestically trends they opposed. Their exodus hastened government appropriation of the "means of production" and the class transformation in turn.

Once full use had been made of established plant facilities, further economic expansion required additional capital investment and additional imported inputs. Castro could not generate the needed capital domestically, available foreign financing was insufficient, and export earnings did not generate adequate revenue to cover new import costs. His problems were compounded by the flight of much of the entrepreneurial, managerial, and professional community, production disruptions caused by the U.S. embargo, and poor planning by inexperienced government cadre.[4] Per-hectare costs of many crops proved to be higher than for sugar,[5] and sugar yields dropped from over six million tons in 1959 to less than four million tons four years later, as land and labor were diverted from production for export to production for the domestic market.[6] The island shifted from having one of the best to having one of the worst export-import ratios in Latin America.[7]

Trade-linked pressures on the one hand and new export opportunities on the other led the government to modify dramatically its development strategy in 1963. It "reverted" to the prerevolutionary emphasis on sugar, this time, though, with a utopian "forward-looking" Marxist twist!

This chapter provides an overview first of Castro's efforts to hasten the transition to Marx's utopian communist stage of development where social relations were to be egalitarian, where people were to be committed to the collective good, and where distribution was to be based on need,[8] and then of his "retreat to socialism" after 1970. Its purpose is mainly to offer a revisionist explanation of the attempted transformation and subsequent "retreat."[9] Although the government portrayed the "push for communism" as ideologically driven, and although studies of Cuba typically portray late 1960s developments as so driven,[10] I will show that policies at the time were rooted in government exigencies and priorities and not merely ideology.[11] The government used moral principles to legitimate policies that addressed its institutional concerns, at the same time that ideology took on a meaning and dynamic of its own to followers of Fidel.

TOWARD A UTOPIAN FUTURE: THE LATTER 1960s "PUSH FOR COMMUNISM"

In line with Marx, Castro portrayed communism as the highest and most ideal stage of development, a stage that followed feudalism, capitalism, and socialism.[12] Marx had argued that under communism people would contribute according to their capacity and be rewarded according to need. And drawing also on Lenin, Castro envisioned that a "vanguard party" would facilitate such a transition.[13] It was in 1965, as noted in chapter 1, that Castro established the Communist Party as the sole political party, with a "vanguard," guiding function. Castro's vision was influenced by Ché Guevara as well, even after the Argentine-born revolutionary no longer held a top government post and no longer lived in Cuba, and then was killed (in 1967) while attempting to "make revolution" in Bolivia. Castro drew most on Ché's ideas after Ché lost out in an open debate about the appropriate development strategy for Cuba that occurred between 1962 and 1965.[14]

Government Initiatives

With the "transition to communism" private ownership (with the partial exception of agriculture) became a matter of history. Also, the "law of value," along with other market forces, officially became inconsequential, in line with Ché's proposed "budgetary system" of economic organization. State appropriation of the "means of production" at the time centered on the two sectors where private ownership of any significance had escaped earlier nationalizations—agriculture and private retail trade. A 1959 agrarian reform had nationalized only agricultural holdings over 402 hectares. A second reform in 1963 led roughly 76 percent of the total land area and 63 percent of the cultivated land to pass to state hands.[15]

The "push for communism" entailed additional agrarian restructuring. The government, for one thing, deprived workers on the newly formed state farms of private plots previously allotted them, and it pressed (but did not force) remaining private farmers to incorporate their properties into the state sector. Second, the historical significance of private ownership was transformed for remaining independent farmers: the farmers were to help out on state farms, to sell all their produce to the state (at low prices), to cooperate with state plans, and to hire no labor. The government, furthermore, encouraged private farmers to organize Mutual Aid Brigades that tended collectively to harvesting and other tasks, and to form credit and service cooperatives. And it rented land at such a low price from private landowners who held on to their parcels that peasant landowners had to work part-time on state farms.[16]

In the cities Castro nationalized remaining small businesses. In the spring of 1968 the so-called Revolutionary Offensive absorbed into the public sector some 55,000 to 56,000 small businesses, especially retail food and service shops but also other stores, bars, restaurants, and snack and artisan shops. As a result, the one sector besides agriculture where private activity had partially escaped earlier nationalizations officially passed to state hands.[17]

The elimination of most private ownership, together with wage increases for the poorest paid workers and a guaranteed employment policy, served to equalize earnings. Indeed, the initiatives led Cuba to come to have the most egalitarian distribution of wealth in Latin America.[18] And through rationing the government sought (beginning in 1962) to equalize consumption at prices affordable to all.

The egalitarian emphasis came with a promotion of Ché's vision of the "new man."[19] Workers were exhorted to labor for society rather than for personal gain.[20] In place of material reward for overtime work and exceptional productivity, workers individually and collectively were to labor hard out of a sense of moral commitment. Rewards for "socialist emulation" and "fraternal competition" consisted of diplomas, pennants, flags, and titles. Sections, departments, and factories, as well as individuals, competed for these nonmaterial "rewards."[21]

In a similar egalitarian and collectivistic spirit, the government expanded free social services. All education, medical care, social security, day care, and much housing were provided free of charge, with access to them more equitable and need-based than ever before. Money lost much of its historical meaning in the process, as Marx argued it should in a utopian communist society.

Meanwhile, the government attacked social distinctions and privilege. Drawing on idealistic societal visions advanced by Marx, as well as by Cuba's independence hero José Martí, Castro urged the breakdown of barriers between manual and nonmanual labor. City dwellers, including professionals, were exhorted to volunteer for seasonal agriculture activity and other tasks. By 1970, 40 to 57 percent of the labor force worked part-time in agriculture, mainly in sugar-related activity.[22]

The egalitarian, antielitist emphasis involved a campaign against bureaucracy as well. Bureaucratic problems—the proliferation of administrative personnel, bureaucratic inertia, and red tape, and the creation of a privileged stratum removed from the masses—were portrayed as "unsavory holdovers from the past" that were exacerbated by inexperience and by copying "countries of the socialist camp that were weighted down with bureaucratism."[23]

Newly created state organizations facilitated the "push for communism." Membership in the prestigious Vanguard Peasant Movement and in the Vanguard Worker Movement, for example, was restricted to private farmers and workers, respectively, who conformed with state-set norms. To become a Vanguard Worker, as 18 percent of the labor force had in 1969, laborers had to overfulfill their average daily production schedule, meet all standards of quality, contribute to a reduction of production costs, do voluntary work, belong to the militia, maintain "correct behavior," and have a positive attitude toward skill improvement and political involvement.[24]

Although workers were guaranteed year-round employment (or earnings) and the previously noted social benefits, they were to labor more for less material reward and they lost the right to strike and to organize independently of the state. And although at the grass-roots level workers could elect their union leadership (a right they exercised in 1966 to reelect only 26 percent of all incumbents and to select leaders who, in the main, were not Party militants),[25] Castro and the Party appointed top union officials.[26] Unification of the labor movement, combined with centralized government and Party control over it, led to labor losing the bargaining power it had enjoyed, in some years, prior to the revolution. In due course the labor movement became little more than a "transmission belt" between the revolution's leadership and rank-and-file workers.[27]

Some of the functions previously assumed by unions passed to new Labor Councils. Council membership, however, was confined to workers who complied with government-set norms, and Labor Councils came to have little authority, especially in matters of planning and wage determination.[28]

Similarly, ANAP, the private farmers' organization formed shortly after Castro came to power, assisted in the agrarian transformation. Headed also by a Castro and Party-approved appointee, the organization's other officers were at first required to be peasants employing no more than two farm workers and later to be peasants employing no farm hands, to own no more than 67 hectares, and to have been involved in no counterrevolutionary or "antisocial" acts.[29] ANAP's organizational cadre, in essence, were confined to private farmers conforming with state regulations at the time, people most apt to assist the government in transforming private farming.[30]

Meanwhile, the very government that guaranteed workers the right to employment also regulated and recorded their behavior with the introduction of an identity card "labor file" system in 1969. Identity cards listed the worker's merits and demerits. Demerits included absenteeism, on-the-job negligence, nonfulfillment of work quotas, and abandonment of work without authorization; merits included Vanguard Worker status, overfulfillment of work quotas, involvement in unremunerated overtime work, and voluntary labor contributions, such as cane cutting.

Why the "Push for Communism"?

The measures associated with the "push for communism" appeared ideologically grounded and, to many analysts, economically irrational.[31] But the morally justified "push for communism" resulted not specifically from the ideological fervor of new Party converts. Rather, that ideology was advanced and Party believers in the philosophy were given voice because the ideas were consistent with the government's economic and political priorities at the time. From the vantage point of the government, the policies were not irrational, though their intended effects often were not accomplished.

As evidence of the economic irrationality of the "radicalization of the revolution," critics noted that productivity on holdings nationalized before 1963 was lower than on remaining private properties, and that most state farms operated at a loss. Yet from the state's point of view, by constricting the activities of small farmers *economy-wide*, export production could be maximized even if at the expense of *individual* farm production and profit. The second agrarian reform formally increased state control over what was produced, and as a consequence, more land and labor could be channeled to address the state's balance-of-payments needs, to promote the government's new emphasis on export-led growth, and to increase government appropriation of farm surplus. Government efforts to expand its revenue base prior to the second agrarian reform—by taxing private production—had proved ineffective. There was no tradition of property and income taxation on which to build, and private farmers evaded taxes (a form of resistance consistent with their own economic interests).

Around the time of the second agrarian reform, the government shifted from the "inwardly" to the "outwardly" oriented growth strategy. Import substitution had involved import dependency (for inputs) at a time when Castro de-emphasized exports. The Soviets, who became the island's main source of imports and exports after the United States terminated all trade, refused to tolerate the growing trade imbalance, but they also agreed to step up their purchases of Cuban sugar, at prearranged prices. Cuba's new international alliance, in essence, compelled Castro to reemphasize sugar.

In its drive to maximize sugar yields, the government consolidated newly expropriated holdings and centralized control over farm activity. Land and labor could thereby be diverted to production for export as never before. Edward Boorstein, who worked for the Cuban government at the time, claimed that Cuba's heavy dependence on exports required such centralized, autocratic control over production.[32] There thus was a pragmatic and not merely an ideological basis for the second land reform and the subordination of private-to state-sector agricultural production.

Similarly, the government deprived state farm workers of private plots not merely because private production was inconsistent with utopian communist principles; it did so also because workers lavished, in its view, too much attention on their private parcels.[33] Agriculturalists had tended to use the holdings as they wanted, for private profit; they as a consequence produced goods for the more profitable domestic market, not, as the government then wanted, for export.

The Revolutionary Offensive had material roots as well. Castro had a repugnance for the unproductive petty bourgeoisie. But he was hostile to the sector also because it attracted people away from productive jobs. Some 27 to 34 percent of proprietors surveyed (in at least three provinces and in the city of Havana) had been workers before setting themselves up in business.[34] The sector had attracted workers because of the money to be made. Shopowners could charge high prices because "too much money chased too few goods." Most importantly, the nationalization of the sector freed labor for the sugar sector, to permit record yields. About one-fourth of the persons in Havana province whose businesses were appropriated in conjunction with the Revolutionary Offensive went into agriculture.

Similarly, the government had pragmatic as well as moral reasons for the urban cane-cutting mobilizations. First, the government had difficulty recruiting permanent workers for backbreaking sugar work. Second, voluntary labor, in principle, minimized wage costs at a time when ever more workers were needed for stepped-up sugar targets. Had the government relied on monetary incentives to attract urban labor to agriculture, it would have had to increase its wage bill substantially. Urban earnings were then much higher than farm earnings, as reflected in industrial/agricultural wage differentials, and people would not willingly take income losses: in the mid-1960s farm workers earned, on average, only 51 percent as much as industrial workers.[35] Since city jobs, in addition, were considered more prestigious, the monetary enticement to do disdained cane-cutting would have had to be sizable. Moreover, it would have been costly to pay year-round wages, which Castro guaranteed, to the large labor force needed for projected historically unprecedented sugar yields, given that work in the sector was largely seasonal in nature. Not yet mechanized, harvesting and other stages of production required hundreds of thousands of laborers.

The emphasis on moral incentives and on rewarding "each according to need" also helped contain the government's wage bill. The mean wages for all but the poorest state employees declined, after having increased during Castro's first years of rule: average earnings dropped about 12 percent between 1966 and 1971, following an increase of 3 percent between 1962 and 1966.[36] In restricting wage earnings the government freed monies for investment, another priority at the time. Gross investment, as a share of the national (gross material) product, rose from 16 percent in 1962 to 25 percent five years later.[37]

Even the antibureaucratic campaign was designed not merely to attack repugnant vestiges of capitalism, as the government proclaimed. The government hoped thereby to improve administrative efficiency, partly to free labor for more productive work, especially in agriculture. Castro also hoped to undermine a new class in the making, comprised of functionaries who had nothing to defend except their own positions.[38]

The moral crusade of the time, in essence, helped legitimate policies that otherwise would have been unpopular. It legitimated policies that involved material deprivations for all but the poorest paid workers and the appropriation and change in meaning of private property; it also countered a centuries-old elitist repugnance toward manual labor. In so doing it eased, in principle, the transition to a sugar-based external growth strategy and the subordination of consumption to investment.

The government also had political reasons for certain of the initiatives—for the second agrarian reform and the Revolutionary Offensive, in particular. The first land reform had left much of the medium-sized rural bourgeosie intact, a bourgeoisie that was in its great majority hostile to the revolution. Landowners spread rumors and pessimism in the countryside, they sabotaged production, and they provided a social base—especially in the Escambray Mountains in southern Las Villas Province—for counterrevolutionary CIA-armed guerrilla bands.[39] There had been bloody clashes between farmers and state troops in the region in the early 1960s, and some teachers and literacy brigade members, who had come from the cities at Castro's inspiration and instigation to educate the illiterate, were murdered. The second reform liquidated this counterrevolutionary bourgeosie.[49] Meanwhile, in nationalizing small businesses Castro hoped to eliminate urban-based opposition to the revolution.

Another political conflict in the early 1960s that may have contributed to the 1963 reform centered in southern Matanzas Province. There, a struggle arose between agricultural workers and their peasant employers, neither of whom had benefited much from the 1959 agrarian reform. The government sided with the workers who pressed for the nationalization of peasant holdings. Peasant opposition to land expropriations resulted in the burning of sugarcane, assassination of officials, sacking of property, and agricultural sabotage; peasants had no formal political channels for recourse. Their opposition was so fierce and so destructive to production that the government ultimately returned expropriated holdings there to peasants. The nationalization of holdings elsewhere in the country, though, was not reversed.[41]

Impact of the "Push for Communism"

From the standpoint of sugar *production*, the reforms paid off. Sugar output rose from a 1963 low of less than 4 metric tons to an all-time high of 8.5 million tons in 1970. And with sugar's increased importance to the economy, export's contribution to the national product rose from about 16 percent in 1963 to 25 percent in 1970 (see Appendix, Table 1.1).

But the government failed to reach its 1970 10-million-ton sugar target, and production in the rest of the farm sector and in industry suffered as priority was given to sugar. The 1970 national product barely exceeded that of 1965, and on a per capita basis it dropped (see Appendix, Table 2.1). The economy was in such turmoil that long-term planning, a purported advantage of socialism, was suspended.[42]

The policies failed not merely or mainly because they were ideologically driven and economically irrational in their conception. They failed also because of unanticipated unfavorable conditions in the external sector and because Castro overestimated his ability to remake society.

Problems arose in the external sector in part because the Soviets cut back assistance out of opposition to the revolution's radicalization.[43] Moscow opposed both Castro's efforts to "export revolution" (described in more detail in chapter 7) and his domestic "push for communism." The Soviets at the time advocated "peaceful coexistence" internationally, and "socialism" and the organizational and remunerative features it purportedly implied at home. Indicative of tensions at the time between the two new allies, the number of agreements between Havana and Moscow declined and Moscow reduced oil deliveries.[44] But Cuba's problems also derived from low world sugar prices. Since the Soviets only purchased, by agreement, 36 to 56 percent of Cuba's sugar exports between 1966 and 1970,[45] Havana had counted on supplementary world market sales when it promoted the 10-million-ton sugar target (the "push for communism" notwithstanding). Cuba's ability to turn its increased sugar yields into increased earnings was impaired, however, by the world market price of the sweet plunging to under two cents a pound in 1968, below production costs. In 1970, when the island produced its record sugar harvest, the world market price was only 3.8 cents, still less than half of what it had been in 1963 when the government made the commitment to the "big sugar push."[46] Cuba proved to be part of its own problem: in expanding the world's sugar supply it depressed the world price.

Domestic conditions made matters worse. For one, the efficiency of the urban labor mobilized to help in seasonal sugar tasks was low, and the temporary absence of labor in the urban economy contributed to the decline in production and productivity there. Second, bureaucratization remained a serious problem despite the official antibureaucratic campaign. Implementation of the "budgetary system" turned plant managers into local-level bureaucrats, and the nationalization of commerce in conjunction with the Revolutionary Offensive brought bureaucracy to every block. In agriculture the expansion of state control along with ownership created such labor problems that the military was called in to regiment farm work.[47]

Moreover, foot-dragging, absenteeism, black-market activity, and other forms of quiet resistance became widespread, adversely affecting productivity in the state economy. The government's moral campaign had failed to convince enough of the population, as workers and consumers, of the virtues of the theoretically utopian society-in-the-making. Without institutional means to express discontent, aggrieved folk turned to covert means. People resented both the material sacrifices they were called upon to make and the backbreaking cane-cutting, and their motivation to work accordingly deteriorated. A time-loss study conducted in 1968 of more than two hundred enterprises, for example, revealed that one-quarter to one-half of the workday was wasted owing partly to poor discipline.[48] Meanwhile, daily absentee rates reached 20 to 29 percent in some regions of the country in 1970, and people withdrew from the workforce.[49] In Oriente, the cradle of the revolution, 52 percent of the agricultural workers were absent from work in August 1970 (and 23 percent were absent five months later).[50]

Data on formal work center–based labor conflicts that went to appeal similarly suggest how severe the problem of absenteeism (plus negligence and disobedience) had become: 58 percent of all the appeals in 1969 centered on such matters.[51] The greatest number of conflicts occurred in the sectors best organized prior to the revolution, not because their objective conditions were worse but because their expectations undoubtedly were higher, they were more politicized, and they had experience in using institutional channels of grievance articulation.

Meanwhile, islanders sabotaged government efforts to regulate distribution in the name of the lofty communist principle, "To each according to need." They turned to the black market to purchase goods unavailable through the ration system and to purchase quantities in excess of their official allotments. Private farmers took advantage of excess liquidity that stimulated black-market deals; they were in a good position to do so in that consumers wanted fruits, vegetables, and coffee, intensive-care crops that require labor but limited capital inputs, the resources private farmers had. In due course, private farmers became some of the wealthiest Cubans.[52]

Consumers and producers in essence resisted internalizing the utopian communist value system the state propagated. Despite the government's control of the mass media and the school system, and despite ideological work by the mass organizations and the newly consolidated ruling party, workers resented and resisted working more for less material gain. The state's preoccupation with capital accumulation—through both the subordination of production for the domestic market to production for export and the promotion of investment over consumption—conflicted with workers' concern with their level of well-being and with control over their own labor. Dissatisfied islanders did not, in the main, articulate their grievances through formal organizational and political channels because formal and informal controls made such channels ineffective and personally risky, but that did not keep them from defying policies they disliked in covert ways.

The strategy of the late 1960s, as a result, proved to be catastrophic both politically and economically. Although there appears to have been a logic to late 1960s reforms, government initiatives generated unintended consequences and their effective implementation was impaired by conditions Castro had not anticipated.

BACK FROM THE FUTURE:
THE 1970S AND THE EARLY 1980S "RETREAT TO SOCIALISM"

That Castro survived the crisis of 1970 was in no small part attributable to his brilliant handling of the situation. That year, in his annual July 26 speech commemorating his Moncada attack and the official beginning of the revolution, he transformed himself into a humble human being. He told the populace that they were all responsible for the failure, but he more than anyone. He offered to resign, an offer the crowds refused to accept. His charismatic claims to rule were thereby reasserted.

But recuperation from the political and economic crisis hinged on structural reforms as well. Officially, the revolutionary leadership had erred in trying to "skip" and "combine" stages. Conditions would improve, the government argued, with a "retreat" to socialism, and its attendant organizational and moral emphasis—following the example of the Soviet Union.

Policy Reforms

The government reemphasized, as in the early revolutionary years, economic diversification, and it encouraged economic and political decentralization, including contained market reforms and democratization measures. The changes were said to be consistent with and appropriate to a socialist stage of development.

While economic diversification involved a reemphasis on import substitution—above all, industrialization, sugar was not neglected. However, it received less priority, targets were lowered, and efforts were made to mechanize production. The proportion of cane cut by combine harvesters rose from 2 percent in 1971 to 62 percent by 1984;[53] consequently, one-fourth as many canecutters were used in the latter as in the former year. With less need for labor the government could promote production of the sweet for export without excessive economic centralization and without depressing production for the domestic market. Under the circumstances, the government even raised sugar targets to higher levels than in 1970. It aimed for eleven to twelve million tons by 1990, and for thirteen to fourteen million tons by the year 2000. Officials counted on guaranteed sales to the Soviet Union and other Soviet-bloc countries. Said Castro, "The sugar we will produce in the next five-year period, as well as in the next fifteen years, has already been sold to the socialist countries."[54]

Meanwhile, the organization of labor was democratized, though again mainly at the local level. The Minister of Labor publicly acknowledged that there had come to be no one who defended the worker, so much so that workers with grievances "did not know where to turn."[55] Local union elections resulted, as in 1966, in a major leadership shake-up. Some 73 percent of the officials elected were new to their posts.[56] The massive ousting of incumbents, as in 1966, reflected workers' dissatisfaction with official labor policies and with people associated with those policies.

Changes, however, were not confined to "who rules" labor at the local level. Over 26,000 new union locals were established, and there was a revitalization of union activity at the local level.[57] Worker assemblies were held regularly again. Workers participated in meetings where production targets, health and safety, worker education, and labor discipline were discussed. The assemblies also provided workers with an opportunity to air grievances against management.[58] And workers were formally incorporated into the enterprise decision-making process, through representation on management boards.

In 1973, at the Thirteenth Congress of the CTC, the Cuban Labor Confederation, organized labor came out for policies more favorable to workers' material interests than in the 1960s: for production and productivity-linked pay, pay for overtime work, limits to the number of double shifts per month, and a 55-hour maximum work week. The CTC also supported the "socialist principle" of economic remuneration: reward hinging on "contribution."

The government shifted its strategy accordingly. Bonuses and other productivity incentives could amount to 25 percent of a worker's take-home pay.[59] By 1975 over two-thirds of the labor force received pay for overtime and double-shift work, and the following year over half of all workers had their jobs, in Cuban parlance, "normed," that is, they had their pay scale tied to the quality and quantity of work they purportedly performed.[60] Meanwhile, the government increased the supply of such consumer goods as refrigerators and televisions and it expanded the housing stock, linking access to them to "economic contribution." Distribution of the coveted goods in short supply occurred through work centers. The housing, moreover, was built by enterprise workers who formed so-called minibrigades (described in more detail in chapter 6), a new form of collective voluntary labor reminiscent of the cane-cutting mobilizations of the late 1960s.

Workers agreed to allocate the goods enterprises received and the dwellings enterprise workers built among themselves, on the basis of merit as well as need—that is, on the basis of work record, plus family size and living conditions. In so doing they participated in the allocative process and shared responsibility for any resulting material inequities.

The government also made a concerted effort to facilitate women's participation in the labor force, as no other Latin American government had. It emphasized gender equality, consistent with the egalitarian spirit of the preceding decade. The 1976 Constitution codified the government's new public concern with women's rights—women's equal rights in marriage, employment, earnings, and education. Sex discrimination was made punishable by a withholding of ration rights and imprisonment.[61] The 1976 legal formalization of women's rights followed on the heels of the promulgation of a Family Code that, among its specifications, noted that men were to share housework when women were gainfully employed.

To make it easier for women to combine work and family life the government did not merely change the law and the moral code; it also assumed responsibility for tasks that women previously had, and it eased remaining household tasks. An expansion of public day-care facilities, for example, made it easier for women to combine work with childrearing. By the mid-1970s facilities were almost three times greater, in 1980 over five times greater, and in 1985 they were nearly six times greater than in the mid-1960s.[62] Meanwhile, the government expanded semi–boarding school facilities. Semi–boarding schools offered children of working women free lunches and free child care during nonschool hours (including school vacations). As of 1980–81 about one-fifth of all children attended such schools.[63]

To ease remaining household tasks the government initiated a shopping-bag plan. Employed women could leave a list of desired items at the store in the morning and pick the goods up after work. The government also earmarked electrical appliances that reduced the burdens of housework for working women, and it made laundry services available at hours suited to working women.[64] Meanwhile, its 1974 Maternity Law granted working women a paid maternity leave and rights to absent themselves from work to attend to children's health needs. Such measures were consistent with the Marxist view that women's emancipation hinged on their economic participation. Castro proudly referred to women's incorporation into the workforce as the "revolution within the revolution."

Concomitantly, the government sought to debureaucratize and democratize its own administration and to make it more responsive to citizens' concerns through newly formed Organs of Popular Power (OPP) (as described in in chapter 1). The new local administrative units were ultimately responsible to JUCEPLAN, the state planning agency, but municipalities, through the OPP, acquired some latitude in choosing projects and selecting enterprise directors. Delegates to the municipal Popular Power assemblies, moreover, it will be remembered, were chosen by the population-at-large in multicandidate elections.

Yet in 1980 a new pay scale, the first since 1963, was put into effect. It reduced the earnings spread among manual workers, while raising the earning potential of (and wage spread among) technicians, executives, and (to a lesser extent) administrative and service personnel.[65] Accordingly, the wage reform reversed the egalitarian emphasis of Castro's first decade of rule and the spirit of equality associated with the "revolution within the revolution."

The 1980 wage reform was not the only policy associated with the "retreat to socialism" that turned on labor. Already in 1971 an antiloafing law had been promulgated that made work for men an obligation and no longer merely a "socialist right." The 1971 law also deprived workers guilty of absenteeism of vacations and social benefits (including the work canteen), and, in extreme cases, ordered their transfer to work camps.[66] And another law called for the repeal of a 1968 pension and retirement benefits decree. Meanwhile, survey data suggest that workers in the mid-1970s saw the main function of unions as improving production and educating members,[67] not as defending workers' rights.

Between the mid-1970s and mid-1980s several market-related reforms also were introduced. For one, a new management and planning system (the SDPE, the System of Economic Management and Planning) was initiated—modeled, in many respects, on 1965 Soviet reforms. Premised on self-financing, profit incentives, decentralization, and efficiency,[68] it involved an incorporation of market features into the state sector. Profit incentives included a "stimulation fund," which could be used for social and cultural purposes, small investments, and productivity-linked employee bonuses. Under the SDPE enterprises could also use up to 30 percent of their profits for purchases from the private sector, and managers could hire and fire workers (within limits) and employ workers on a piecework basis.[69] Profit incentives were to serve as a corrective to the "command economy" enterprise tendency to hoard labor and other resources. With the right to retain a portion of profits, managers in principle had an incentive to minimize their wage and supply bills.

In the latter 1970s and early 1980s changes occurred in the state farm sector as well, involving, in part, market reforms. In the sugar sector agro-industrial complexes were created, which merged agricultural and industrial processes under a single management structure. Authorities at the same time permitted some state farm workers to have private plots again, to engage in collaborative subsistence farming, and to take responsibility for specific portions of state lands. And because state farm managers, like other state managers, acquired the right to fire labor, farm workers became more vulnerable to profit and other market-related pressures than ever before under Castro.

Market reforms were not confined to the state sector. They came to include tolerance of new private economic activity in agriculture and the service sector and, in the early 1980s, in commerce and housing as well. Farmers were pressured less to work on state farms, to cooperate with official agricultural plans, and to sell their holdings to the state. The number of private farmers who affiliated with state plans consequently dropped—by half, for example, between 1973 and 1977—and government farm purchases declined from about 20,000 between 1967 and 1970 to fewer than 1,500 a year subsequently.[70] Tobacco-growing, at least in key provinces, reverted entirely to the private sector.[71]

At the same time that the government became more tolerant of private farm production, it encouraged cooperative over independent farming.[72] Castro spoke of cooperatives as a "higher" form of economic organization, in line with Marxist collectivistic principles. To entice farmers to form cooperatives, the government added material to moral incentives. Incentives included the reserving of new farm machinery for state farms and cooperatives; charging cooperative members lower interest rates on loans and lower tax rates on earnings than independent producers; and extending social security coverage to cooperative members but not to independent farmers. The number of production cooperatives in due course rose from forty-four in 1977 to over 1,400 in 1984, with production cooperatives coming to involve about 45 percent and credit and service cooperatives an additional 41 percent of the land that had remained in private hands.[73] ANAP, at its Fifth Congress in 1977, endorsed the cooperativization drive that pressed for the demise of independent farming. As in the 1960s, it supported official policy.

Meanwhile, the government allowed ever more goods to be available off the ration system—to the point that in 1980 the percentage of total consumer spending on purchases of rationed goods dropped to 30 percent from nearly 100 percent ten years earlier.[74] Yet the government continued its commitment to the poor by still distributing basic foods through the *libreta*, the ration book.

The government also permitted so-called farmers' markets, where private farmers and state farm employees alike could market any surplus they produced beyond their commitments to the state. Until then, farmers could only legally market their surplus on their own land. Prices at the new markets were determined between buyers and sellers, and there were few restrictions on what could be sold. In early 1981, an estimated 50 to 80 percent of families frequented the markets at least once a month, and by mid-decade the markets supplied more than 80 percent of the perishables consumed by islanders.[75]

The government also began to market nonrationed goods itself, through a newly established "parallel market" system. At the "parallel markets," items sold for higher prices than through the ration system. Much of the food sold at the new state outlets was to come from private producers.

The government also legalized certain private-service activities. Individuals could offer such services as appliance and auto repair work, carpentry, plumbing, gardening, and private housing construction for a fee—if licensed and done on a self-employed basis. Tolerance of private-service work spurred a boom in the private sector in building construction, the stock of housing having remained grossly inadequate even with the minibrigade program. In 1984 three times more dwelling units were built privately than in any previous year under Castro.[76]

While these market reforms were justified as necessary and appropriate for a "socialist stage," other market reforms defied nationalist as well as "socialist" principles. The government, for one thing, began to encourage foreign investment, reversing its ownership stance since the early revolutionary years. It encouraged contract manufacturing and joint ventures, beginning in 1977. Then, in 1982 it went so far as to issue a foreign investment code, which formalized its efforts to attract private capital from abroad. Sectors opened to foreign investors included tourism, light industry, medical equipment, medicine, construction, and agro-industry. Investors were promised tax-free use of land, tax exemptions on imported materials, and free repatriation of profits. The 1982 reform allowed foreign investors up to 49 percent ownership in local enterprises.

Initially opposed to tourism on moral grounds because of the gambling, gangsterism, and prostitution with which it had been associated under the Old Regime, in the late 1970s Castro modified his stance here too. He argued that tourism could be regulated to avoid the degenerating effect it had had before the revolution.

Cuba also affiliated with associations outside the Soviet bloc, and it expanded its Western trade. It was a member of the International Sugar Organization (ISO) and it joined the newly formed Latin American and Caribbean Sugar Exporters' Association, for example. The Western bloc, in turn, came to account for 41 percent of island trade in 1974. Cuba even increased its trade with U.S.-based multinationals through third countries, as Washington modified the embargo. Washington responded to pressure from foreign governments and U.S. firms that sought to take advantage of Cuba's mid-1970s growing hard currency import market.[77]

Cuba's opening to the West occurred at the same time that its ties with the Soviet bloc became more formalized. Cuba in 1972 became an official member of the Council for Mutual Economic Assistance (COMECON). With developing-country status, economic relations vis-à-vis the Soviet superpower became more beneficial to the island. The Soviets agreed to an increase in the price they paid for island sugar without raising the price charged Havana for their oil commensurately, to the point that terms of trade between the two countries favored the island as never before. Also, the Soviets provided new long-term low-interest financing, and they agreed to allow Cuba to postpone repayment of its outstanding debt until 1986.[78]

Why the Official "Retreat to Socialism" and the Opening to Capitalism?

If the government had economic and political reasons for the policies of the late 1960s, it should have them for the post-1970 period as well. Reforms associated with the official "retreat to socialism" should be rooted in new economic and political concerns and in efforts to resolve old problems. Economic concerns included improving production and productivity, minimizing government fiscal expenditures (except if offset by revenue gains), and raising badly needed revenue first for imports and then also for foreign debt payments. Governmental efforts to address such concerns should explain policies both consistent and inconsistent with the ruling ideology of the time. Again, were policy primarily ideologically driven, only initiatives consistent with the moral precepts the leadership then espoused should have been put into effect.

Policies focusing on problems the "push for communism" failed to address—and indeed exacerbated—included the consumer-oriented initiatives: the wage reforms, government allotments of appliances and other coveted manufactures, plus housing and the establishment of the farmers' markets and the "parallel market" system. In raising consumption the government hoped to reduce political discontent in a manner that raised productivity. Labor had influenced the shift in consumer-oriented policy, though only indirectly and informally—through workplace disobedience (namely, absenteeism and low productivity).

Leadership concern with minimizing expenditures was reflected, in principle, in the minibrigade housing program, where the government only provided the construction materials. Enterprises provided, free of charge, the labor. When minibrigades proved to be inefficient the government opened construction to private builders, theoretically reducing state-sector expenditures even more.

The antiloafing law was premised on principles that were the antithesis to those of minibrigade voluntarism. The law was a response to the failure of moral incentives to induce islanders to work. Thus, it too can be explained at the economic level, though, in contrast to the minibrigade program, not also at the ideological level.

While Castro's mid-1970s commitment to the "revolution within the revolution" was, like the minibrigades, reminiscent of the late 1960s in its ideological rationale, as Castro himself admitted it was also a question of "elemental necessity" for economic development that women work because "the male work force will not be enough."[76] When Cuba experienced an economic boom in 1974, linked to record-high world sugar prices, Castro saw women as a relatively untapped source of labor. Under the circumstances, Marxism provided a moral rationale both for inducing women to work and for minimizing male resistance to working wives.

The government understood that moral suasion alone would not bring women permanently into the labor force. In the 1960s, in the absence of state supports, women's participation in the labor force had barely increased: it rose only from 13 percent in 1956 to 18 percent in 1970 (see Appendix, Table 2.2).

If the government had material reasons for encouraging women to work in the mid-1970s, its emphasis on gender equality and the "revolution within the revolution," and its fiscal commitments to facilitating women's participation in the labor force, should vary with the demand for labor. Already in 1976 women were officially excluded from nearly three hundred jobs. They were excluded ostensibly for health reasons, but not all the work from which they were barred can be so explained.[80] Then in the early 1980s the government reduced social supports for working women, and its Five Year Plan called for no increase in the rate of women's participation in the labor force.[81] The government reduced the rate of day-care expansion, and it began to charge on an "ability to pay basis" for day care and noontime meals at work.[82] Since in 1973 day-care centers were believed to accommodate less than 10 percent of the women who wanted to work,[83] the slowdown cannot be explained by women's needs having been met. Meanwhile, in discourse the government and Party ceased to exhort women to work, and little mention was made of gender issues.[84] Castro himself made it clear that the incorporation of women into the workforce would have to be slowed down unless the growth of the economy picked up.[85]

The shift in the state's stance toward women came after the mid-1970s economic boom turned bust and changing demographics plus mechanization reduced the demand for labor. The unemployment rate is estimated to have risen above 5 percent in 1976 (from 1 percent in 1970). And in the early 1980s a baby boom generation, born in the first years of Castro's rule, reached working age, increasing the pool of people in search of work; at the same time, mechanization of sugar production freed men who previously had been employed in the sector for other lines of work, and the availability of schoolchildren (from newly created rural boarding schools) as well as of people in military brigades helped meet peak seasonal state-sector labor needs. Under the combination of circumstances, the government had less need for women to work and therefore less interest in absorbing the costs of the social programs that facilitated their participation in the labor force.

Even the OPP was structured to address economic along with political concerns. The contained democratization gave citizens at the grass-roots level not merely the opportunity to determine "who rules" but also an opportunity to pressure for improved quality of services.[86] To the extent that complaints were acted upon, the OPP contributed both to more efficient use of existing resources and to improved citizen satisfaction.

In turn, the loosening of controls over private agriculture were tied to changing government economic priorities and changing labor demands, along with political considerations. With successful mechanization of sugar production the partial deregulation of private farm activity could address peasant concerns and consumer demand at the same time that government export exigencies could be sustained. In "liberating" peasants Castro revitalized his rural support base, which had weakened in the late 1960s.[87] And Castro could thereby also improve his popularity in the cities since the private sector produced much of the food city dwellers consumed, when not pressured, as in the "push for communism," to partake in export-related activities.

But why other than ideological reasons might the government have encouraged cooperatives over independent farming? For one thing, the government believed that large-scale farming was more efficient than small-scale farming in that it allowed for economies of scale. The Soviets encouraged such a bias toward "bigness." Second, cooperatives could make better use of the island's expanding production of farm manufactures than could small independent farms.[88]

The "market opening" in the food distribution system, in turn, responded to producer and consumer along with government disquietude. Consumers had been pleased with the low prices of rationed goods, but they found their quotas insufficient and the quality of rationed goods poor. And producers preferred the (legitimate) opportunities to prosper that the private markets allowed; the government paid below the market price for peasant purchases. Meanwhile, in reducing the role of rationing the government could cut its expenditures, stimulate production, and undermine the conditions that created the black market. The government subsidized the price of goods sold through the ration system, at the same time that it kept down the price it paid private producers for their yields. Also, the ration system was costly to administer and the low prices induced people to buy their full allotment of goods even when they had no use for items, an unnecessary expense the state was forced to absorb. Furthermore, by restricting sales of exportable items (and cattle, to build up the domestic stock), the farmers' markets were not to conflict with the government's continued concern with producing for export.[89]

Finally, Castro's mid-1970s stepped-up Western trade and bank borrowing and, later in the decade, the promotion of foreign investment and tourism (which picked up at the very time of formalized and increased Soviet-bloc integration) are also explicable at the economic level. Castro allowed for the "capitalist backsliding," without ever acknowledging this at the level of discourse, to take advantage of what he saw as a "window of opportunity." He took advantage of record-high world market sugar prices, which rose from under two cents a pound in 1968 to sixty-eight cents a pound in November 1974. The Soviets even helped him take advantage of the favorable world market situation by allowing the island to sell some of their contracted sugar to Western-bloc countries. Castro wanted the Western sales to generate hard currency for Western purchases. Soviet manufactures typically were more expensive than and inferior in quality to comparable Western equivalents, and they did not always arrive on schedule, causing production stoppages and bottlenecks. Meanwhile, rubles earned from Soviet-bloc exports could not be used for Western purchases, for the ruble was not a convertible currency.[90] It was precisely Castro's quest for Western goods that led him to borrow from Western banks and governments, when the opportunity arose in the mid-1970s,[91] even though the financing was on far less favorable terms than the Soviets'.

Only when the seeming "window of opportunity" turned bust did Castro outrightly defy the nationalist principles he earlier had championed by encouraging foreign investment and tourism.[92] By 1977 the price of sugar dropped to a yearly average of eight cents,[93] down from a yearly average of thirty cents just three years earlier. Cuba was left with the problem of repaying Western loans contracted when world market sugar prices had been much higher, and with few goods that hard currency customers would buy. Castro hoped foreign investment and tourism would stimulate hard currency earnings for loan repayments.

Impact of the "Retreat to Socialism" and the Opening to the West

The continued if reduced emphasis on sugar, and the ability and willingness to market the sweet in Western as well as Soviet-bloc markets, paid off by the mid-1970s as never before. When the world market sugar price reached a record high in 1974, Cuba's export earnings spiraled,[94] and the West came to account, as previously noted, for as much as 41 percent of the island's foreign trade, up from a low of 17 percent in 1962.[95] Although Castro's government had exported more sugar in half the years prior to 1974, in no year had the commodity accounted for as large a share or amount of export earnings as in 1974. Trade earnings were only partly a function of the volume of exports. Moreover, Moscow responded to the high world market prices not only by releasing Cuba from contracted commitments but also by raising the price it paid Cuba for the sweet. Favorable world market conditions thereby had a positive effect on Cuba's relations with the Soviet Union as well.

Partly because of improvements in the external sector, the country experienced an impressive economic recovery (see Appendix, Table 2.1). Cuba's growth rate, estimated to average 14 percent annually between 1971 and 1975, ranked among the highest in Latin America at the time.[96] Concurrently, its export-import ratio rose from .80 in 1970 to .95 in 1975, with the ratio jumping from one of the lowest to one of the highest in the region in the five-year period.[97]

Sectors of the domestic economy that had done poorly in the late 1960s, in turn, rebounded, including industry. Output of about two-thirds of the island's major industrial items improved. The total value of industrial production rose about 35 percent in the first half of the 1970s. Yields of most nonsugar crops also improved, although typically not to levels of the early import-substitution years. The improvements contributed to a rise in per capita consumption of most durables and nondurables, suggesting that Cubans on the whole benefited from the boom.[98]

By 1976, however, the growth rate was down to 4 percent.[99] Noted organizational changes may have been necessary for the economic recovery of the early 1970s, but they were not sufficient to allow a continued high rate of growth when the world sugar price dropped. With the decline in sugar earnings, the country's export–national product ratio and its trade balance, as well as its growth rate, deteriorated. Hard currency sugar-export earnings (from sales to the industrial West) dropped from a high of $719.9 million in 1975 to $157 million three years later.[100] The drop in export earnings quickly reversed the mid-1970s improved export-import ratio.[101]

The Western-based growth strategy began to backfire in the latter 1970s also because Castro was left with a large debt contracted when world market sugar prices had been high and commercial interest rates low. The Western debt rose from $660 million in 1974 to $1,338 million in 1975 and to $2,100 million two years later.[102] With the debt rising much faster than hard currency export earnings, the island's Western debt, relative to its hard currency export earnings, jumped from 62 percent in 1974 and 117 percent in 1975 to 268 percent in 1977. Cuba shifted from having one of the better to having one of the worst hard currency debt–export ratios in the region (see Appendix, Table 2.3).

The mounting hard currency debt and the deterioration in Western trade compelled the government to modify its five-year development program. Long-term planning accordingly was undermined again, by changed global market conditions. Investments and Western technology imports had to be slashed and austerity measures initiated.[103]

Relations with COMECON shielded Cuba from the full impact of the unfavorable world market conditions. Indeed, the new low-interest Soviet loans and improved Cuban-Soviet terms of trade reduced Cuba's Soviet debt burden; the Soviets, moreover, did not readjust the price they paid for island sugar "downward" as world market sugar prices plunged. Although in the course of the 1970s the debt rose in absolute value, Havana's Soviet debt–national product and especially its Soviet debt–Soviet export ratio improved, according to available information.[104]

But relations with the Soviet Union were not without their problems either. Aside from Cuba's inability to use trade-earned rubles to purchase Western goods and to repay its accumulating Western debt, and aside from the poor quality and high prices charged for items other than oil, the Soviet Union and other Soviet-bloc countries were willing to purchase only a limited range of Cuban products. Cuba's Soviet-bloc COMECON integration continued the country's prerevolutionary monoproduct export dependence at a time when other countries were diversifying their exports (see Appendix, Table 1.1). Soviet willingness to keep high the price it paid for island sugar meant that Cuba could produce nothing else as profitably. Moreover, most Soviet funding covered—according to Western sources—Cuba's trade deficit with the superpower. The funding therefore failed to address the root cause of the island's continued Soviet-bloc balance-of-payments problem: its inability to generate sufficient export revenue to offset import needs or to advance import substitution to the point that trade was less vital to the economy.

An economic recuperation in the early 1980s suggests that the various reforms of the latter 1970s finally paid off. United Nations sources estimated Cuba's 1981–83 gross social product growth rate in current pesos to have been 23 percent, and the average yearly growth rate in constant pesos to have been around 7 percent.[105] Even if the figures are somewhat exaggerated, the island appears to have been more immune to a world recession at the time than other countries in the region: the average GDP growth rate for Latin America during this period was negative (-2.8) and only 11 percent in the fastest-growing economy in the region. And the economy did well in the early 1980s by regional standards even after the world market price of sugar dropped to five cents in 1984, from a yearly average of twenty-eight cents of 1980.

By the early 1980s Cuba made significant strides in a number of areas of production. Capital goods, chemicals, medicines, electronics, computers, and steel are sectors that experienced improvement. Indicative of the growth, engineering and the capital goods sector accounted for 13 percent of industrial production in 1983, up from 1 percent in 1959.[106] Output of citrus, fish, eggs, nickel, cement, and electricity also by then expanded severalfold over their 1959 levels. With some exceptions, though, production in the consumer goods industries was less impressive.

Agriculture output also improved, in both the state and private sectors.[107] The private sector was stimulated by a hike in state procurement prices, release from former obligations to work part-time on state farms, and the ability to hire help once again. And state as well as private sector workers produced more than they were obligated to sell to the official procurement agency, to profit from the lucrative farmers' markets.

Even when macro indicators suggested improvements, however, the "market opening" and associated reforms generated problems—from the government's vantage point, as distinct from producers' and consumers'. Agriculturalists, for one thing, quickly discovered that they could prosper by staggering the farming of crops, by concentrating on varieties that they were not obligated to sell to the state, and by selling their poorest quality output to the state while reserving the best for the more lucrative farmers' markets. Second, although it would appear that the market reforms would reduce fiscal expenditures, the private sector came to compete for scarce state resources. Public resources intended for state farms began to be used for private gain. Farmers manipulated the market reforms to their own advantage, at the government's expense. Third, private farmers also took advantage (illegally) of domestic demand for goods the government reserved, for its own fiscal reasons, for export. In particular, the government restricted domestic coffee consumption, through rationing, because the commodity was one of the few products Cuba could sell in hard currency markets. With domestic demand for the bean greatly unsatisfied through the official distribution system, farmers could sell the crop at substantial profit illegally. Accordingly, consumers and producers sabotaged state efforts to maximize coffee export earnings.

Distributors as well manipulated the market opening to their own advantage. They manipulated sales so as to maximize their earnings at consumers' expense.[108] In particular, they created scarcities by limiting what they sold at any point in time, to drive prices up. They also engaged in new illicit activity, although the farmers' markets legalized sales that had been illegal in the late 1960s. Farmers tended not to market the goods themselves, even though they were supposed to. Instead, they often relied on an emergent stratum of intermediaries. Middlemen were seen in Castro's Cuba as a parasitic, unproductive class, a class whose labor should be put to more productive use. In pursuit of profits, vendors, moreover, falsified documents, sold meat that was not officially inspected, and marketed goods stolen from government warehouses. Many of them, along with farmers, spent their new profits on luxury goods available only on the black market; farmers did so in part because government regulations, designed to encourage cooperatives over independent farming, prevented them from investing their earnings productively. As noted, machinery was made available, at low interest rates, to cooperatives and state farms only.

Apparently because vendors and farmers not only profited at the public's expense but because they also siphoned off surplus that the state itself wished to appropriate, new market regulations were issued in the early 1980s. The government increased the amount farmers had to sell to the official procurement agency and required farmers to fulfill their official contracts before marketing goods privately (imposing a penalty on farmers who failed to comply). Meanwhile, to enhance its earnings the government instituted a progressive tax (ranging from 5 to 20 percent) in May 1983, on the gross income of individual farmers and the net income of cooperatives, and it required private vendors to pay a 20 percent tax on gross sales and private farmers to pay their own crop insurance (which, until then, the government had provided).

At the same time, the government imposed a lower sales tax (only 5 percent) on producers who sold directly to the official procurement agency, and it raised the price it paid farmers for output exceeding contracted quantities.[109] The measures were to stimulate sales to the state for the new official "parallel market." The government could profit from "parallel market" sales since goods channeled there were more in line with farmers' markets' prices than with prices of goods distributed through the highly subsidized ration system.

Cooperatives, the "higher" form of economic organization that allowed for economies of scale, generated some problems, in turn. They gave rise to illicit extra-agricultural activities and to speculation by middlemen,[110] and many operated at a loss.[111]

While the legalization of private-service work was well received and while it corrected deficiencies and delays in work done through official channels, it too generated problems because the government failed to regulate it effectively. Workers took advantage of the opportunities for private profit, pilfering supplies from their work centers for private use and absenting themselves from work to pursue private jobs.[112] Private-service work thereby undermined state-sector production at the same time that the quality of service work improved.

Within the state sector even the incorporation of women into the labor force caused problems. Women's participation in the labor force rose from 18 percent in 1970 to 31 percent ten years later (see Appendix, Table 2.2), a 72 percent increase compared to a 38 percent increase between 1953 and 1970. Women, however, were harder hit than men by the 1976 economic downturn. They came to account for the majority of the unemployed while still a minority of the employed, and their unemployment rate soared while men's dipped. Men's unemployment rate dropped from 2.2 percent in 1974 to 1.7 percent in 1976 while the women's rate rose from 9.7 to 13.6 percent during the two-year period.[113] Women proved to function somewhat as a labor reserve.

From the government's vantage point, women entered the labor force beyond what the economic plan called for. Women's participation in the labor force continued to rise, to 37 percent in the mid-1980s. Cuba came to have, according to available information, the highest female labor force participation rate in Latin America,[114] especially in so-called formal-sector jobs. Whereas in the rest of the region many women held low-paying informal-sector jobs that offered no social benefits or income guarantees, in Cuba most women, as state employees, held jobs that offered a secure salary as well as pension, unemployment insurance, and other benefits.

Women's increased participation in the labor force, in the absence of official encouragement, was partially a lingering effect of the state's mid-1970s moral campaign to get women to work and the increased social supports it extended to working women. However, their increased participation in the labor force was also a response to women's changed social and economic situation. For one, women's educational upgrading must have induced them to want to work. As of 1980, women constituted 42 percent of postsecondary students,[115] and Cuban education had a pragmatic bent. The school program combined work with classroom studies. As a result, girls not only acquired work experience before completing their formal education but they also obviously were taught, through school, to value work. Second, the divorce rate had risen considerably (although the officially registered increase is *partly* a statistical artifact of the liberalization of divorce legislation); it rose among women of all ages, including among women of the most employable ages. The proportion of women from ages fifteen to forty-nine who were divorced or separated rose from 1.6 percent in 1953 to 9.3 percent in 1979, a high rate by international standards. Divorced women (followed by single females) constituted the largest category of working women.[116]

But the expanded availability of consumer goods in the 1970s and early 1980s gave married as well as single women reason to work.[117] For every hundred homes with electricity, the percentage with television sets, for example, rose from 33 to 74, with refrigerators from 15 to 38 percent, with washing machines from 6 to 34 percent, and with radios from 42 to 105 percent between 1975 and 1980.[118] With purchasing power largely (though not entirely) dependent on income, women both as heads and members of households had reason to work.

The SDPE, the new management system that incorporated market features, ran up against problems as well. Its impact was constrained by the nonmarket, resource-poor economy in which it was embedded. Both official studies and privately conducted interviews with enterprise administrators and other economic-planning personnel who emigrated to the United States suggest that the SDPE was encumbered by many snags.[119] It met with bureaucratic resistance, especially from old managers and administrators who felt threatened by the reform—state cadre who pursued their own covert forms of disobedience. And the irrational administrative pricing structure, combined with scarcities, caused additional problems. Pricing and most investment decisions remained centrally determined.[120]

Implementation of the SDPE was also impeded by informal worker-managerial ties. Although the new management system formally strengthened managerial prerogatives at labor's expense, friendship and camaraderie prevented managers from punishing workers for substandard work and attendance. Castro spoke to the issue. He quite remarkably portrayed the classless society as a problem, not a solution, created by socialism! Said he, industrial discipline and efficiency were being undermined by the classless structure of management and the labor force on which the revolution prided itself.[121] A CTC leader similarly complained of the "good neighbor spirit, the family cosiness" that needed to be wiped out.[122] And the main Party newspaper attacked "weak-willed managers."[123] Managers were chastised in the official newspaper for allowing workers to collect a full salary for four hours of work a day and for tolerating absenteeism and worker resistance to night shifts. The criticisms undoubtedly were used to justify increasing managerial authority.

Indicative of the problems the SDPE encountered, the profit-based "stimulation fund" was slow to take effect. Although by 1983 some 43 percent of all enterprises had such funds, the right to retain earnings proved at best a weak productivity incentive, for insufficient goods were available for enterprises to purchase with profits. And the "stimulation fund" soon thereafter was rescinded. Central authorities thereby reined in managerial autonomy at the same time that labor's rights remained circumscribed.[124]

Survey data suggest that, prior to the implementation of the SDPE, workers had felt their participation in enterprise affairs to be meaningful. A 1975 study found that 85 percent of the fifty-seven surveyed workers felt labor should be consulted about enterprise matters, and 58 percent of them felt worker input to be influential.[125] Another survey conducted the following year, of 355 workers, reported 80 percent to feel that they "always or nearly always" made a personal meaningful intervention at production assemblies.[126] And in a 1977 survey of one thousand randomly selected workers in large Havana enterprises, the majority of six different strata of laborers claimed to participate actively in monthly production meetings. They also spoke of management receptivity to their suggestions.[127] While the enterprises, on the one hand, were not randomly selected, and interviewees, on the other hand, may not have felt entirely free to express their views, the surveys suggest that labor, following the union and economic restructuring of the early 1970s, did feel that their concerns were being addressed—probably to an extent they had not felt in the latter 1960s. The results of union elections in 1978 further confirmed labor satisfaction. Almost half of incumbent local leaders were reelected, twice as many as earlier in the decade.[128]

Even if worker satisfaction improved, the 1970s reforms left part of the population discontent but reluctant to channel grievances through Popular Power. While Popular Power purportedly had extended democracy to the grass-roots level, continued grievances led a number of islanders to ram their way into embassy compounds in search of political asylum. These islanders, like the middle and upper classes between 1959 and 1961, preferred "exiting" to pressing for change at home. The government's response was to allow them, and others, a one-time opportunity to leave in 1980, from the port of Mariel—an opportunity that 125,000 Cubans took advantage of. The desire to leave is believed to have been partly stirred by the new tourism, by visiting émigrés who came with lavish consumer goods and who spoke of the good life in the United States.

Meanwhile, political turmoil rocked the state apparatus itself. In 1980 Cuba experienced its greatest ministerial shake-up under Castro. Eleven ministers were ousted.[129] Functionaries associated with policies that fell from favor were removed from office.

CONCLUSION

A nationalist and populist, in power Castro set in motion dynamics that contributed to state ownership of most of the economy, a major redistribution of wealth, and a welfare-type state (described in greater detail in chapter 5). Organizationally and ideologically, Castro drew on the Soviet system, but in a manner that built on Cuban traditions, Cuban history, and Cuban "exceptionalism."

In the course of the first decade of the revolution, Castro pushed for a "rapid transition to communism," "combining" the transitions to socialism and communism. He launched what from a Marxist perspective was a utopian project when his efforts to promote diversified "inwardly" oriented development created problems in the external sector he could not ignore. The government expanded its role in the economy, and it emphasized equality, distribution on the basis of need, and a diminution of social distinctions. Concealed at the ideological level, the government promoted exports over production for the domestic economy and investment over consumption.

When the "push for communism" proved to generate new problems while leaving earlier problems unresolved, Castro called for a "retreat to socialism." The "retreat" was associated with a strengthening and formalization of ties with the Soviet Union and other Soviet-bloc countries, an emphasis on distribution on the basis of economic "contribution," not need, and market reforms. The "retreat," in turn, concealed an opening to Western trade, investment, and bank borrowing.

The Western opening more than the "socialist reforms" stimulated an economic boom in the mid-1970s. However, world market conditions turned all too quickly against Cuba, the effects of which have haunted the government ever since, as ensuing chapters show.

That global economic and political conditions in general and global market forces in particular have been of consequence reveals the limits of "socialism in one bloc," let alone one small island. It also reveals the necessity of examining how and why market forces are of consequence to regimes committed to socialism and communism—analytically as well as empirically. For these reasons, socialist "mode of production" and Soviet "dependency models" prove wanting: while premised on different assumptions, they both leave important aspects of the "push for communism" and "retreat to socialism" unexplained, misunderstood, and unaccounted for.

Although the economy by the mid-1980s showed signs of recuperation from the 1970 abyss, and although the market reforms were politically popular, the growth left fundamental fiscal problems unresolved. As a consequence, the government shifted its development strategy once again in 1986, a shift it justified in the name of both Marxist-Leninist and Guevarist principles. If the government "retreated" from communism to socialism in the early 1970s, ideological purists might say there had been excessive "backsliding" toward capitalism a decade later; those purists came to include the government and Party leadership.

Chapter Three

THE LATE 1980s CAMPAIGN TO "RECTIFY ERRORS AND NEGATIVE TENDENCIES"

SOCIALIST RENEGADE OR RETROGRADE

IN THE ERA OF PERESTROIKA?

IN 1986 THE GOVERNMENT launched a campaign to "rectify errors and negative tendencies." The campaign stressed values and organizing principles somewhat akin to those of the late 1960s rapid "push for communism," when many of Ché Guevara's philosophical ideas were put into practice: moral incentives, an expansion of the state's role in the economy, and collective and voluntary labor. The national leadership argued that the revolution had gone astray and that the Rectification Process (RP) would correct this.

A reining in of the early 1980s "market opening" might seem economically and politically irrational in that the opening had stimulated economic growth and had been, in the main, politically popular. The reforms also were out of sync with world trends in that the clampdown occurred at a time when other Soviet-bloc Communist countries opened up to market forces and, by the decade's end, abandoned their commitment to socialist economies and "vanguard party" rule. And in the United States the new emphasis on "rectification" was puzzling because Castro's Cuba had been portrayed as a Soviet pawn. The Soviets, under the leadership of Mikhail Gorbachev, then advocated *perestroika* and *glasnost*, economic and political liberalization, not increased ideological orthodoxy. Castro took public issue with *perestroika*, while still heavily dependent on the Soviet superpower for trade.

Supporters and critics of "rectification" alike have tended to take the government's discourse at face value: supporters pointing to areas in need of improvement,[1] critics pointing to its ideologically driven irrationality.[2] I, by contrast, will show that policy initiatives in the latter 1980s were rooted in emergent government concerns, not primarily in new ideological fervor and commitments, and that those concerns explain why the government reemphasized moral principles it had downplayed for two decades. The national leadership turned to ideology to help legitimate policies that it had material reasons to implement, policies that would have been politically risky to implement if not ideologically justified. Despite economic growth in the early 1980s, the government's fiscal problems had mounted; the government turned to austerity and other measures, justified in the name of "rectification," to address the matter.

If the national leadership had material and not merely or mainly ideological reasons for initiating the RP, then policy initiatives at the time might be consistent with the ideology propagated but not necessarily so. And policies, whether or not ideologically justified, should address state economic concerns. The RP will be shown, with time, not to have resolved economic problems, but not because it was irrationally driven by ideology.

The moral themes and policies linked to the RP are delineated below, after which the roots of the strategy shift are explored. There follows a discussion of the impact of the RP in the 1980s.

THE MORAL CAMPAIGN FOR "RECTIFICATION"

The RP, as Castro asserted, involved a "battle of ideas,"[3] political and ideological work to correct "negative tendencies." There was a trend toward mercantilism and economism that had to be corrected, in his view.[4]

With moral indignation Castro spoke of the injustices committed in the early 1980s by people who had put their own interests above the collective good, when the government tolerated market reforms. In one of his first speeches on the struggle against negative tendencies Castro specified that "socialism must be built with awareness and with moral incentives."[5] On another occasion he noted that the country was going downhill in moral terms with inevitable economic and political consequences. Workers were corrupted by attempting to solve all problems with money.[6]

Castro found fault with the values guiding people in all walks of life, not merely with workers. "Our technocrats and bureaucrats," he noted, "were suffering from and transmitting a sort of ideological AIDS . . . that was destroying the revolution's defenses."[7] And "two-bit capitalists" were criticized for profiteering at the public's expense.

Enterprises, in addition to individuals, were criticized for selling out to capitalism. Groups of enterprises, fired Fidel, were "teaming up with capitalist hucksters . . . playing at capitalism, beginning to think and act like capitalists, forgetting about the country."[8]

With the RP, profiteers were considered the new mercenary, destroying the society from within by exercising a petty-bourgeois type of mentality. Castro argued that one of the negative trends of the revolution had been the shift from the idealism of the late 1960s, which led to neglect of the "historical necessity" of the socialist distribution formula, to a more dangerous emphasis on economic mechanisms "to try to solve everything."[9]

Ché Guevara symbolized the values guiding the "rectification process." Newspaper and journal articles appeared on Ché, and two of Cuba's most prestigious awards went to a book on the revolutionary martyr.[10] In a speech marking the twentieth year since Ché's death, Castro commented that the country was rectifying all that was a negation of Ché's ideas, Ché's style, and Ché's spirit.[11] Castro mentioned that islanders were to rectify those things—and there were many—that strayed from revolutionary spirit, revolutionary work, revolutionary virtue, revolutionary effort, and revolutionary responsibility.

POLICY CHANGES ASSOCIATED WITH THE "RECTIFICATION PROCESS"

At the policy level the RP, like earlier revolutionary policies, had no formal blueprint. But the purported drive for ideological purity was associated with a variety of policy changes. The campaign centered on a clampdown on certain market features and profiteering and a reemphasis on collective forms of labor organization. But certain policies of the latter 1980s, as during the 1970s "retreat to socialism," were more characteristic of an ideal-typical capitalist than an ideal-typical socialist economy.

"Rectification" was associated, for one, with a clampdown on the incipient housing market allowed earlier in the decade. The government announced the reform had been a mistake shortly after defending it at the February 1986 Party Congress. The country's leadership complained that the market opening in housing had given rise to speculation and profiteering, and to the construction of homes for large sums of money with resources and materials taken from the state. In 1988 the National Assembly ruled that the state was to be a compulsory partner in the buying and selling of homes, to prevent a "free market" and transactions for profit.

At the same time, the government revived the minibrigade program that had been initiated in the early 1970s when ideology had been downplayed. Minibrigades, it will be remembered, involved workers temporarily released from their work centers. In the 1980s they also included people not otherwise employed—for example, students, school dropouts, retirees, housewives, and jobless members of the labor force. They were called upon, in conjunction with the RP, to build not only housing but also "social projects," such as health care units, schools, daycare centers, and other facilities.

As described in more detail in chapter 6, released workers continued to receive their salary from their place of employment, where they were expected to return after completing their construction work stint, as in the 1970s. But unlike in the 1970s, the government this time agreed to reimburse enterprises for the wage labor paid to minibrigade members. The enterprises therefore no longer had to absorb the wage costs of the released labor. Minibrigade members who were not at the time employed were paid directly by the state. Known to work twice as many hours as on their regular jobs,[12] *minibrigadistas* both completed buildings begun by professional construction workers and initiated their own projects.

Minibrigades helped address an "error" of the preceding period: neglect of social needs. The Cuban economist José Luis Rodríguez noted that day care, hospital facilities, and housing had been allowed to deteriorate.[13] He noted, for example, that demand for some 20,000 child care "slots" remained unsatisfied, and that the housing stock deficit rose from 754,800 in 1971 to 888,000 in 1985, despite the boom in private housing construction in the early 1980s.

Cubans not incorporated into minibrigades also were called upon to help out in construction and local improvements. In 1987 the Communist Party put forward the slogan "forty hours of voluntary work on community projects." That year more than 400,000 people met the challenge, contributing twenty million hours of voluntary labor.[14] Two years later, in commemoration of the October Revolution in the USSR and the Sixteenth Congress of the Cuban Workers Confederation (CTC), there was a "Red Sunday" mobilization, in which over two million workers reportedly contributed a day's voluntary labor.[15]

Voluntary labor extolled the values stressed in the RP. Minibrigade work was said to involve the "communist work spirit," a "recovery of the work spirit" advocated by Ché.[16] It also was consistent with the previously mentioned Marxist and Guevarist concern of breaking down barriers between manual and intellectual labor. Castro spoke of the virtues of professionals creating with their hands as well as their intellect, and of how professionals can learn from workers; the breakdown of manual/nonmanual distinctions contributed, he added, to feelings of fraternity and equality. Yet the reliance on labor mobilizations over the years, when both downplaying *and* exhalting Guevarist principles, suggests that such mobilizations were not driven merely by ideology.

The RP also included, in May 1986, the closing of the farmers' markets permitted since 1980. The markets as well were said to have been a mistake in that they generated inequities and "too many millionaires." In commerce, as in construction, middlemen typically prospered at consumers' expense. But the markets had allowed people to enjoy a better selection of foods than before.

Agriculture was affected not merely by the termination of the private market outlets but also by a continued de-emphasis on private independent farming. The government did not transform the cooperatives that had been formed since the latter 1970s into state farms, but it continued to encourage remaining independent farmers to join cooperatives, a "higher" form (as previously noted) of private economic activity from a Marxist perspective. By 1989 cooperatives came to absorb 86 percent of all land not held by the state, and the portion of total land operated by independent farmers dropped to 2 percent.[17]

Cooperatives did not go uncriticized during the RP, though. "Flaws" that needed to be corrected included inefficient management, poor implementation of technology, and improper use of land, labor, machinery, and other resources. The correction of "errors" was to reduce the number of unprofitable cooperatives, which had increased from 11 to 30 percent in the first half of the 1980s.[18]

"Rectification" reined in much of the "market opening" in the service sector as well. After having permitted, since 1976, private-service work, the government prohibited private manufacturing and street vending, and it derided self-employment. The clampdown was consistent with the other antimarket policies. Both the providers and consumers of the services lost out.

The government, in addition, promoted worker brigades and construction contingents. Contingents and brigades were to have responsiblity for the use and administration of their own raw materials, labor, energy supply, and salary fund. While seemingly more consistent with socialist than capitalist organizational principles, brigades were first introduced in the early 1980s, during the period of market reform,[19] and they incorporated market features in that they were responsible for their own cost accounting. Moreover, a bonus system was designed to induce members to minimize costs and maximize productivity. Funds saved were, in part, to be distributed to members, in proportion to each person's basic wage. The bonus could be as much as 40 percent of basic earnings. Some brigades also paid for piecework, either on an individual or collective basis.

Construction contingents put emphasis on team spirit, quality circles, and hands-on management.[20] The most famous, a model for others, was the Blas Roca contingent. It included 1,280 workers in 1988.[21] By the end of 1989 some 28,000 Cubans were involved in contingents, and the number increased to 33,000 by early 1990.[22] Like minibrigades, the contingents were not subject to labor regulations. Participants were known to work twelve- to fifteen-hour days.

Only select workers were eligible for brigades and contingents. Workers were chosen on the basis of their productivity and labor discipline.[23] Brigades drew on highly motivated laborers with "above-average political commitment"; they all included Party cells. Brigade membership brought economic reward to politically loyal folk.

The government and Party at the same time called for a "rectification of errors" in more conventional forms of employment. The "errors" involved rule by the "bureaucratic method," policies generating income inequities, excessive emphasis on material reward, and inefficiencies in the use of labor. It is uncertain whether labor problems were worse then than in years past, but the national leadership, as previously noted, was most inclined to admit problems during transition periods, to help legitimate policy shifts. Official acknowledgment when launching the RP of high absenteeism and high labor turnover during the preceding decade implied that the "market opening" had not resolved problems of labor discipline. *Granma*, in conjunction with the rectification campaign, on a number of occasions alluded to labor instability and absenteeism. And Castro highlighted the severity of the problem of worker discipline in noting that a textile plant in the eastern city of Santiago de Cuba had an absentee rate of 25 percent (a sector with typically high turnover rates), and that members of certain cooperatives worked merely four- to five-hour days.[24]

Work "norms,"[25] the job obligations required for receipt of basic wages, were said to have become so slack by the mid-1980s that almost all workers fulfilled them four to five times over, and work shifts had often been shortened, with millions of overtime hours reported.[26] As part of the RP, 241 workplaces were inspected in Granma Province. Over 4,200 workers were reported to have been overpaid because of mistaken interpretations of existing legislation, faulty implementation of norms, incorrect use of the principle of linking wages to norms, and lack of control and supervision. Deliberate foot-dragging, or creeping inefficiency in the normal workday, allowed workers to increase their earnings through overtime work. Labor, in essence, had manipulated work rules to their own advantage, at enterprises' and the government's expense.[27] Decentralization and other reforms had increased labor's power, but once again through informal worker not formal union channels. Seen in this light, the national leadership may have promoted brigades and contingents in part to bypass and undermine growing grass-roots labor power.

Rectification, not suprisingly, included efforts to restructure work norms. The government tried to increase job performance requirements for receipt of basic wages. And payments for overfulfillment of norms fell from 6 to 3 percent of the average worker's basic wage between 1985 and 1987.[28] Yet in contrast to the late 1960s, no ceiling was placed on bonuses for exceptionally productive workers.[29] Said Castro, "Although we recognize that there is room for bonuses under socialism, they must be the result of good work . . . not because of trumped-up profits, inflated prices and charging 10,000 pesos for what actually cost 500."[30]

Along with attacking "excessive" material earnings, the government addressed the issue of unequal earnings. It raised wages for the lowest-paid workers (in agriculture) 40 percent.

The RP involved an attack on bureaucratic tendencies, in turn. Rule by the "bureaucratic method" was criticized once again. Drawing on Marxism-Leninism, Castro argued that anyone who ruled or managed "from above," without contact with the masses, was guilty of relying unjustifiably on the bureaucratic method. An article in the Party paper, entitled "The Military Chief as a Bureaucrat," criticized any official who acted selfishly, technocratically, and passively. The same article also stated that anyone who either violated rules and regulations or tolerated infractions by others was guilty of resorting to bureaucratic methods.[31] Employees of the state were hereby targeted for need of "rectification." The government even sought to reform the SDPE, the state enterprise management system implemented gradually since the latter 1970s—first by expanding market features of the system but then by reining in the system altogether. In 1986 managers gained greater control over the movement of stocks and supplies. Yet a few years later they lost their discretionary power. Central authorities limited enterprise rights to retain profits, and in 1990 Castro trashed the system. Ten years, he said, had been wasted from the time the economic management and planning system had been put into practice.[32] He pressed for greater economic centralization as supplies became ever more scarce (with to-be-described import cutbacks and recession-linked austerity measures).

The government, meanwhile, remained committed to minimizing the role of state-regulated rationing. Rationing accounted for about a quarter of family consumption in the latter 1980s, down markedly from 95 percent in 1970 and down somewhat from 30 percent in 1980. Only when new shortages arose, such as of toothpaste in 1988, were goods that had unrestricted sales put back on rationing.[33] The nonrationed goods were sold largely through state "parallel market" outlets after the closing of the farmers' markets. Indeed, the "parallel market" system was expanded with the RP.[34] Surplus quantities of both rationed goods and luxury items were made available through these outlets, at nonsubsidized prices set by the state. Newly established state-run agricultural produce markets (*agromercados*) were also established, in Havana; they offered greater variety and better quality food than the *acopio* (subsidized) outlets where rationed goods were sold.[35]

The values stressed with "rectification" would lead us to expect promotion of worker interests along with a de-emphasis on market features. Yet the RP was associated with the introduction of some labor policies more characteristic of an ideal-typical capitalist than socialist economy, and the nonunionized "informal" sector of capitalist economies at that. Castro himself attacked worker prerogatives. In a speech in January 1989 he asserted that laws had been enacted that provided undue labor protection. He advocated discarding all paternalism and increasing labor discipline.[36]

In the latter 1980s the government came out against employment security, wage guarantees, and unemployment and seniority rights.[37] Jobs in industry that needed to be staffed were no longer to be filled on the basis of years of service but on the basis of qualification and skill. Even organized labor defended the attack on seniority rights. Delegates to the Fifth Congress of the National Union of Light Industry Workers, for example, in 1989 passed a motion supported by their union leadership to eliminate such rights. They conceded job rights for their membership, for the sake of increased productivity. Organized labor took such a sacrificial stance at the urging of its leadership, handpicked, as noted, by Fidel and his most trusted collaborators.

In 1988 the white-collar stratum, in turn, was subject to attack. The government ordered the number of administrative jobs to be slashed by 6,300 and the number of managerial jobs by 16,400.[38] The government obviously felt the managerial stratum, in particular, to have grown too large, and possibly also too dependent. Not surprisingly, under the circumstances, unemployment rose—to an estimated 6 percent of the labor force.[39] The government praised enterprises that reduced their payrolls, and it castigated others that did not. For example, the National Science Center and two power plants, which reduced their staffs by half, were praised, while the tourist sector was chastised for not so doing. Yet released workers, in the spirit of the revolution, received unemployment compensation until relocated to new jobs.

But employed workers in some instances ceased to be guaranteed a basic wage, reversing Castro's initial wage policy. In the professional construction sector, for example, workers were to be paid according to performance and the amount of time worked.[40] Since production in the sector increasingly was halted because of supply shortages, workers had to shoulder costs of conditions not of their making. And the right of state enterprises to hire on a piecework basis further undermined worker security and rights to a minimum wage.

Other labor policies of the late 1980s attacked institutional rigidities without either undermining worker employment rights or subjecting workers to market-type insecurities. The *multioficio* (multiple-job, or "broader job profile") principle is illustrative of the attack on institutional rigidities. The *multioficio* system permitted managers to call on employees for diverse economic tasks, to combine a number of work norms (job descriptions). Management at many workplaces had, previous to the reform, experienced difficulty assigning laborers to tasks for which they had not officially been hired[41]—owing to labor refusal to do other work. The *multioficio* system allowed for more efficient use of labor, but it weakened informal worker control over the labor process.

The government at the same time attempted to reduce the number of job classifications. The number of job classifications had jumped from 10,000 in 1975 to 14,000 in 1983, after the 1980 wage reform had increased earnings for workers in skilled categories.[42] The rise in job classifications reflected yet another way that labor had manipulated the system to its own advantage. Like the "broad job profile" principle, fewer job classifications allowed for greater flexibility in the use of labor in a manner that weakened labor's power.

The government, in addition, initiated consumer policies that caused islanders' living standards to drop. The government reduced supplies of milk, petroleum, sugar, kerosene, and textiles and raised the price of consumer goods, transport, and electricity. Urban transport fares doubled, and electricity tariffs increased about 30 percent. Prices of some rationed goods had never before been raised. The price hikes occurred, moreover, at a time when the average monthly wage fell slightly (from 188 pesos in 1986 to 184 pesos in 1987).[43] Simultaneously, the government cut food subsidies to state agencies. It stopped providing snacks at work centers, and it replaced the afternoon meal (until then offered at child care institutions) with a snack.

Meanwhile, the government aggressively pursued Western economic ties, and it initiated new forms of economic ownership of a capitalist sort, the rhetoric of "rectification" notwithstanding. Annual Western trade at the time amounted only to some 14 percent of total trade, far less than the 41 percent reached in 1974, but the government sought Western management expertise, Western assistance in export markets, and Western investment. Joint venture agreements were reached in electronics, mechanical engineering, petrochemicals, pharmaceuticals, textiles, and tourism. Julio García Oliveras, then president of Cuba's Chamber of Commerce, noted that the "Russians turned our technicians into captains and sergeants of industry but now we are looking to the West . . . to turn us into business executives."[44] Various plants available for joint ventures began to be publicized.[45] Moreover, when in Brazil to attend the inauguration of President Collor de Mello in March 1990, Castro hinted that restrictions on foreign investment and the setting up of joint ventures, as specified in the 1982 Foreign Investment Code, might be relaxed.[46] Castro appeared more open to foreign investment during the period of "rectification" than in years past, at the same time that he criticized individuals and enterprises for "teaming up with capitalist hucksters . . . playing at capitalism, [and] beginning to think and act like capitalists."

Government ministries as well as state agencies directly sponsored joint production and distribution deals with foreign public and private entities. The Cuban Public Health Ministry, for example, signed an agreement for cooperation in quality control in medicine production, joint production and distribution of medicines, and a bilateral consultancy in 1990.[47]

The state agency, Cubatabaco, even went so far as to try to take over private foreign cigar companies, though with only one success, the British Knight Brothers Company. Cubatabaco, in addition, aggressively manipulated its foreign contracts. It sought to introduce cheaper brands, for example, under the Davidoff label and said that it would continue to market cigars under the foreign brand name when the overseas company announced a severing of relations.[48]

Sociedades anónimas (SAs), semiautonomous state agencies, moreover, grew in number and significance, above all in the foreign trade sector.[49] The SAs operated with considerable autonomy from day-to-day budgetary constraints of ministers of state, at home and abroad, for profit and hard currency. Among the best known were Cubanacán, set up in 1987 to attract foreign investment for hotel development; Contex, a fashion enterprise; and Artex, a promoter of live music and performing arts.

Cubanacán promoted package beach holidays, conferences, and health tourism. It was responsible for the construction of most new tourist accommodations and for bringing in a quarter of all foreign visitors at the end of the 1980s. Companies from Spain, Venezuela, Mexico, and Italy invested in Cubanacán hotels, to the tune of around $40 to $100 million each.[50] In May 1990, Cubanacán opened its first joint venture hotel. No less than 40 percent of its development was targeted to take place through such joint ventures.[51]

In 1988 another mixed-enterprise tourist agency, Gaviota, was established, aimed at the high-income tourist market. It opened a health resort in the Escambray Mountains and a small hunting reserve in Pinar del Río Province, and it advanced plans for marinas and other tourist attractions.[52] Begun with an $88 million government loan, it issued stock and secured both foreign and domestic shareholders. Foreign shareholders included investors from Latin America, Spain, and France.

The government, partly through the promotion of such SAs and foreign investment,[53] aggressively encouraged Western tourism during the period of "rectification." Tourism had been the island's second largest hard currency earner at the eve of the revolution, but it was subsequently discouraged, as previously noted, on moral grounds, for contributing to societal decadence. The government encouraged tourism even in the aftermath of the 1980 Mariel mass emigration. Islander pressures to leave had been attributed partly to contact with visiting U.S. émigrés. The turnabout even included development of Cayo Largo as a free port for cruise ships, without customs or immigration restrictions,[54] and the granting of special concessions to foreign investors in the sector. A Spanish-Cuban joint venture hotel at Varadero beach, for example, was given rights to greater flexibility in hiring and firing workers than fully owned Cuban state enterprises and agencies.[55] The number of tourists in due course rose, from some 130,000 in 1980 to 326,000 by the decade's end.

The government, meanwhile, sought to profit from the émigrés who had earlier fled Cuba in opposition to the revolution through means other than tourism. Shipments of cash and goods, as well as transportation, visas, and hotel bookings, became sources of émigré revenue.[56] Visiting émigrés came to contribute some $100 million to $125 million a year to the state coffer (when reintroducing a ban on U.S. travel to Cuba, lifted by President Carter, President Reagan exempted émigrés). A *sociedad anónima*, Cubapak, moreover, was set up specifically to handle dollars and packages sent by exiles in the United States to their families in Cuba.

A number of the SAs demonstrated an entrepreneurial spirit through the diversification of their ventures. Cubanacán, for example, quickly moved beyond its initial tourism mission. By the end of the 1980s it had negotiated an $80 million contract with Brazil to export meningitis B vaccine (Cuba at the time being one of the few countries with the vaccine).[57] Then, in January 1990, Cubanacán negotiated a second Brazilian pharmaceutic contract, with the Rio de Janeiro municipal government, for sale of 16,000 bottles of *melagenina* medicine used in the treatment of vitiligo, a skin disease.[58] Cubanacán, in addition, established clinics abroad to treat vitiligo with the exported medicine (discussed in more detail in chapter 7).

Cimex, registered in Panama, became the largest SA. Although initially set up to capitalize on visiting émigrés, by the end of the 1980s it included forty-eight subsidiaries and twelve associated companies that operated in seventeen countries. It by then ran tourist shops and a car rental enterprise; it arranged flights and accommodations; and it organized tours. Havanatur, a Cimex subsidiary with tourist offices abroad, brought half a million tourists to Cuba between 1979 and 1989. It became the biggest tour operator selling holidays in Cuba.

Cimex's involvement in tourism spurred ventures, in turn, in trade, manufacturing, finance, and consulting. It came to export seafood, meat products, sugar, cigars, rum, software developed by the sugar industry, and biotechnology products, and it imported for island hard currency stores and for any entity with money to pay. Cimex, in addition, set up a small merchant fleet in Panama to deliver goods in the Caribbean. Over the years it developed expertise in international law, which it subsequently marketed through Consultoria Jurídica Internacional. It also became one of the main depositors in Cuba's Banco Financiero, a bank operating in international stock and commodity markets. Cimex's subsidiary Caribsugar, which refined, imported, and exported sugar, in turn operated in overseas financial markets, and its subsidiary Afinco oversaw investments in tourism.

While the *sociedades anónimas* operated with considerable autonomy of the central government, they did not operate entirely independently of each other. Available evidence indicates that they shared common management and directorates, simultaneously and sequentially—a practice known in market economies to enhance corporate power. The Cimex vice president responsible for tourism, for example, was involved in Hava-natur, a Cimex subsidiary, but also in Cubapak and Cimesportes (set up to handle commercial activity associated with the 1991 Pan American Games in Cuba). Similarly, a president of Cimex served as president of the Banco Financiero.

In sum, "rectification" in practice diverged from and at times contra-dicted the rhetoric of the campaign. While assigning new life to Marxist-Leninist and Guevarist moral principles, the government and Party imple-mented certain reforms and tolerated practices of the preceding period that involved market features, that undermined revolutionary and pre-revolutionary won labor gains, and that led living standards to drop. While inexplicable at the ideological level, the policies are explicable at the political and, as indicated below, economic levels. Government policy will be shown to be rooted in an effort to address fiscal and political concerns. Yet the promotion of voluntary labor, brigades, contingents, and cooperatives, and the clampdown on private independent economic activity, reveal how government and Party commitment to socialism in-duced a somewhat distinctive response to concerns shared with capitalist states in the Third World. Many other Third World governments imple-mented neoliberal economic reforms in response to similar fiscal crises at the time. State exigencies influenced policy choices but in no way prede-termined them. Accordingly, government commitment to socialist values was of consequence, but Marxist-Leninist ideology was not *the* driving force behind "rectification" reforms.

State Efforts to Address Emergent Problems

Although Cuba experienced—according to official sources—an impres-sive growth rate during the period of the "market opening," at a time when many other Latin American countries did poorly, the country's im-pressive economic performance concealed growing fiscal problems. Cu-bans benefited from the "market opening," but often at the state's ex-pense. The "opening" did not address and, in some respects, adversely affected the state's ability to generate revenue to meet its fiscal needs—to repay foreign loans and to finance domestic expenditures (see Appendix, Table 2.3 and Table 3.1).

The early 1980s economic expansion had been tied, in part, to im-ports, including from Western-bloc countries, and not merely to domestic market reforms. But the government's capacity to finance hard currency imports deteriorated in the mid-1980s with a plunge first in sugar then in oil export earnings. In the 1980s, it will be remembered, Moscow had allowed Havana to reexport some of its oil for hard currency, oil reexports briefly becoming the island's main source of hard currency. Oil reexport earnings, which peaked in 1985, dropped about 50 percent the following year. Meanwhile, the price of sugar plunged from a near record average annual high of twenty-seven cents in 1980 to four cents in the middle of the decade. The 1985 world market sugar price was the lowest in nominal terms since 1970, and in real terms since the Depression of the 1930s.[59] As a result, sugar hard currency earnings dropped 80 percent between 1981 and 1985.

Castro addressed the problem of the shortfall in hard currency at the opening session of the Third Party Congress in February 1986 and again at the closing session in December of the same year. Noted he, "We are going to face problems such as delays in importing raw materials, an inability to import some spare parts or delays in obtaining them, as a result of the severe constraints we face regarding convertible currency balances, constraints which are greater than ever."[60] On yet other occasions he hinted that the RP was specifically tied to island hard currency needs.

Cuba needed and wanted hard currency not merely to finance Western imports but also to service its mounting Western debt. The Western debt, which had stabilized briefly in the early 1980s, jumped from 3.6 billion pesos in 1985 to nearly 5 billion pesos the following year. (*Note*: A peso, at the official—and overvalued—exchange rate, was roughly equivalent to the U.S. dollar.) Moreover, no new loans were forthcoming and Castro failed in his efforts, unlike in years past, to reschedule loan payments that were due. The only loan he successfully negotiated totaled $97 million, from the Paris Club. The financing was to help service the island's foreign debt, not to initiate new undertakings. Under the circumstances debt payments were suspended.

The government's problems were further compounded by the fall in the value of the dollar, over which it had no control. Hard currency commodity trade is negotiated in dollars, while the island's Western loans were necessarily contracted in other hard currencies owing to the continued U.S. embargo.

Western commentators viewed the drop in Western trade as an indication of the anticapitalist bent of the Rectification Process, consistent with the ideology of the campaign. Increased COMECON trade dependence was not, however, of Cuba's own choosing. The Soviet Union and Soviet-bloc countries came to account for 86 percent of Cuba's total trade in 1986, but largely because Western opportunities contracted. With limited hard currency export possibilities and with no access to new Western loans, Cuba could trade little with market economies.

Several policies associated with the RP that were antithetical to socialist moral principles and the new ruling ideological emphasis reflected state efforts to address the mounting hard currency crisis. For one, the SAs that encouraged an entrepreneurial spirit and foreign investment were designed to generate hard currency. Second, austerity policies were partly designed to increase the supply of goods available for hard currency export. The government, for example, increased the amount of textiles earmarked for export while decreasing textile rations, and it slashed sugar and motor vehicle gas allocations to increase the amount of each item available for export. The government also raised the electricity tariff to encourage more rational electricity use, so as to free petroleum for sale abroad. Third, tourism was tolerated during "rectification" because it generated hard currency. The government earned around $200 million in convertible currency from tourism in 1989, a fivefold increase over 1980.[62] As of the latter 1980s only sugar, fish, and oil reexports brought in more hard currency than tourism.[63] Tourism came to generate about 12 percent of the value of hard currency merchandise trade, up from 3 percent in 1981.[64] Cuba's competitive advantage came not merely from its beautiful beaches. The cost of a holiday, on average, was less than elsewhere in the Caribbean.[65]

The underlying fiscal crisis that induced the RP had roots, however, in the domestic as well as the external sector. In 1983, during the purportedly "good years" of the early 1980s, the government ran a 266 million peso budget deficit. The deficit improved the following year, after which it deteriorated again (see Appendix, Table 3.1). In conjunction with the RP, the government sought to reduce domestic expenditures and increase domestic revenue (with, as discussed below, mixed results), plus improve hard currency earnings.

On the domestic front there is reason to believe that the market reforms stimulated production and that they raised the earning power of many Cubans. But individuals and enterprises benefited partly at the state's expense—in ways that macro economic data conceal. The disjunction between private and state interests is well illustrated in agriculture. Private producers manipulated the "market opening" to their own advantage. At the time, they sold their poorest quality output to the state. In so doing they maximized the quality of goods they could market privately for profit, while minimizing that which the state could. Similarly, in marketing privately produce pledged to the state, in exchange for credit, seed, and other input, the government absorbed farm expenditures while farmers appropriated profits. And when farmers diverted goods that were supposed to be exported, such as coffee, to the domestic market when consumers were willing to pay more than the official procurement price, the state was deprived of much-needed trade earnings, while farmers and intermediaries prospered. At the same time, government expenses rose. The state had to raise the price it paid farmers for crops, to induce producers to sell to the official procurement agency rather than market their goods privately.

By restricting private trade the government could, in principle, better control what agriculturalists produced, minimize diversion of goods from the export to the domestic market, and profit more from domestic sales. The government could profit by buying foods from farmers at one price and selling them to the public at state "parallel market" outlets for more;[66] efforts to profit from private commerce through taxation of the activity had failed.[67] The government indeed took advantage of the closing of the farmers' markets to raise some "parallel market" retail prices.

The farmers' markets also undermined government efforts to promote agricultural cooperatives. Peasants, Castro claimed, were resistant to join a cooperative when they could earn more money by producing and selling on their own.[68] The government, it will be shown, had certain economic and not merely ideological reasons for encouraging farm cooperatives.

Production in the state sector, moreover, had suffered—in both the city and the countryside—as labor and supplies were diverted to private activity. People stole resources from their state jobs for sideline activity; they absented themselves from work to profit from private initiatives while drawing their official wage; and they sought early retirement, collecting state pensions while pursuing private endeavors. The workforce, in essence, manipulated the situation to their own advantage. They pursued the best of both worlds, at the state's expense: the wage, unemployment, and retirement guarantees associated with state employment, and the opportunities for additional income that market activity allowed. In clamping down on private production and service activity, government agencies were, in 1988, to produce ten times more, and to contribute 250 to 300 million pesos to the state (as well as to make about three hundred items cheaper for consumers).[69] Restrictions on private activity, accordingly, were to enhance state revenue and output.

Even the market reforms in the state sector had created problems for the government that the RP was designed to address. Under the SDPE state enterprises could retain a portion of the profits they generated. To profit, enterprises hoarded material and labor inputs, to assure themselves adequate supplies—a tendency previously noted to be characteristic of scarcity economies,[70] but one that the reform had been designed to mitigate. Managers, in essence, used state resources for their own ends. In reflecting on the pre-"rectification" period Castro noted, with dismay, that "Enterprises were asking constantly for more men instead of controlling . . . their work."[71] Payrolls had become inflated as enterprises competed for scarce labor. The government had ultimately to absorb the wage costs since the enterprises were state-owned, and the wage bill was state-financed. Quite possibly, the mandate to slash 16,400 managerial posts was designed to rein in a stratum that had abused the SDPE.[72]

The market reforms also had led to enterprise concentration on the most profitable economic activity, not necessarily the full range of activity needed for the smooth functioning of the economy and the fulfillment of state plans. Here too enterprises manipulated the system to their own advantage, with the state (and, ultimately, the consumer) having to bear the costs. What was profitable to an enterprise and its labor force was not necessarily equally profitable and beneficial to the government. As a result, the "right" things were not always produced, and projects (such as in construction) were left unfinished because the value of the final stages of building were lower than the initial stages.[73] Earth-moving and placement of foundations was worth the most.[74] Indeed, at the time of the launching of the RP, the number of unfinished projects had allegedly gotten out of hand.

Completion of state construction projects also apparently suffered because workers absented themselves to build private housing, taking state equipment with them. Castro publicly castigated an individual who exemplified the abuses occurring in the construction sector—a man who borrowed, from different state enterprises, a crane, a cement mixer, and a truck to build a house that, if he were to sell it, would bring him 40,000 pesos. The equipment, meanwhile, was not available at the work sites.

The restructuring of work norms and the attack on "unwarranted" bonuses were, similarly, in principle cost-saving measures. They were designed to minimize idle and inefficient labor, to tie wage payments to efficiency, and to reduce the wage bill. During the latter 1980s the government frequently addressed the issue of productivity. It made mention of the need to take full advantage of the workday, to respect the workday at every job site, and to work better with more dedication and quality.[75]

The ideological work associated with "rectification," meanwhile, was designed to restore work discipline along with revolutionary purity.[76] Said Castro, the RP involved a "Battle of ideas . . . that can be transferred into material wealth."[77] And on another occasion, he asserted that the RP would save hundreds of millions of pesos,[78] revealing that it was not just a political and ideological matter but economic as well. He also warned that "we have to be careful not to fall into . . . errors of excessive idealism. . . . We must be careful, prudent, cautious, and wise and not do anything which could hamper production."[79]

With RP-linked consumer import cutbacks, and production slowdowns caused by a reduction in imported inputs, the government had added reason to stress work as a revolutionary duty, not as an opportunity for personal gain. Castro acknowledged this matter as well. "Right now," he said, "the Revolution is not able to provide a counterpart to that effort in money because there is no counterpart in goods."[80] The RP, in essence, made a virtue out of necessity, just as emphasis on moral incentives had done two decades earlier.

Even the wage increase granted the poorest paid workers addressed state economic concerns. This socially just measure involved an added fiscal expenditure at a time of budgetary belt-tightening. Though seemingly inconsistent with the fiscal austerity emphasis of the time, it was designed in no small part to attract labor to such poorly paid sectors as agriculture, and to reduce labor turnover in low-paid industries. Unable to strike for higher wages, workers in those sectors had been voting with their feet. Laborers opted, when possible, for better paying, less backbreaking work, to the point that farm hands had come to be in short supply and farm labor turnover was high. Reportedly, the 1987–88 sugar crop suffered from labor shortages in the planting, cutting, and transporting stages, and high labor turnover hurt the profitability of the sector.[81] A wage raise for canecutters is said to have helped attract eight thousand laborers in the latter 1980s.

The collective forms of economic organization promoted in the latter 1980s—worker brigades and contingents, agricultural cooperatives, and construction minibrigades—in turn were consistent with government economic concerns at the time. That is, the state had economic and not merely political and ideological reasons for promoting the collective forms of labor organization. The worker brigades were designed to increase labor productivity, including in sectors where labor turnover and absenteeism had been high because the work was hard and dirty.[82] In 1988 brigades were reported to have cut unit costs by as much as 50 percent.[83] Brigade workers were deployed as shock troops to resolve problems or complete priority projects quickly.[84] They typically worked long hours in return for higher pay, better housing and food, and coveted consumer durables, such as air conditioners and refrigerators.

The moral campaign for minibrigade participation even concealed state economic interests. For one thing, although *minibrigadistas* had proved themselves in the past to be less efficient than professional construction workers, they involved minimal direct labor costs to the state. They, in principle, involved "unnecessary" labor that enterprises had hoarded. Second, minibrigades could be called upon to complete work that professional construction workers had abandoned when it was less profitable to finish than to start projects; they accordingly permitted better use of material as well as human resources. Third, the minibrigade movement addressed a labor recruitment problem the state faced. The government had difficulty attracting labor to do menial, backbreaking building except when it was highly profitable (as it had been in the private sector with the market opening in the early 1980s). Finally, minibrigades allowed for employment flexibility. They were not subject, as were professional state construction workers, to labor laws. They could be expanded and contracted with the availability of building supplies, and they could be asked to work long hours. Minibrigade workers reputedly labored sixty to seventy hours a week.[85] Even though they were less efficient than professional construction workers, in relying on them the government avoided the fiscal and political costs involved in laying off professional builders during "bad times." Unemployed workers received 70 percent of their former salary while not contributing to the economy. The government, as noted, had become sufficiently concerned with the problem of periodic unemployment in the construction sector, with cutbacks in essential hard currency supply imports, to reduce construction worker wage guarantees—a politically unpopular move. It was easier, both economically and politically, to slow down completion of minibrigade housing than to reduce construction employment and wages when bottlenecks arose.

Agricultural cooperatives, in turn, in principle permitted economies of scale, and not merely a "higher" form of social organization consonant with Marxist principles. As the rural population became more educated and resistant to farm work,[86] a more capital-intensive organization of agriculture made sense, from the state's vantage point (though only in the sectors of agriculture not requiring, as in coffee and tobacco, intensive-care work). Large farm units could make better use of farm equipment than small land holdings, and the government (as noted earlier) gave cooperatives, along with state farms, priority access to equipment and low-interest loans for machine purchases.[87] In the first half of the 1980s the machine industry in the sugar sector had doubled its production, and by the end of the decade Cuba manufactured over six thousand cane havesters.[88]

If there were "underlying" economic reasons for reforms rooted in the domestically oriented economy that the state justified ideologically, in the name of "rectification," the same was true of reforms for which the state had no such justification. The labor policies that eroded worker employment security and earnings, in violation of socialist principles, addressed state economizing concerns. Tolerance of part-time hiring and payment on a piecework basis, elimination of seniority rights, and encouragement of employment cutbacks encourage labor efficiency while minimizing non-productivity-linked labor expenditures.

The consumer austerity policies associated with the Rectification Process that caused islanders' living standards to drop similarly addressed state fiscal concerns. Price hikes and consumer cutbacks were designed to reduce state fiscal outlays, as well as in certain instances to increase, as noted, the stock of goods available for hard currency export. Thus the population suffered as the state tried to address its own fiscal problems.

The government may have had political reasons as well for launching the RP. Although designed in part to undermine black-market activity, the "market opening" had contributed to an increase in certain crimes, with implications for the moral order. People turned to illegal means to attain then-legitimate ends—private profiteering. Some self-employed reportedly had several people working for them, and dozens of others selling their products, in violation of the law. In addition, Castro noted that thousands of small farmers, private truckers, state vendors, and managers of small places got rich robbing, bribing, and corrupting others. People would steal truckloads of goods and sell the cargo for profit, and factory employees would use, as noted, machines and raw materials for their own personal profit. Reports also disclosed theft by managers of small places, such as cafeterias and ice cream parlors.[89] They were said to be stealing 100 to 200 pesos a day. Doctors, in turn, sold medical notes to excuse employees from work and to permit early retirement. It was disclosed, for example, that several doctors in Pinar del Río Province sold medical releases for 1,500 pesos each to persons wanting to retire before the legal age. People purchased the certificates to collect pensions while having the freedom to make money in private pursuits.[90] State-employed doctors thus were accomplices in employee maneuvers for personal gain, at the state's expense.

Enterprises as well as individuals violated the law. Castro castigated enterprises for stealing to pretend that they were profitable and selling materials officially alloted them for profit.[91] Fifteen municipal enterprises in Havana responsible for house repairs, for example, were said to be guilty of such illegal activity. Price rigging, in addition, became rampant: enterprises prospered by overcharging for the items they produced and the services they offered. As Castro noted, by charging high prices, considerably above costs, "Any outfit can be profitable."[92] According to a study of 451 enterprises in 1986, four out of ten were found guilty of price violations (especially in the restaurant sector, which underweighed and overpriced food).[93] Enterprises were, in Castro's words, becoming the sorcerer's apprentice, that is, apprentice capitalists.[94] Inspectors confiscated 21.4 million pesos in profits earned by enterprises in violation of state pricing policy. While the crackdown undoubtedly was motivated by moral considerations, government efforts to curtail the illicit profiteering brought millions of pesos to its coffer; it accordingly addressed its fiscal concerns as well.

The scope of illegal activity was such that crimes relating to dereliction of duty and abuse of office were among the few crimes for which penalties were increased in the Penal Code adopted at the end of 1987. The new code, designed to improve rationality and efficiency in the legal system, was a reform associated with "rectification."

Given that the RP addressed government economic and moral concerns, the underlying rationale behind it and Gorbachev's *perestroika* were less dissimilar than the U.S. government and media and even Castro himself conveyed. Both the Cuban and the Soviet governments emphasized efficiency and selective market features, and they attacked corruption. Havana, in contrast to Moscow, cracked down on private commerce and other private activity, but not because Castro was obsessed with, and blinded by, Marxist orthodoxy. The different leadership responses to shared problems reflect discretionary power possible under state socialism, as well as Castro's political independence from the Kremlin. By the end of the 1980s even ideological differences between *perestroika* and "rectification" waned. The Cuban leadership came to put less public emphasis on the values that Ché stood for then than when launching the RP in 1986, and Gorbachev increasingly emphasized sheer regime survival. The deepening economic and political crisis in the Soviet Union, meanwhile, gave Castro ever less reason to adopt Soviet-style "liberalization" reforms.

IMPACT OF THE "RECTIFICATION PROCESS"

By the end of the 1980s the RP resolved neither the state's economic nor its political problems. But problems persisted because of unforeseen changes abroad at least as much as because of "errors of rectification."[95]

If a major reason for launching the "rectification process" was fiscal, the success of the campaign might be measured by the government's ability to rein in the foreign debt and improve the balance between domestic revenue and expenditures. To government dismay, the island's hard currency foreign debt continued to mount (see Appendix, Table 2.3). Estimated at close to $3.6 billion in 1985, by the decade's end the debt had doubled.[96]

The RP, in essence, failed to keep the hard currency debt from mounting. However, the debt undoubtedly would have been greater had the government not restricted Western imports, in conjunction with the RP. Moreover, the debt increased in the main for reasons beyond the government's control. Seventy-two percent of the increase in the debt was attributed to the depreciation of the dollar.[97] Also, hard currency merchandise export earnings never recuperated to levels of the early 1980s owing to the low value commodity exports commanded abroad, not to a drop in the volume of goods exported. The government's problems were further compounded by its continued inability to negotiate new hard currency bank loans. Cuba was locked out of all but the most costly form of hard currency financing—suppliers' credits. The problem of foreign financing was exacerbated by the precipitous cutoff in Soviet-bloc development aid in the latter 1980s, the only bilateral aid of any significance it had received. COMECON aid dropped from an estimated $888 million in 1984 to $1.9 million at the decade's end.[98]

Partly because the government's fiscal strength was so tied to the external sector, the RP did not resolve domestic budgetary problems either. As revealed in Table 3.1 (see Appendix), the balance between revenue and expenditures improved between 1985 and 1986, but it deteriorated dramatically thereafter. Revenue remained relatively constant while expenditures climbed.

The deficit might have been worse in the absence of RP reforms. Government earnings increased, for example, with the closing of the farmers' markets. In 1988 "parallel market" sales rose by 13 million pesos.[99] Even from the state's vantage point, though, fiscal gains must be weighed against other costs and losses. Indeed, in 1988 total sales declined by 70 million pesos, possibly because agriculturalists produced less once the closing of the farmers' markets curtailed their opportunities to prosper. Since a drop in consumption is not politically popular, the government created new problems while addressing its fiscal needs.

Economic conditions in general were not good the first two years of the RP. After a slugggish year in 1986, the economy took a nosedive in 1987. Government efforts notwithstanding, in 1987 the gross national product (GSP) decreased by about 4 percent (in constant 1981 pesos).[100] Yet, the English Economist Intelligence Unit attributed the economic slowdown more to conditions beyond Cuba's control than to errors of the campaign to "correct errors and negative tendencies":[101] in its view the economy was adversely affected in the first few years of the RP by Hurricane Kate and low world sugar prices, low world oil prices which reduced petroleum (re)export earnings, the devaluation of the dollar, and the cumulative impact of long drought. The combined effect of these "exogenous" forces was a continued low capacity to import, affecting consumption and the ability to finance production-related imports.

The economy took a slight turn for the better in 1988: the GSP grew by more than 2 percent that year. Cuban authorities attributed the growth to the ongoing process of "rectification."[102] But the value of production in 1988 still was slightly below that of 1985 (in constant pesos). And by the decade's end the economy did barely better than before the launching of the RP (see Appendix, Table 2.1).

Certain sectors specifically targeted with the Rectification Process, nonetheless, showed impressive gains: construction increased 16 percent and sugar about 10 percent between 1986 and 1987 (versus, on average, 4.5 percent yearly between 1981 and 1985).[103] Housing completions, in turn, rose—from 28,542 in 1986 to 30,495 by the close of the 1980s.[104] However, minibrigades built far fewer of the housing units than their official attention conveyed. They were responsible for only one-sixth of all units built in 1989.

Expansion of the sugar industry, moreover, served as a base for developing the engineering and cane derivatives industry. By 1990 the sugar industry included building-board plants, distilleries, pharmaceuticals, cosmetics, and torula yeast (for animal feed) plants. The sector also produced about 10 percent of the energy generated domestically, including energy for its own use, through the burning of bagasse (a cane derivative).[105] The export of sugar by-products also increased. Annual exports of sugar-related animal feed, for example, doubled in the 1980s.[106]

But nonsugar agriculture, also targeted with "rectification," fared less well. According to data on state farm procurements and state farm productivity, during the latter 1980s state procurement of only six of eleven basic agricultural products improved, from both state and private sources, and total procurement of tubers and tobacco was less in 1989 than in 1980. State procurement of nine of the eleven products from state farms and of eight of the products from private producers had increased in the first half of the 1980s, when the farmers' markets operated. State acquisition of key foods, from private as well as state farms, therefore increased more during the "market opening" than subsequently, when the state, in principle, had greater control of the marketing system.[107]

Data on output per unit of land also reveal disappointing results with "rectification." In the state sector output per unit of land improved for only five of the eleven basic crops in the latter 1980s, whereas it had improved for eight crops both between 1975 and 1980 and between 1980 and 1985. Land productivity deteriorated in the state sector in the latter 1980s despite an increase then in state farm employment and in farm wages.[108] Government efforts to spur farm output with increased material incentives did not counter other factors adversely affecting farmwork at the time, such as reduced imports of herbicides, pesticides, machinery, and spare parts.

The cooperative movement also ran up against difficulties. Despite government promotion of cooperatives, the number of cooperatives, the land held by cooperatives, and the number of agriculturalists in cooperatives all diminished in the latter 1980s.[109] The government did not compel *campesinos* to remain in cooperatives against their will (unlike forced collectivization under Stalin). Some *campesinos* joined only long enough to take advantage of retirement benefits that affiliation entitled them to.

And the advantages of affiliation with cooperatives may have diminished if low-interest loans made available to the sector could not be used to import farm inputs, with "rectification" austerity restrictions.

Wholesale trade in food, in turn, deteriorated in the latter 1980s. Between 1985 and 1989 the volume of sales of nine of fourteen key items dropped in the wholesale sector—more than in any period since the early 1970s.[110] Yet, state retail-sector sales showed record increases. Why the difference in the performance of the two sectors? Retail trade through state channels undoubtedly improved as a direct result of the closing of the farmers' markets. Food that had been diverted to the private markets were channeled through the state system with "rectification." Here the state gained. The wholesale sector, by contrast, suffered in the latter 1980s from the general drop in state farm productivity.[111]

Islander access to domestically produced consumer nondurables, however, was poor throughout the 1980s, but especially during the period of "rectification."[112] In the 1980s industrial gains were concentrated in heavy industry, not in production of items that folk could directly appreciate.

More surprisingly, social consumption trends were the opposite of what regime rhetoric suggested. The government conveyed the impression that social expenditures were emphasized with "rectification" while personal consumption was not. Yet social consumption outlays, in constant prices, declined 5 percent between 1985 and 1989 while personal consumption expenditures increased 6 percent. (However, personal consumption rose at a slower rate during "rectification" than in the preceding decade.)[113] While day-care and medical care services expanded, the government quietly cut back work center and day-care meal subsidies and other social programs. And per capita hospital bed facilities improved less in the late than in the early 1980s, while university matriculation in 1989 was down to levels of the mid-1980s.[114] Thus, the rhethoric of "rectification" concealed a contraction of certain social outlays.

State preoccupation with its own fiscal concerns did not result in a diminution of the proportion of the national income allotted to overall consumption. Between 1985 and 1989 the proportion increased slightly, from 46 to 50 percent, while the proportion allotted to investment dropped from 14 to 9 percent.[115] The state did not put its investment priorities ahead of consumer concerns, as it had in the latter 1960s. (Consumption suffered mainly because the economy in general did poorly.)

The RP, meanwhile, left other problems unresolved. For one, despite the "battle of ideas" bureaucratic inadequacies remained. A Cuban survey found most respondents critical of mistreatment, and poor and slow service.[116] Islanders were critical of the behavior of functionaries, of their "bureaucratic methods." Through "rectification" the government failed to regulate effectively its employees. Second, illegal activity persisted despite efforts to rein it in with "rectification." A 1988 audit of commerce found that nearly half the 125,000 retail establishments scrutinized violated price and other regulations. The number of violations in wholesale outlets was not made public, but it was noted that the outlets received 12 million pesos in undeclared earnings.[117] Similarly, 460 audits of state ministries uncovered 19 million pesos of undeclared earnings. People, individually and on an enterprise basis, took advantage of their positions for their own ends. "Rectification" did not convince them to do otherwise.

A decree issued in 1989 extended the range of petty criminal offenses to include customer grievances in the retail sector. New offenses included the ignoring of customers by sales assistants, nondisplay or nonrevision of price lists, nonpresentation of menus in restaurants, and "package sales," that is, a store manager's refusal to sell customers articles in short supply unless they also bought items in large stock.[118] The national leadership must have issued the decree because of widespread discontent with the delivery of services. Moral suasion, in conjunction with the campaign to "rectify errors and negative tendencies," had not induced low-level bureaucrats to be responsive to consumers.

The government's ability to remake society was impaired not merely by administrators, clerical workers, and other white-collar employees, however. It was also impaired by the indifference and disobedience of manual workers, the proletariat in whose name the leadership claimed to rule. Despite "rectification" emphasis on productivity and socialist morality, absenteeism, at least in certain sectors, remained high. It was reported to reach 20 percent in a sector of the clothing industry, as high as it had been in certain sectors in 1970. And according to the Minister of Health, people still frequently feined illness.

Not least important, in addressing economic problems the government and Party generated political problems. People did not happily accept cutbacks in earnings, purchasing power, and the stock of consumer goods. Workers also probably were not happy with the diminution of their labor power. The entire national committee of the sugar workers' union was replaced in March 1989, apparently because it failed to secure worker conformity with new labor norms.[119] Worker dissatisfaction once again took the form of foot-dragging and absenteeism, not public protest.

The RP, moreover, may have increased criminal activity unwittingly. The RP, for example, had the unintended effect of sparking new illicit activity. People turned to illegitimate means to attain coveted goods when legitimate means were curtailed. In particular, in closing the farmers' markets the government made illegal private commerce that previously had been legal; it did not eliminate private trade. A black market immediately emerged, and persons illegally started to sell places at the front of queues for goods that came to be in short supply.[120]

The black market reflected the disparity between supply and demand: the failure of RP policies to keep the stock of goods available through legitimate channels in line with the money people had at their disposal. It also reflected the state's inability to contain material aspirations and to impose its will when in conflict with people's priorities. Government efforts to promote savings over consumer spending were ineffective. Islanders preferred to defy the state, quietly and illicitly.

The closing of the farmers' markets probably also transferred some problems from the private to the state sector. Quite possibly auditors would have found fewer price and other irregularities in the retail and wholesale trade in 1988 had the farmers' markets still operated. Employees in commerce may have been faced with new opportunities for private, albeit illegal, gain as consumers turned to the official distribution system for more purchases than before and austerity policies resulted in supply shortages.

Public revelations of serious criminal involvements by high-level ministerial and military officers in 1989 illustrate how ineffective the moral campaign for "rectification" was even among the bureaucratic elite. The RP was subverted by the very cadre called upon to carry it out. The state's hard currency preoccupation became an instrument of high-level private abuse of office, an unintended consequence of island dealings with the capitalist world. Functionaries took advantage of their privileged access to foreign exchange, both to enrich themselves and to build up informal followings in the Latin American patron-client tradition.

In an effort to put an end to alleged high-level corruption, illicit activity, and immoral conduct, the government publicized the trials of key accused culprits, and it punished harshly those it claimed were most guilty: four top-ranking officials were executed, and others were imprisoned or dismissed from office. The government hoped that the crackdown and the public shame associated with the televised trials would not only punish the accused but also stop future abuse of office.[121]

Accusations against the main individuals singled out suggest widespread abuse of office. José Abrantes, responsible for Castro's safety for some thirty years, for example, was sentenced to a prison term of twenty years for purported abuse of power, neglect of duty, and misuse of monies.[122] He was found guilty of converting pesos into dollars at black-market rates, contracting construction projects in hard currency using Ministry of the Interior (MININT) resources and convict labor, granting visas illegally, purchasing some 1,300 vehicles valued at $4 million mainly for members of his ministry, and concealing information from the state, including about drug trafficking by MININT officials.

The Ministries of Transportation and the Armed Forces were singled out as other major loci of corruption. The transporation minister was sentenced to twenty years in prison for embezzlement, abuse of power, and unlawful use of financial and material resources. He purportedly purchased two hundred cars illegally for $840,000 in hard currency. Meanwhile, as noted in chapter 1, Arnaldo Ochoa, one of the revolution's most esteemed generals, was one of the four who were executed. He was officially condemned to death for high treason.

Why Castro sanctioned such harsh treatment of the accused remains unknown. If the official explanation is taken at face value, Fidel's most trusted disciples had become more concerned with making a living from their alleged calling, and making it illicitly, than with serving the revolution. Even if the official explanation is true, their illicit dealings do not alone explain the severity of their treatment. Quite possibly the accused were penalized also for criticizing Castro, for disagreeing with him on the appropriate path for Cuban socialism (e.g., on whether Cuba should implement *perestroika*-style reforms), or for attempting to build up their own informal bases of power, which Castro considered unacceptable. Whatever the real reason, it is noteworthy that Castro defined the problem as criminal rather than political misbehavior, in contrast to the Escalante affair of the early 1960s. If ideology guided policies during the period of "rectification," one would not expect Castro to have depoliticized publicly problems he had with his inner circle of disciples.

The SAs and foreign companies with local operations became, in turn, instruments of corrupt dealings. In 1989 fifteen companies were told that they could no longer employ Cuban representatives,[123] and thirty-two local offices of foreign companies were closed to tighten foreign exchange controls.[124] Meanwhile, it was through Cimex as well as other Cuban enterprises that Abrantes reputedly conducted business with MININT financial reserves. Thus, not only did the government promote capitalist-type ventures while advocating revolutionary purity but those very ventures became bases of corruption. The government's need for hard currency created conditions for new abuses of office.

The hard currency obsession even led Castro to support the creation of state institutions to evade the law: however, not law of his government's own making. The government established an agency, known as the MC (Moneda Convertible), under the Ministry of the Interior, that had as its mission finding ways to evade the U.S. embargo. The MC was to attain goods the government wanted but could not obtain legally, owing to Washington's continued refusal to allow bilateral trade. Once created,

the MC became a loci of much of the above-mentioned illicit activity committed by Castro's "inner circle."[125]

The 1989 trials implied that the criminal activity was rooted in the
misbehavior of selective individuals. However, extraordinary numbers of
ordinary folk collaborated with the accused, especially as consumers of
illegally obtained goods. They did so for structurally induced reasons—
their inability to attain coveted goods legally. "Rectification" did not
tame people's material wants. And the trials did not put an end to petty
and organized crime, even in the short run. Reported crimes increased
between 1989 and 1990. The worst crimes were said to be "economic."
Illustrative of economic crimes, ninety-one audits in the first half of 1990
disclosed 25 million pesos that were unaccounted for.[126]

CONCLUSION

Official propagations conveyed the impression that the RP was ideologically driven by a renewed official commitment to Marxist-Leninist and
Guevarist principles. Had the RP been, first and foremost, ideologically
driven, policy initiatives should have been consistent with the values and
morality the state stressed at the time. Yet many government initiatives
were inconsistent with "rectification" morality. The government promoted foreign investment, tourism, and capitalist-like ventures that it had
originally condemned on moral grounds—policies more characteristic of
an ideal-typical capitalist than socialist society. The government also implemented a number of policies that defied the interests of the proletariat
in whose name it claimed to rule. Collective forms of labor promoted at
the time—brigades, contingents, and minibrigades—provided the government with means to undermine union authority and historically won
union rights. In exchange for material benefits, brigade and contingent
workers conceded the eight-hour day, a right organized labor had strug-
gled to attain before the revolution.

Rectification reforms that are inexplicable at the ideological level are
explicable at the institutional level. Reforms at odds with the moral precepts of "rectification," in principle, helped address mounting government fiscal problems, problems that the economic boom of the early
1980s had left unresolved. The policies were to increase state earnings,
above all desperately needed hard currency earnings, and to reduce state
expenditures.

An economic logic to the launching of the RP notwithstanding, "rectification" reforms were not predetermined by state exigencies. Other Soviet-bloc countries and China, not to mention Third World Western-bloc
countries, responded differently, in certain respects, to similar fiscal con-

cerns. *Within* the context of economic constraints, ideology and political considerations shaped the strategy the state selected. Castro's government clamped down on certain market features at a time when the rest of the world feverishly sought to remove market "fetters."

Rectification rhetoric helped legitimate economically induced austerity policies and stepped-up demands on labor. Resentment about, and resistance to, new material deprivations and demands on labor might well have been greater had the government not defended the policies in the name of fundamental revolutionary objectives. At the time, price hikes in many other Latin American countries had sparked protests and other acts of defiance,[127] and dissatisfaction with economic and political conditions led the people of Eastern Europe to bring their regimes down.

While Cubans did not rally to the anti-Communist, prodemocracy tide that swept Eastern Europe and China, neither the common man nor high-level bureaucrats fully internalized the values stressed with "rectification." Cubans engaged in foot-dragging; they absented themselves from work; they abused their offices; and they partook in other illicit activity. The leadership shake-up in the latter 1980s revealed that the very cadre called upon to implement the campaign "to rectify errors and negative tendencies" did not practice what they preached. The shake-up reflected a crisis *within* the state, and not merely among subjects of the state. Since the trials and personnel changes left the conditions that induced abuse of office unresolved, the government addressed the manifest but not the root cause of the problem.

Moreover, the RP never effectively resolved the government's fiscal problems. While its fiscal situation might have been worse had certain practices tolerated during the "market opening" not been reined in, unforeseen changes abroad added fuel to the fire. At the decade's end the government's budgetary deficit and hard currency debt continued to mount, while imports from COMECON countries became more costly, fewer, and unpredictable. By the start of the third decade of Castro's rule the Soviet bloc became the principal source of Cuba's problems, not a source of their solution.

The crisis caused by the collapse of Soviet-bloc Communism made the moral issues raised by the Rectification Process a luxury the state could no longer afford. To address the crisis the government ushered in a "special period in peacetime," to try to "save the revolution."

Chapter Four

FROM COMMUNIST SOLIDARITY TO
COMMUNIST SOLITARY

THE 1990s "SPECIAL PERIOD IN PEACETIME"

WHILE THE RECTIFICATION process of the 1980s left many economic and political problems unresolved, with the collapse of East European Communism conditions in Cuba went from bad to worse. The collapse of Soviet-bloc Communism made the government's vulnerability to global market forces greater than ever. Castro did not passively acquiesce to the "new world order." He implemented reforms consistent with socialist ideological and organizational principles, but more than in years past he "reverted" also to market measures and even to precapitalist survival strategies. He implemented political reforms as well. But the populace did not passively acquiesce either, even if they did not take to the streets to bring down the state as did their former Soviet-bloc comrades.

FROM COMMUNIST SOLIDARITY TO COMMUNIST SOLITARY

COMECON (Council for Mutual Economic Assistance) had guaranteed Cuba markets at prearranged prices, and the trade had not required hard currency. By the start of the 1990s, though, former Soviet-bloc governments insisted on trade terms more favorable to them and on hard currency as the unit of exchange. In addition, they refused to contract medium- and long-term trade agreements, and they did not always honor contracts formally agreed upon.

COMECON countries issued no Five Year Plan for the 1991–1995 period. The European countries insisted on prices set annually on a bilateral basis, thereby de facto dissolving the basis of the multicountry-bloc association. Disinterested in solidarity with, and assistance to, the less developed world, Poland, Hungary, and Czechoslovakia spoke of forming a European only organization,[1] and by 1991 they concerned themselves with joining the European Economic Community (EEC) and qualifying for EEC privileges.[2] That year they dissolved COMECON. The post-Communist governments dropped all moral, political, and economic commitment to Cuba.

The changed relations with East Europe evoked a war of words. Castro asserted, on one occasion, that "we defend each country's and each Party's sacred right to independence," and on another occasion that "we respect the right of any country even to build capitalism."[3] However, soon after economic relations with the former Eastern-bloc European countries soured, Castro became contemptuous, in public, of the poor quality of East European imports. Hungarian buses were chided for getting "six kilometers to the gallon and fill[ing] the city with exhaust fumes."[4] And Castro accused the Bulgarians of sending forklift trucks that "could find no other market."[5] Adding fuel to the fire, he noted that Cuba would no longer accept East European "rubbish."[6]

Castro noted that the quality of East European imports had not changed, only that Cuba's ability to criticize their quality and to admit why they had traded with COMECON countries had. "If we didn't have the money to buy something of better quality . . . we often ended up buying ones made in the socialist countries."[7] In the same speech he acknowledged that "there was a time when saying that something from a sister socialist nation was no good seemed to be an antisocialist stand." He was quick to add that socialism did not by definition produce inferior goods, to justify Cuba's continued commitment to the form of economic organization. "What does socialism have to do with the quality of equipment? . . . Socialism can turn out many good things . . . and capitalism also produces a lot of junk."

The war of words picked up as trade unraveled. Not only did the former COMECON countries refuse to enter into long-term agreements (which would facilitate the Cuban government's ability to plan ahead); Bulgaria, Czechoslovakia (both before and after it subdivided), and Hungary also refused to sign various trade agreements up for renewal, and they did not deliver several items previously promised.[8] Czechoslovakia, in addition, cut credit lines.[9]

While the East European countries—which, after Communism, redefined themselves as Central European—combined had accounted for only about 15 percent of Cuba's trade, they were a vital source of key products, such as trucks, buses, electric generators, centrifuges for sugar mills, and spare parts. A shipment of Hungarian buses had to be cannibalized, for example, for spare parts, to keep existing transportation service in operation.[10]

The dissolution of COMECON occurred just as some industrial export agreements appeared to be reducing Cuba's role within the "international socialist division of labor" as a commodity exporter. In the high-tech field Cuba had contracted 103 assignments associated with the Integrated Program for Scientific and Technical Progress. By 1990, though, the number fell to thirty-four. Cuba also had begun to produce garments in a *maquila*-like manner for a Bulgarian enterprise.[11]

The breakup of COMECON cost Cuba traditional export deals as well. Cuba had counted on East Europe for some 15 percent of its sugar trade. Between the 1988–89 and 1990–91 harvests, however, sugar exports to the former Soviet-bloc countries dropped from 469,000 to 55,000 tons.[12] With German reunification, any ex–East German deficit was covered by the former West Germany or by European Community (EEC) surplus; the former COMECON member automatically joined the EEC when the two Germanies united.

German reunification hurt Cuba in other ways. Although East Germany had only accounted for 5 percent of island imports and 6 percent of its exports, with reunification Cuba lost an important source of aid and military equipment and an important source of key supplies. Cuba had been the East European country's largest recipient of development aid.[13]

When trade with former COMECON partners continued, terms of trade turned against Cuba. Before trade with Hungary came to a standstill in 1991, the Hungarian company, Ikarus, for instance, unilaterally raised the price it charged Cuba for buses—20 percent in 1989 alone. Hungary's main commercial importance to Cuba had been as a supplier of buses.

Economic and not merely political considerations contributed to the East European price hikes. Enterprises and governments there were no longer bound by "solidarity" commitments and no longer subject to Soviet pressure to sacrifice their own material interests. At the same time, enterprises sought to pass on rising production costs to customers. Enterprise costs rose as post-Communist governments terminated subsidies and price controls. Enterprises, in addition, tried to charge what the market would bear, to maximize their profits. They became more profit-driven once freed from Communist state constraints.

Insistence on hard currency as the medium of exchange added to Cuba's problems. Already in the mid-1980s, the island, as noted, had come to have one of the worst hard currency debt/export ratios in Latin America because of difficulties generating convertible currency revenue.[14]

Between 1989 and 1991 Castro was much less publicly antagonistic toward the Soviets than toward the other East Europeans. Officially, relations between the two countries continued on "mutually advantageous" terms.[15] But with the dissolution of the Soviet Union and Gorbachev's fall from grace, trade ties, in the words of Cubans, "dissolved like a meringue." Cuba experienced cutbacks and delays in deliveries and a rise in transport costs. Since the Soviets in the latter 1980s had provided about

70 percent of Cuba's imports and they purchased nearly that portion of island exports,[16] the deterioration in bilateral relations with the former superpower was of much greater consequence than the collapse of East European trade.[17] Imports of foodstuffs, raw materials, and manufactures all came to a near standstill. By 1991 little arrived other than oil, and oil deliveries themselves dwindled.

Reduced oil deliveries meant that Cuba could no longer reexport oil for much-needed hard currency. For a period in the 1980s, it will be remembered, oil reexports had been Cuba's main source of Western currency.[18] Oil cutbacks thereby impaired even island Western trade possibilities, just when they were most needed.

Trade subsidies, the main form of Soviet aid, also ended. While charging the world market price for oil the Soviets did continue, through 1991, to pay over the world market price for island sugar. But they insisted on prices closer to the prevailing world market rate, less than the EEC-Lomé Pact price.[19] Then with the dissolution of the Soviet Union in December 1991, Moscow began to pay Cuba no more than the going world market price—one-fourth the rate it had paid a few years earlier.[20]

On the bright side, Moscow increased its purchases of island biotechnology products, pharmaceuticals, and high-tech medical equipment[21] (as will be described in more detail later in the chapter). The value of these export contracts rose from a modest sum to some $800 million in 1991.[22] There had been plans for Cuba also to become a *maquiladora* of sorts for the then still Soviet Union: for low-wage island workers to assemble Soviet televisions, radios, tape recorders, computer keyboards, and video display units (VDUs), and to manufacture clothing for the once superpower's home market.[23]

Initially, Soviet domestic economic problems, more than political tensions, accounted for the deterioration in trade relations. Indeed, while *perestroika* and *glasnost*-type reforms were in full force in the USSR, 1989 and 1990 protocols called for increased exchanges of goods with Cuba. Gorbachev even continued after the collapse of COMECON to supply the island with some military equipment, and he sided with Cuba against the United States in the UN-Geneva Human Rights Commission when the post-Communist Central European countries did not.

Emergent political tensions *within* the Soviet Union, already before its dissolution, added fuel to the fire, however. Soviet politicians began to disagree openly about the issue of continued aid to Cuba. So-called liberal reformers, most notably Boris Yeltsin, favored slashing aid, if not trade. He and his allies depicted Cuba as a Brezhnev-era police state. They also argued that aiding Cuba was a drag on the budget, exacerbating Soviet fiscal problems. "Conservatives," by contrast, argued that Moscow should continue offering military and economic aid as long as the United

States refused to normalize relations with the island. But Castro's main Soviet supporters, in the military and the security apparatus, were swept from power with the failed Soviet coup of August 1991 and then Gorbachev's fall from power. Soviet-Cuban economic relations thereby became prey to political struggles six thousand miles apart.

Cuba's problems with the Soviet Union came to be at the enterprise and not merely the state-to-state level. Soviet enterprises ceased to abide with bilaterally negotiated contracts. As in the other East European countries, in the Soviet Union enterprises became more profit-oriented and preoccupied with hard currency sales. Enterprise negotiations also became more cumbersome. While the two governments signed protocols, Cuba had to negotiate contracts product by product with individual Soviet suppliers. Formerly having only sixty-two Soviet institutions to deal with, Cuba found itself faced with some 25,000 enterprises (many plagued with production problems) that had gained authorization to engage in trade dealings.[24] To make matters worse, Soviet merchant fleets at times paralyzed deliveries by demanding hard currency payments. For this reason they refused, for example, to load a substantial portion of Cuba's 1989–90 citrus crop, leaving Havana with no major foreign market for the perishables.

With the December 1991 breakup of the Soviet Union, Cuba's trade problems mounted.[25] Indicative of problems to ensue, under the leadership of Yeltsin the Russian Republic passed a bill (in 1990, when the USSR was officially still intact) to invalidate contracts signed between the Soviet government and other countries. The central government opposed the bill, but with the formation of the Commonwealth of Independent States (CIS), under Yeltsin's tutelage, republics ceased to be bound by former deals. Yeltsin, as already indicated, was no friend of Cuba's, and his republic, Russia, produced about 80 percent of Soviet oil.

To make matters worse, Cuba's once favorable financing ground to a halt. In 1992, Moscow extended no new credits (Cuba having previously received, according to Castro, $1.463 billion a year in credits from Moscow—and an additional $162 million from Eastern Europe). Moreover, Moscow insisted on converting the accumulated debt of 15 billion rubles into dollars.[26] At the official exchange rate Cuba owed $24 to $25 billion, but the real value in hard currency was much lower—estimated to be somewhere between $1 to $2 billion at the exchange rate then prevailing in Soviet hard currency auctions.[27] To maximize the money it extracted from Havana, Moscow resisted accepting the real hard currency value of the debt while insisting on commodity trade at world market prices.

Meanwhile, in 1990 the Soviets stopped shipments of arms. According to Raúl Castro, Moscow had provided some $10 billion in armaments gratis.[28] The cutback came just when Cuba could no longer count on its once ally for defense purposes. Castro was forced, as a consequence, to rely on the world market for future military supplies, as well as for imports for the civilian economy. All told, the Cubans assessed the cost of the collapse of Soviet-bloc relations at $5.7 billion in 1992.[29] They lost 70 percent of their purchasing power in three years.

China was the only remaining Communist country with which Cuba's trade relations improved. In 1990, China became the island's second most important trade partner, with trade worth between $500 and $600 million.[30] A five-year agreement for the 1991 to 1995 period involved an exchange of sugar, citrus, nickel, iron, pharmaceuticals, medical equipment, and for the first time, biotechnology products, in exchange for foodstuffs, bicycle parts, and financing for electrical fan and bicycle factories and fish breeding. And in 1992 the two countries initiated a joint venture, their first ever, for production of medical equipment.[31] However, trade between the two countries amounted only to about one-fourth the value of the island's total market economy trade, and it too was denominated in hard currency; the relationship showed little sign of being premised on "Communist solidarity."

Washington, meanwhile, stepped up its efforts to tilt the Communist "domino" collapse in Cuba's direction. Washington had argued, since Castro's early years of rule, that Cuba's ties with the Soviet Union stood in the way of improved economic and diplomatic relations. And in the 1970s Washington added that Cuba's African military missions (detailed in chapter 7) were a barrier to any normalization of relations. Yet as of the early 1990s, Washington was on good terms with Moscow, Cuban-Soviet relations had soured, and Cuba had withdrawn all troops from Africa. Rather than the changed circumstances resulting in improved relations between the closest of neighbors, George Bush, then president, instead imposed new conditions for normalization of relations: political reform. Said he, "Freedom and democracy, Mr. Castro! Not sometime . . . but now!" Bush added that U.S.-Cuban relations could improve if Castro allowed free elections and a UN investigation into human rights abuses, if he released political prisoners, and if he put a stop to subversive activity in Latin America.[32]

Washington maintained a hard line toward Cuba while improving relations not only with Gorbachev's Communist government, before its collapse, but also with China after Beijing's repression of a prodemocratic movement there (and with Vietnam after Hanoi shared information regarding U.S. prisoners of war). To justify his China policy President Bush used the opposite rationale that he articulated in his Cuban stance. He argued that isolating China was not the best way to pressure for democratic reform.

Emergent domestic political forces in the United States, and Bush's conservative political ties, combined with China's greater potential economic importance, help explain why Washington treated Cuba differently than China. A wealthy and aggressive Florida-based Cuban-American anti-Castro lobby, dominated by Jorge Mas Canosa's Cuban-American National Foundation (CANF), became influential under the conservative Reagan and Bush administrations.

Reflecting the growing power of the Cuban-American anti-Castro lobby, Florida Republican Sen. Connie Mack sponsored a bill to prevent subsidiaries of U.S. companies overseas from trading with Cuba; subsidiary trade with other remaining Communist countries was not subject to the same restraint. The bill, passed by Congress in 1990, sought to reinstate the subsidiary trade restrictions lifted in the mid-1970s. In this instance, though, President Bush kept the law from going into effect, vetoing the bill. Exxon, IBM, ITT, and other large U.S. companies that benefited from third-country trade with Cuba (worth about $300 million at the time) lobbied against the bill.[33] Bush also was influenced by Canadian and other government opposition to the legislation. The foreign governments resented Washington's interference in their domestic trade dealings.

The anti-Cuban bloc refused, however, to take "no" for an answer. It put forth a new bill called the Cuban Democracy Act. Bush had opposed the bill until Bill Clinton, when campaigning, courted the Florida vote in the 1992 presidential election. Though closely tied to the Republican party, the CANF contributed $120,000 to Clinton's electoral campaign. Under the circumstances, Bush decided to support the bill and very deliberately signed it in Miami on the eve of the election. Sponsored by Robert Torricelli, the bill not only prohibited U.S. overseas subsidiaries from trading with Cuba; it also banned ships that landed in Cuba from U.S. ports for six months, it allowed for the withholding of U.S. aid to any country that traded with Cuba, and it authorized the U.S. president to give assistance to Cuban dissidents. U.S. subsidiaries affected by the new law by then accounted for about 18 percent of Cuba's $4 billion hard currency imports.[34] The restriction on ship landings hurt Cuba the most: transportation costs rose some 40 percent.[34]

Washington's stepped-up efforts to destabilize Castro's government included denial of rights to a U.S. television network to broadcast the Cuban-held 1991 Pan American Games. Bush sought thereby to deprive Havana of millions of dollars.[35] Though the Bush administration subsequently acquiesced, Cuba had to settle for a much less lucrative deal. The U.S. government, moreover, refused to allow the Organizing Committee to import the drug-testing equipment typically used at Pan American Games.[36]

Washington also stepped up efforts to undermine Havana's ability to profit from the émigré community. It restricted the remittances Cuban-Americans were allowed to send relatives in Cuba, and it limited the fees payable to the Cuban government for visa processing.[37]

Washington even sought Soviet assistance in subverting Castro's government. In one instance, the U.S. Treasury reached an agreement with Gorbachev's government to purchase Soviet nickel, banned since 1962, but only on condition that Moscow certify that shipments contained no Cuban nickel.[38] Nickel was Cuba's second most important export, the Soviet Union had been its chief customer, and Moscow had assisted development of the sector. Second, in 1990 Washington took advantage of the Soviet's mounting economic vulnerability by making aid to the troubled country conditional on Moscow's cutting economic links with Cuba[39]—a condition Gorbachev initially refused to accept, on the grounds that he would not tolerate U.S. pressure over a bilateral matter. The then still Soviet head of state noted that he wanted Cuban-U.S. relations to normalize before weaning the island of aid.[40] He considered U.S.-Cuban hostilities anachronistic in the post–Cold War era. In the fall of 1991, however, he finally conceded to U.S. pressure after the attempted coup d'état left his claims to rule ever more fragile and U.S. support all the more crucial. Third, Gorbachev's successor, Yeltsin, in 1992 accepted U.S. financing to purchase two million tons of sugar on the open market, a credit designed to keep Moscow from purchasing the sweet from Cuba.[41] Then, shortly after he was elected, President Clinton put additional pressure on Moscow. At his 1993 summit meeting with Yeltsin in Vancouver he insisted on Russian cessation of oil deliveries to Cuba as a precondition for U.S. aid,[42] even though the commodity was sold on an entirely commercial basis at the time.

Although the General Assembly of the United Nations in 1992 passed a resolution calling for an end to the embargo, Washington's Western European allies made matters worse for Cuba. While opposed to Washington's interference in their own trade dealings (with some countries refusing to cooperate with the 1992 Cuban Democracy Act), the aid ministry of the newly unified Germany announced that his country would send no aid to Cuba until Castro initiated political reforms. And the newly elected conservative government in Sweden cut off aid to Cuba. The Spanish socialist government even cut direct economic assistance from $2.5 million to $500,000; it denied Spanish exporter and investor requests for a credit line and credit guarantees; and it helped Cuban human rights activists.[43] In 1992, Cuba was the only Latin American country to receive no EEC aid.[44]

Cuba in the early 1990s also faced difficulties with its Latin American neighbors. Cuba lost regional allies when a U.S. intervention ousted Panama's Gen. Manuel Noriega in December 1989 and when the Sandinistas were defeated in the February 1990 Nicaraguan elections. In addition to these political setbacks, Cuba's debts to a number of countries in the region heightened economic tensions; they did not, however, prevent Latin American trade and investment (as detailed below).

"SPECIAL PERIOD IN PEACETIME" ECONOMIC AND LABOR REFORMS

Castro responded to the crisis created by the changed world situation by calling, in late 1990, for a "special period in peacetime." The Special Period, a euphemism for a siege economy, involved sacrifices and reforms "to save the revolution." Though "Socialism or Death" became Castro's slogan of the time, policy initiatives drew, as noted, on features associated with not merely ideal-typical socialist but also capitalist and even precapitalist societies. Noted Castro at a Congress of the Federation of University Students, "This is no time for theorizing but instead for advancing, resisting, and overcoming."[45] With the revolution's future at stake, Carlos Lage, executive secretary of the Council of Ministers in charge of the Special Period economic policy, assumed an importance surpassed only by Fidel (although Raúl remained titularly second in command and next in line).

Socialist-Style Strategies

Consistent with the moral aims of socialism, some reforms were inspired by egalitarian and collectivist principles, and they reflected a continued commitment to a planned economy. Other measures involved the more repressive aspects of socialism as it has evolved historically in practice.

The government began by promoting an ambitious "Food Program"[46] designed to make the country as self-sufficient as possible and to offset the island's declining import capacity.[47] Here Castro appeared to "revert" to the agricultural diversification strategy he had promoted during his first years in power, a project abandoned within four years because of the balance-of-payments problem it caused. But in contrast to the earlier effort, the new program had decades of experience on which to draw.

The program centered on an expansion of irrigation facilities; an expansion of rice, banana, plaintain, root and green vegetable production (partly through irrigation-based increases in land productivity, partly through converting some 20,000 hectares of land from sugarcane cultivation to vegetable production); fish breeding; fifty new hog-breeding centers; 1,800 new poultry sheds; and one thousand new dairies (about two hundred per year).[48] Illustrative of the scope of the program, the new poultry farms were to raise egg and chicken meat production by 10 percent and vegetable production by 50 percent. Yet as Castro admitted with dismay, the project had to be developed without feed, without fertilizer, and almost without fuel, and for these and other reasons its results were disappointing (except for vegetables and tubers).[49]

The Food Program targeted the distributive system as well as production, for about one-third of all crops rotted before reaching consumers. Transport and storage facilities were extremely inadequate. Consequently, the government constructed new distribution centers, storage facilities, and canneries.[50]

Energy conservation was another central component of the Special Period, owing to the massive cutbacks in former Soviet-bloc oil deliveries and the rise in the price charged Cuba. When launching the austerity program, the government reduced petroleum supplies to both the state sector and private consumers by 50 percent, it cut back state investments, and it closed down a number of oil-guzzling factories, most notably cement and nickel plants. It also called for a 10 percent cut in domestic electricity consumption (though, independently of the mandate, power cuts soon became routine).[51] By 1993 electricity was often off six to seven hours a day, making work ever more difficult. In agriculture the government, moreover, reduced the use of fuel-driven tractors and plows. Unfortunately for Cuba, most Soviet-assisted projects and equipment were fuel inefficient.

Transportation also was affected. The government used its authority to halve the number of taxis in operation and then to make them available almost exclusively to tourists. It also cut back bus runs—in Havana by some 30 percent in 1991, and more subsequently. As an alternative islanders could not, however, easily rely on cars, even if they owned one, because gas allotments were slashed and drivers had to wait in line up to five hours to fill their tanks.[52] Hard currency–paying foreigners had priority access to gas.

The economic crisis led in turn to greater state control of the printed word, and to more limited access to information. A 60 percent cut in Soviet newsprint deliveries led the government to slash domestic publishing. Castro called for the conversion of two daily newspapers, *Juventud Rebelde* and *Trabajadores*, into weeklies; for cutbacks in the page length, page size, number of copies, and frequency of publication of the Party paper, *Granma*;[53] for reduced regional press allocations; and for the closing of the armed forces newspaper. By 1992 it was difficult to find a newspaper. *Juventud Rebelde*, at the time of the cutback, had articulated some of the disquietude surfacing among the younger generation.

The publishing industry, which normally put out some five hundred new books a year, ground to a halt as well. Except for some school books, no new works were printed.[54] The publishing cutbacks followed on the heels of a state ban on sales of the Spanish language editions of *Moscow News* and *Sputnik*, in 1988. These publications were outlawed for political, not economic reasons: for promoting "bourgeois democracy and capitalism." Identified with *glasnost* and *perestroika*, the journals contained articles not only critical of the Soviet Union but also of Cuba. They had been selling out in recent years, after having collected dust in kiosks before then. The outlawing of the Soviet publications was unambiguously a form of cultural repression.

For energy-related reasons television broadcasting also was reduced, to forty-eight hours a week in 1991 and more subsequently. Islanders were left with little entertainment even within the confines of their homes. As the country became an increasingly noninformational society, proximity to Florida nonetheless allowed islanders access to U.S. radio programs—including to the Washington-financed Radio Martí, and other anti-Castro stations. The foreign competition resulted in less state control over radio than other media programming. Phone-in programs, in which islanders could air grievances, became popular.

The launching of the Special Period was also associated with stepped-up rationing, and with gradual reductions over time in official allotments (described in more detail in chapter 5). It will be remembered that the government had very deliberately reduced the role of rationing since 1970. However, as goods became scarce it sought, in its own words, "to equalize sacrifice" and to keep goods at prices everyone could afford.[55] Rationing was confined, in the main, to basic necessities. The *libreta*, the ration book, entitled everyone in 1992 to five pounds of rice, twenty ounces of beans, six pounds of sugar, two portions of fish, four ounces of coffee, and sixteen eggs per month. Milk was reserved for children under seven years of age.

Without rationing, scarcities would have caused prices to spiral beyond the means of low-income earners. But not one citizen, according to Castro, was to go without sustenance. "How could a capitalist country accomplish this?" he asked rhetorically.[56] Special Period rationing, however, followed on the heels of cutbacks already in effect for milk, petroleum, textiles, and kerosene, and on hikes in prices charged for consumer goods, transportation, and electricity just a few years before, in conjunction with "rectification." The new and more draconian austerity measures were largely the direct and indirect result of the near-total collapse of trade with former Soviet-bloc countries. Cutbacks in Soviet grain deliveries, for example, meant less grain-based feed for chicken and cattle, and less wheat for bread, although the loss of the Soviet-bloc market for citrus meant more fruit for islanders.

However principled government rationing was, people came to spend hours in queues for meager pickings. And they were forced to make numerous trips to stores just to attain their paltry official allotments, because on any one day not all items were available. Under the circumstances shopping became an obsession and caused people to miss work. A family typically spent fifteen hours a week in food lines, the burden of shopping falling disproportionally on women (in 1993, however, it became legal to pay someone to stand in the *colas*, the lines, and time spent in lines stabilized as distribution became better organized and there was less to buy). Although the Family Code specified that spouses were to share housework when wives worked, men continued to leave most family matters to women, even as household responsibilities became more onerous.

Despite the crisis, Castro remained committed to providing social services. He prided himself in speeches for not closing a single school, day-care center, or hospital, and for not leaving a single person destitute. But circumstances led him to call for no expansion of social services and no new housing construction, and to cut food allotments—in quality and quantity—to schools and day-care centers. Said Castro, "If in five years we don't build housing, if that's the price for saving the revolution, then we'll spend five years without building them."[57]

In an effort to coordinate schooling with declining employment opportunities, the leadership cut back university admissions. The title and subtitles of a *Granma* article reflected official reversal of the earlier commitment to higher education and professional training: "CAN WE DEVELOP WITHOUT MANUAL LABORERS?: Should We Go on Turning Out Tens of Thousands of University Graduates When We Already Have Over 380,000 Professionals? Not Everyone Should Be an Engineer, a Professional or an Intermediate-Level Technician."[58]

Already beginning in the latter 1980s, it will be remembered, the government had selectively reduced university admissions. The number of students enrolled at the university level on a per capita basis tapered off after 1987–88.[59] The government emphasized educational programs that trained students in careers for which there was demand. It accordingly promoted polytechnical studies. Whereas 60 percent of the vacancies for ninth-grade graduates had been in university-track senior high schools and 40 percent in polytechnics prior to the Special Period, the Ministry of Education called for a reversal of the proportions. To "retrack" children some senior high schools in the countryside in 1991 were converted into agricultural polytechnical institutes.[60] But the Ministry of Education even considered eliminating training of intermediate-level technicians when factories were closed down because supplies were not forthcoming.

The government no longer wanted to shoulder the costs of massively upgrading the educational levels of the children of the revolution. It was fiscally costly to invest in schooling for which there were no jobs. It was politically risky to "overeducate" youth as well—to raise professional expectations that could not be met.

From a comparative vantage point, Cubans could afford no expansion of social services. As detailed in the next chapter, Cuba offered more low-cost institutional day care than any country in Latin America, and it had the lowest infant mortality and highest life-expectancy rates in the region. Moreover, Cuba's primary and secondary school pupil/teacher and enrollment ratios were exceptionally high by Latin American standards at the eve of the Special Period (see Appendix, Tables 4.1 and 5.2). Yet the lid on social investment followed on the heels of previously described social consumption cutbacks, during the period of "rectification," and the halt in housing construction occurred despite pent-up demand and despite overseas sales of cement. The government gave hard currency exports priority over islanders' needs and wants as its deficit rose.

Not surprisingly, termination of construction projects, plant shutdowns and slowdowns, and investment cutbacks reduced employment opportunities. It was for this reason that the government, as noted, shifted its education policy. At first Castro called for a reduction of the work week (but not the workday), to prevent layoffs. Particularly popular was the suspension of work on Saturday. "At worst," he said, "the worker will get more free time but he will never be left out in the street without a job or penniless."[61] "Everyone will be assured of income sufficient to meet his needs."[62] Castro sought to keep Cubans from experiencing the insecurities and destitution that economic recessions had in market economies.

With the contraction of job opportunities the government announced a change in its unemployment policy, which had it gone into effect according to plan would have reintroduced a labor scheme more consonant with an ideal-typical capitalist than ideal-typical socialist society. Workers who lost their jobs were given the right, according to the new policy, to select from three alternative jobs. If they refused the options, they were entitled to unemployment insurance, first for three and later for one month.[63] Previously Castro had placed no limits on unemployment compensation.

The new labor regulations distinguished between two types of unemployed workers: "surplus workers" who were temporarily or permanently transferred to other jobs of similar complexity, as near as possible to where they lived, and "available workers" who could not be relocated. "Surplus workers" could maintain their old salary if it was higher than the pay scale of the new job, and they continued to be considered employees of the earlier workplace. "Available workers" were entitled to 60 percent of their previous salary. But if they refused to accept a job transfer (or training), they received only one month's full salary.[64] Cutting unemployment benefits was, in principle, revenue-saving. But it would also help direct labor to where it was then needed—in the countryside, for the newly launched Food Program. The government understood that workers with a guaranteed income would have been disinclined to take up manual work in the fields.

While changing compensation regulations the government concealed how pervasive unemployment was. A *Granma* headline in May 1991, for example, denied the problem altogether in noting that "There Is No Unemployment in Cuba."[65] Yet one university professor informed me that about half the labor force in the light-industry sector and about half the workforce in many ministries around that time had been let go.

By 1993 underemployment was much more widespread than unemployment: Cuban economists estimated one-third of the labor force to be underemployed compared to only about 7 percent (in 1989) unemployed.[66] The government by then had stopped both enforcing its fiscal belt-tightening unemployment policy and pressing city dwellers to work in the fields. The political risks of firing "unnecessary" labor and insisting that they do farm work they disliked became too great, as the potential numbers involved came to be massive. Under the circumstances the government chose to subsidize urban employment. But in so doing it not only exacerbated its fiscal problems; it also contributed to too much money in circulation relative to the supply of goods (the effects of which are detailed below).

To meet labor needs in the one sector where the demand for labor increased, agriculture, the government made use of a variety of collective and voluntary work strategies, consistent with socialist and Guevarist strategies previously deployed. For one, it set up agricultural brigades, or *contingentes*. The thirty brigades operating in 1991, with two hundred cadre each, were modeled after the privileged productive Blas Roca construction contingents (described in chapter 3).[67] And Blas Roca contingents were redirected to agriculture. *Contingentes* signed up for two-year stints. They were expected to work twelve-hour days, six days a week, as model workers. In return for waiving the historically won labor right to an eight-hour workday, they were rewarded with relatively good living conditions and wages (68 percent above the average wage) and certain control over the work process. *Contingentes* (in all sectors) were up to 52 percent more efficient than ordinary workers.

Urban volunteers supplemented the work both of *contingentes* and of the permanent agricultural workforce, especially around Havana.[68] But because they proved to be costly and inefficient, by the end of 1993 they were phased out.

The mobilizations (described in more detail in chapter 6) outwardly resembled those of the latter 1960s which the government had halted for both economic and political reasons. However, the Special Period's voluntary brigades differed in important respects. Most urban workers in the 1990s did not have to cut cane, despised arduous work, and their rural stints were shorter. Also, the mobilizations were much better organized, and they had their attractions. Many of the *campamentos* that housed the volunteers had the ambience of a summer camp, a diversion for city folk who otherwise could not easily get away, given the stringent gas rationing. Further, food at the *campamentos* was more plentiful than back home, and volunteers might establish informal food-supply networks to draw on subsequently. At the same time, though, the idealism of the 1960s was nowhere to be found. Islanders did not feel that they were helping to construct a utopian communist society, and the government did not try to convince them that they were.

Yet the government did not rely exclusively on collective and voluntary labor strategies to address agricultural-related needs. Aside from market strategies (described below), it called on the armed forces at times to help out both in the fields and in transporting produce to markets. The top leadership must have felt the military to be more reliable for certain tasks than civilians, for there was no shortage of labor at the time.

Marketlike Reforms

To "save the revolution" the government also introduced market-type reforms. It did so in both the externally and the domestically oriented sectors.

All trade relations, first and foremost, came to be contracted in hard currency, though not by Cuba's own doing. Cuba, as a consequence, was pressed to develop internationally competitive products and new marketing networks. As of 1991 the island's hard currency exports amounted only to an estimated $3.3 billion. Though a 9 percent increase over the preceeding year, they did not begin to compensate for the decline in Soviet-bloc trade and they did not begin to cover import needs; hard currency imports increased 45 percent, and more imports would have been desired.[69]

To compete in the "new world order," Castro courted foreign investment as never before. He publicly defended the "creeping privatization" and economic "denationalization" involved. Said he, the revolution will make no concessions on principles. Capitalists could contribute capital, experience, and markets. "We're not dogmatic, no, we're realistic. . . . We do all this with a practical attitude, we're not violating any principles of socialism."[70] "Capital yes, capitalism no" became the slogan of the day.

Castro was not alone in his revisionist view. In 1991 the then head of the Cuban Chamber of Commerce, a Central Committee member, noted that "we have to think like capitalists but continue being socialists." In an interview he commented jocularly that he had to remove the statue of Lenin from his office so that Lenin "would not hear the kind of business we've been discussing." Yet he felt the opening to foreign capital was not ideal. "For us privatization does not mean going forward, but a step backward to the situation of thirty years ago."[71]

Granma, in the process, took on a tone expected of a *Business Week*, not a "vanguard party" newspaper. Stories began to appear almost weekly on potential or actual hard currency deals. Front-page headlines like "Negotiations with Italian Business to Increase" or "Incentives for Mexican Firm in Cuba and Vice Versa" became commonplace.

The government encouraged mainly hard currency–generating cooperative, or "associated production," agreements, along with joint ventures and marketing deals. By 1991 businessmen from twenty-six countries invested some $500 million.[72] And by mid-1993 around 280 companies from thirty-six countries had representatives in Cuba, mainly for trade-related activity, and eighty businesses had been created by Cuban and foreign capital combined.[73] The government created Consultores Asociados, S.A. (CONAS) to provide support and advisory services to potential foreign investors, and it gave the State Committee for Economic Collaboration (CECE), the bureaucracy set up initially to deal with Soviet foreign aid, authority to coordinate, promote, and negotiate foreign investment deals on a case-by-case basis. Joint ventures operated autonomously from the state and independently of centralized planning.[74]

Private foreign investment was courted in nearly all sectors. The government sought foreign investment both for existing as well as new ventures. But the "antidiluvian" nature and scale of Soviet-bloc-built factories, plus Special Period uncertainties, were disincentives to potential investors. In the main, plants built with Soviet-bloc assistance ran the risk of becoming tombstones of bygone "Communist solidarity." To offset such obstacles, the government exempted investors from compliance with labor laws, and it allowed for unlimited profit repatriation for up to ten years.[75] The government also agreed to bear construction and infrastructural costs.

Foreign ownership creeped up not only from zero to 49 percent, in compliance with the 1982 Investment Code, but in some instances to majority ownership. Accordingly, both labor and the government were "squeezed," to "save socialism." The CTC, the labor confederation, supported the economic restructuring.[76] It did not, at least publicly, contest the concessions workers were called upon to make. As in the past, it took the *oficialista* position.

Foreign investment concentrated in the hard currency earning sector. Profits from import-substitution ventures appeared too limited. Both overseas businessmen and the Cuban government were disinterested in peso profits. The main initial sector to attract investment was tourism. Billed as an "industry without smokestacks," the government hoped its beautiful beaches would generate even more hard currency than in the latter 1980s. The sector grossed an estimated $500 million in 1992 and $700 million the following year, up from $200 million in 1989. Cubanacán boasted 100 percent returns to investments in five years. Over 424,000 tourists came, and the government aimed to more than double the number by the mid-1990s.[77] However, the government netted no more than half of gross earnings, and the sector was import-intensive.

Sociedades anónimas (SAs), such as Cubanacán, aggressively promoted foreign investment in tourism. Cubanacán also sought foreign hotel management contracts. Designed to ensure quality management, the contracts (along with foreign investor rights to repatriate profits) cut further into the money Cuba made from such ventures. At the same time, Cubanacán diversified its involvements, indicative of the new role SAs had begun to assume in the latter 1980s. Aside from building hotels and related infrastructure, it organized conventions, managed restaurants and shops, and operated taxis, rent-a-car services, and tours. It also developed import enterprises and represented twenty-seven foreign firms whose products it promoted, while continuing to serve since the latter 1980s as the exclusive exporter of certain medicines and to export some other products on a smaller scale.[78]

But other sectors attracted foreign investment as well. Cuba negotiated production-sharing contracts with French, Brazilian, Swedish, and Canadian firms for offshore oil exploration, with Italian, Spanish, and Latin American companies to retool the steel industry (the private Cuban bank, Banco Financiero, also becoming a shareholder in the steel enterprise, Siderurgica Acinox), and with a Canadian firm to develop the nickel industry. The state also contracted Benetton, of Italy, to set up hard currency clothing stores.[79] Desperate for capital and people with entrepreneurial talent, the government even talked of allowing Cuban-American investment.

Some ventures involved debt-for-equity swaps. Mexican companies, in this connection, were offered a 50 percent share in tourist, industrial, and citrus undertakings, and Argentinians considered an exchange of Cuban medical technology for debt reduction. The biggest shared risk venture as of 1993—a textile business valued at over $1 billion—was designed to have a substantial portion of the firm's export earnings go to Mexican debt repayment.[80]

Cuban enterprises came to compete among themselves for foreign investment and hard currency business. Foreign tourist operators noted tension, for example, between the national airline, Cubana de Aviación, and Cubanacán for control over internal and international flights.[81] And the competition picked up as the tourist enterprise, Gaviota, introduced its own airline service for Latin America. Enterprises were pressured to be self-financing in hard currency.

In its drive to attract tourists the government played on the image of the "old Havana." Three of the main Cuban organs that operate resorts—Cubatur, Cubanacán, and Cimex—hosted a Playboy trip around the time the Special Period was launched. The government allowed the magazine to feature an article on the "girls of Cuba," contingent on coverage of the island's tourist facilities.[82] Even the Ministry of Tourism began to run travel advertisements abroad featuring string bikini–clad sexy Cuban girls. If that were not enough, in 1991 the government opened a Tropicana nightclub in Santiago de Cuba,[83] a club capitalizing on the name of Havana's most famous prerevolutionary nightspot. The government's interest in hard currency led it to play on its prerevolutionary reputation and to reverse its earlier puritanical stance on such matters.

But the government did not merely promote the status quo ante. It also played on contemporary internationally "politically corrrect" motifs. In 1992, for example, Cuba offered "ecotourism" which "celebrates and protects nature." Special tours were offered for zoologists, ornithologists, geologists, and other naturalists.[84]

Tourism contributed to an officially sanctioned two-tier economy. Cubans referred to the disparity between the high life of tourists and their own austere, declining standard of living as economic apartheid. Foreign tourists, who frequented dollar restaurants and dollar stores and used dollar taxis, ate food and used transportation that Cubans could not, and they spent no time in queues for goods and services. The government's need for hard currency led it not only to reverse its initial puritanical antitourist stance but also to give foreigners preferential treatment.

Indicative of the "apartheid," on a twelve-day trip in 1991 I changed only fifteen U.S. dollars into enough pesos to cover nonhotel-linked expenses; in 1992 and 1993 I exchanged no money. Aside from books, there was nothing I could buy with pesos since most goods in stores for Cubans were rationed, and I had to have dollars to buy items in the tourist shops. Tourist taxi drivers even refused payment of a small portion of the fare in local currency, and they gave change in a new special tourist-sector currency. Ironically, the dollar served as the tourist currency, despite the embargo and despite Americans comprising a minority of all tourists (aside from visiting émigrés).

In its aggressive pursuit of convertible currency, the government expanded dollar stores that sold food, clothing, and other items. Initially it only allowed tourists and other foreigners to patronize the stores, though they could shop for islanders not permitted to hold dollars. In mid-1993, however, the government decriminalized islanders' possession of dollars. Since then, Cubans have been able to shop on their own in special stores, the government thereby appropriating hard currency that until then had been illegally circulating in the economy (discussed in more detail below).

While remaining publicly committed to "equality of sacrifice," Cubans with close ties to émigrés were the main beneficiaries, along with tourist-sector workers, of the dollars stores. Emigré contacts became a major material asset in other ways as well. On visits to Cuba exiles brought suitcases full of consumer goods for their island relatives, whom they also gave money (the remittances estimated to exceed net tourist earnings). Emigrés who never struck it rich in the United States complained of how expensive it was to visit their Cuban kin. No longer were exiles a source of political disgrace, the *gusanos* of the early revolutionary years.

While he was president, however, Bush did his best to limit Cuba's hard currency tourist earnings: by obstructing foreign investment, by restricting U.S. travel to the island, and by limiting the amount of money that U.S. citizens exempt from the embargo (such as journalists and academics as well as visiting émigrés) could bring or send to the island. A Spanish company, for example, abandoned a large project to develop tourism in Cayo Coco, allegedly because the United States pressured one of the Spanish directors, with U.S. business dealings, to pull out.[85] But with 60 percent of all Caribbean vacationers coming from the States, the continuation of the ban on U.S. Cuban travel had the most damaging effect on island tourist earnings. At the time of this writing, President Clinton has continued to enforce Reagan's travel restrictions.

Along with tourism, the government promoted biotechnology for hard currency. Initially the sector was developed without foreign investment, but foreign support came to be important for the overseas marketing of products. No other country, with the possible exception of Japan, assigned such high priority to biotechnology.[86] Exports of the sumptuous Center of Genetic Engineering and Biotechnology rose from zero in 1988 to an estimnated $800 million two years later.[87] In 1991 the center received the National Export Prize, a prize introduced that year to encourage export excellence. Products of the center and other research institutes came to include epidermal growth factor (which helps to regenerate skin), a drug (PPG) that washes cholesterol out of the blood, and meningitis and hepatitis B vaccines. Buyers of these products included the former Soviet Union and Brazil, and to a lesser extent India, Sweden, Finland, Italy, Spain, Mexico, Peru, Chile, Panama, Costa Rica, and Venezuela.[88] Cuba's competitive advantage was the low prices it charged.

In the early 1990s, Cuban economists were optimistic about biotechnology's future prospects. In 1991 the sector was self-financing, and it generated capital for its own development.[89] However, purchases from the former Soviet Union became unpredictable, and export prospects were constrained by international competition and the oligopolistic nature of the international pharmaceutical market, by difficulties in marketing products in countries that recognized U.S., European, and Japanese patents, and by Cuba's weak marketing skills. Under the circumstances the island's best hope for developing the sector rested not in fighting but in allying with its overseas competitors, through joint ventures.

The government, meanwhile, did not neglect traditional commodity exports for hard currency. Shortages of fuel, fertilizers, and spare parts, combined with labor demoralization and adverse weather conditions, however, made the 8-million-ton sugar yields of the 1980s a matter of history and the projected 11 to 14 million tons for the 1990s an unfulfilled utopian dream. The 1992 harvest yielded 7 million tons, the 1993 harvest only 4.2 million tons.[90] The 1993 drop cost Cuba about $500 million in hard currency, equivalent to 1992 tourism earnings. The harvest had not been so low in three decades. But the problem with sugar was not merely the volume; it was also the value the commodity commanded in the world market. Castro referred to the price as the "garbage heap of the world market" (nine cents per pound in 1991 and 1992, and only slightly higher in 1993). In the fall of 1992 he claimed the purchasing power of sugar to be at its all-time post-1959 low: a ton of sugar being worth 1.4 tons of oil, in contrast to 7.5 tons thirty years earlier. Cuba had to spend half to two-thirds of its sugar earnings to import about half as much oil as just a few years earlier, when not dependent on world market dealings.[91]

Meanwhile, hard currency nickel export earnings improved, though not to the point that they offset Soviet-bloc purchasing losses. The island's hard currency export potential continued to be jeopardized by U.S. pressure on other countries, along with the Soviet Union, not to purchase the Cuban mineral.

The government also promoted nonsugar farm exports. To do so it opened the sector to foreign investment, though not land ownership. A joint citrus venture with a group of Chilean companies, considered a model for other investors, centered on the modernization of packhouses, new machinery, improved packing, and worker training.[92] Cuba had the potential of becoming a leading world citrus producer, but Castro had in years past failed to break into hard currency markets. The country had, by default not design, relied almost exclusively on sales to Soviet-bloc countries—where the quality of products did not have to be internationally competitive.

While relying increasingly on foreign investment, technology, and markets, Castro portrayed foreign capital as the source of island problems, as well as the basis of their solution. He was quick to blame, for example, the March 1993 "storm of the century," estimated to have caused a billion dollars in damage, on "capitalism, imperialism, and consumer society" and their environmental effects.[93] Here Castro incorporated the growing international concern with environmental matters into his political discourse, just as he capitalized on that concern in the development of the tourist sector.

Meanwhile, the Special Period "market opening" was not confined to the external sector. It also affected domestic pricing. The government planned to end enterprise price subsidies.[94] Firms were to pay the "real" prices at which Cuba purchased goods from abroad. Retail prices were not to be affected, undoubtedly because Castro understood that the termination of food subsidies, like massive unemployment, was too politically explosive. There were lessons to be learned from Poland, and from the previously noted protests in market economies sparked by neoliberal reforms. Thus, the government continued a retail price policy that was, from its vantage point, politically rational, but fiscally irrational from a neoclassical economic perspective. When the government was forced to choose, politics received priority.

The "market opening" also affected the organization of work. In the tourist sector not only were foreign managers entitled to fire workers; workers in the sector also became eligible for new bonuses, tied to the quality of the services they provided. Moreover, in the prime tourist area, Varadero, the government allowed workers, for reasons to be explained, to retain tips (though they were to share them collectively).

In turn, in agriculture the government offered material incentives as never before. It paid Havana residents who committed themselves to work two years in agriculture more than 400 pesos a month, the top of the state's wage scale; it extended bonus payments to farmers who exceeded average deliveries to the state; it initiated yield-related wages in sugar, rice, pig and dairy farming, and an across-the-board 20 percent productivity bonus; it raised the average wage paid farm workers to the point that they no longer were the poorest-paid sector; and it raised the amount it paid for produce sold to the official collection agency.[95] Although these measures increased government expenditures at a time of fiscal belt-tightening, they were designed to improve farm production and productivity, address subsistence needs, and, where possible, generate much-needed export earnings. "You can't have agricultural workers," conceded Castro, "unless you pay them adequate wages, unless they are properly taken care of, unless they have homes and day-care centers for their children."[96] Castro recognized that if moral incentives did not work in the 1960s, a time of idealism, then they would not work now.

The government, meanwhile, transformed thousands of its holdings into cooperatives with unprecedented autonomy. It rescinded control over land use and labor, as well as revenue appropriation, to minimize its costs and losses at a time of crisis. The cooperatives received few subsidies.[97] (By contrast, the cooperative moment of the 1970s and 1980s had targeted private independent farms.)

Castro even hinted at incentives for all workers "who do more, and a little less in the rationing card to those who do less." A subsistence threat was a far cry from the 1960s utopian communist principle of rewarding people "according to need."

Castro also became more tolerant of domestically oriented private economic activity. The 1991 Party Congress, as detailed below, relegalized private family-based service work, and the government authorized private pig breeding in Havana Province (though, in principle, for family consumption, not commercialization). Pork is Cubans' favorite meat, and a source of much-loved lard. Said Castro in a speech before the National Assembly, "We've declared a general amnesty for pigs."[98] The measure was designed to help people supplement the paucity of rationed meat and undermine a huge black market in pork that had developed. Some 15,000 people reportedly bought pigs within days after the authorization.[99] Pig raising until then, however, had been outlawed not merely because it was inconsistent with "socialist principles" but also because it was considered a health hazard; the crisis therefore led the government to sacrifice health and not just ideological principles.

The government "conceded" to contained private activity partly in response to "popular pressure"; but it did so also in recognition that the private sector succeeded at times where the state sector did not. The government even turned to the private sector for advice. In 1991 high-yield farmers received certificates accrediting them as advisers for the Council of Ministers' committee for the Food Program. They were to serve as consultants.[100] As of 1991 private farmers still accounted for over half the bean, tobacco, and garden vegetable production, though for under 20 percent of all cane and citrus production.[101] There remained 144,000 private farmers on 22 percent of the cultivated land and 34 percent of the pastureland. They concentrated on labor-intensive crops where they continued to have a comparative advantage relative to state farms.

The private-state distinction in many respects remained more formal than real. For one, the government helped provide private farmers with seasonal labor needs (at a fixed price), and it continued to provide financing for private agriculture. Second, the government also used its influence over ANAP, the private farmers' organization, to get its 1992 Congress to reprimand members who did not comply with state contracts. But illegal farmer activity (described in more detail below) revealed that the government's control over and containment of the sector was collapsing.

Finally, remaining state enterprises were encouraged to adapt new marketlike features. The government introduced, in early 1991, a profit-sharing scheme in about one hundred enterprises that had previously been applied in enterprises run by the armed forces. The scheme involved higher earnings for increased output at the enterprise, not the individual,[102] level. And self-financing, especially in hard currency, became the order of the day for about one-fourth of all enterprises (as of 1993). In conjunction with the self-financing mandate, the government allowed firms to negotiate trade deals on their own. Even academic and sports institutes became mini-hard currency hustlers, marketing publications and services in convertible currency markets.

Precapitalist Survival Strategies

Castro also "reverted" to precapitalist-type strategies to deal with the crisis. He did so in a variety of ways, at the level of discourse as well as policy. He went so far as to plan "Option Zero," the survival strategy to be pursued under conditions of total economic isolation.

Castro, for example, turned to nineteenth-century symbolism to legitimate Special Period reforms. He portrayed the Special Period as but one additional struggle in the country's long history—dating back to the struggle for national independence—to control its destiny. In speech after speech Castro portrayed the country's independence and not merely the revolution and socialism to be at stake. A speech commemorating the anniversary of the Bay of Pigs invasion was indicative:

> "We will tell the imperialists, no, you can't do what you want with us! . . . And if we have to put up with material deprivation we will put up with it, because we can never forget that those who began our independence struggle spent ten years in the woods . . . and when some of them got tired and thought that it was impossible to fight under such difficult conditions . . . and wanted the Zanjón Pact's peace without independence, [Antonio] Maceo said 'No!' And along with Maceo, the best representatives of that heroic people said 'No!' and the eternal Baraguá Protest was born to confront the Zanjón Pact. That is who we are: the heirs of Maceo, the heirs of Baraguá, the heirs of Martí."[103]

In that same Bay of Pigs speech he added that not only were the mothers of the revolutionary fighters present. "Spiritually present here, too, are the mother of the Maceo brothers, Martí's mother, the mothers of the fighters who started the wars of independence, the mothers of the men who took part in the Baraguá Protest. . . . If necessary we will die like they did, defending the revolution and the nation!"[104]

Castro's (delayed) 1992 annual speech commemorating the 1953 Moncada attack was similarly telling. He asserted that "every last drop of sweat and every last drop of blood that have been spilled throughout our history, from 1868 until today, are at stake."[105]

Meanwhile, the one hundred fortieth anniversary of the birth of Martí became the occasion for the first torchlight celebration in forty years. It was billed by the Party as "another yes for Cuba; another show of patriotic and revolutionary feeling and . . . support for the Party, the government and Fidel, as well as a celebration in honor of Martí."[106]

Castro made use of historical symbolism to justify policies both reformist and restrictive in nature. He drew an analogy between austerity measures caused by cutbacks in Soviet imports and the country's nineteenth-century independence struggle. When the once superpower slashed newsprint deliveries, Castro proclaimed that "even if it were like the times of *El Cubano Libre*, printed in the woods during the war of independence, our newspapers will keep coming out, even if it's just one page once a week."[107]

Farmers, meanwhile, were required to substitute manual labor and draft animals for the mechanized equipment the government had proudly manufactured and made available to state farms and cooperatives since the 1970s. The national leadership aimed to harvest 70 percent of the sugar crop by hand in 1993, the very percentage it had succeeded in mechanizing in a twenty-year drive.[108] The machinery required petroleum now better reserved, in its view, for other purposes. Farmers of all crops were pressed, in turn, to weed manually again, once Soviet-bloc pesticides stopped arriving. Here too Castro made virtue of necessity, pointing out how much better the "new" methods were for the environment;[109] and here too Castro incorporated contemporary international environmental discourse into his seemingly "hard-line" Communist orthodoxy. He went on to tell the National Assembly in March 1993 that the revolution and socialism had to be saved with a machete in hand, with lathes to make spare parts, and with hoes for weeding.[110]

The crisis, moreover, contributed to deindustrialization, by default not design—to an unraveling both of Castro's "History Will Absolve Me" and of Ché's industrial developmental vision. Nearly half of all factories were shut down or forced to operate on a much reduced scale, for lack of imported raw materials, spare parts, and petroleum. Until the previously cited Mexican joint venture, the textile and apparel industry, for example, had come to a complete standstill. Cement, nickel, construction material, and chemical plants, among others, that the Soviets had helped build were hit by the drastic cutback in Soviet (and then CIS) imports, by irregularities in deliveries, and by the exodus of some 1,200 technicians in 1990.[111] And the opening of the nearly completed Soviet-assisted nuclear power plant was put on hold when Moscow insisted on hard currency payments. Though controversial, the plant was expected to have lowered oil import needs by 1.2 million tons a year. Cuba had invested around $1.2 billion of its own in the project, a project that Raúl Castro acknowledged stood like an abandoned Egyptian pyramid.[112]

Foreign direct investment allowed for gradual reindustrialization, but on a much reduced scale and mainly only for industries geared toward the export market. Islanders were still left without consumer manufactures. Recycling and repair became the order of the day, a reason why the government relaxed restrictions on private-service work.

Recognizing the limits of the Food Program, the government exhorted city dwellers to set up fruit and vegetable "victory gardens" in residential neighborhoods: in backyards, empty lots, and open spaces. As of mid-1992 there were more than one million such gardens, tended to by families, neighborhood groups, workers, and students. City dwellers, in essence, were to help produce their own subsistence needs.

For transportation people had to turn to bicycles in place of buses, trucks, and cars. The government purchased a million two-wheelers from China, which it sold to students for 60 pesos and to workers for 120 pesos. By the close of 1992 *habañeros*, as Havana residents are called, relied on bicycles for one-third of all their trips; about half of all households had one or more bikes, mainly acquired since the start of the Special Period; and one-fourth of all bicycle owners used their two-wheelers to commute to and from work.[113] The government, deciding that bicycles would be the mode of transportation "of the future," set up among the few new factories five that were to produce half a million two-wheelers within five years. And for transport of goods the government aimed to replace half the truck fleet with 60,000 Chinese cargo tricycles.[114] Symbolic of the transportation mode "of the future," the armed forces began to ride bicycles in the annual May Day parade.

Granma referred to bicycle use as the "transportation revolution," and the government organized an international bicycle conference in 1993 which it called "Bikes: Vehicle for the Twenty-First Century."[115] Bicycling, the leadership claimed, was good both for islanders and for the environment. It guaranteed "health for all" and contributed to a modern "ecotopia" by not polluting. "We've entered the bicycle era," noted Castro, "but after this Special Period disappears we mustn't abandon this wonderful custom because of what it means to our health."[116] Here too Castro drew on contemporary industrial-country discourse.

The transportation "revolution" created new problems while reducing dependence on oil-guzzling cars and buses. Bikeriding increased people's appetites just when food became more scarce. With bikes in short supply, theft of two-wheelers also rose, and people were angered over having to carry their 48-pound mode of transport up flights of stairs to their offices and apartments for security purposes.[117]

Horsedrawn carriages even became "fashionable." They carried people who could not bike, and were used for cargo transport and rubbish collection. The main newspaper reported that in Bayamo, in Granma Province, nine million people used such carriages for travel in 1992.[118]

With electricity cutbacks islanders also turned to candlelight for night-time vision. The government went so far as to encourage islanders to make their own candles, to produce their own lighting by preindustrial techniques. Candles were not the only product islanders were asked to make. Women were encouraged to make soap and sew cloth shoes for their children. And for cooking women were to rely, as in times past, increasingly on charcoal fires. Vilma Espín, head of the FMC, which for three decades had pressed for the liberation of women from housework, now urged women to take on time-consuming preindustrial tasks. And the weekly magazine *Bohemia* introduced a "Practical Solutions" column that informed readers of how to make their own products at home.

Meanwhile, the government, which (as will be described in chapter 5) had aimed to become a "world medical power," exhorted the ill to make use of "grandmother remedies." Doctors were encouraged to prescribe such cures, and even to grow their own supplies. Modern university-trained doctors, a source of revolutionary pride, were to transform themselves, when possible, into old-fashioned medicine men (and women). The government urged islanders to rely on traditional herbal cures at the same time that it assigned high priority to the production of pharmaceuticals for export. As it sought to address its own hard currency needs, islanders were left without such basic medicines as aspirin.

DEMOCRATIZATION IN FORM AND PRACTICE

Castro did not confine reforms to the economic domain. Measures were taken to democratize governance, despite and partly because of the crisis. But the political reforms were more democratic in form than substance, and Castro turned to a range of nondemocratic political strategies as well to "save the revolution."

Castro not surprisingly stepped up his identification of political as well as economic initiatives with nationalism. Heroic leaders of Cuba's lengthy nineteenth-century struggle for national independence were raised from their graves to justify current concerns and commitments. A manifesto issued at the 1992 Congress of the UJC, the Party's youth division, highlighted loyalty to Martí along with love of "Fidel with all our hearts as we would love a dear father."[119] At the congress Castro linked the revered national hero of independence to socialist ideals. And the then UJC head, Roberto Robaina, echoed Castro in asserting that "Cuban youth are saying, to paraphrase the words of José Martí, that a congress of revolutionary youth, inaugurated in the depths of a people's shelter, can do more than an empire."[120] The UJC Congress was launched in a new People's Tunnel, constructed for defense in case of a U.S. military attack.

Specific Special Period political events and reform initiatives were very deliberately identified with days important in the country's independence struggle. Castro, for example, scheduled the opening of the 1991 Party Congress on October 10, the official anniversary of the start of Cuba's war of independence (the Cry of Yara), the 1993 elections on February 24, the anniversary of the so-called second war of independence, when José Martí and Máximo Gómez "dared stage an uprising," and the early 1993 National Assembly meeting on March 15, the anniversary of the Baraguá Protest.[121] Castro scheduled the 1993 elections on February 24, even though it fell on a Wednesday; a Sunday would have been preferable for working people.

In addition to using history to legitimate his continued claims to rule, Castro drew on his personal charisma. He made almost daily public and televised appearances. His presence in the 1992 potato harvest was especially visible. But the effectiveness of charisma hinges, as noted, on continued proof of worth, made increasingly difficult by Special Period circumstances.

Recognizing the limits both of charisma and of traditional claims to legitimacy, Castro also initiated institutional reforms, to "perfect institutions." In this vein he launched another antibureaucratic campaign and called for Party reforms. In conjunction with the antibureaucratic campaign, the Party was reorganized at all levels.[122] The number of people on the Party's payroll decreased by two-thirds. At the national level, Central Committee departments were halved (from nineteen to nine) and their staff slashed 50 percent, and the Central Committee's Secretariat was disbanded. The number of posts on provincial committees also was halved.

In streamlining the size of the Party bureaucracy, the state attacked oligarchic tendencies. In some departments half the people in appointed posts changed. The Party leadership used the opportunity to weed out ineffective and "problem" cadre and to give select and critical constituencies, such as youth, greater representation within the "vanguard" institution.[123] Meanwhile, rank-and-file cadre at the municipal and provincial levels were given the right to elect committee members by direct secret vote for the first time. Top Party functionaries could no longer choose committee members and have their choices ratified by subordinates in a show of hands. A nascent Party "reformist" faction in principle thereby gained the means for greater influence over internal Party matters.[124]

Party-run educational institutions, in turn, were revamped. The Party's school of higher political studies began to downplay Marxist-Leninism and concentrate on Castro's political thoughts.[125] But precluded from consideration was a multiparty system. Castro claimed that Cuba had its own form of democracy. "There's no country in the world," said he, "where the people participate in shaping their fate as much as in ours." He also claimed that "No other regime is as democratic as a socialist regime."[126] It was a "people's" or revolutionary democracy, premised on close ties between the Party and the populace, not democracy premised on multiparty politics.[127] Castro argued that one party "befits the long revolutionary stage," a single party "like the one founded by José Martí to carry out the war of independence."[128]

Democratization involved ordinary citizens. In the so-called *llamamiento* (calling) preceding the 1991 Party Congress, over three million people participated in national "kvetching" sessions.[129] Over a million opinions were voiced on fifty topics. Citizen complaints centered on problems of "everyday life": on transportation, education, housing, recreation facilities, the food supply, services, excessive nonwork-related meetings, and crime, as well as on disillusion with the mass organizations and bureaucratism. People even talked of disbanding the FMC. The *llamamiento* gave islanders a chance for democratic input at a time when their former Soviet-bloc comrades brought Communism to its heels.

The *llamamiento* gave people a sense of "popular" involvement, reinforced by some subsequent policy changes. Complaints about education policy, for example, are believed to have contributed to the replacement of a much disliked minister of education and to the shelving of plans to send more city students to preuniversity boarding schools in the countryside. Urban families had complained about their children leaving home at such an early age. However, the *llamamiento* proved to be a one-shot affair; there were no follow-up sessions where people could, en masse, articulate grievances without fear of reprisal.

The actual 1991 Party Congress laid the groundwork for additional Party and government democratization. It agreed to open the Party to religious believers, thereby making it less exclusionary, and to have secret direct elections for representatives of all levels of the Popular Power system, not just, as had been the case until then, at the municipal level.

There also was a major turnover in leadership. Fidel and Raúl remained officially first and second in command. However, about half of the Party's 225-person Central Committee and the 25-member Political Bureau were replaced,[130] consistent with the previously mentioned Party shakeup. Also, the Council of State underwent over a 50 percent turnover. Such an officially sanctioned generational turnover was rather unprecedented in the Communist world. It was designed to counter growing political disinterest and disquietude among youth who never experienced firsthand the Old Order, and to allow for intergenerational political continuity.

Three-quarters of a year after the congress the National Assembly approved constitutional reforms. While the amended Constitution legitimated democratization, it was implemented in a less democratic fashion than the original 1976 document in that the revised document was not submitted to the populace for discussion and approval. The revised Constitution recognized People's Councils, designed to make governance more responsive to community-based concerns (see chapter 6), an essential part of local-level governance; it called for direct elections for all levels of the Popular Power system, in line with the 1991 Party Congress mandate; and it guaranteed freedom of religion and freedom of expression, in accordance with the goals of a socialist society. In the economic domain the amended Constitution guaranteed property rights of foreign investors, and it put an end to the state's monopoly of foreign trade. Individuals and companies could now, according to the country's main legal document, independently import and export and negotiate business deals.[131] Meanwhile, former references to the international socialist community and the Soviet Union were dropped.

Between November 1992 and February 1993 electoral reforms specified in the revised Constitution were put into effect. Elections for municipal assemblies continued, by law, to include no fewer than two and no more than eight candidates, with up to 50 percent of the elected delegates eligible for the National and Provincial assemblies. At the provincial and national levels Candidacy Commissions, comprised of representatives of the diverse mass organizations and presided over by a CTC representative, selected the slate of candidates: they put forth only one candidate per district, and the electorate was encouraged to vote for the "entire slate, for the nation." Technically, dissidents could run for office. However, they needed to run as individuals, not as representatives of political organizations, and they needed to be approved by the Candidacy Commissions at the respective provincial and national levels; as a result, none ran.

The elections, as implemented, were noteworthy in several respects. For one, at the provincial and national levels they functioned as plebiscites, Castro—himself a candidate (along with most of the top leadership)—even acknowledging that this was so.[132] Castro turned the elections into a "yes for Cuba," into a show of unity, of commitment to nationalism more than to Communist Party rule. (After the elections "yes for Cuba" signs remained while Party signs were rarely visible.) And 88 percent of all voters responded to his request for a "united vote," for the entire slate of candidates.[133] Second, turnout for the Provincial and National Assembly elections was high, even in the absence of electoral choices. Ninety-three percent of all eligible voters, according to official figures, participated in the December 1992 Municipal Assembly elections,[134] 99 percent in the February 1993 Provincial and National Assembly elections.[135] Third, the elections, like the high-level Party replacements at the 1991 Party Congress, resulted in a remarkable "circulation of elites." Fifty-three percent of the town councillors elected in December, and 75 and 83 percent of the Provincial and National Assembly delegates and deputies, respectively, elected in February 1993, were new to the job.[136] Their average age was forty-three. Many of the new deputies had widespread appeal, to the young and other constituencies.

Yet the deputy selection, approved by the Candidacy Commission, suggests the electoral opening was designed to extend symbolic more than real power. The new National Assembly included two religious leaders, nine athletes and trainers (among them the popular baseball player Victor Mesa), and Silvio Rodríguez, Pablo Milanes, and twenty-three other artists, singers, writers, and poets, people without political experience.[137] Castro could tolerate the "opening" to non-Party apparatchiks because the National Assembly so far had never opposed him once he spoke on an issue.

At the same time, the national leadership tried, as in years past, to disentangle the Party from routine administration. With the Party closely identified with governance, and discontent mounting with hardships, people increasingly viewed the Party, according to official sources, as the "ugly duckling," and they blamed it for "everything" that went wrong.[138] But the national leadership was in a bind that prompted contradictory policies. Despite interest in "depoliticizing" administration so that grievances over the delivery of goods and services would not evoke anti-Party sentiment, it sought, in light of the crisis, to increase its control over "particularistic" concerns. To safeguard "interests of the Revolution over and above those of local or business interests" the Political Bureau promoted far-reaching participation of Communists in production;[139] it thereby politicized the very administration it sought to depoliticize. Political appointees, moreover, tend not necessarily to be the most technically qualified, and they are predisposed to make decisions on the basis of political, not economic, considerations. The government faced a "Red versus expert" dilemma.

The Party also tried to strengthen ties with civil society, above all with youth. It did so not merely by bringing the younger generation into top political and administrative posts, but also by implementing policies and programs that appealed to them. The leadership, for example, eased international travel restrictions, lowering the minimum age from forty-five for men and forty for women to twenty for both genders in 1991. Youth had been unhappy with the travel restriction, and the collapse of Eastern European Communism deprived some 30,000 students a year of Soviet-bloc scholarships and travel.[140] The lowered age cleverly directed frustration toward the United States, which granted visas to only about one-tenth of the 20,000 yearly visitors permitted by U.S. law.[141]

The national leadership also sought to entertain youth who had no place to go, on weekends and vacations, with the cutback in petroleum rationing. Under Robaina, a rising political star at the time, the UJC sponsored large outdoor concerts by Cuba's hottest music groups.[142] Robaina himself embodied the "new generation" with his informal, outgoing style. He recognized that ideology and politics could in themselves no longer captivate the hearts and minds of youth.

Reforms even extended to the military. Compulsory military service dropped from three to two years. And troops began to focus on producing food for their own subsistence, on land owned by the armed forces. "We've defined beans as more important than cannons at this moment," Raúl Castro noted.[143] He publicly acknowledged that the armed forces were "too big and too costly in relation to the country's economic development." The changes reflected no post–Cold War "peace dividend," the government simultaneously having constructed, as noted, People's Tunnels for defense purposes. The Cold War had not ended from the vantage point of the Cuban-U.S. relations.

But the government "tooketh with one hand what it gaveth with another." It became more repressive while promoting democratic reforms and downsizing the military. Both the 1991 Pan American Games and the Party Congress were preceded by clampdowns on prodemocracy groups,[144] groups described in more detail below. Dissidents began to be confronted with *actos de repudio*, by newly formed Ministry of Interior Rapid Response Brigades. The "goon squads" were verbally and physically abusive. Unpopular, even among Party loyalists,[145] they reflected the government's growing inability to rely on the mass organizations to regulate life informally at the grass-roots level.

The experiences of two dissident group leaders were telling. María Elena Cruz, a poetry prizewinner turned dissident, distributed leaflets in her apartment building about a prodemocracy meeting she planned. The Rapid Response Brigades, in an *acto de repudio*, went after her: they stormed into her quarters, dragged her down the stairs, and forced her to eat some of her writings. The media discredited her in turn; it portrayed her as poorly educated (having a seventh grade education) and mentally unstable, and it accused her of having ties to Cuban exiles with CIA connections. She was sentenced to over two years in jail on charges of spreading antigovernment propaganda (and was released in the summer of 1993). Meanwhile, Elizardo Sánchez, a former philosophy professor who headed the small Cuban Commission for Human Rights and National Reconciliation, and the Democratic Socialists, spent nine years in jail between 1982 and 1992. Upon his release in 1992, a Rapid Response Brigade beat him unconscious. He was arrested again for violating the peace and defaming Castro.[146]

Cultural repression also picked up. In 1991 a Cuban film, *Alice in Wondertown*, was banned after a brief showing. The film's allegoric depiction of a depressing corrupt "Wondertown" was more than the government would tolerate, as Cuban reality became ever more bleak. The same year the writers' union, at the Party's urging, accused ten of its members of having taken part in an "enemy operation": in signing a "declaration of Cuban intellectuals" which called for democratic reforms on the island.[147] Then, in 1992 two film directors were tried for "enemy propaganda" and "contempt" for a film, *Just Another Day*. That same year, Carlos Aldana, then the Party's chief of ideology, called on journalists to "have the courage to be *oficialista*," implying that they were not sufficiently so.[148]

Before the close of 1992, Aldana was stripped of his political and administrative posts. Like recent predecessors who had fallen out of favor, he was officially dismissed for alleged corrupt dealings, not for ideological or political "deviationism." The "Western" media was quick to presume he fell from favor for his "reformist" influence.[149] If the official reason is taken at face value, the government continued to be unable to stop corruption at the highest level; if the foreign version is correct, the political system allowed little room for change and it stunted a new generation of leadership from effectively evolving.

PEOPLE'S RESPONSES TO THE "SPECIAL PERIOD"

While islanders did not follow the example of their once East European comrades and turn to the streets to bring down the state, outward quiescence concealed growing disquietude. Covert acts of defiance had the effect if not the intent of weakening governmental authority and governmental control over production, consumption, indeed everyday life.

Already at the eve of the Special Period a Party-conducted survey revealed certain misgivings among ordinary people. Respondents may not have felt fully free to speak their mind, but in November 1990 only half of them said they were satisfied with their material situation.[150] Despite free education, free health care, inexpensive if not free housing, and rationed food, two-thirds of the people interviewed said the cost of living was high and about one-third felt their salary unjust.[151] But dissatisfaction was as much a function of expectations and aspirations as of income. The higher-income respondents voiced the most complaints:[152] they were most inclined to feel their salary unjust and to feel that people working hardest were entitled to more.[153] Such findings suggest that government support may be weakest among the more privileged stratum.

The same survey reported complaints with governance. One of seven complaints centered on bureaucratism: red tape, excessive numbers of meetings, *sociolismo*, abuse of office, private use of government vehicles, corruption, and the like.[154] People attacked Popular Power for being insufficiently responsive to their needs (in part because delegates lacked adequate authority), and they suggested that the FMC be incorporated into the CDR block organization.[155]

The dissatisfaction with Popular Power confirmed findings of a poll published in the summer of 1990 in the weekly magazine *Bohemia*.[156] More than half the people interviewed said Popular Power needed to change, less than a third said they were prepared to serve as a Popular Power assembly delegate, and two out of five respondents felt that they were not participating fully in the governing of the country. The Popular Power reforms previously delineated undoubtedly were designed in part to address the disenchantment picked up in these surveys.

Another nonrandom survey of four hundred adults also conducted before the full impact of Special Period austerity was felt found Castro no longer the nearly ubiquitously esteemed hero he once had been. Three-fourths of the people interviewed did not at the time consider him a hero and most said that Cubans considered him "the most important TV artist" or "a dictator."[157] Most likely, disillusion with Fidel picked up as living standards plunged.

The lines that people had to stand in for rationed goods and for bus transportation, meanwhile, did not merely fuel anger but led to a sharing of grievances and gossip. They served to strengthen informal social networks. *Bolas*, or rumors, snowballed. People added and distorted news as they talked to others. Fact and fiction at times became indistinguishable. Thus, society became stronger as formal organizational life and the state became weaker.

Most unhappy islanders acquiesced. As one Cuban confided, "We feel even when we do nothing and say nothing." And another added that he and his wife even shied from sharing their discontent with their daughter; they feared she might speak up in school and get in trouble.

Despite perceived risks, resistance picked up, people's responses varying with their "opportunity structures." Islanders increasingly voted with their feet and emigrated. In 1990 three dozen islanders sought asylum at European embassies. In 1993 even a daughter of Castro's left. Cubans who successfully attained U.S. travel visas took vacations abroad, from which they, in growing numbers, never returned. The Mariel exodus democratized access to this semilegal route. Air tickets for travel abroad had to be paid in hard currency by people overseas. Since the 1980 mass emigration included a broader socioeconomic range of islanders than earlier waves of defection, a broader range of remaining Cubans had contacts abroad. About one-third of all islanders were in regular contact—through phone conversations, letter-writing, and visits—with folk in the States, and about two-thirds had relatives there.[158] Thus, to leave as well as to attain dollars and goods off the ration system it became useful for Cubans to be hooked into an émigré network.

Unable to attain overseas sponsors, or impatient to wait until the U.S. government granted a visa, others turned to more risk-taking modes of escape: to unseaworthy craft. The United States welcomed some 1,500 "boat people" during the first eight months of 1991, forty times the rate of 1988, then 2,557 in 1992 and 3,656 in 1993.[159] Though they arrived without U.S. visas, the U.S. government warmly received the *balseros* (rafters), and it did so at the same time that it turned away Haitian boat people.[160] The U.S. response was politically motivated: *balseros* were portrayed as heroes of anti-Communism. Yet interviews with the Cuban arrivals showed them to be fleeing a crumbling economy (rooted, above all, in declining aid and trade) more than a political system they despised. They dwelled on existence without underwear, soap, shampoo, and medicines. "Without food," said an arrival at an Immigration and Naturalization Service detention center in Miami, "there was nothing to do but leave."[161]

A limited number of Cubans escaped more dramatically by air. An air force major in 1991 flew a MIG-23 to the United States where he requested asylum, and in January 1992 thirty-four Cubans flew a helicopter to Miami.[162]

Disgruntled people in positions of importance had less risk-taking means to leave. They took advantage of opportunities to travel abroad to defect. Several prominent Cubans with permission for international travel defected in this manner, including Arturo Sandoval, the internationally renowned jazz trumpeter, two ballet stars, dozens of athletes, and a scientist. So too did the director of a radio station and two high-ranking shipping and tourist officials, a vice minister in charge of the state's pricing board and former deputy secretary of COMECON, and a major in the military.[163] Castro's inability to count on the loyalty of government appointees demonstrated a state weakening "from within."

At home, small unofficial political groupings sprouted around such issues as family reunification with émigrés, artistic freedom, support of *perestroika* (before the Soviet Union dissolved), freedom of religious worship, and democracy. Carlos Aldana, before his fall from grace, admitted there to be about fifty such "counterrevolutionary" groups, involving some one thousand people.[164]

Religious gatherings even became politically suspect, at the same time that official religious tolerance increased. In particular, a pilgrimage to the Virgin of Cobre, the much revered patron saint of Cuba, was suspended in 1990. Officials feared the procession would turn into an antigovernment demonstration.[165] The virgin is a syncretic saint. Like *santería*, her appeal derives from Afro-Cuban beliefs merged with Catholicism. As noted in chapter 1, syncretic religions reflect cultural resistance to elite-imposed religious beliefs and possibly resistance to culture and social structure more broadly defined, and they gained (along with Pentecostalism) popularity during the Special Period.[166]

Music became another channel of cultural resistance. Recognizing it as such, the government denied performance licenses to groups who sang in English and who played rock music.[167] The national leadership saw such music as culturally subversive.

Mobilizations for the Food Program, meanwhile, prompted at least one protest. Some city high school students, angry about being sent to the fields to help in Special Period farmwork, staged a minirebellion. They organized a march back to Havana.[168]

The defections, the dissident groups, and the protest movement involved people who did not see formal political channels as means whereby to press for change. Yet electoral dissidence in 1993 was itself noteworthy. Although no opposition candidates ran for office and although the leadership turned the elections into a plebiscite, 7 percent of Cubans, and 15 percent of Havana voters, according to official sources, used the franchise to show opposition to the regime—by spoiling their ballot or casting a blank ballot. And 12 percent refused to comply with the government's call for a "show of unity," by refusing to vote for the entire state of candidates.[169]

While not explicitly political, increased crime reflected growing defiance of state authority as well. Broad-based and varied in form, the illicit activity contributed to a de facto withering away of the state, independently of rule breakers' intent. The anticrime measures initiated in the name of "rectification" in the second half of the 1980s, as well as the widely publicized arrests and executions of Ochoa and other high-level officials in 1989, did not put an end to serious abuse of office. Workplace pilfering and small acts of favoritism, endemic in societies with consumer shortages, for example, picked up;[170] and theft, corruption, and black-market activity reached record levels. In the first half of 1990, 25 million pesos in government funds went unaccounted for. And in 1992 the largest bank robbery in the country's history occurred, and more than two dozen people were arrested for drug trafficking.[171]

To help put a stop to crime the government launched another draconian anticorruption campaign. Five hundred people were arrested. Arrests included catering and tourism workers, police officers, and interior ministry staff, up to quite high levels.[172] They were arrested for theft, embezzlement, speculation, bribery, and hard currency trafficking. Two large crime rings were uncovered involving illegal currency dealings, appropriation of foreign currency from plane landing fees, illegal buying and selling of televisions and other items taken from tourist stores, and dealings in stolen goods:[173] one ring centered around Havana's port, the other around Varadero international airport, led by the customs chief there. Such white-collar crime not only weakened the moral and legal order but also undermined government efforts to maximize its hard currency earnings; as in the late 1980s, official hard currency activity became major loci of illicit dealings, with well-placed individuals trying to appropriate convertible currency for themselves.

But crime involved ordinary citizens, not merely well-placed individuals. In April 1991 the government halted its railway parcel delivery service because too many food parcels sent by city dwellers to relatives in the provinces were stolen en route.[174] And in agriculture crop theft became so rampant that farm laborers requested protection. To address the problem rural authorities in 1991 handed out weapons to "peasant vigilance detachments" on cooperatives.[175] *Campesinos*, in essence, lost control over the fruits of their labor.

Special Period programs had the unintended effect of exacerbating certain crimes. Bike theft, for one, picked up as the demand for two-wheelers far exceeded the supply.[176] Second, prostitution, which symbolized the Old Regime that Castro in 1959 had sought to purify, returned with a vengeance. Growing numbers of prostitutes hung out near the mushrooming hotels frequented by foreigners. University students and others who never would have dreamed of selling their bodies for sex before the revolution began to do so. A lust for dollars, meals in dollar restaurants, and gifts from the dollar stores outweighed the social stigma, the degradation, the health risks, and the fear of arrest.

The new tourism gave rise to other illicit activity as well. Although Cubans could not legally possess dollars until mid-1993, hotel workers and tourist taxi drivers pocketed tips they were supposed to turn over to the government. As a model of what hotel employees were to do, *Granma* publicized a case where workers in a Havana hotel gave a $180,000 check to a Political Bureau member in 1991, with the request that it be given to Fidel.[177] Charismatic rule, as Max Weber pointed out, relies on such gift-giving. But official regulation, Castro's charismatic authoritative claims, and Party publicity to exemplary gift-giving failed to convince most tourist-sector employees to subordinate their own desire for dollars to the state's. Indeed, private tip appropriation became so pervasive that the government in 1993 conceded to tourist-sector workers in Varadero, making legal what had occurred illegally: retention of their private tips. Workers at the time reportedly earned eighty to ninety times as much in tips as salaried workers.[178]

Special Period rationing, though premised on the government's lofty effort to "equalize sacrifice," had the unintended effect of inducing law-breaking. Off-the-books sales of foodstuffs became the most widespread illicit activity. Producers and distributors siphoned off goods for private profiteering, and shop managers routinely set aside stock to sell at premium prices to select customers.[179] With demand so in excess of supply, prices of goods on the black market skyrocketed, a temptation to profit people did not let pass by. The value of black-market trade is estimated to have risen from $2 billion in 1989 to $14.5 billion in mid-1993—exceeding the value of official retail trade.[180] Nearly everyone who could, be they Party loyalists or regime opponents, bought things illegally. Black-market purchases hinged less on people's morality than on their pocketbooks. As a consequence, governmental control over the distributive system caved in, just when it officially increased. Rationing, because of its black-market effect, became part of the problem of consumption, not its solution.

Indicative of ration-induced black-market activity, in 1992 police arrested nineteen people for selling privately thirty-two tons of chicken meat stolen from state stores.[181] And the government uncovered a gasoline coupon ring that had distributed bogus coupons for an estimated 265,000 gallons of gasoline and a 25-person truck driver ring that delivered foods to black marketeers.[182]

The profits to be made through illegal marketeering were reflected in the large disparity between official and unofficial prices. In mid-1992 soap in state stores cost twenty to twenty-five centavos, beans eighteen centavos a pound, cooking oil twenty centavos a container, and rice twelve centavos a bag, whereas on the black market they went, respectively, for fifteen, ten, three, and ten pesos. At the time, people bought chicken in the black market for seventy pesos and cheese for fifty pesos, the equivalent of one-third to one-fourth the average worker's monthly income. A year later, people paid as much as 200 pesos for chicken, more than their average monthly earnings, and the black market price of rice had doubled. Moreover, many manufactured items became attainable only on the black market: for example, jeans for 500 and shoes for 300 pesos.

In turn, tourism and contact with émigrés contributed to a black market in dollars. In mid-1991 the black-market exchange rate for dollars was about ten times the official rate, a year later about forty times, and by the end of 1993 it was about eighty times the official rate. Anyone with access to dollars had a decided advantage in the runaway black market. In illegal dollars chicken and cheese cost no more than a few dollars. As a consequence, the dollar and peso economies were not, as the government had intended, separable. In mid-1993 the illegal dollar economy was estimated to be on the order of $200 million, 60 percent of which was attributed to émigré sources.[183] It was the government's effort to appropriate for itself the illegally circulating hard currency and to rein in the black market that led it to decriminalize islander possession of dollars in mid-1993. Unable to restrict the "dollarization" of the economy, Castro unhappily acceded to it (to the point that the government even offered twenty-five pesos to the dollar, as opposed to the peso per dollar official rate).

Islanders were pressed to sell and not merely buy on the black market. The economic situation induced them to steal from their workplaces as never before to attain sellable items and materials usable for marketable services (such as mechanical repair work).

Arrests proved to no avail, for the illegal activity was rooted not in the crime-prone character of individuals but in socioeconomic conditions: in the paucity of coveted goods available through the ration system, the undervaluation of the peso in an increasingly dollarized economy, and the excess money in circulation (estimated by Castro in his 1993 Twenty-sixth of July speech to total 9 million pesos, more than three times the previous peak, in 1970). And as illicit activity became ever more widespread, moral restraints withered.

The Party even publicly acknowledged the crime and corruption to be embedded in social institutions, not individual maladjustment. A *Granma* article on an anticrime campaign, known officially as *Operación Cascabel* and popularly as *maceta* (flower pot), noted that imprisonment and fines alone cannot maintain social discipline and keep crime at bay.[184] "It is a chimera to expect the police to quickly end all our social disorders." But the article went on to chastise police for being part of the problem. It portrayed some police as lazy and defiant of institutional norms.

Islanders, furthermore, at times defied policies that were not actually laws. Government efforts to deschool and deprofessionalize the population, for example, met with opposition. The revolution had raised expectations beyond the state's Special Period means, and families tried to circumvent placements that implied downward mobility for their children. Not only did too many students still enroll in senior high school because of family preference, but also most students who "conceded" to enroll in polytechnic institutions hoped to train as intermediary-level technicians, with the intent to go on to obtain a university education.[185] Subsequently, government efforts to downscale schooling ran into "popular" resistance. The resistance here too occurred informally, through personal networks; the mass organizations were unresponsive at the neighborhood level to people's concerns.

Government regulation of the world of work also eroded. Absenteeism reached unprecedented levels, though there is no publicly available data to verify this. People's motivation to work waned as there was little to work for. Money came to have little meaning in the legal economy—but not by design as, according to Marxism, it was supposed to do in a utopian communist society. There simply was little to buy through officially sanctioned channels, and the government provided most social needs gratis or for minimum fees. Under the circumstances, material as well as moral incentives became ineffective in the legal economy. The burdens of sheer survival and transport difficulties also led people to miss work with increased regularity, above all women on whom the burdens fell most. Some families spent the equivalent of half an official work week in shopping and other lines. Cutbacks in trade, aid, and investments were far from the government's only economic problems. In its effort to improve productivity, it began to allow selective enterprises (especially where foreign investment and exports were involved) to open their own stores, produce their own food, provide clothing for their employees, and build housing for their workers. In this manner workers' real income increased, they could avoid the time-consuming lines at ration outlets, and they could attain goods otherwise difficult to get in the legal economy. It was hoped that enterprises could thereby stabilize their workforce, reduce absenteeism, and motivate workers to be productive and committed, even if institutionally-based inequities thereby increased.

CONCLUSION

Seemingly against all odds, Castro survived the domino collapse of the Communist Soviet bloc. His capacity to rule, however, was challenged as never before—both from abroad and at home, economically and politically. If ever the government's hold over society was constrained by global and domestic forces, it was during the Special Period.

Imports dropped from some $8 billion in 1989 to about $2 billion three years later. Although the government released no official figures, the national product is believed to have declined, in turn, about 25 percent in 1990 and 15 percent in 1991.[186] The decline was primarily rooted in the plunge in Soviet trade and terms of trade, and in Soviet financing (trade in 1992 down to 7 percent of its 1989 level). Improved relations with market economies and remaining Communist governments did not begin to offset Soviet-bloc losses. And the crisis lowered domestic morale and compliance, further exacerbating economic problems.

The government's economic response to the crisis was multipronged. It involved ideal-typical socialist, capitalist, and precapitalist strategies, although by late 1993 several socialist strategies were too inefficient and costly to be continued. Castro found ideological and moral justification for the diversity of strategies pursued, partly in reinterpreting Marxism-Leninism but also in nationalism and contemporary au courant global discourse. The ruling ideology was flexibly reinterpreted.

Unfortunately for Cuba, the timing of the collapse of Soviet-bloc Communism could not have been worse. The country at the time was at peak dependence on Soviet trade, conservative political dynamics in the United States had stepped up pressure to isolate Cuba economically, and the world market value of Cuba's main commodity export was below production costs while world market prices of vital oil imports were high. Meanwhile, production based on Soviet-bloc technology, initiated over a thirty-year period, was not internationally competitive, except when priced low. Factories that had to be closed down for lack of imported inputs and investment became costly mausoleums of Cold War politics and enormous sunken Cuban capital investments. As a consequence, Cuba found itself worse off than at the eve of the revolution. On top of the costs of Soviet dependence, Cuba was marginalized for political and not merely economic reasons, from Western trade, financing, and tourist markets.

Politically, the government responded to the crisis both with reform and repression. Cuban Communism became increasingly a formal shell under which an increasingly nationalist inclusionary political system took form. But democratization initiatives failed, in the main, to contain discontent. Instead, people of all walks of life defied government authority, most typically in covert and manifestly nonpolitical ways—but in ways that were politically consequential in that the government's capacity to maintain moral and political order eroded in the process. Even regime loyalists indirectly and unintentionally contributed to the erosion of state authority by attempting to avert the deprivations, the downward mobility, and the subsistence crisis that "equality of sacrifice" entailed. How people responded to the crisis varied, in the main, with their personal opportunities, both legal and illegal.

More than ever before, Castro experienced the "weight of history," constraints on his ability to make and remake society as he would have liked. Stepped-up repression was a sign of regime weakness, not strength, as was the rampant expansion of the illicit economy. In response to the crisis Castro cut back social investments that had made the revolution distinctive. However, the next chapter makes apparent that Castro continued to have social accomplishments to his credit even as material conditions became bleak, accomplishments, however, that proved to compound the government's fiscal problems.

Chapter Five

THE IRONY OF SUCCESS

SOCIAL ACCOMPLISHMENTS AND THEIR

UNINTENDED CONSEQUENCES

CASTRO MAY HAVE limited economic accomplishments to his credit, but the social accomplishments of his government have been impressive. The social welfare of a population hinges not merely on a country's material base but on how material resources are utilized. Social policies are, at heart, political; they are contingent on state priorities, on the types of programs governments choose to finance, and the groups targeted. The same monies can be spent on costly capital-intensive programs that benefit a select group of people as on less expensive programs that reach a larger number of folk.

The health welfare accomplishments of the revolution will be shown to be impressive not merely by Cuban standards historically but also by Latin American, Third World, and even First World standards. Castro demonstrated a commitment to health care since his guerrilla days in the Sierra Maestra. The medical system and health welfare became an obsession of his. Hardly a week passed without articles in the Party newspaper highlighting health-sector accomplishments, even during the crisis of the early 1990s.

At the moral level Castro identified health welfare as a basic human right. It was codified as such in the 1976 Constitution. Castro also saw the medical system as a basis for the island's global empowerment. For a while in the 1980s Castro even spoke of developing Cuba into a world medical power.

The class transformation helped make implementation of his moral vision possible, though not inevitable or irreversible. Socialization of the "means of production" undermined corporate and private resistance to the reorganization of medical care—including from private doctors who would lose opportunities to enrich themselves and from wealthy individuals and businesses who would have to be taxed to help finance an expansive, comprehensive system of free medical care. Prerevolutionary doctors who did not want to sacrifice their own lifestyle for the social project indeed opted out: they left quickly and in droves during Castro's first years of rule.

The very social accomplishments of the revolution, however, had the unintended effect of exacerbating the state's fiscal problems. The social accomplishments compounded its fiscal problems not merely because health welfare programs were costly to run but also because the very successes generated new fiscal demands on the state—fiscal burdens that prerevolutionary Cuban governments, contemporary governments in other Latin American countries, and even as wealthy a country as the United States did not assume to the same extent.

HEALTH WELFARE

Government commitment to health welfare is reflected in the scope of publicly provided medical care; it also is reflected in dietary standards when government policies affect what people eat. And the effectiveness of a health welfare system is reflected, in turn, in life expectancy and infant mortality rates.

The Medical Delivery System

Castro's government invested in expanding and democratizing access to the medical delivery system.[1] In principle, doctors provide better quality care than nurses and paraprofessionals because of their more extensive training, but the latter can provide an array of services for which doctors are unnecessary. In resource-poor countries with low health standards, there may be a positive trade-off between large staffs of less expensive paraprofessionals and a small cadre of costly physicians. There may also be a positive trade-off between investment in costly hospital curative and cheaper preventive care. Although many treatments do not require hospitalization, the availability of hospital beds reflects the capability of a delivery system to provide whatever intensive inpatient care might be necessary.

Prior to the revolution the state offered only minimal medical care. People who could afford to, or who qualified through work for care, relied on the private sector.[2] And most medical care was concentrated in Havana.[3] Hospitals typically were either proprietary or religious.

Under Castro, Cuba came to rank among the Latin American countries with the largest number of doctors, nurses, and hospital beds per capita (see Appendix, Table 5.1). Since about half the country's doctors fled the island when the revolution radicalized,[4] the island's stock of trained physicians initially deteriorated. By the 1970s, though, the government had trained a sufficiently large new cohort of doctors that the number of physicians per capita began to surpass prerevolutionary levels. At the start of the decade medical students accounted for one-third of all university enrollments.[5] The stock of doctors was built up to the point that by the end of the 1980s there were more than three doctors to treat islanders for every one that there had been under Batista.[6] With all graduates guaranteed jobs and with nearly all doctors government-employed, the expansion of the medical profession directly reflected the state's commitment to health care.

Medical training was designed to produce a "new professional man." Instead of the Hippocratic oath, medical graduates promised to abide by revolutionary principles. They were asked to agree to serve in rural areas, to not engage in private practice, to promote preventive medicine and human welfare, to strive for scientific excellence and political devotion, to encourage proletarian internationalism, and to defend the revolution.[7] And all graduates upon earning their degree performed rural service in the countryside for three years.

Not only, though, did the government train a new cadre of doctors with new professional principles. It also modified its medical care priorities and restructured the delivery system. The system remained doctor-based, but health units made extensive use of nurses, pharmacists, technicians, and medical and dental assistants. The shift in medical concern was reflected in an even greater improvement in the country's stock of nurses and paraprofessionals than in its stock of doctors (see Appendix, Table 5.1). Although there were fewer nurses than doctors to serve the population before the revolution, the opposite became true as of the mid-1960s. The government, in essence, combined a high- with a lower-skilled, a more expensive with a less expensive, health care staff provisioning strategy.

Castro encouraged low-cost public health campaigns that targeted medically marginal groups early on. Islanders were mobilized for street cleaning and immunization,[8] blood donation, and disease-control campaigns, typically through the block organizations, the Committees for the Defense of the Revolution, but also through the FMC, the women's mass organization. These promotions relied heavily on volunteer labor, and they served until the medical delivery system was well established to vitalize the CDRs as well as the other mass organizations involved; they also helped raise "health consciousness" at the grass-roots level.

The government, meanwhile, promoted outpatient care and reorganized the medical delivery system. The administration of health was centralized and made more uniform while the delivery of services was decentralized. A well-organized system of health centers, known as polyclinics, was initiated to provide ambulatory care throughout the country. The polyclinic-based system delivered a fairly standard set of services and aimed at universal coverage within territorially defined districts. Doctors and support staff were given responsibility for a given group of families within their assigned district.[9]

In the 1980s Castro continued to encourage innovations in the medical system. He went so far as to launch a campaign for a doctor "on every city block" and more doctors for isolated rural areas. The so-called Family Doctor Program, allegedly conceived by Castro himself, involved professionals trained in social and comprehensive general medicine, a closer patient-physician relationship than in the past, and extensive doctor and support staff care.[10] In 1990 the program was extended to workplaces, schools, and day-care centers. The program, which began with ten doctors in 1984, by 1992 included 20,000 physicians overseeing two-thirds of the populace.

In addition to making medical care more extensive, the Family Doctor Program changed the way primary care was delivered and the role of polyclinics. Most doctors and nurses were, in conjunction with the program, to live and work on the city block or in the rural community they served, to comprehend better their patients' psychological and physical problems and to provide immediate and continuous care.[11] They also were responsible for routine community diagnostic care.

The Family Doctor Program represents the first international effort to provide family medicine universally, without charge, as part of an integrated national health system.[12] It was cost-efficient in that it reduced hospitalization and emergency room use.[13]

Expansion of medical care services and facilities does not in itself guarantee use. Since Castro made medical care free to all, cost ceased to be a user impediment. While cultural and other factors might nonetheless inhibit usage, information on medical consultations shows that islanders came over the years to make increased use of the medical system. The average number of consultations per inhabitant, for example, more than tripled between 1963 and 1989.[14]

The medical care system is designed to reach large numbers of people with some possible sacrifice to costly, specialized health needs. Initially the government did not assign high priority to hospital expansion because of the costs involved. At the same time that it invested in training doctors and paraprofessionals and in expanding outpatient facilities, the per capita supply of hospital beds deteriorated—to the point that the population/bed ratio was slightly worse in 1980 than in Castro's second year of rule. In the course of the 1980s, though, the government sought to correct the deficiency of its in-hospital care capacity—to the point that by the end of the decade hospitals had almost twice as many beds, relative to the size of the population, as at the eve of the revolution (see Appendix, Table 5.1). Declining hospital capacity had been singled out (in a Party academic journal) as a problem in need of "rectification" (see chapter 3, note 13). Hospitals offer more specialized treatment than polyclinics and family doctors.

A showpiece specialized hospital in Havana that serves the entire island (as well as foreign patients) absorbed 10 percent of the annual health budget in 1983. The hospital offers CAT scanner, NMR (nuclear magnetic resonance), and organ transplant services.[15] The hospital exemplifies how the government increasingly promoted expensive capital-intensive care along with cheaper paraprofessional and preventive community-oriented care.

In the 1980s the government added other costly high-tech components to the medical care system. Import substitution had by then advanced in the medical, pharmaceutical, and biotechnical fields to the point that the island manufactured over two hundred new biomedical products, a total of nine hundred drugs, and electronic medical equipment and medical software. Cuba by then also produced vaccines and offered medical treatments that few other countries did,[16] and Cuban doctors performed organ and heart transplants, genetic engineering, and microsurgery. Announced Castro confidently (even in the midst of Special Period hardships): "I am certain that . . . there will be no product in the universal pharmacopoeia that we won't be able to produce, nor will there be any international medical equipment that we will not be able to produce besides the new products we'll be able to create." [17] Eighty percent of drugs consumed in Cuba were by the early 1990s manufactured on the island, and the government designated pharmaceuticals a priority sector to develop for export.

In the context of Latin America, Castro's Cuba alone offered a universal, institutionalized system of free rural and urban health care. In only four other countries did more than 50 percent of the population officially have medical-care coverage,[18] and it is doubtful whether even in the four (especially Brazil) the quality of care for low-income groups compared to Cuba's.[19] In the capitalist countries in the region, public and private medical facilities remain more doctor-oriented, more concentrated in the major cities, and less accessible to the masses, and government-subsidized health care is available, in the main, only to the fraction of the labor force who work for the state or formal-sector private firms. Also, the diversity of Cuba's health care offerings were exceptional by regional and Third World standards: the high-tech along with low-tech curative and preventive care.

Cubans are generally happy with their medical care. When asked in a 1989 survey, during the period of "rectification," about attitudes toward the health system, most respondents articulated satisfaction. Eighty-two percent of the people said that the quality of health services was "very good."[20] The new Family Doctor Program was evaluated especially positively. Two-thirds of the respondents, though, felt the quality left something to be desired (the criticism lending credibility to the Party-sponsored survey). Women, who tend most to family needs, and highly educated respondents raised the most reservations. The greater dissatisfaction voiced by more educated folk reflects, undoubtedly, their higher expectations, not their receipt of inferior medical care.

Even with the fiscal crisis of the early 1990s Castro remained committed to providing free, universal medical care. Some services actually expanded. In the 1991–92 school year, for example, 1,400 new doctors were placed in educational centers. But admissions to medical school were cut back. Already in the years immediately preceding the Special Period the national leadership had come to feel that the country was "overproducing" doctors. The government came to view the quality of physical plant facilities more problematic than hospital service.[21]

The main effect of the Special Period was on medical supplies, not medical personnel. Despite advancements in pharmaceutical production, the industry required imported components: an import dependence that the market economies in the region had experienced as well when emphasizing import-substitution industrialization. Unfortunately for Castro's social project, imports for the pharmaceutical industry and the medical system in general had to be slashed with the Special Period trade crisis. The Cuban Democracy Act, moreover, raised the cost of health care imports as Cuba had to find more distant suppliers of products.[22]

The government tried to continue to provide drugs to people with special medical needs, but medication for non-life-threatening ailments became hard to come by. Drugs for headaches and stomachaches, as noted in chapter 4, all but disappeared. Islanders experienced such shortages almost immediately after Castro boasted in 1991 that "there will be no product in the universal pharmacopoeia that we won't be able to produce." Doctors also began to have to consume a lot of their day trying to track down supplies around the country. The crisis caused by the collapse of Soviet-bloc Communism thereby hurt the social project that Castro had developed so creatively and independently of foreign influence.

Meanwhile, in greater need for hard currency than ever before, the Cuban government assigned higher priority to production of pharmaceuticals for export than to production for Cubans. Hard currency exigencies led Castro to sacrifice his people's needs. He advocated traditional herbal medicinal cures for Cubans (as noted in the previous chapter) while promoting modern medicine for export. The modern domestic medical establishment remained intact, but what were doctors and their clinics and hospitals without adequate medical supplies? As of 1993 medical facilities ran the risk of becoming museums of Castro's once showpiece social project, just as shut-down industries became mausoleums of bygone oil-guzzling Soviet-financed development.

Nutrition

Health welfare depends, of course, not only on the size and scope of a medical delivery system but also on nutrition. Because the government regulates the production and distribution of food, its policies directly influence dietary patterns. Data on per capita caloric and per capita protein intake reflect diet. The latter is a better indicator of nutrition, but it accounts for only one source of nutrients. Because poor people often consume insufficient calories, total caloric consumption must also be addressed.

Available information on per capita protein and caloric consumption suggests that Cuban nutritional standards deteriorated during the 1960s and then improved. While average daily protein intake surpassed pre-revolutionary levels by 1970, it took about two decades for average caloric consumption to surpass prerevolutionary levels (see Appendix, Table 5.2). In the mid-1950s daily per capita intake was higher than the estimated requirement (2,460), but the diet was not well balanced. Rich and poor alike sought a diet high in carbohydrates.[23]

The deterioration in nutritional standards in the 1960s came first with the restructuring of agriculture and then with the "push for communism," when production for domestic consumption was sacrificed for record sugar export yields and when the government emphasized investment over consumption. The state's preoccupation then with trade-based economic exigencies, legitimated in the name of lofty moral principles, came at the populace's dietary expense—as well as at the expense of material consumption.

Nutritional standards improved once the government, after the crisis of 1970, reemphasized production for domestic consumption. Caloric and protein intake improved especially in the early 1980s, when the farmers' markets flourished and when agriculturalists were motivated by economic opportunities to improve their yields—that is, when the state regulated agricultural production and distribution least.

From a regional vantage point, by the end of the 1980s Cubans' caloric intake compared more favorably with their Latin American neighbors' than did their protein intake, even though it took longer under Castro for the average daily caloric consumption to exceed prerevolutionary levels than it took protein intake. The country's regional ranking on caloric intake improved by two by 1970 while its regional ranking on protein intake deteriorated under Castro until the mid-1980s.

The improvements of the 1980s, by national and regional standards, proved, however, short-lived. Average daily caloric intake declined to an estimated 2,000 by April 1993, a decrease of some 30 percent from 1989 and below the minimal essential level specified in the mid-1950s.[24] And it dropped just when routine living required more calories: when islanders had to take up bicycle riding as their principal means of transport. Government efforts to improve the food supply through the ambitious Food Program failed. With food scarce, the government became a de facto administrative weight watcher: it monitored how much and what people ate through the reintroduction of—in the legal distribution system—near total rationing. While the government sought to guarantee everyone minimal nutrition and calories under the circumstances, it did so with different foods than people were accustomed to. In place of milk, beef, eggs, and chicken, people were to eat tubers, a traditional source of protein—a diet modification that did not please the cosmopolitan folk. Many people as a result lost weight. While they looked better, the weight loss was not of their own choosing.

Government efforts to guarantee everyone adequate food at affordable prices failed for several reasons. Output suffered from exceptionally heavy rains and import cutbacks. Over half of all protein and calories consumed depended, directly and indirectly, on imports that had to be slashed. And government efforts failed also because producers and distributors, as previously noted, siphoned foods off to the ever more lucrative black market. International assistance that poured in after the March "storm of the century" was insufficient to counter the deterioration in official provisioning. By 1993 the food available through the ration system came to cover about half of a family's monthly needs.

Nutritional deficiencies with the crisis of the 1990s mounted to the point that new health problems arose. In particular, some 40,000 islanders, as of June 1993, lost their eyesight owing to an epidemic of optic neuritis.[25] The government's response revealed, however, its continued commitment to ordinary people's health welfare: the government immediately began to distribute vitamin tablets to all islanders, it involved 18,000 Family Doctors in diagnosis, and it supplied sixty support centers with appropriate specialists and equipment. By the fall of 1993 the illness was under control and no new cases were reported.

Although there are no publicly available studies documenting dietary patterns by socioeconomic class, protein and caloric intake, like health care, undoubtedly improved among low-income groups until the 1990s even when per capita intake did not (and more among low-income groups in Cuba than in other Latin American countries). Even during the "bad times" of the latter 1960s and the Special Period, few islanders suffered from hunger and starvation. Employment, wage, and housing policies raised the purchasing power of rural and urban poor, while the rationing of basic foods guaranteed all an affordably priced diet that met, in the main, minimal nutritional standards. Also, people of all ages received free meals under Castro: the employed through their work centers and children through their schools.[25]

Between the mid-1970s and mid-1980s official policy was most tolerant of dietary inequities. The farmers' markets and the "parallel market" meant a diminished role for rationing, along with greater food production, while the wage reform increased the food-purchasing power of top income earners. Since the government never abandoned rationing of basic foods and it remained committed to its free midday meal program, the lowest socioeconomic stratum undoubtedly did better, in relative and absolute terms, in Cuba than elsewhere in the region even during these years. Indeed, in the 1980s other governments in the region cut back food subsidies, in conjunction with "neoliberal" economic reforms.

The reintroduction—in principle—of near-total food rationing during the 1990s Special Period officially equalized dietary consumption among socioeconomic strata once again, when scarcities would have driven up food prices had distribution not been regulated. But, as noted, affordably priced dietary equity became more an official ideal than a reality, as the government lost its ability to contain black-market activity. Islanders increasingly manipulated food production and distribution to their own advantage when scarcities, resulting initially from drastic import cutbacks, set in. In so doing they undermined state efforts to provide all Cubans with an equally healthy, ample, affordable diet.

Life Expectancy and Infant Mortality

What effect did the expansion and democratization of the health care delivery system and nutritional patterns, as well as other social policies, have on life expectancy? As indicated in the Appendix, Table 5.2, average life expectancy rose from fifty-nine years before the revolution to seventy-six years in 1992. While life expectancy was already impressive by Latin American standards before the revolution, Cuba's regional ranking improved under Castro: the country came to have the highest life expectancy, up from the third highest under the Old Regime.[26] Cuban life expectancy came to be exceptional even by industrial Western and former Eastern European-bloc standards. In fact, *in the early 1990s men tended to die younger in the United States than in Cuba*.[27] No doubt the expansion and reorganization of the medical delivery system, with its emphasis on preventive care and free and relatively equal access, contributed to the island's improved life expectancy, as did the regulation of diet through rationing.

Meanwhile, government social policy contributed to a marked decline in the infant mortality rate.[28] But whereas Cuba already had the lowest Latin American infant mortality rate before the revolution, available data suggest that the rate increased under Castro before it declined, and Cuba lost its top regional ranking for some years under Castro. Health care may have deteriorated under Castro until a new generation of medical cadre were trained to replace the physicians who left, until the health care delivery system was fully reorganized, and until nutritional standards improved. It also may be that the increase in infant mortality registered during Castro's first decade of rule reflected improved data collection, not a worsening in health care: in 1969, for example, 98 percent of all deaths were reported, whereas in 1956 it is thought that only 53 percent were reported.[29]

Ambiguity of data notwithstanding, beginning in the 1970s Cuba unquestionably guaranteed newborns a better chance of survival than before the revolution and by 1980 a better chance of survival again than in any other Latin American country. Between 1970 and 1992 the infant mortality rate plunged from 36 to 10.2 per one thousand live births (see Appendix, Table 5.2). The release of the annual figures was a source of official pride, and the government continued to publicize the yearly rate during the Special Period when it refused to release economic performance figures.[30]

In its effort to improve children's life expectancy the government shifted its strategy over the years.[31] New approaches were needed to target at-risk babies that existing programs failed to reach. Until 1970 the emphasis was on low-cost immunizations and reduction of infectious diseases and diarrhea. In the 1970s perinatal and respiratory problems were targeted. With perinatal diseases and congenital problems the main causes of infant deaths in the 1980s, Castro ordered perinatal intensive-care units in all maternal-infant hospitals, and therapeutic abortions to mothers found, through genetic screening, to be carrying babies with congenital abnormalities. Meanwhile, pregnant mothers responded to government efforts to improve perinatal care. Average obstetric visits per delivery rose from four in 1965 and seven in 1970 to fifteen by the end of the 1980s.[32]

The government made a concerted effort to improve children's life expectancy upon birth as well. With nearly 100 percent of all babies born in hospitals, staff were on hand to attend to any birth-related problems. Then, during the first and most precarious year of life, babies were expected to be seen by their pediatrician twice a month (and more if there were problems), and doctors, often accompanied by nurses, were mandated to visit babies' homes at least once.[33] Working women, meanwhile, were entitled, under the 1974 Maternity Law, to miss work to tend to their children's medical needs.

The Family Doctor Program contributed, in turn, to lowering children's death rate. Where the program was set up, infant mortality rates fell below the national average.[34] In the remote Escambray Mountains, for example, the rate dropped from 20 to 6 per thousand after the Family Doctor Program was initiated there.

Infant survival rates, like life expectancy rates, came to compare quite favorably with those of the more industrial countries. In 1990 the children's death rate in Havana was about half that in Washington, D.C., and the overall U.S. rate was only slightly lower than Cuba's.[35] The quality and quantity of medical care in the United States is much more class- and race-based than in Cuba. Though infant mortality rates continued in the prerevolutionary tradition to vary with socioeconomic status, "class" variations, as measured (imperfectly) by the mother's education level, and differences between richer and poorer provinces, diminished over the years.[36]

Fertility Decline

Cuba's birth and fertility rates, like its life expectancy and infant mortality rates, have come to resemble the First World's more than the Third World's. Although Cuba's rates were already low by regional standards before the revolution,[37] the island moved from having the third lowest to the lowest rates under Castro. The fertility and especially the birth rates actually rose in Castro's first years of rule (see Appendix, Table 5.3), but they subsequently declined.[38] After reaching record lows around 1980, they picked up briefly in the mid-1980s, partly (but only partly) because the boomlet of the early revolutionary years reached childbearing age.

Since women of all ages came under Castro to have fewer children, the drop in the fertility rate is not attributable merely to a postponement of child raising. Indeed, the drop in the fertility rate as of the 1970s was especially dramatic among women over twenty-four, and it was the decline in the birthrate among women over twenty-four that distinguished Cuba at the time from other countries in the region. In the early 1970s, when the island's birthrate plunged, fourteen Latin American countries had a lower birthrate among women fifteen to nineteen years of age than did Cuba, whereas only one, none, and two countries had lower rates among women aged twenty-five to twenty-nine, thirty to thirty-four, and thirty-five to thirty-nine, respectively.[39]

Women appear to be having fewer children by choice. Women entering their reproductive years have expressed disinterest in children. According to a 1978 government study, women in conjugal relationships expected, on average, to have no more than two children. Among the childless women who were interviewed, 42 percent of those under twenty, 32 percent aged twenty to twenty-four, and 42 percent aged thirty to thirty-four said they did not want any children. Meanwhile, among the women aged twenty to twenty-four, 38 percent of those with one child and 83 percent of those with two children expressed no interest in additional children.[40] Comparative evidence suggests that Cuban women want fewer children than women in other Latin American countries.

With the infant mortality rate now so low, mothers may aspire to have no more children than they want in the long run. In countries where health conditions take their toll on children, families recognize that they cannot count on all their babies surviving. Cuba's low infant mortality rate does not in itself, however, account for the low birthrate. Otherwise, countries with similar infant mortality rates should have similar birthrates. However, Costa Rica's birthrate was much higher than Cuba's (25 per 1,000 people in 1990), even though the death rate among children under one year of age in the two countries was nearly identical (Costa Rica's was 3 per 1,000 higher than Cuba's).[41]

Changes in the health care delivery system made it possible for women's ideal family size to become reality. As of the 1980s, 70 percent of all families used birth control, more than in any other country.[42] Abortion services and contraceptives became readily accessible, at minimal if any cost. Once medical care became a basic right of all Cubans and medical facilities were extended throughout the island, Cuba came to have the fifth highest-known abortion rate *in the world*—surpassed, in the 1970s, only by Bulgaria, Japan, Romania, and the USSR.[43] Abortion on demand is exceptional in Latin America. In the late 1970s intrauterine devices (IUDs) and then birth control pills replaced abortions as the primary means of fertility control; they became readily available, at low cost, at least up until the Special Period.[44]

Thus, socialist medicine on the one hand, and women's (if not family) desires on the other, enabled Cuba to accomplish what most Third World governments now aspire to: a substantial drop in their population growth rate. While governments used to believe there was strength in numbers, they have come to see high population growth rates as a weight on their economies, contributing to potentially politically explosive mass poverty. Cuba, unlike China, lowered the birthrate without coercion, without a massive ideological campaign, and without offering direct material incentives to families with few children. The urban prerevolutionary cultural heritage predisposed Cubans to relatively small families, but the medical delivery system, combined with other social conditions to be discussed, contributed to a dramatic drop in the birthrate under Castro.

SOCIAL AND FISCAL RAMIFICATIONS OF THE
DEMOGRAPHIC REVOLUTION

The demographic revolution has had both social and fiscal ramifications. Demographically, the increase in life expectancy, together with the decline in the fertility rate, contributed to a "graying" of the population. Since the state absorbed many of the costs of old age, the demographic revolution generated new fiscal burdens. Society's gain in this respect was at the state's expense. Governments in the capitalist countries in the region were not faced with comparable demands on their fiscal resources.

Cuban demographers lauded the positive aspects of the demographic changes.[45] The fertility rate, however, dropped so low that the population stopped reproducing itself (see Appendix, Table 5.3). By the start of the 1980s Cuba was the only one of the twenty principal Latin American countries to have a projected reproduction rate lower than that necessary for the society to maintain its population.[46]

In addition, Cuba's population has "grayed," including in comparison to other countries in the region. The percentage of the population over sixty-five rose from 4 to 11 between 1960 and 1981 (see Appendix, Table 5.4), and whereas in 1960 four countries in the region had a larger proportion of their population sixty-five years or older, twenty-one years later no country did. In the course of the 1980s the proportion of the population over sixty-five actually declined, while the proportion aged fifteen to sixty-four increased. The "coming of age" of the baby boomlet of Castro's first years of rule accounts for the age distributional shift in the 1980s. Since the proportion of the population under fifteen dipped dramatically during the decade, from 30 to 23 percent, the "graying" trend will resume in the years to come. The 1980s "bulge" of fifteen to sixty-four years old was temporary, not symptomatic of a more youthful long-term tendency.

The old-age costs absorbed by the state increased for both structural and demographic reasons. For one, the proportion of the population eligible for pension benefits rose not merely because of the "graying" of the population since the revolution but also because the number of workers qualifying for the old-age insurance picked up. The proportion of the population working for the state increased with the "socialization of the economy," to the point that, in 1989, 94 percent of the labor force were state employees,[47] state workers automatically qualifying for pensions. Thus, the very social forces that contributed to the expansion of state ownership of units of production and distribution contributed to the expansion of the labor force qualifying for pensions. Women could retire at fifty-five, men at sixty, with full benefits if they worked twenty-five years for the state.[48] As of the 1980s farm cooperative members also qualified for pensions, leaving little of the population ineligible for retirement benefits. The percentage of the labor force qualifying for pensions is estimated to have increased over 30 percent in the process. Meanwhile, Castro saw to it that retiree benefits were made more uniform.[49]

Costs to the state rose, in addition, because Castro's government financed nearly the entire social security system. Before the revolution, salaried employees and private employers (and consumers, through highly priced monopoly-sector goods and services) absorbed most social security costs; only professionals were heavily subsidized by the government.[50]

As a result of the demographic and structural changes, government pension outlays rose substantially. Between 1959 and 1978, for example, they increased 344 percent (in current pesos).[51] The growth in the costs was rooted in the aging of the population and the expansion of the eligible elderly population more than in increased individual annual average benefits,[52] for the number of pensioned Cubans increased 323 percent while expenditures *per* retired or pensioned person increased only 5 percent.[53]

Although the increase in pension outlays through the 1970s was rooted primarily in the growth in the number of eligible elderly, a law promulgated in 1979 increased state *per capita* expenditures as well. The 1979 law tied pension benefits to salary, whereas the earlier law (in effect since 1963) had set a pension ceiling of 250 pesos per month. The newer law specified that workers could qualify for a pension worth up to 90 percent of their average salary when employed.[54] Since the 1980 wage reform raised the basic earnings of most state civilian employees, especially of state managers and administrators, state pension outlays were thereby driven upward.

As a result of these changes state social security expenditures (which exclude health care expenditures) outstripped state social security revenue since the mid-1970s (see Appendix, Table 5.5). The government counted on an employment tax to finance the outlays, but the tax increasingly did not cover costs. A law required employers (in state enterprises and agencies) to pay 10 percent of their wage bill, self-employed to pay 10 percent of their estimated income, and agricultural cooperatives to pay 3 percent of their anticipated average daily income to the social security fund.[55] Pensions accounted for the largest of the social security expenditures and for a growing percentage of those expenditures. Between 1971 and 1989 pension expenditures as a proportion of total social security expenditures rose from 64 to 81 percent, and in 1990 they may have risen to 83 percent.

Castro maintained his public commitment to social welfare even when he introduced austerity measures in the mid-1980s. At the eve of launching the Rectification Process he proudly asserted that "we do not take such measures as leaving senior citizens without help, reducing pensions for retired people, giving less medical care to the sick, or less resources to hospitals and schools; we do not sacrifice our social programs."[56] Although total social consumption expenditures actually declined during the RP, the government remained publicly committed to a range of concerns of the elderly, and its words here were matched by deeds. The government, moreover, approached the "graying" of its population from a social and not merely medical perspective. It established old people's clubs, closely linked to the Family Doctor Program; there were some 4,500 in 1990.[57] The centers targeted the generation that had helped "make" the revolution but who were now senior citizens. The number of centers increased even during the Special Period. The facilities drew primarily on domestic, not imported resources: on labor in abundant supply, not scarce hard currency.

During the Special Period social security outlays increased as well. However, the purchasing power of pension payments fell appreciably for reasons the government could not control. Pensions could cover purchases in the official economy but not the inflationary prices of the black market. By 1993, as the official economy no longer sufficed, a typical household spent 50 to 70 percent of its income on black-market goods. As a consequence, at the same time that state pension expenditures rose, pensioner needs went unmet as never before.

The official medical policy compounded the government's fiscal problems. The government financed medical care directly, not, like social security, through a specific enterprise tax. Indicative of rising medical expenditures, the health budget increased 25-fold between 1959 and 1983.[58]

Not only was medical care free, expansive, and increasingly capital-intensive but also the causes of death shifted to those characteristic of the industrial West's, causes expensive to treat. Cubans have come to die, in the main, of heart failure and cancer. Even if treatment expenditures for such ailments are less in Cuba than in, for example, the United States, where medicine is big business, treatments often involve costly procedures and in-hospital care. State costs increased also because the number of elderly in old-age homes picked up as islanders began to live longer and the younger generation shunned caring for aging kin. The number in such homes more than doubled between 1965 and 1989, beds in old-age homes accounting, in the 1980s, for about 15 percent of all hospital beds.[59]

Few other Latin American governments provide comparable social and health welfare coverage. Typically, the other governments assume, like prerevolutionary Cuban governments, a *portion* of medical and pension costs, and only for workers in the modern bureaucratic and industrial sectors of their respective economies.[60] And in most countries these workers constitute a small fraction of the total labor force.

Health care expenditures, like social security expenditures, thus came to weigh heavily on the economy. According to available evidence, Cuba ranked fourth among Latin American countries in the 1980s in the weight of public health outlays and first in social security expenditure outlays (as a percentage of the national product).[61]

The government, meanwhile, faced problems financing the expenditures through economic expansion. Between 1962 and 1989 social security disbursements, excluding medical outlays, increased 744 percent while the national product increased by only 338 percent. The social security deficit was equivalent to 8.5 percent of the national product as of the mid-1980s, the highest in the region.[62]

The economic crisis caused by the collapse of Soviet-bloc Communism made matters worse. Although the Soviets provided relatively little direct aid to finance social expenditures,[63] aid for other development and defense projects had freed Cuban government monies that might otherwise have had to be allocated to such ends. Moreover, of greater importance, the cutoff in COMECON trade caused the economy to contract precipitously (as previously noted) at the same time that social welfare and unemployment expenditures increased. To make matters worse, to attract foreign capital during the Special Period the government allowed private investors to repatriate profits while the state absorbed social costs of their labor force not covered by the enterprise wage tax.

In light of the growing fiscal problems, the government might have tried to reduce pension expenditures. But such a reduction would have been politically unpopular, for the pension system had contributed to a type of "welfare dependency." Cubans tended to save little, and a previously mentioned 1989 study published in May 1990 found that few people aspired to save for old age.[64] Moreover, during the Special Period, as noted, the purchasing power of pensions dropped precipitously as families had to turn to costly black-market purchases for subsistence.

Alternatively, the government might for economic reasons have raised the retirement age. Given that Cubans are living longer, such a change in retirement policy might make social as well as fiscal sense. But from the state's point of view unemployment costs must be weighed against retirement costs. The unemployment rate undoubtedly would rise if the retirement age were raised.

In principle, the state could create jobs to absorb a larger labor force age pool; however, that too is costly. Moreover, this alternative became inconsistent first with the government's growing concern with labor efficiency and, during the Special Period, with employment cutbacks. If a choice needed to be made, it was in the government's economic interest to have younger rather than older workers employed. Young workers tend to be more productive, and youth unemployment can be politically explosive.

THE IMPACT OF THE "REVOLUTION WITHIN THE REVOLUTION": WOMEN'S PARTICIPATION IN THE LABOR FORCE

One strategy for addressing growing social welfare (and other) revenue needs is through mobilization of previously unutilized and underutilized labor resources. The larger the number of employed in the fifteen to sixty-four age group relative to older people, the more readily can the social costs of the elderly be financed by surplus generated by the working population. Since the proportion of the population of working age (fifteen to sixty-four) rose in the 1980s (see Appendix, Table 5.4), the labor pool to finance old-age costs improved at the time. Yet viewed from a regional vantage point, Cuba was in the worst position to rely on future generations to finance old-age expenditures. By 1989 no other of the twenty principal Latin American countries had such a small percentage of its population under fifteen years of age as did Cuba, and only one country had a lower population growth rate projected for the immediate future.[65]

Women, however, were a source of productive labor on which the government could draw. As noted in chapter 2, beginning in the 1970s the government encouraged women to work and they entered the labor force in record numbers—more so in Cuba than in most other countries in the region. Since most women (as well as men) worked for the state, the government was in a good position to appropriate directly the fruits of their labor.

The number of working women could potentially be expanded to the point that nearly all employable were economically active. Women would thereby contribute more to the productive process and to state accumulation in turn. However, this strategy would pose problems for the government as well. For one, as previously noted, not only are jobs costly to create but there already were insufficient jobs for those in search of work, and women bear, disproportionally, the brunt of unemployment. Second, the more women work, the more likely the fertility rate will drop even lower than it already has. Fertility rates vary with women's labor force participation.[66] The fertility rate dropped dramatically precisely when women's work rate picked up in the 1970s.[67] Work may not keep women from having children, but it inclines them to have fewer.[68]

Studies that permit comparisons of fertility patterns among economically active and nonactive women indicate that working women, on average, have fewer children than nonworking women, but that the impact of work has diminished as all women have increasingly tended to have smaller families.[69] Although the studies capture women's fertility and labor force experiences only at the time of the investigation, and not at the end of their reproductive and productive years, and although the sample bases of the studies differ, they do suggest that work affects family size.[70]

The drop in the birthrate can be traced to women's changed job opportunities and not merely to their increased participation in the labor force. With nearly all full-time economically active women (about 98 percent) working for the state, they qualify for an array of social benefits that relatively fewer women receive in other Latin American countries (where they tend to be more concentrated in informal-sector jobs). However, the demands of formal-sector work, such as inflexible hours and constraints on bringing children to offices, undoubtedly make working women more reluctant to have children in Cuba.

Moreover, women's improved formal-sector opportunities, and not merely their formal-sector employment, seem to contribute to the fertility decline. A 1982 FMC–University of Havana study, for example, found that fertility rates varied with women's occupational status. In three communities surveyed women "workers" (in agriculture and other economic sectors) had the highest fertility rates and women professionals, *técnicas*, and managers had the lowest rates; and daughters in the three communities were much more likely than their mothers both to hold higher status jobs and to have fewer children.[71] Since national employment data show women to be increasingly moving into jobs associated with low fertility rates, the success of the revolution in advancing gender equality undermines the government's ability to count on future generations to generate the resources to finance the welfare state.[72]

In essence, the state's concern with reproducing the population makes the employment of women, especially in high-status jobs, a problematic economic strategy. The 1974 Maternity Law did not stem the tide of fertility decline, even though it offers working women generous maternity and early infant-care benefits. While the birthrate might have declined more in its absence, the rate continued to drop after the promulgation of that law.

Assuming that women's formal-sector work has contributed to the fertility decline, the government's more lax stance toward private economic activity in the early 1980s may be a factor explaining why the fertility rate then briefly rose—the only time it rose since the mid-1960s (see Appendix, Table 5.3). The "market opening" may have encouraged women who might otherwise have sought formal-sector jobs to work part-time, in their homes, and in other ways more congenial to child-raising than bureaucratized jobs. (Improved material conditions at the time may also have inclined more women to have children then.)

Formal-sector employment induces women to have fewer children because women still assume primary responsibliity for housework and childcare. The "double duty" is physically and emotionally exhausting, and it became all the more so during the Special Period in the 1990s (as described in chapter 4). The strains of "double duty," and the financial independence that comes with women's formal-sector employment, undoubtedly contributed to the rise in the divorce rate.[73] Already on the increase in the 1970s, the divorce rate rose an additional 45 percent in the 1980s: it rose to the point that Cuba had one of the highest divorce rates in the world.[74] One of every two marriages ended in divorce, and the average length of marriage was less than five years.[75] Marriage-breakup and employment, separately and in combination, lower the likelihood that women have children.[76]

The government and Party never acknowledged, at least not publicly, the "contradiction" between the need to reproduce the society and women's participation in the labor force. There is no evidence that the government's declining emphasis on the "revolution within the revolution" was rooted in demographic considerations. Nor did Cuban demographers point to the problem. Hernández Castellón and Catasus Cervera,[77] for example, claimed that as women came to assume an increasingly active role in the society they limited the size of their family and that in so doing they helped the state, in the absence of a structured family planning program,[73] to reach the desired family size. Alvarez Vázquez,[78] in turn, saw no conflict between women's social duty to participate actively in the development of the new society—politically and socially as well as economically—and their personal duty to reproduce. She saw Cuban women *resolving* the dilemma by having fewer children.

In sum, as women joined the labor force in record numbers they added to the country's productive capacity. However, their participation in the labor force was contingent on costly fiscal outlays (described in chapter 2), and it contributed to a drop in the fertility rate and to a "graying" of the population in turn. The state's diminished concern with women's participation in the labor force as of the 1980s appeared rooted more in a male gender bias in times of shrinking demand for labor than in a concern with the impact of women's employment on the fertility rate.

CONCLUSION

Cuba's experience under Castro highlights possible social if not economic benefits of socialism. Its demographic profile has come to resemble that of highly industrial countries more than Third World nations. Policies that address islanders' needs from cradle to grave, and that have opened employment opportunities for women, contributed to a "demographic revolution."

The revolution's social accomplishments were shown, however, to generate unintended fiscal problems for the state. The government assumed the health and retirement costs of the increasingly long-living population. Social security expenditures came to outstrip social security revenue, and social expenditures in general increased more rapidly than the state's productive capacity. The very successes of socialism thus exacerbated the state's fiscal problems.[79]

The state's success at reducing infant mortality partly offset the impact of the declining fertility rate on the country's ability both to reproduce itself demographically and to maintain a labor force that could generate revenue to finance the needs of the aging population. The universalization of health care, emphasis on frequent visits to doctors by pregnant women and infants in the first year of life, promotion of medical programs that targeted at-risk populations, special food rationing for pregnant women, and the promulgation of the 1974 Maternity Law entitling women to absent themselves from work to tend to the medical needs of their children all suggest that the government was willing to underwrite costs to minimize infant mortality.

The government might further counter the trend in fertility decline with a pronatal moral campaign. Families might be made to feel that they have a patriotic duty to have children. The government might also tie work and other benefits to family size. However, such material incentives as family allowances were ineffective in former Soviet-bloc countries, and they have been ineffective in Western market economies as well.[80] There is reason to believe that they would be ineffective in Cuba as well. As Cuban demographer Alvarez Vázquez notes,[81] such material incentives as dietary supplements for pregnant women and families with young children, job-related maternity benefits, and free medical care are unlikely to induce families to have more children because the island's population by now considers such benefits basic rights, not privileges.

Immigration is not a viable option for expanding the size of the productive workforce to finance the costs of the "graying" population either. The government would have to make domestic conditions more attractive to entice foreign labor to come. There has been little foreign desire to migrate to Cuba; otherwise, more foreigners would be entering the country, illegally if not legally. Some people did immigrate to Cuba during Castro's first decade of rule out of solidarity with the revolution's efforts to create a more humane and just society; by the Special Period, though, many of them had left and others did not come. There is, of course, no reason for the government to encourage migration as long as the domestic labor supply suffices, except of skilled labor in short supply. Unemployed labor would only add to the state's social and economic problems. And, as noted, with the Special Period unemployment and especially underemployment became problems as never before in Castro's Cuba.

Alternatively, the government might encourage men to assume more household responsibilities. It could thereby address its production and reproduction concerns simultaneously, in a manner consistent with its avowed commitment to Marxist principles of gender equality. The Family Code could provide the basis for such a moral campaign. But, as noted, to date the code has not persuaded men to relieve women of the "double duty."[82] Moreover, should the government attempt to enforce the code it would undoubtedly antagonize men whose political support it needs and wants.

While the Cuban experience was shaped by the change of the dominant "mode of production," on a number of social indicators Cuba already did well before the revolution. Accordingly, Castro had an impressive social base on which to build. The Cuban experience also reflected Castro's personal priorities. Castro based his claims to legitimacy largely on health welfare provisioning. Socialization of the "means of production" enabled him to invest heavily in social programs, but the economic and class transformation did not make such investment inevitable. Cutbacks in admissions to medical schools, the deterioration in hospital physical plant facilities, and declining nutrition standards in the early 1990s, all ripple effects of the collapse of Soviet-bloc "solidarity," point to the fact that neither government will nor the "mode of production" are all-determining. With the Special Period crisis Castro did his best to maintain his commitment to social welfare provisioning, above all to programs requiring no hard currency imports. However, his ability to carry out his social project met up with ever more difficulties, to the point that by the end of 1993 there was talk of starting to charge for certain goods and services proudly presented until then free of charge. By then the deficit had reached 4.2 billion pesos, about three times more than just four years earlier (see Appendix, Table 3.1).

Chapter Six

"A MAXIMUM OF RURALISM,
A MINIMUM OF URBANISM"

FROM IDEALISM TO REALISM

CASTRO LONG CONCERNED himself with rural/urban inequities. He did so since his guerrilla days in the Sierra Maestra. The inequities date back, in Cuba as elsewhere in Latin America, to the colonial period, when the cities, above all the imperial outposts, were favored over the hinterland.[1] And cities were favored again in the twentieth century, especially after World War II, as countries in the region promoted import-substitution industrialization.

Urbanization per se, of course, does not distinguish Latin America from the countries that industrialized first. But urbanization in Latin America and the industrialized West has differed in important respects: in Latin America the rates of city growth have been higher, relative to the level of industrialization, and more concentrated in the main national city; a smaller percentage of the urban labor force has attained jobs in industry because the sector, dependent on foreign capital and technology, has been less labor absorbing than early manufacturing in the first industrial countries; more of the urban population must find ways to eke out a living in petty entrepreneurial activity or in small businesses that offer no job security, no social benefits, and pay poorly; and more city folk have had to house themselves in makeshift quarters that are unhygienic and deficient in urban and social services because the available stock is too costly and too limited. Typically also the benefits of industry have been more concentrated in a small professional and business class in Latin America than in the countries that industrialized first.

Despite deplorable urban conditions, rural folk in Latin America have been flocking in recent decades to the cities, and mainly to the principal city of each country. They have done so because rural conditions, even worse than urban, have deteriorated with population pressure and the modernization of agriculture, which, while more efficient, has diminished the demand for labor.

The characteristics—rapid demographic growth, urbanization that outpaces the expansion of industrial jobs, proliferation of squatter settlements, widespread poverty and dependence of the labor force on informal-sector work that offers no economic and social security, and highly inequitable distributions of the benefits of industrialization—have been so common in the main cities of each Latin American country that they have been presumed to be by-products of "dependent development"— that is, of capitalist development in countries industrializing late and dependent on capital-intensive, imported technologies. They prove however, to be the result not merely of invisible "forces of production." They are the result also of governments that in the process of supporting import-substitution industrialization promoted policies favoring the class interests of industrialists, at the expense, above all, of the peasantry.[2]

If these problems are rooted in late capitalist development, Cuba's socialist transformation might resolve them: improve rural conditions so that pressures to migrate are less, improve urban conditions so that fewer city dwellers are ill-housed, ill-fed, and without urban and social amenities, and improve the distribution of the benefits of development among all socioeconomic groups. Given Castro's commitment to rural injustices even prior to taking power, there is added reason to think that Cuba's revolution might make a difference here.

Castro, in power, indeed addressed these matters. His efforts to break historical disparities between the city and the countryside appeared as ideologically driven as his concerns with speeding the "push to communism" in the 1960s and with "rectifying errors and negative tendencies" in the 1980s. The maxim "A maximum of ruralism, a minimum of urbanism" appeared to guide state initiatives, especially during the first decade of the revolution. But as argued before, if government policy is first and foremost ideologically driven, initiatives should be consistent with the principles espoused, and policy shifts should be accompanied if not preceded by shifts in government moral commitments. If the government implements policies that defy the principles it claims guide its initiatives, if policies are not ideologically justified, and if official initiatives advance political and economic concerns of the state, ideology can be assumed not to be the only and, in some instances, not the main determinant of social policy. In essence, the government and Party may use ideology more to legitimate than to guide policies.

The government proves to have modified its rural/urban policies quite dramatically on a number of occasions.[3] Although the government conveyed the impression that at least certain modifications were ideologically driven, the changes were responses to the same forces as shifts in national economic policies. Developments in the city and the countryside were affected by national policies, municipal and provincial governments enjoying little decision-making autonomy.[4] But neither city dwellers nor country folk were mere passive subjects of priorities set by Castro and his inner circle. They defied the law, resisted collaboration, and limited their productivity when averse to state initiatives.

THE 1960s "A MAXIMUM OF RURALISM, A MINIMUM OF URBANISM": IDEALISTIC AND PRAGMATIC

Before the revolution Cuba was the fourth most urban nation in Latin America (see Appendix, Table 6.1). Thirty-five percent of the population lived in urban areas, communities of 20,000 or more inhabitants, in the mid- to latter 1950s. With one-fifth of its population in Havana, Cuba also ranked fourth in the region in single-city population concentration. By regional standards Cuba therefore was exceptionally urban, and its urban population was exceptionally concentrated in a single city.

People had flocked to Havana because it was the most important city economically. Seventy-five percent of national industry (excluding sugar) was located there, and 90 percent of all foreign trade passed through its port.[5] It was also an important educational center, and the island's only university was located there.

Havana symbolized the "high" and the "low" life of the Old Regime. It was, in part, a privileged city. Most new housing built in the five years preceding the revolution, mainly large residences and luxury apartments, was concentrated in Havana.[6] The beautiful bayside city's posh neighborhoods rivaled the most elegant in the United States. Only about 6 percent of the city's population lived in shantytowns—a very small proportion by Latin American standards. (However, shantytowns began to proliferate throughout the continent mainly only in the 1960s, after the revolution.) And rent control, in effect since 1939, kept the cost of shelter low for many less fortunate city dwellers who were tenants.

But prerevolutionary Havana was also notorious for corruption, gambling, and prostitution. The city was the "Las Vegas of the Caribbean" to many U.S. tourists.

Almost immediately upon taking power Castro sought to put a break to the rate of urban growth and to transform the quality of urban and especially rural life. During his first decade in power Havana's share of the national population held steady while other cities became demographically more important. And Cuba's Latin American ranking on measures of urbanization dropped—that is, people in a number of other countries in the region became more concentrated in the principal city and more concentrated in cities with a population over 20,000 (see Appendix, Table 6.1). From a demographic vantage point, the revolution served to make one of Latin America's most urbanized and most concentrated urban populations more like the rest of the region. Had prerevolutionary trends continued, Cuba undoubtedly would have remained one of the more urban, single-city-centered countries in the region.

The decline, from a comparative vantage point, in the demographic significance of island cities was partly rooted in changing population trends. For one, the families who fled Cuba as the revolution radicalized were mainly from Havana, and about one-tenth of the population emigrated. Second, a shift occurred after the revolution in internal migration patterns. Before the revolution Havana absorbed 52 percent of internal migration, but in the 1970s it absorbed only 12 percent.[7] Third, the drop in the island's urban fertility rate (after the 1960s baby boomlet) contributed to Havana's declining demographic importance. Urbanization elsewhere in Latin America typically was not associated with a comparable fertility drop.

But the halt in Havana's growth rate was the result also of deliberate government policy.[8] Early on Castro tried to transform the culture of Havana. He and his revolutionary purists outlawed gambling and prostitution. Havana ceased to be a magnet for islanders in search of excitement. Meanwhile, the radicalization of the revolution expanded government control over where and how people lived—through the administration of the ration system, residence permits, and, later, worker identity cards.[9]

While making life in the capital less attractive, Castro made provincial living more attractive. His government constructed more new communities than any other Latin American government, and it stabilized former communities with mobile populations (*bateyes*). Between 1959 and 1962 it built eighty-three new towns and settlements, housing, on average, three hundred to five hundred people each. They included services typically found elsewhere in the region only in cities, and only in the better-off urban neighborhoods at that. The planned communities were built with schools and medical facilities, and the dwelling units had electricity and sanitary facilities. The government even furnished apartments. Often the new communities offered employment opportunities as well, especially when associated with agricultural development projects. Castro had in mind a modern, "urbanized" countryside, in contrast to the traditional Latin American rural way of life.

Castro's pro-rural and pro-provincial strategy involved other components which, combined, further reduced reason for urban migration. Castro's 1959 agrarian reform rewarded some 100,000 humble rural folk with legal rights to land. At the time, no other Latin American country had redistributed land "to the tiller" on a significant scale. And Castro's government alone came to guarantee farm workers year-round employment (and income). In the 1960s, as indicated in chapter 2, it also raised wages in agriculture more than in other sectors, and in the latter half of the decade agriculture was the one sector where the mean salary increased. The urban/rural wage gap thereby diminished. Wealth became more equitably distributed in the cities with the nationalizations first of large businesses and then, in 1968 with the so-called Revolutionary Offensive, of small businesses.

Castro also broke with the Latin American tradition in investing substantially in rural education and medical care, and not merely in the newly constructed communities. His concern with educating rural folk had already been articulated in his 1953 Moncada defense trial. Said he, "A serious error is being made in Latin America: where the inhabitants depend almost exclusively on the products of the soil for their livelihood, the education stress, contradictorally, is on urban rather than farm life."[10] Yet in the decade of the 1960s his government did not consistently favor the countryside over the city, official discourse notwithstanding: the percentage of elementary students graduating and receiving scholarships, and the student/faculty ratio, remained better in urban than rural areas (see Appendix, Table 6.2). And Castro's ambitious health welfare programs in many respects targeted rural areas more in the early than latter 1960s (see Appendix, Table 6.3).

Cuban urban statistics are, however, inflated by a governmental redefinition of "urban." An island community became defined as "urban" not necessarily on the basis of population; it became so defined also if it provided such social amenities as running water, medical assistance, schools, and paved streets and street lighting. By definition, therefore, most urban communities came to have such amenities. The redefinition reflected a social in contrast to a demographic definition of cities.

Castro's concern with rural health welfare, as well as with rural education, was articulated in his Moncada defense trial. The "greatness and prosperity of our country," he asserted, "depends on a healthy and vigorous rural population. . . . Ninety percent of rural children are consumed by parasites. . . . Society is . . . criminally indifferent to the mass murder of so many thousands of children who die every year of lack of facilities, agonizing with pain."[11] Consistent with this outrage, his guerrilla comrades provided free medical care to peasants in the Sierra Maestra in the latter 1950s, and when in power he immediately improved rural hospital facilities, almost nonexistent under the Old Order.[12]

Castro made certain that the new doctors his government trained would break with the prerevolutionary tradition of locating mainly in Havana. In addition to requiring all medical students to serve in rural posts, as part of their training, his government expanded rural medical training, facilities, and job opportunities.

Castro broke in yet another way with the Latin American urban bias: in his economic investment policy. As noted, with import-substitution industrialization economic investment was confined mainly to the principal cities of the region—where infrastructure was best developed, and where skilled labor and other resources were concentrated.[13] But Castro made a concerted effort to locate new industries near natural resources and in previously underdeveloped areas.[14] He also developed provincial ports to reduce the importance of Havana for trade.

The government, in particular, promoted a plan to develop the impoverished Oriente region as a "growth pole." Around Nicaro-Moa it promoted nickel, iron, steel, oil refining, and other heavy industry, new port facilities, and a new city, Levissa, intended to house 130,000 people.[15] A variety of industrial investments were also made in Santiago de Cuba, the main city in the region. Accordingly, the area where Castro centered his guerrilla movement was amply rewarded.

While breaking with Latin American precedent in investing heavily in the countryside and in provincial cities, Castro did not entirely neglect Havana. Architecturally, the revolution initially inspired creative building design—social, not socialist, architecture which drew on a variety of architectural techniques and concepts.[16] Inspired by the élan of the time, Cubanacán, the Havana art school, broke with prerevolutionary architectural canons. It was modern and innovative in design, though elitist in concept and costly.

In his first years in power Castro also invested in two conventional large pricey housing developments, East Havana and El Cotorro, and his government helped finance private construction. The developments were premised on middle-class design concepts then in vogue in the United States, although they were built to house industrial workers and urban poor removed from blight areas. East Havana was conceived as an ambitious 100,000-unit development comprised of neighborhoods integrated into superblocks. Situated on a beautiful site overlooking Havana Bay (on land that, prior to the revolution, such firms as Skidmore, Owings, and Merrill, and such world renowned architects as Oscar Niemeyer and José Luis Sert, had been approached to design luxury housing for), East Havana included high-rise and walk-up residential buildings, community facilities, and commercial areas.[17] Many of the original squalor families the government relocated in the high-rise were unaccustomed to apartment living. Resentful, they abused the buildings, and many ultimately moved away. The government's utopian urban-planning vision conflicted with city folk's customary way of life, and they let it be known. Only 1,500 of the planned 100,000 units ultimately were built.[18]

The government also helped finance private housing. For example, it established a National Institute for Savings and Housing (INAV) in 1959 to fund construction of single-family homes. During its first year of operation INAV constructed 10,000 new units.[19] Then, the government established a Self-Help Mutual Aid Program. However, the two programs were short-lived as they were costly and an inefficient solution to housing needs, and from a political and ideological perspective they kept families isolated.

Castro's class bias concomitantly led him to address tenant concerns. He was initially less antiurban than antibourgeoisie. Even though prerevolutionary rent control legislation had kept many rents low, new legislation halted evictions, rolled back rents by as much as 50 percent, and relieved residents of rundown tenements who had paid sixty monthly payments of rental obligations altogether. A 1960 Urban Reform Law, in turn, allowed tenants to acquire the housing they inhabited.[20] Castro argued that each rural and urban family should have decent housing and the right to own their own home or apartment. Just as each rural family should be able to own its own tract of land, so too should each urban family have the right to own property. Fidel made mention of such housing rights in his 1953 Moncada defense as well.[21] The 1960 law led 50 percent of urban tenants to become homeowners.[22] Beneficiaries paid for the units in monthly installments equal to the rent they previously paid, for five to twenty years. Former owners of nontenement buildings were compensated and given lifetime pensions.

Later in the decade fiscal considerations led the government to postpone the day of universal home ownership, though it guaranteed that *no one* spent more than 10 percent of their family income on rent.[23] Then in 1971 the government exempted the poorest income earners (those earning less than twenty-six pesos a month) from rent payments, just as it previously had exempted tenement dwellers from such payments. The government meanwhile sympathized with the "petty" rentier class. Small property owners benefited from tax exemptions, and they were allowed to have rental units, provided that they lived in the buildings and charged tenants no more than 150 pesos a month.

The government was not, however, so kind to large urban proprietors. Laws passed in 1959 forced the sale of vacant land and regulated the sale and use of land. The government, in addition, ended urban and suburban land speculation, outlawed large rental operations, regulated purchase and sales agreements, called for expropriation without compensation of all tenement buildings, and cancelled all mortgages and loans.

But in addressing tenant and small proprietor concerns the government left unresolved the problem of insufficient housing. The early housing projects accommodated only a small fraction of urban folk, and the still-standing prerevolutionary building stock left much to be desired, in quality as well as quantity. Much of it was in a state of disrepair, to the point that the number of Havana residents living in buildings on the verge of collapse rose.[24] Meanwhile, demand for housing increased as the younger generation came of age and started their own families.

Toward the end of the 1960s the government developed a low-cost construction strategy, involving prefabricated units. Industrialized construction was perceived to be more efficient, and congruent with socialist objectives.[25] This type of housing initially was mainly built outside Havana. The first large-scale project, in Santiago, was conceived to rehouse 40,000 former slum and shantytown dwellers (one-sixth of the eastern city's population). Named symbolically after the country's independence hero, José Martí, the complex included, like other new housing, social services, electricity, and other infrastructure. The housing units were produced at a plant donated by the Soviet Union, with the project design drawing on a French-inspired Soviet system. Residents were asked to pay 10 percent of their income as rent (in line with the official rental policy at the time), and an additional 2 percent to amortize furniture costs.

The government's main investment in Havana in the late 1960s was in the area surrounding the city. In 1967 it initiated a Green Belt project, designed to make the capital self-sufficient in food. The Belt was to produce subsistence crops and coffee for export. It promoted a redefinition of urban as well as country living that further broke down historical differences between the city and the countryside: on the one hand, farmers participating in the Green Belt program received housing in new fully "urbanized" communities, equipped with day-care centers, schools, and polyclinics, while, on the other hand, city dwellers helped out in seasonal Green Belt farm activity. This was the period when *habaneros*, Havana residents, also helped in cane-cutting. The utopian project, however, died a quiet death. It had been poorly conceived and poorly organized, and it involved people without necessary farm skills and motivation.

The latter 1960s' emphasis on "a minimum of urbanism, a maximum of ruralism" and on a diminution of rural-urban distinctions appeared morally inspired. As one of Castro's longtime trusted collaborators, Carlos Rafael Rodríguez, noted in a speech, "Our capital today is the stagnant capital of a country in development," whereas prior to the revolution Havana was "the developed capital of an underdeveloped country."[26] Rural prioritization was deliberate.

But moral principles alone did not guide policy. Some investments diverged from what the discourse would suggest. The government, for example, retained an urban educational bias, although that bias perhaps would have been greater had the leadership not been officially committed to reducing rural/urban disparities. Furthermore, the commitment to "a maximum of ruralism" peaked when the government had economic reasons for promoting rural development, with the "big sugar push."

In sum, during the first decade of the revolution Castro broke with the urban Latin American tradition in a number of ways and in so doing revealed how socialism can make a difference. Urban property relations and the usage of urban property were "debourgeoisified." Nationalization of ever more of the economy enabled the government to alter architectural styles, construction strategies and techniques, and access to social services, and in so doing to change the historical meaning, to a large extent, of urban and rural living. In a number of ways the government reduced historical differences between the city and the countryside by "ruralizing" the former and "urbanizing" the latter. And it sought to reduce the importance of the capital city, demographically and economically, along with class disparities. The break with the Latin American tradition was morally justified and consistent with the goals of speeding up the "transition to communism." But the morally justified project was a creative response to externally rooted constraints and opportunities and it was promoted with this end in view. The government had to redress the balance-of-payments problem resulting from its initial import-substitution prioritization.

THE NEW URBANISM OF THE 1970s AND EARLY 1980s

For reasons described in chapter 2, the "push for communism" proved a fiasco, economically and politically. The government failed to convince city dwellers of the virtues of "ruralizing" their lifestyle and conceding historical privileges. Its ability to remake society was here constrained by islander resistance. Few besides the poor fared better than before the revolution. The failure of the externally based sugar growth strategy, plus brewing urban discontent, led the government to modify its urban along with its macro economic policy in the 1970s.

City concerns as a result received more attention. Government investment in Havana, for one, picked up, though without ideological fanfare comparable to the late 1960s "maximum of ruralism" maxim. Second, habañeros stopped having to work seasonally in agriculture. Yet Castro continued to promote developments that broke with the Latin American urban tradition, and he did not turn his back on provincial folk, as Latin American governments typically did.

The government argued that "realistic" and "technical rational" considerations, not elemental justice, called for the policy shift. It asserted that investments were to be located in the capital because the city had good facilities, infrastructure to support the new industries, a concentrated consumer market, and a disciplined, skilled, and experienced labor force.[27]

Castro was most innovative in the field of housing. Because state-built construction in the provinces in the 1960s had met up with many problems, Castro was reluctant to draw on that strategy to address Havana's housing deficit. Bottlenecks caused by supply and equipment problems impaired output, and projects proved to be more costly than planned. Also, an ambitious urban housing program required much labor. Under the circumstances, he called on enterprises and their workforce to help build apartment complexes, and quickly. Enterprises provided the labor, the government the building materials and architectural plans. The so-called minibrigade program, mentioned in chapter 2, was responsible for 65 percent of all new housing in 1972 and 1973,[28] with some 40 percent of the minibrigade construction concentrated in and around Havana. Construction of new housing peaked in the capital in 1974. That year over 8,000 units were built, up from 500 units four years earlier.[29] The new building made minimal use of professional architects and construction workers.

Each minibrigade consisted of thirty-three to thirty-five workers, released from their ordinary work commitments for up to two years. The work centers could retain 40 percent of the housing their workers built. Minibrigades involved collective voluntary labor, consistent with Guevarist principles, but at a time when such principles were publicly downplayed. The construction strategy was promoted because it was well suited to labor market conditions and urban political priorities at the time. The economy then was especially robust and demand for labor in more attractive jobs was high. Under the circumstances there were pragmatic along with moral reasons for the mode of building. Indeed, labor shortages in the professional construction sector were so acute in Havana then that builders were brought in from the eastern provinces to help in state-built projects.

Not only was the mode of construction innovative; so too was the process of housing allocation. Employees in the work centers that built the housing decided collectively who, on the basis of need and work performance, should get to live in the new apartments. Asserted Fidel, "In the case of two workers with equal need, the one with the largest sense of social responsibility and merit should have priority";[30] this view was consistent with the "socialist distribution principle." While the allocative scheme favored workers in large enterprises who could best afford to release employees for construction work, it left less room for corruption and elite favoritism than centrally controlled housing allocations.[31] At the same time housing was not contingent on ability to pay, as in market economies. People paid for the same quality housing according to their economic means. Rents continued to be pegged to family income.

The most ambitious minibrigade-built project was Alamar, on the outskirts of Havana. Built on land that had been held for speculative purposes before the revolution, it housed some 30,000 people by 1978. In addition to housing, the plan called for thirty-two day-care centers, eighteen semi–boarding schools, six theaters, sports and health facilities, and industrial plants (employing mainly women).[32] Minibrigade teams helped build the social and economic structures as well as the apartment complexes. Although the government was responsible for the project plan, some design modifications were made in response to resident concerns. Balconies and service patios were, for example, added in response to criticisms raised by the first residents.

While premised on different construction and financing principles than earlier projects, the effort to use design to create a meaningful social community was no more successful here. A standing joke about Alamar is that "everything's there now but the city." Alamar is large, isolated, and impersonal, and some distance from where most people can find work. The prefabricated apartment units also do not allow residents to modify their dwellings as their family needs change and their income allows, or to easily use their quarters for income-generating rental and commercial purposes, as shantytown dwellers can.

Moreover, despite worker input into housing design and the allocative process, the government never relinquished political control over the areas *minibrigadistas* built. Not only had Castro made it clear that access to housing was partly contingent on workers' sense of social responsibility, but also state-linked mass organizations, such as the CDRs and the FMC, established a footing in housing developments once residents moved in. Aside from concerning themselves with community maintenance, the CDRs established informal social and formal political control in the new dwelling complexes. Their influence, however, was probably never as great as regime critics claimed, and their influence diminished over the years. Symbolic of CDR failure to enforce Party hegemony at the grass-roots level, the poet who in 1991 became an outspoken dissident, María Elena Cruz Varola (see p. 118), lived in Alamar, and it was there that she tried to organize her antigovernment meetings.

The minibrigade program represented a proactive state-financed and state-directed approach to urban housing that contrasted with the largely reactive governmental approach elsewhere in the region at the time.[33] The other Latin American governments tolerated poor people's private solutions to their housing needs—individual shantytown home construction on property typically illegally staked out. The governments over the years often legalized and urbanized areas settled by squatters, after which market forces drove up the value and cost of housing there. The Cuban approach thus allowed for better urban and community planning and better hygiene, and for a ceiling on the costs of shelter; but it did so, as noted, at the cost of flexibility and maximum use of housing for income-generating purposes. While the government never adequately addressed the demand for housing, it did improve the quality, even from a regional vantage point. According to official sources, by the end of the 1970s some 91 percent of urban units had running water and an even higher percentage had electricity, and about half had sewerage facilities.[34] Castro had provided thousands of homes in low-income neighborhoods with electricity and other infrastructure, even where no new housing was built. In only three other Latin American countries did a greater percentage of urban dwellers have running water in their homes, although in seven other countries the proportion with sewerage facilities was higher.[35] It should be remembered, though, that such infrastructure became a criterion for classifying communities as urban in Cuba.

The changed definition of "rural" made the Cuban countryside, in turn, appear more underdeveloped. Only about 10 percent of Cuban-defined rural housing units at the time had water and 6 percent had sewerage facilities.[36] A higher percentage of rural folk in half the other principal Latin American countries had running water in their homes and in five countries more had sewerage facilities. Rural amenities appear statistically unimpressive because relatively unpopulated communities that in other countries would be considered "rural" are "factored out" and reclassified as "urban" when they offer social services.

But the government's concern with urban housing quickly waned. The number of units built in the capital dropped to 3,500 yearly by the latter 1970s. Unmet housing needs may have contributed to the mass emigration from the port of Mariel in 1980. The vast majority of the 125,000 who took advantage of the possibility to leave that year had resided in and near the capital.[37] The dashing of housing expectations, following the contraction of the much-publicized minibrigade program, may have fueled discontent—as did contact with visiting émigrés. All too frequently divorced couples had to continue living together or with former in-laws, at times even with new spouses.

Minibrigade housing was perceived to be of lower quality and even higher cost than equivalent buildings erected by state brigades. The programs involved labor lacking construction experience, and minibrigade labor costs were high because the workers received their regular salaries, which were higher on average than wages paid to full-time unskilled construction employees, from their workplaces. Meanwhile, with the implementation of the New Management System, enterprise managers became more reluctant to release labor for construction work, because with fewer workers their productivity, and profits in turn, might be down.

There followed a period of "benign neglect" in which the government turned to market forces to resolve housing as well as other urban economic needs. The "market" proved to generate more housing than the government and minibrigades ever had, highlighting how much demand had been left unsatisfied. In the early 1980s construction grew faster than any other economic sector. Of the 398,000 housing units built between 1981 and 1986, 63 percent were privately constructed, and the private construction during the five-year period accounted for 85 percent of all housing built between 1959 and 1980. Even in 1984, when new dwelling completions dropped to 60,000, the number was over three times greater than in the peak year of construction prior to 1980.[38]

In the latter 1970s and early 1980s more attention also was given, indirectly, to maintenance and repair work. During the first decade and a half of the revolution, the government's restriction of private contract work contributed to building decay. First the legalization of independent private contract work and then a 1984 housing law helped address maintenance problems; the 1984 law also helped address tenure, inheritance, and payment issues that had accumulated over the years.[39] Many families had engaged in informal unauthorized sales, swaps, and other arrangements, and private builders not infrequently had constructed housing on sites attained illegally. Unsatisfied demand for housing until then under Castro had led to widespread evasion of the laws, as city dwellers had quietly sought their own solution to their housing needs and aspirations, and builders took advantage of the situation. Islanders did not simply acquiesce to state priorities at the time.

The 1984 housing law also called for the conversion of leaseholders in government-owned housing into homeowners. Within four years 450,000 former leaseholders had their rents converted into monthly payments for home purchases and another 330,000 were granted title at no cost.[40] Castro here renewed his earlier commitment to make everyone homeowner. Meanwhile, Castro legalized private rentals and in so doing also allowed for more efficient use of the existing housing stock. More families could be accommodated with minimal additional material outlays. And the law also facilitated family construction by making low-interest financing available for building.

The national government at the time concentrated its scarce resources where "the market" was ineffective in stimulating construction and where it wanted to direct labor.[41] More than a quarter of the government-constructed housing planned for the early 1980s, for example, was to be located in cane-growing areas: the national leadership called for 58,000 state-built units to be built in such areas, compared to only 33,000 in more densely populated Havana. Another 10,000 or so homes were to be built on cooperative farms as an incentive to remaining private agriculturalists to give up independent farming. It will be remembered that, beginning in the latter 1970s, the government promoted cooperative farming in the nonstate sector.

At the Third Party Congress in February 1986, Castro reconfirmed that agro-industrial development projects would receive priority housing. The government would assume responsibility for about half the housing projected for the upcoming Five Year Plan; the other half was to be built privately.

Meanwhile, investment in rural social services continued to improve and, in some respects, to improve more in the countryside than in the cities. Beginning in the 1970s the elementary school student/faculty ratio came to be better in rural than in urban areas, and the percentage of scholarship students also came to be greater in the countryside than in the cities (see Appendix, Table 6.2).

Enrollments in basic secondary school picked up after 1970, increasing nearly fourfold between 1970 and 1980 and declining somewhat thereafter.[42] So-called Schools in the Countryside accounted for much of the enrollment increase; these were new boarding schools where children worked half a day in farm-related activity and studied the other half.[43] Since the boarders may be city children, there is no way of telling, from available information, what proportion were city and what proportion were rural children.

Access to medical care, in turn, continued to improve in the countryside, as in the 1960s. However, facilities and use of facilities never favored rural residents as much as in the mid-1960s (see Appendix, Table 6.3). The slight urban bias notwithstanding, Havana's population/hospital bed ratio deteriorated between 1970 and 1985 from 82:1 to 102:1.[44] This deterioration was considered in the latter 1980s to be a problem in need of "rectification."

Urban improvements that occurred through government and government-tolerated market channels, beginning in the latter 1970s, did not occur at rural folk's expense. Peasant producers prospered with the farmers' markets, and the government raised state farm wages more than industrial wages. Between 1980 and 1985 farm wages increased 42 percent while industrial wages rose "only" 24 percent.[45] The period of market reforms accordingly was associated with improvements in the state as well as the private sector, and in the countryside as well as cities.

Although both government policy and the "market opening" gave an air of improvements in both urban and rural areas, as of 1986 over 11,000 Havana households, and more than 45,000 individuals, lived either in shelters or in units declared dangerously uninhabitable. And half the housing stock was still in need of repair.[46] Havana had sixty-one shantytowns (out of 416 island-wide), and building collapse became frequent. The main beneficiaries of the "market opening" had been the more affluent islanders who could afford the private housing prices.[47]

Revelations about tenements and shantytowns became public as the government launched the campaign to "rectify errors and negative tendencies." Castro noted that the neglect of Havana was a result of "negative tendencies and wrong ideas." Lingering effects of the "maximum of ruralism and minimum of urbanism" campaign were, the government now acknowledged, in need of correction.

THE "RECTIFICATION OF URBAN ERRORS" IN THE LATTER 1980s

As noted in chapter 3, the government, with no forewarning, suddenly announced that the "market opening" in the housing sector had been a mistake. It shifted its stance shortly after defending it at the February 1986 Party Congress. While addressing city dwellers' housing needs more than in years past, the "market opening" in the housing sector had undermined state production and it left the economically and socially most marginal islanders with unresolved housing needs. Workers were noted to have pilfered enterprises for supplies, to have absented themselves from work to build private housing, and to use state enterprise building equipment for private gain.

Despite the new Guevarist-like rhetoric of "rectification," market features were not entirely reined in. The government issued a ban on builders taking private jobs and on property advertisements in the media. It also tightened control over sales and rentals, including over the price of housing (which had risen exorbitantly in the 1980s). But within such constraints private housing activity was tolerated.

The government's attempt to undermine private profiteering had, in certain respects, the opposite effect. Speculation became rampant.[48] Because new regulations discouraged construction, the housing stock did not grow apace with demand. Probably more than earlier in the decade, in the latter 1980s prices rose to levels only the more affluent (or people pooling their financial resources) could afford.[49] Government efforts to keep costs of private sales down for low-income groups were "sabotaged" by people turning to covert means of attaining housing.

As also noted in chapter 3, the RP was associated with the revival of the minibrigade program. The program again centered in Havana. In 1987 some 20,000 to 29,000 workers participated in minibrigades; two years later 35,000 did. As in the 1970s, they built social and other facilities along with housing.[50] In 1989, for example, they were responsible for the construction of six hundred home/offices for doctors (for the government's "doctor on each city block" campaign) and about fifty day-care centers along with 5,000 housing units.[51] The following year minibrigade members worked on 25,000 dwellings, and the number of completed day-care centers rose to 110.[52] Decentralization of the administration of the program meant that building was more responsive to neighborhood needs than in the 1970s.

In relying on minibrigades rather than professional construction workers for state construction projects and in appropriating most minibrigade-built units for its own allocation, the government found itself in political trouble. City dwellers resented doing low-prestige, manual construction work if they did not directly benefit from it. They resented, in particular, building the Expo-Cuba Center and facilities for the Pan American Games that the government planned to turn over to tourism after the regional sports competition. To make their views felt, they staged work slowdowns and some of them insisted on building larger units than appropriate for dwelling sites in order to accommodate more families.[53] Confronted with the anger and worker foot-dragging, the government increased the share of minibrigade units that work centers could retain for themselves: it increased the percentage from 40 percent in the 1970s to 50 percent and, in 1989, to 60 percent.[54] Moreover, minibrigade participants became entitled to units in the buildings they constructed; in the 1970s, it will be remembered, workers collectively decided who most merited the housing enterprise laborers constructed. Housing became heavily politicized as demand went much unsatisfied.

The minibrigade program, however, proved less ambitious than projected. Only half the dwelling units planned for 1987 were built, and only slightly over one-quarter of the dwelling units begun in 1990 were finished. The 7,000 completed in 1990 amounted to only about 11 percent of the annual number completed privately, on average, between 1981 and 1986. Although pre-Rectification construction had been criticized for leaving many buildings unfinished as workers concentrated on the most profitable stages of production, minibrigade building, for different reasons, was no better. Necessary cutbacks in building imports in the latter 1980s impeded construction.

By the end of the 1980s, Havana's problems proved far from solved. Insufficient numbers of new units were built to compensate for the deterioration of old buildings. Indeed, the RP left the city with housing problems alleged to be characteristic of the capitalist, not socialist, Third World—tenements and shantytowns. Castro acknowledged that approximately 3 percent of Havana residents (60,000 to 90,000 people) lived in shantytowns, some 210,000 folk in 7,000 "tenement areas" where families were overcrowded, and 63,000 in sixty neighborhoods and ninety-six small zones judged to be unhealthy.[55] Housing continued to be so bad that some 3,000 residents lived in special shelters. Another 16,000 *habañeros* qualified for shelters but preferred to continue living in their old domiciles at their own risk. All told, by the decade's end about 14 percent of the nation's capital lived in slums, unhealthy areas, or homes that were in a very poor state of repair, while 20 percent of Havana housing units lacked electricity and running water. The "rectification campaign" had not improved city blight. The number of people with inadequate housing in Havana exceeded the population of Camaguey, Cuba's third largest city!

Havana's problems were, moreover, compounded by overcrowding in dwellings in good condition, by sewerage problems, by streets in need of construction and repair, and by transport and food distributional problems. To help address unmet housing needs the government announced plans to build 10,000 units in the capital in 1990, and 20,000 the following year.

The government claimed commitment to "rectifying errors" as urban discontent and social problems mounted. Slums were loci of crime. Governmental political discrimination in its housing allocations had the unintended effect of exacerbating social disorder. The government had rewarded the most active and hardworking slum dwellers with new housing, leaving behind the most socially marginal people.

Meanwhile, the rural/urban earning gap, as reflected in state agricultural versus industrial wages, nearly disappeared—a situation unprecedented in the history of Latin America. But the decline in the differential during the period of "rectification" was tied to a *drop* in average industrial wages along with an increase in average farm wages. The decline in average industrial wages received no attention in official public discourse.

Thus at the same time that the government very publicly acknowledged that city conditions were in need of "rectification," in practice it left urban problems and city folk's material yearnings not merely unresolved but in some respects worse. The mounting fiscal problems delineated in chapter 3 led the government to quietly "squeeze" the urban populace.

A "MAXIMUM OF RURALISM" IN THE 1990s: PRAGMATISM WITHOUT IDEALISM

By the early 1990s the state tried coming full circle, in practice if not words. With the crisis brought about by the collapse of Soviet-bloc Communism and the shortage of foreign exchange to trade in the "new world order," the government (as noted in chapter 4) assigned increased priority to food production. The agricultural emphasis was first and foremost rooted in a subsistence crisis tied to the sudden changes in the external sector.

In the name of a defensive commitment to "Socialism or Death," not a "maximum of ruralism" and an idealistic "push for communism," the government tried to de-urbanize the population and further reduce rural/urban differences. While the prorural emphasis was reminiscent of the latter 1960s, in contrast to the earlier period the government in the 1990s relied more on material incentives and market-type tactics to get civilian cooperation. City dwellers, it had learned the hard way, would not easily give up their urban way of life: if this was true in the 1960s, when there was enthusiasm and belief in a possible utopian future, it was more true in the 1990s when increased deprivations put an end to any remaining idealism.

The sudden trade and fiscal crisis brought the minibrigade program, so identified with the Rectification Process, to a near halt. The government's announced intention to build 20,000 units in 1991, under the circumstances, never materialized. Emphasis was given to completion of projects begun before the Special Period, but even here the government gave building for the Pan American Games priority over unfinished dwellings. Cuba' had committed itself to holding the Games in 1986, when the economy was in better shape.

Habañeros were angry. When informed that the housing for the Pan American athletes was to be used for tourism after the Games were over, minibrigade laborers working on the project not only staged a work stoppage but they went so far as to destroy some of the building machinery: tourism would address the state's hard currency needs, at their expense.

Pressured to complete the construction in time for the Games, the government agreed that only a portion of the new units would be used for tourism, the same portion of minibrigade construction that it had been withholding from the work centers involved in building projects. Workers defended their interests once again the way they most effectively could—informally, not through formal political or union channels.

Even after the Games, completion of microbrigade housing continued to drag on, due to lack of materials. The one success story involved construction of some 5,000 low-cost housing units (between April 1992 and May 1993) with locally available "rustic" materials, by community work brigades in coordination with local governments and ministries.[57]

As agriculture became a top priority the government concentrated its resources there. As noted in chapter 4, farm laborers were offered wage and productivity incentives, and the only new housing the government ordered was linked to agricultural projects, the urban blight notwithstanding. At the same time, though, that the government favored the countryside, its initiatives met up with a multiplicity of problems.

Through 1993 rural/urban material and social disparities diminished, and not only because agricultural economic opportunities improved while urban opportunities deteriorated. They diminished also because city dwellers were called upon once again to help out in agriculture. The mobilizations, alluded to in chapter 4, centered in Havana. People in the country's most populated city were to help develop their own food supply, in the area surrounding the city. As of May 1991, 117,000 Havana residents had participated in the crash Food Program; by the end of 1992 some 500,000 had.[58] They typically were mobilized through their work centers, which were contacted according to demand by the authorities in charge of the mobilizations. Participation was not obligatory. Workers who rallied to the call typically did so because they thought it advantageous to do so: to get work merits or to increase prospects of job promotion, to produce food for their work center canteen, to get better meals than in the city, and to stake out possible sources of private and illicit food supplies for their families in the cities. As petroleum-based travel became a luxury of the past, the farm stints even became viewed as an escape from the doldrums of city life. Yet the government phased out the mobilizations in 1993 because they proved too problematic.

Gone were the days of the late 1960s when at least certain urban folk believed that they were helping to build a new society, through their voluntary labor. Indicative of the growing resistance to march to the government's calling, more than half of the 117,000 who as of May 1991 had partaken in the brief agricultural stints were members of the Party or the UJC, the Party's youth division.[59] With only about 10 percent of the population belonging to the Party, a small fraction of non-Party members initially volunteered; with time, though, Party members seem to have been joined by others, as the subsistence crisis worsened.

Rural/urban distinctions diminished also as city dwellers took up gardening near where they lived, worked, and studied. As noted in chapter 4, in mid-1992 urban neighborhood groups, workers, and students tended some one million fruit and vegetable gardens to supplement meager rationed food allotments: one of the precapitalist-type coping strategies initiated during the Special Period.

The urban mobilizations always were meant to be temporary, for four or five years, until a permanent in-resident rural labor force was established. The government had planned to construct forty-two communities.[60] Then, the sudden transformation of state farms into cooperatives in 1993 put a near-halt to the demand for city labor.

Havana, meanwhile, became deindustrialized, as the country in general did. The social and economic significance of Havana accordingly broke, even more than in years past, with the Latin American urban tradition, but for externally rooted reasons beyond Castro's control, not because of the inherent dynamics of socialism or a moral commitment to a "maximum of ruralism."

One political administrative reform introduced around the time of the Special Period, that of People's Councils, initially centered in Havana. The ninety-three councils were comprised of Popular Power delegates, together with local representatives of the mass organizations (the CDRs, the FMC, and the CTC) and social and administrative agencies. Unlike Popular Power delegates, the ninety-three council leaders, selected by council members in each district, were to work full time in their administrative role, for the same salary they earned at the job they held before assuming their post. The payment marks a break with the mid-1970s–initiated Popular Power policy of not separating the political-administrative from the productive stratum, premised on Marx's ideal of having workers with "working men's wages" serve as officials (see chapter 1). Prompted by the severity of the city's crisis, the national leadership felt the need to have full-time functionaries available to tend to local problems. The reform also gave a sense of state responsiveness to city folk's concerns at a time of new unprecedented deprivations.

Council delegates were expected to report to authorities about local factory, medical, energy, food distribution, cafeteria, and other matters; curb local waste of human and material resources; avert stealing and corruption; and mobilize neighbors for community tasks. While they varied, in practice, in how seriously they pursued their mission, in reporting directly to central authorities local problems were to be resolved more easily and quickly than through the intact Popular Power structure: council delegates, at least initially, were empowered to bypass entrenched bureaucratic redtape and overcome inertia in dealing with problems at hand. Because district council leaders were to have "strong political authority" and to "behave as revolutionaries regardless of whether or not they were Party members,"[61] their tasks were obviously conceived as political and not merely administrative.

Why were People's Councils initially established only in Havana? They undoubtedly were designed to help further centralize political control where challenges to the state were most probable. *Habañeros* whose living standards plunged were well aware of changes abroad; this made the densely populated city a likely location of political trouble to the powers that be. *Habañeros* could be expected to defy Party hegemony before isolated folk in the provinces.

While the role of the councils remained unclear to many city folk, Castro considered them sufficiently effective and consistent with the reformist image he sought to convey to extend them to other regions of the island in 1992. The Havana reform thus became the basis of national reform, a reform incorporated into the Constitution approved at the Party Congress that year. Yet, without resources the councils could do little.

CONCLUSION

The experience of Castro's Cuba suggests that socialism can counter the Latin American urban bias favoring urban over rural and middle- and upper- over lower- and working-class interests. But changes have not been unilinear or automatic by-products of dynamics unleashed by the class transformation and the new dominant "mode of production." The class transformation, namely the elimination first of the bourgeoisie and then the petty bourgeoisie, did, however, make some of the changes possible. It allowed Castro to use the powers of the state to intervene over the years in diverse nontraditional ways.

Castro sought, first and foremost, to change the importance and meaning of cities, and to reduce the importance of the principal city over society. He tried to "ruralize" the city by involving city folk in farm labor, and he "urbanized" the countryside, reducing centuries-old rural/urban differences and inequities in the process. He allocated state monies for rural and provincial urban education, medical care, housing, and employment, as no other Latin American government ever had. But he simultaneously targeted lower socioeconomic groups in the cities; unlike in the capitalist countries in the region they were not left to the vagaries of the market and prey to laissez-faire government housing and employment policies.

The moral underpinnings for these reforms were articulated by Castro at his Moncada defense trial in 1953. Had moral principles alone determined policy, Castro's commitment to "a minimum of urbanism, a maximum of ruralism" should have persisted over the years, both in words and deeds. Yet Castro was not consistently committed to the countryside over the city, his policies were not always consistent with the rural/urban emphasis he preached, and he at times implemented prorural policies that he made no effort to legitimate ideologically. He shifted his policies as domestic and global economic conditions changed, and as policies in effect generated unintended political and economic consequences. Both the opportunities opened up by the Soviets in the 1960s and the collapse of those opportunities a quarter of a centery later led the government to emphasize a "maximum of ruralism," though in the latter period without ideological fanfare. In the intermediate years city folk's concerns were addressed in diverse ways, through a combination of state initiatives and state tolerance of contained "market forces."

City dwellers were not, however, mere passive subjects of macro economic forces and ruling elite–defined national priorities. Depending on
circumstances, some opted for emigration; those who stayed resisted par-
taking in activity they disliked and they sought illegal solutions to concerns of theirs that the government did not address.

Meanwhile, the weight of the past persisted. Cuba remained highly
urbanized and Havana its most important city. Island socialism left problems dating back to the capitalist epoch unresolved. Nonetheless, new
problems also arose—that of housing in particular. The collapse of Soviet-bloc Communism and the island's international trade dashed hopes
of "rectifying" earlier urban neglect, and urban living conditions deteriorated by default, not deliberate design, as never before.

Chapter Seven

INTERNATIONALISM

UNRESOLVED SOCIAL, economic, and political problems at home never kept Castro from extending aid to other Third World countries. In the course of the 1970s he even became seemingly more preoccupied with overseas than with domestic matters.

Cuba's international commitments were exceptional for a country of its size and economic status. Since the largest overseas commitments were coordinated with the Soviet Union, it would appear that the initiatives were at Moscow's behest. Judging by official statements, however, Cuban internationalism, the official term for overseas commitments, was morally inspired by the revolution, quite independently of the Soviet Union. Yet shifts in the scale and scope of Cuban internationalism over the years, commitments assumed independently of the Soviet Union and sometimes in opposition to Soviet foreign policy, and commitments inconsistent with officially articulated moral priorities cannot be explained from either point of view. Cuba will be shown to have had reasons of its own for "going international," though those objectives were not always achieved.

Overseas Activities

Castro in his 1953 Moncada defense speech demonstrated an international as well as a domestic social and economic vision. However, in power overseas commitments changed with time. This is true both for Cuba's overseas military commitments and its civilian commitments, the latter least well known outside Cuba and the primary focus of this chapter.

Military Assistance

In the 1960s Castro's government trained and aided a variety of guerrilla movements in Latin America. Cuban assistance notwithstanding, the movements remained small and insignificant. The Cubans did, however, train and arm a then little-known fifty-person Nicaraguan group, the Frente Sandinista de Liberación Nacional (FSLN), which within the next decade and a half grew in force to the point that it took power.

The government's Latin American strategy at the time was encapsulated in Ché's famous exhortation to create "two, three, many Vietnams."[1] If the small southeast Asian country could successfully contest United States imperialism, a whole continent would stand an even better chance, he argued. His "two, three, many Vietnams," in turn, built on his guerrilla "foco" theory, which he developed along with the then revolutionary Regis Debray.[2] Practicing what he preached, Ché sacrificed his life for his global transformatory vision. It was when organizing a peasant guerrilla movement in Bolivia that he was captured and murdered in 1967 by the military government there. In death as much as in life, Ché symbolized the revolution's commitment to internationalism.

Castro laid the foundation for African involvements in the 1960s as well. Cuba provided Algeria, shortly after it attained independence from France, with some arms and troops when that North African nation was attacked by Morocco. Castro's government also supported national liberation movements and "progressive" governments in Angola, Guinea-Bissseau, Mozambique, and Congo-Brazzaville in the course of the decade.

During Castro's second decade of rule, Cuba's African commitments surged. Havana began to offer extensive conventional military assistance, including logistical support and training, to established governments. The Cubans provided advisory and training missions in Sierra Leone, Equatorial Guinea, and Somalia. And for the first time they also sent large numbers of combat troops, to Angola and Ethiopia, and smaller contingents to Libya, the Congo, and some other countries in the region. By 1978 Cuba had some 38,000 to 40,000 military cadre in Africa, up from about 750 to 1,000 a decade earlier.[3] In the 1980s the number rose even higher, with about 50,000 troops stationed for some years in Angola alone. By the decade's end half a million troops had served in Africa, some 377,000 in Angola.[4]

The Angolan mission had the greatest impact. The Cubans helped Agostinho Neto's Popular Movement for the Liberation of Angola (MPLA) consolidate power when the Portuguese pulled out, and they subsequently helped the MPLA fend off U.S. and South African–backed rebels. In 1988 massive Cuban aid resulted in a military victory of such proportions, in Cuito Cuanavale, as to change the political dynamics in southern Africa. Fidel was so obsessed with Cuito Cuanavale that, by his own admission, he spent 80 percent of his time planning each move of island forces there.[5] The victory left the Angolan government in a position of strength from which to negotiate a regional settlement. The following year Cuba, South Africa, and the United States agreed not to support their Angolan allies and to grant Namibia independence (in conjunction with UN Security Council Resolution 435). As part of the accord Cuba agreed to withdraw all its military forces serving in Angola by 1991. Keeping to the agreement, Castro did not step up military assistance when the Angolan government was subsequently attacked by rebel forces.

Cuba's other main African mission, in Ethiopia, was never either as extensive or as consequential. Castro had initially aided the Eritrean rebels when Haile Selassie ruled. Then, when the Ethiopian government was headed by the self-proclaimed Marxist Col. Mengistu Haile Mariam, Castro helped Addis Ababa win the Ogaden war with neighboring Somalia. After the two African countries made peace, Cuba cut back its military mission there. Cuba refused to be drawn into subsequent Ethiopian government domestic conflicts, including struggles with Eritrean rebels and the movement that in 1991 drove Mengistu from power. At its peak Cuba's military mission in Ethiopia involved, according to Western sources, 10,500 to 15,000 islanders. By the mid-1980s the mission dropped to about 3,000, and by the end of the decade remaining troops there too were sent home.[6]

The military involvements in Africa in the 1970s had no parallel in the Americas, despite Castro's initial regional focus. Castro acknowledged, in his report to the Communist Party's First Congress in 1975, that Latin America was not yet on the eve of the kind of overall changes that lead to sudden socialist transformations. Following the failure of his regional guerrilla strategy in the 1960s, Castro sought to improve government-to-government relations. The changed strategy became viable in the early 1970s because countries such as Peru under Gen. Juan Velasco Alvarado, Chile under Salvador Allende, and to a lesser extent Argentina under Juan Perón came to have progressive governments. Latin American governments had stopped acquiescing to U.S. pressures to isolate Cuba, so that they were willing to reestablish diplomatic and economic relations with Havana.

Although extremely repressive governments became entrenched in the larger South American countries in the course of the decade, including in Chile and Argentina, socialist governments gained power in Nicaragua and Grenada, Guyana came to be headed by a self-identifying Left-leaning leader, and rebels in El Salvador began to be a serious political force. The shifting tide led Castro to express newfound optimism by the twenty-fifth anniversary of the Cuban revolution. He then claimed that revolution was inevitable, even without Cuba's instigation: "Cuba cannot export revolution. Neither can the USA prevent it."[7]

Despite the newfound optimism, Castro provided little military assistance to rebel forces in the region. In 1978 Cuba offered the Sandinista insurgents in Nicaragua (who by then had substantial mass support) training, advice, and military equipment; however, it contributed less aid than did some other Latin American countries. Only *after* the Sandinista victory the following year did Havana's military assistance pick up. The

Cubans then began to help train the Sandinista government in weaponry use and national security.

The size of the Nicaraguan mission was never confirmed. The Reagan administration claimed that Cuba had some 3,000 military personnel in Nicaragua in early 1984, and about 800 two years later,[8] while Castro claimed that island military advisers in Nicaragua numbered about 200 in 1983, and the then Sandinista head of state, Daniel Ortega, admitted to 800 Cuban advisers in his country in 1985.[9]

Whatever the size of Cuba's Nicaraguan military mission, which by all counts was minimal compared to the Angolan and Ethiopian missions, Washington exaggerated Castro's radicalizing role in the Sandinista revolution. Castro assisted and sympathized with the Sandinistas, but he was a restraining force there as well. To avoid problems that Cuba had experienced, Castro urged the Sandinistas to maintain good relations with as many countries as possible, avoid excessive dependence on the Soviet Union, minimize conflicts with the United States, and "go slow" on building a socialist economy to limit flight of capital and skilled cadre.[10] He also resisted a Sandinista request for troops to help contain antigovernment rebels; instead he sent General Ochoa to oversee an overhaul of the Nicaraguan army.[11]

In the same year that the Sandinistas ousted Anastasio Somoza from office, Maurice Bishop's socialist New JEWEL (Joint Endeavor for Welfare, Education, and Liberation) Movement took power in Grenada. Cuba was no more instrumental in the turn of events there than in Nicaragua, and it supplied Bishop, once head of state, with only limited light arms and a few dozen security advisers.[12] Most aid to Bishop's government was civilian in nature (described below).[13]

Military assistance in Latin America was not confined to regimes sharing a common ideological outlook. Castro, for example, aided Panama's Gen. Manuel Noriega militarily the last two years the Central American governed. Documents indicate that Cuba shipped more than 80,000 weapons to Panama, trained hundreds of Panamanian officers in sabotage operations, and helped set up an intelligence agency. Castro's interest in assisting Noriega was pragmatic. Panama was Cuba's main trade link to the capitalist world, and the government's embassy there served as a conduit to guerrilla movements and leftist parties in the hemisphere.[14]

In the 1980s El Salvador was the one main country in Latin America where Cuba aided rebels. There, Castro helped unify guerrilla factions, contributing to the formation of the Farabundo Martí Front for National Liberation (FMLN)—a unifying role he had previously played in the Nicaraguan anti-Somoza struggle. Although Cuba trained and armed guerrillas battling the El Salvadorian government, it provided the rebels with minimal weaponry after the failure of the "final offensive" of January

1981.[15] Indeed, also as in Nicaragua, in El Salvador Castro was a constraining force. He advocated a negotiated settlement, which helped pave the way to the 1992 ceasefire.[16]

In the rest of the Third World, Cuba's military presence was even more modest than in Latin America. Havana sent small contingents to Southeast Asian countries and somewhat more substantial ones to some Middle Eastern countries. In the 1970s Cuba sent combat units to Syria, and advisory and training missions to South Yemen, Iraq, and Lebanon. Western sources believe the military mission to Iraq involved at its peak in the 1980s some 2,000 cadre.[17]

Thus, the scale and scope of Cuban military internationalism changed over the years. It expanded in the mid- and latter 1970s, just after the West had come to account for 41 percent of the island's foreign trade and just when the government began to initiate domestic market reforms. And overseas military commitments began to wane in the latter 1980s when the government's Guevarist-linked campaign to "rectify errors and negative tendencies," taken at face value, would suggest the opposite: increased internationalism, to create "two, three, many Vietnams." They contracted even more, not surprisingly, when the armed forces became preoccupied with their own subsistence needs during the Special Period.

Civilian Assistance

Civilian assistance, minimal in the 1960s, expanded in the latter 1970s, when military internationalism did. By the 1980s Cuba accounted for nearly one-fifth of all Soviet-bloc economic technicians working in the Third World, with only 2.5 percent of the bloc's population, and between 1982 and 1985 Cuba had one civilian aid worker for every 625 inhabitants while the United States had only one worker in the Peace Corps and the Agency for International Development (AID) for every 34,704 inhabitants.[18] Although the civilian program involved fewer Cubans than the military program, more countries received civilian than military assistance. Over 111,000 Cubans had worked on overseas civilian missions by the close of the 1980s.[19]

Construction was an important component of the island's overseas civilian program.[20] The government offered materials, organizational and planning advice, builders, and topographic surveys. Construction aid began modestly in Peru in 1970, when island workers helped repair damage caused by an earthquake there. The program expanded in the mid-1970s with the building of a hospital, highway, hotel, several poultry complexes, and thirteen milking barns in North Vietnam. At the close of the Vietnam War, Cuba sent an additional nine hundred workers to help in national reconstruction. Construction assistance grew rapidly in the latter 1970s, to the point that some 7,900 Cubans—3 percent of the island's construction labor force—worked on overseas assignments. Between 1978 and 1979 the number of construction workers abroad more than doubled. Angola and Ethiopia received especially large contingents. Cubans contracted to build a sawmill, waterworks, a school, port and airport work, housing, and part of a conference center in Angola. In Ethiopia, and also in Laos, Guinea, and Tanzania, Cuban brigades built roads, airports, schools, and other facilities. And in Jamaica during Michael Manley's initial Left-leaning administration (1972–1980), Cubans built housing, dams, and factories for the manufacture of prefabricated building units.

Cuba's principal building projects in the 1980s were in the Middle East and North Africa (in South Yemen, Algeria, Iraq, and Libya), and in Nicaragua and Grenada. In the course of the decade construction projects tapered off, though not by the government's own choosing. While all told over 33,000 Cuban workers participated in building assignments in some twenty Asian, African, and Latin American countries, as of 1989 there were no more construction workers abroad than in 1979. The government had hoped by 1981 to have 15,000 to 20,000 construction workers abroad on a yearly basis,[21] double the peak number in the 1970s.

From the U.S. vantage point, Cuba's most controversial civilian assistance project was the construction of an airport in Grenada. Cuba agreed to build a $50 to $71 million airport, and to absorb about half the cost. It had competed with British, Canadian, and French firms for the contract.[22] The Reagan administration claimed that the airport was to be used for military purposes: a rationale for the U.S. invasion of Grenada in 1983 that brought the Left-leaning government there to an abrupt halt. The New JEWEL Movement's head of state, Maurice Bishop, all along insisted that the airport was intended primarily for tourism (a claim affirmed by the English company that supplied and installed airport electrical and technical equipment). The Reagan administration used the construction project as a pretext for undermining a regime sympathetic to Cuba.[23]

Cuba also offered extensive educational and medical aid. The medical assistance program dates back to 1963, but it too expanded dramatically in the 1970s.[24] The number of medical cadre abroad rose from 700 in 1977 to some 2,000 three years later, and to about 3,000 by the end of the 1980s.[25] By 1990 more than 30,000 doctors, dentists, nurses, and paramedics had served on international missions in more than twenty countries; they had treated about sixty million people. At its peak 10 percent of the island's doctors were stationed abroad.[26] Cuba came to have more doctors abroad than the World Health Organization (WHO).[27]

Health care internationalists provided medical training; they shared medical information in symposia; they wrote public health literature; they conducted vaccination and other health prevention programs; and they offered outpatient care. Over the years the services they offered became more sophisticated, and they came to include curative as well as preventive care, including surgery and obstetrics.

In the 1970s Jamaica, under Michael Manley's first administration, was a major recipient of medical aid. Before Manley was voted out of office in 1980, Cuban medical brigades had treated one million patients there.[28]

In the 1980s Cuba had especially large medical missions in Nicaragua and Iraq. In Nicaragua several thousand health workers offered consultations, performed some 140,000 operations, and delivered about 50,000 babies.[29] The island's largest African medical missions were in Angola and Ethiopia, but it had health contingents in Mozambique, Cape Verde, Equatorial Guinea, Guinea-Bissau, and São Tomé. Cuba, moreover, was the first country to provide medical aid to Namibia after it attained independence at the end of the decade. Guyana under Forbes Burnham, Grenada under Maurice Bishop, Peru under Alan García, and Bolivia under civilian governments also received medical aid from Cuba at the time.

Castro over the years was also quick to send medical emergency relief to countries in need. To Nicaragua, Iran, and the Soviet Union, as well as Peru, Cuba sent medical-related earthquake relief. And after the Chernobyl nuclear accident Cuba announced plans to treat 10,000 victims, a commitment Havana continued to honor even after the Soviet Union outlawed its Communist Party and then broke apart.[30] Cuba also treated nearly three hundred Soviets injured in the Afghanistan war in 1990 and 1991, one-third with surgery. Thus, Cuba even provided the very country on which it was heavily dependent for aid and trade with medical care.

While tapering off overseas military missions, Castro continued to be committed to medical internationalism. In a major speech in January 1989 he noted that Cuba would have 10,000 doctors ready for international cooperation by the year 2000, 13 percent of the projected stock of doctors. He hoped medical contingents would be the type of mission the country carried out then, so that "when I talk about heroism, I'm not just talking about heroism on the battlefield, the military field, but also civilian heroism."[31] Yet a year after announcing his ambitious program, only seventy-nine of all graduating doctors were assigned to international service.[32] And in 1993 Cuba still had only 3,000 health professionals abroad, the same number as in 1989.

The medical assistance program centered in Cuba as well as abroad. Domestically it involved training and treating foreigners. In the mid-

1980s some 1,800 scholarship students from seventy-five Third World countries were enrolled either in intermediary-level or in postgraduate medical courses. Meanwhile, Cuban medics treated foreign patients in special facilities set aside in major hospitals. Nicaraguans here too were major beneficiaries. Between 1979 and 1991 some 6,000 patients from the Central American country received gratis medical care in Cuba (over 1,000 after the Sandinistas were voted out of office).[34] The Cuban government set aside two small hospitals for exclusive use of Nicaraguans who could not get proper medical attention at home. Medical care, as detailed below, even came to be promoted as a form of tourism.

The medical training was but one aspect of Castro's educational assistance program, a program also based partly overseas and partly on island soil. Between 1963 and 1989, over 26,000 teachers worked abroad in thirty countries.[35] At its peak in 1981, 2 percent of all island teachers worked on overseas assignments.[36] In Africa, Cuban teachers exceeded many-fold the number of UNESCO employees there.[37] Island internationalists abroad taught tens of thousands to read and write and hundreds of thousands received primary through university education.

Cuba played an especially important educational (as well as medical) role in Nicaragua. The Sandinistas, who modeled their literacy program partly on Cuba's, turned to Castro for literacy and educational assistance upon taking power.[38] By 1983 some 2,000 islanders worked in the Central American country,[39] many in remote places their Nicaraguan colleagues resisted going to. Castro and the Sandinistas shared a common language as well as a similar political perspective.

But Cuba's overseas educational program, like other components of its internationalism, dropped precipitously by the end of the 1980s. In 1989 only .4 percent of all island teachers worked abroad. The Nicaraguan program, for example, ended when the Sandinistas lost power.[40]

Beginning in 1977 Cuba educated many foreign students domestically, including after overseas internationalism tapered off. The Isle of Pines, renamed the Isle of Youth after the revolution, became transformed from a prerevolutionary prison into an educational showcase; Castro himself had been incarcerated there when convicted for his 1953 failed effort to depose Batista militarily. The scholarship program developed to the point that in 1989 there were 25,000 foreign students.[41] And in 1992, in the midst of the Special Period crisis, Cuba still hosted 21,000 foreign scholarship students (about 12,000 from sub-Saharan Africa).[42] Foreign students worked part-time, typically in agriculture, to help defray educational and living expenses, just as Cuban students did. Cuba at the time had more foreign students per capita than any other country in the world.[43] Even the United States, with much greater economic resources, funded only 7,000 scholarships for Third World students in the mid-1980s.[44]

Cuba, moreover, offered economic assistance. In 1979 it had some 14,000 economic and technical aid personnel overseas. It offered assistance in agriculture, sugar cultivation and refining, mining, fishing, transportation, cattle raising, irrigation, industry (basic, light, food, sugar, power and machine industry), economic and physical planning, management, and commodity trading. In the late 1980s Cuban economic cooperation agreements also included communications, radio and television, banking, labor, and social security advisers.[45]

As with the other components of the civilian program, economic assistance expanded in the course of the 1970s. In 1978 Cuba sent hundreds of economic specialists to Ethiopia, and two years later seven hundred technicians to Mozambique.[46] In 1980 Cuba also sent the People's Republic of the Congo livestock and dairy industry aid, Ethiopia two hundred specimens of its best breed of cattle, and South Yemen technicians and specialists in livestock, poultry farming, mining, fishing, tobacco growing, education and sports, maritime transport, and port and shipyard work.[47] In addition, more than 2,000 Cubans worked in Angola, as sugar specialists, pulp and paper personnel, and lumberjacks;[48] and Nicaragua was the recipient of at least $50 million in economic aid.[49]

Economic assistance also included training of foreign personnel, either abroad or in Cuba. By the end of the 1980s Cuba trained, on the island, some 3,500 Third World technicians, in fields such as agriculture, economics, and construction.[50] And Cuba sent technicians to Vietnam to train local persons in hotel and restaurant management, and to Guinea-Bissau, the Republic of Equatorial Guinea, and Somalia to train nationals in economics (as well as in education and public health).

CECE, the State Committee for Economic Collaboration, coordinated much of the overseas economic assistance activity. By the end of the 1980s it had contracts with thirty-seven African and Middle East countries, ten Latin American and Caribbean countries, and ten countries in Asia and Oceania.[51]

In the throes of the early 1990s crisis Cuba continued not merely to provide international aid but to expand certain offerings. In particular, it turned its sports prowess into a form of internationalism to an extent it previously had not. In 1992 six hundred sports trainers (especially of baseball) worked abroad in thirty-nine countries, three times as many as just one year earlier. Cuba also offered sports medicine. A spokesperson for INDER, the National Institute of Sports, Physical Education, and Recreation, said that Cuba's superb performance at the Pan American Games had sparked interest in contracting Cuban athletic personnel.[52]

On a number of occasions Cuba stepped in with civilian aid when the United States pulled out. In such instances the Cubans benefited from U.S. foreign aid politics. Cuba expanded its economic assistance to Ethiopia, for example, when the Reagan administration halted all economic aid to the African government. The United States terminated its aid program in the impoverished country when the Herare government criticized Washington's South African policy.[53] Similarly, Cuba signed a major cooperative agreement with Zimbabwe—involving agriculture and sugar industry assistance, as well as education and public health aid—after the Reagan administration halted aid to the African government.[54] Cuba's relations with Guyana, in turn, improved after the Reagan administration vetoed an Inter-American Development Bank loan to the South American country; the United States stopped aid because of the Guyanese government's then socialist leanings.

Civilian assistance was never confined to politically sympathetic governments, however. In the Americas, for example, Cuba sent specially crossbred cattle, noted for their productivity and resistance to heat, to Venezuela and Ecuador.[55] And it provided Nicaragua with medical aid, as noted, after its Sandinista allies were voted out of office.[56]

Civilian assistance, in its various forms, dominated Cuba's overseas programs in Latin America. Before Castro became heavily involved in Angola in 1975, more Cubans were posted in Jamaica than in any other country. After Manley's electoral defeat in 1980 and the Sandinista victory in 1979, Nicaragua came to receive the most aid in the region. Aid to the Central American country picked up to the point that in 1982 Cuba promised $130 million in agricultural and industrial machinery, and construction equipment, plus 3,800 technicians, doctors, and teachers, and food and medicine. That same year approximately 1,200 Nicaraguans also went to Cuba for technical training. In Nicaragua Cuba's civilian assistance increased as its military presence declined. Some 4,000 to 6,000 civilian internationalists were reportedly in the Central American country in 1985.[57]

Slightly less than eight hundred Cubans were in Grenada providing civilian assistance when the U.S. invasion brought Castro's aid program to an abrupt halt. Castro assisted the New JEWEL Movement in a literacy campaign, health care provisioning, development of the fishing industry, and road construction, as well as in the building of the airport that proved to be the movement's undoing. While the Granadian program was not Cuba's largest, Havana had a major presence there. Cuba provided one-fifth of all Maurice Bishop's foreign aid, more than any other single country.[58]

Cuba's assistance to the Burnham government in Guyana also was ambitious.[59] Havana trained technicians there in health and education, and it provided the South American country with technology for its sugar industry plus cattle to build up the local beef and dairy industries. In 1990, 120 island doctors and paramedics, in addition, worked there. For some years following Manley's 1980 electoral defeat in Jamaica, Guyana was the only member of CARICOM (the Caribbean Common Market) to be on friendly relations with Cuba.

All told, Africa (above all, Angola) received the largest civilian as well as military contingents. However, the mix of civilian and military assistance varied considerably by region. Until the 1980s Cuba offered almost exclusively civilian aid to Latin America, military aid to the Middle East, and a combination of the two to Africa and Indochina. In the course of the 1980s the civilian component became more important in Africa, while military aid to sympathetic governments in Nicaragua and Grenada, and to rebels in El Salvador, picked up; the military missions to Nicaragua and Grenada, though, ground to a halt when the Left-leaning governments there were ousted. Nonetheless, Central American military missions, even at their peak, were much smaller than the civilian missions, and much smaller than the military missions sent to Angola and Ethiopia. Moreover, Cuba never sent troops to its regional allies.

In sum, Cuba offered foreign assistance since Castro's early years in power, but the scale and scope of its offerings changed with time. When overseas military missions contracted at the end of the 1980s, Havana remained as committed as ever to its overseas civilian programs. Yet the number of internationalists serving on civilian missions also then contracted, though less than the number on military missions.

Why did Cuba offer such extensive foreign aid through the 1980s when other Third World countries did not, when domestic economic problems were far from resolved, and when the government itself was a recipient of foreign aid? Possible explanations are explored below.

CUBA AS A SOVIET SURROGATE

Resource-poor Cuba might, as noted, have undertaken overseas commitments at the insistence of the Soviet Union or it might have been made to believe that "socialist internationalism" was a prerequisite for continued Soviet assistance.

U.S. officials and the press depicted Cuba both as a helpless pawn of Soviet imperialist interests and as a willing Soviet collaborator. U.S. Senator Daniel Moynihan, for example, referred to the *fidelistas* as nothing more than the "Gurkhas of the Russian Empire," stirring up trouble on Moscow's behalf and functioning as a vehicle for indirect Soviet subversion and eventual domination of targeted developing countries.[60]

While it is impossible to determine, on the basis of available information, the precise nature of Cuban-Soviet relations, if Cuba had been a Soviet surrogate it should not have extended aid to countries with which Moscow had hostile relations. Also, there should be evidence of Cuban-Soviet overseas coordination, and Cuban overseas involvements should vary with ups and downs in Cuban-Soviet relations and shifts in Soviet foreign policy (including its demise as a superpower). Moreover, if Cuba operated *primarily* as a Soviet puppet, the Cubans should have had no major reasons of their own for promoting internationalism.

In the 1960s Cuba could hardly be said to have been a Soviet pawn. Moscow disapproved of Cuba's overseas activities, just as it disapproved of Castro's domestic emphasis then on the "rapid transition to communism." When Castro and Ché promoted "one, two, many Vietnams," Moscow's Cold War stance was "peaceful coexistence." If the Soviet Union had any influence on Castro's decision to "go international" during the course of the decade, it may have been the converse of conventional wisdom. After being excluded, in 1962, from Moscow-Washington discussions related to the Cuban Missile Crisis, Castro may have felt that internationalism would help him secure reliable foreign allies.

And Wayne Smith, the head of the U.S. Interest Section in Cuba under President Carter, has even argued that Cuba's policy of "exporting revolution" was, in the 1960s, more a by-product of U.S. than Soviet policy![61] In support of his claim he noted that Castro proposed, in a 1964 interview with Richard Eder of the *New York Times*, to withhold material support from Latin American revolutionaries if the United States would cease its own hostile actions against Cuba. In Castro's major annual Twenty-sixth of July speech later that year, he repeated the proposal. With his overture to the United States rebuffed, Castro returned with a vengeance to the export of revolution as a policy and to armed struggle as a tactic. To the Soviets this smacked of "infantile adventurism."

Some analyses which acknowledge that Cuban internationalism initially occurred *despite* the Soviet Union argue that beginning in the 1970s it occurred *because* of the Soviet Union. One observer, for instance, claims that after the first decade of Castro's rule "the politics of clientelism replaced Havana's freewheeling zealousness of the 1960s."[62] The Soviet invasion of Czechoslovakia in 1968 is seen as a turning point in Cuban-Soviet relations. Afterwards Castro moderated his proguerrilla line, and the Soviet Union purportedly rewarded him for so doing with increased economic assistance.

It is indisputable that in the 1970s and 1980s Cuba and the Soviet Union advanced complementary and coordinated overseas military programs, in contrast to the 1960s. Cuban internationalism in essence came to be linked to the Soviet's Cold War global hegemonic project. Yet no other Soviet-bloc member became as internationally committed as Cuba, suggesting that the involvements were not a prerequisite of bloc affiliation.

Cuban-Soviet collaboration was especially apparent in Somalia, Ethiopia, Angola, Syria, and Indochina. Especially in the larger overseas programs the support of both countries was crucial. The Soviets provided equipment and financing while the Cubans provided personnel. Cuban troops would have been much less effective without Soviet matériel.

In the 1970s the Cuban government itself admitted close international collaboration with the Soviets. It even claimed the alliance to be a permanent feature of its international policy. Yet the Cuban leadership always claimed to assume the overseas commitments willingly and on its own. Castro noted that his country, for example, decided on its own to send troops to Angola in 1975, to help the newly independent country stave off a South African invasion. Said he, "The USSR had always helped the people of the Portuguese colonies in their struggle for independence, . . . but it never requested that a single Cuban be sent to that country [Angola]. . . . A decision of that nature could only be made by us."[63] Castro had already established ties with the MPLA in the 1960s, about a decade before committing troops. He had established ties with the MPLA through Ché.

Most U.S. studies—including by such agencies as the Center for Naval Analysis, which does classified research—concur that Cuba did not "go international" at the behest of Moscow, even when the two countries collaborated in their overseas ventures.[64] Such studies note that Cuba had a consistent foreign policy since Castro first came to power, and that it aided revolutionary movements that the Soviets scathed. The Soviets even had diplomatic, trade, and credit relations with some of the governments Castro's government tried to subvert.

Evidence suggests that Cuba initiated the commitment of massive combat troops to Angola.[65] In 1974 Cuba extended aid to Angola when the USSR pulled out and gave the then MPLA leader, Agostinho Neto, a "chilly reception" in Moscow. The Soviets resumed their aid to Angola only *after* the Cuban military buildup had begun. Moreover, in May 1977 a faction within the MPLA, which felt that Neto was not sufficiently pro-Soviet, organized a coup to topple him. While there is no strong evidence that the Kremlin was directly involved in the plot, reportedly the Soviets knew of the maneuver beforehand but did not warn the Angolan head of state. Havana, by contrast, stood firmly behind Neto and helped put down the uprising.[66] Although Cuba's aid to Col. Mengistu in Ethiopia, in his struggle with Somalia over the Ogaden, appears to have been more closely coordinated with Moscow from the onset, Havana is believed to have resisted Soviet pressure to commit Cuban units to crush the Eritrean rebels.

According to a former member of the Ministry of Foreign Relations and former diplomat, Castro lobbied the Soviets for aid for Third World countries. The Soviets had little interest in subsidizing "other Cubas," and to the extent that they were interested in Africa their concern centered on the large countries, such as South Africa and Egypt.[67] Meanwhile, Moscow was even less interested in Latin America than Africa. Havana formulated its own foreign policy toward Central America and the Caribbean, with the Soviet Union more a follower than a leader. Cuba, for instance, took the lead in establishing close relations with Bishop's New JEWEL Movement in Grenada, subsequently persuading the Soviet Union also to extend aid. The Soviets viewed the region as an unwelcome distraction, especially once embroiled in the Afghan civil war,[68] while Cuba valued close regional ties.

Internationalism actually became an arena of tension between Moscow and Havana. Havana and Moscow, for example, differed on their stance toward the Grenadians responsible for overthrowing Maurice Bishop (prior to the U.S. invasion) as well as on Cuba's Ethiopian troop reduction in the mid-1980s. In late 1985 Western diplomats in Havana also believed they detected Central American policy disagreements between Cuba and the Soviet Union.

Ironically, at the same time that Cuba was portrayed in the United States as a Soviet puppet, Castro captured the leadership of the Non-Aligned Movement. Castro served as the organization's chairperson from 1979 until 1983; he was rewarded largely for his country's activist Third World role. Cuba's stance against racist South Africa in Angola, in particular, was widely hailed in the less developed world.[69] The attitude of the Non-Aligned Movement toward Cuba ultimately changed, but only after Havana refused to criticize the Soviet invasion of Afghanistan.

If Cuba engaged in internationalism at the superpower's urging, its foreign policy, moreover, should have shifted with the Soviet's under Gorbachev. The cutback in Cuba's overseas military commitments in the latter 1980s certainly was consistent with Gorbachev's noninterventionist policy. Since Cuban internationalists relied on Soviet matériel, Moscow's global retrenchment gave Cuba reason to reduce its foreign armed forces involvements. Yet Castro reduced the size of the island's Ethiopian contingent and he offered to withdraw military aid to Angola and Nicaragua before Gorbachev took power. Moreover, even once Gorbachev was in office Cuba had reasons of its own to pull out of Angola, the country where it was most heavily committed: it had succeeded in getting South Africa out of Angola, it had suffered relatively high casualties in the civil war there, and Cubans were contracting AIDS.[70] Under the circumstances islander resistance to serving on international missions picked up; that is, informal domestic pressures contributed to the government's decision to pull out of Angola, just as they had contributed to domestic policy reforms over the years.

Proponents of the Soviet surrogate thesis have argued not only that Moscow determined when and whether Cuba "went international" but also that Cuba complied because of its economic dependence on the superpower. However, the foreign policy of the two countries most diverged in the late 1960s when island trade dependence on the superpower rose to a record high. Moreover, Cuba expanded its overseas commitments—both military and civilian—around the time its Western trade ties peaked, in the mid-1970s. There thus was no correlation between Cuban trade dependence on the Soviets and Cuban-Soviet internationalist collaboration.

A Soviet scholar, Sergei Tagor, gives a more nuanced interpretation of Soviet influence on Cuban military internationalism.[71] In his view it was the military-security power bloc and not the Soviet state as such that influenced Cuban militarism, including its overseas component. Until the attempted coup d'état of 1991, the military remained powerful in the Soviet Union. The influence of the armed forces within the Soviet power bloc helps explain why military aid to Cuba remained high ($1.2 billion) through 1989, while other Soviet aid began to be slashed. Well-supplied and well-trained by the Soviet armed forces, Cuba could take on overseas involvements even if the aid was not extended with this end in view.

None of the Soviet surrogate discussions have focused on Cuba's civilian assistance programs. Since there is little evidence that Cuba coordinated its educational, construction, medical, and technical assistance programs with Moscow, and since Cuba remained committed to expanding civilian programs in the very countries where it had pulled out militarily, either the military and civilian components of Cuban internationalism have different roots (and must be understood accordingly) or Cuba had its own reasons for extending foreign assistance, whatever form it took.

While the Cuban government did not "go international" simply at the behest of the USSR, in the 1970s and 1980s Cuban and Soviet foreign policies converged, and in large military ventures the two countries coordinated their involvements. Cuban internationalism helped advance Soviet interests in the Third World, but at a cost the Moscow-based Communist government could no longer bear once its own economy and domestic support began to crumble in the latter 1980s. Indeed, the Soviet surrogate thesis lost all meaning when the once superpower broke up and the new republics were preoccupied with their own internal problems.

Moral Bases for Overseas Involvements

At his 1953 defense trial for the attack on the Moncada barracks, Castro noted that "Cuban policy in the Americas would be one of close solidarity with the domestic people on this continent and . . . those politically persecuted by bloody tyrants oppressing our sister nations would find generous asylum, brotherhood, and bread in the land of Martí."[72] In power Fidel built on this internationalist vision, but his official rationale for so doing changed and became more multifaceted. He appealed, on different occasions, to anti-imperialist, anticolonial, anti-Zionist, Marxist-Leninist proletarian, racial, and revolutionary sentiments in promoting internationalism. While certain of the moral appeals were linked to the Soviet Union, others were not.

Castro's early foreign policy has been traced to revolutionary messianism and revolutionary romanticism.[73] During the 1960s Castro pressed upon Cubans that "the duty of every revolutionary is to make revolution."[74] And in reference to Latin America he spoke of the need to "transform the Andes into the Sierra Maestra of Latin America."

Yet Castro also turned to the heroes of the island's nineteenth-century struggle for independence—to Antonio Maceo, José Martí, and Máximo Gómez, for example—as sources of inspiration and legitimation for internationalism, just as he turned to them for justification of domestic policies. The heroes helped convey an image of a nation seeking to control its own destiny.

Although Castro did not officially draw on Marxist-Leninist doctrine to spur internationalism during his first years in power, he subsequently did. When Cuba took steps to institutionalize the revolution in the mid-1970s, it even formalized its official commitment to world socialism, communism, and international proletarian solidarity. Proletarian internationalism, a commitment to help ideological brethren seize and consolidate power, was linked to Marx's famous dictum "workers of the world unite," to destroy capitalism. The 1975 First Party Congress Resolution on International Policy specified that Cuba subordinated its interests to the general interests of socialism and communism (and national liberation of peoples), so as to defeat imperialism and eliminate colonialism.[75] Similarly, the 1976 Constitution expressed Cuba's commitment to "the principles of proletarian internationalism and the combative solidarity of the peoples." The 1992 revised Constitution reaffirmed the island's commitment to internationalism—above all, its ties to Latin America and the Caribbean, though it deleted mention of Soviet solidarity.[76]

The moral basis of Cuban internationalism was tied to pancontinental racial solidarity in turn. Castro, in his April 1976 speech commemorating the fifteenth anniversary of Cuba's Bay of Pigs victory, asserted that:

"At Girón [the Bay of Pigs], African blood was shed, that of the selfless descendants of a people who were slaves before they became workers. . . . And in Africa, together with the blood of the heroic fighters of Angola, Cuban blood . . . also flowed. The victory in Angola was the twin sister of the victory at Girón. . . . Angola represents an African Girón."[77]

Cuban forces in Africa were, in the main, black and mulatto.

Cuban involvement was portrayed as the island's debt to its African-American heritage. Castro here again drew on historical symbolism. The military mission to Angola was even called "Operation Carlota," in homage to an exceptional African woman who, as a slave in Cuba, headed two rebellions against colonial oppression.

Fidel played on racial and national symbolism up until the day he held funeral ceremonies in homage to the Cubans killed in Africa. The day selected was December 7 (1989), the anniversary of the death of Maceo, the dark-skinned hero of the island's nineteenth-century independence movement.

In a similar vein, Fidel's brother Raúl, as head of the Ministry of the Armed Forces, noted in a speech that "those who in good faith ignore the historical antecedents of our presence in Angola are mistaken when they search for its origins in foolish geopolitical explanations derived from the Cold War or East-West global conflicts."[78] In the same speech he asserted that "as Latin Africans we Cubans . . . had an historical debt to Africa, one of the vital roots of our nationality." This speech occurred when Cuba withdrew its last troops from Angola in 1991, the result of an accord endorsed both by the United States and the Soviet Union!

While there is reason to believe that Castro was morally committed to internationalism for a variety of reasons, its expansion in the 1970s and its contraction in the latter 1980s cannot be explained by a sudden surge and then diminution of commitment to other Third World countries. Moreover, overseas involvements expanded when ideology was officially downplayed in relation to domestic policies. What changed in the mid-1970s was a "window of opportunity," to which Castro responded.

That "window of opportunity" involved changes both at home and abroad. At home, a large military establishment that had been built up to fend off a possible U.S. invasion became available to take on new missions by the 1970s. The armed forces by then were professionalized and well trained (with Soviet assistance) but less preoccupied both with internal security and a U.S. attack than during Castro's first decade of rule. At the same time, the armed forces' informal power within the domestic power bloc had increased and they had Fidel's brother Raúl as their leader and chief spokesperson. Because military internationalism added to their stature and gave them a new raison d'être, they supported it. Accordingly, internal state dynamics may well have contributed to the government's decision to commit large numbers of cadre to overseas missions. Meanwhile, the massive expansion of schooling under Castro made islanders, socialized to value "proletarian internationalism," a pool that could be drawn upon for overseas missions.

Abroad, the disintegration of the Portuguese colonial empire in Africa, and the emergence of self-identifying Marxist and Left-leaning governments in diverse parts of the Third World, offered opportunities for new international allies and new opportunities for Cuba to increase its influence and stature. Cuba could more easily "move in" also because the Vietnam War and Watergate, and the latter 1970s recession, disinclined Washington to take on new commitments at the time.

Thus, Castro's moral commitment to internationalism, combined with the "window of opportunity," help account for the scope of overseas involvements and their expansion in the mid-1970s. Yet Havana became less purist as its internationalism expanded. Marxist governments were not the only beneficiaries of aid and not all Marxist Third World governments were aid recipients. Some governments awarded aid were exceptionally repressive. Havana aided Equatorial Guinea, one of the world's most repressive regimes, for example. Moreover, it sided with Ethiopia, as noted, in its conflict with Somalia, even though Somalia had been a self-proclaimed Marxist-Leninist state and a beneficiary of island aid up to two months before Cuba sent massive support to Col. Mengistu.[79] And Castro continued to aid the Dergue (as Mengistu's military junta was called) even after the African government killed hundreds of thousands and possibly millions of civilians. Saddam Hussein's non-Marxist government in Iraq, in addition, was a recipient of aid, even after it invaded Kuwait and after the Soviets sided with the Western powers in the 1991 Gulf War.

THE ECONOMICS OF INTERNATIONALISM

While professing moral reasons for internationalism, since the latter 1970s Castro took economic considerations into account when expanding overseas commitments—especially in conjunction with civilian assignments. Concealed at the ideological level, such economic considerations have largely escaped the popular and scholarly imagination. What economic benefits might accrue to the island from internationalism, and have the economic benefits outweighed costs incurred?

Economic Benefits

Cuba could, in principle, benefit economically from international missions in several ways. It could charge for services rendered, and aid projects might pave the way for trade. Also, until the Soviet Union became preoccupied with its own internal problems, Moscow might have rewarded Havana for advancing its global interests.

The island's internationalist commitments purportedly paved the way to stepped-up Soviet aid.[80] But Moscow provided Cuba with extensive aid (including trade subsidies) even when, in the 1960s, it disapproved of island support of overseas guerrilla movements. Moreover, Moscow offered Cuba more new low-interest financing in 1972 than later in the decade, and it agreed to raise the price it paid for island sugar to a record high around the same time; that is, Soviet aid picked up before Castro committed massive troops and other internationalists to Africa, at a time when island trade with the West rose to record levels.[81] Cuba therefore could not have been rewarded for advancing Soviet global hegemonic interests. While Moscow provided Havana with perhaps its largest delivery of weapons in the early 1980s, after Cuba had collaborated extensively on overseas missions, it may have done so to help Cuba meet stepped-up U.S. security threats under President Reagan. Whatever the reason for stepped-up military aid, Castro remained committed to civilian internationalism when Moscow turned "inward," initially under Gorbachev.

Even if there is no link between Cuban overseas commitments and Soviet economic assistance, Cuba benefited materially from some of its overseas programs. Beginning in the latter 1970s certain countries were charged for "services rendered," though typically on an ability-to-pay basis.

Havana never disclosed how much it earned from service contracts. In the absence of full disclosures, available information is likely to be a conservative estimate of total overseas earnings.[82] In 1977 Cuban internationalists generated an estimated $50 million in hard currency, about 9 percent of the value of commodity exports to capitalist countries that year; two years later Cuba received $115 million in U.S. dollars for a construction and technical aid contract with Libya, and $25 million (apparently also in U.S. dollars) for another contract with Angola.[83] The two agreements alone generated 18 percent of the value of Cuba's 1979 hard currency trade.[84] Earnings in 1980 seem not to have been as good: that year, according to a Department of Commerce source, Cuba's overseas human capital ventures possibly generated $100 million, 6 percent of the value of the island's Western commodity exports.[85]

If 1980 was a bad year, earnings from internationalism subsequently rebounded. In 1981 Cuba is believed to have received $250 million for its military and civilian operations in Angola, and some $100 million for technicians and construction personnel working in such countries as Algeria, Libya, and Iraq.[86] And later in the decade Cuba reportedly received about $400 million a year for military assistance to Angola, which, if true, was equivalent to about one-third the island's convertible currency trade earnings at the time.[87] Cuba seems to have considered war-torn impoverished but oil-rich Angola capable of paying for certain services rendered.[88]

Havana began to pursue hard currency contracts when its own hard currency needs mounted in the latter 1970s, following the plunge in world sugar prices and the rise in its Western debt. That is, programs *justified in terms of socialist and proletarian internationalism began to be promoted, in part, to improve island market economy relations!* Official ideology and moral claims concealed the government's redirection of internationalism to address its emergent hard currency needs.

Construction became a major source of hard currency earnings, although most construction continued to be offered free of charge.[89] Between 1977 and the mid-1980s UNECA, the Cuban overseas construction contractor, secured deals worth more than $400 million. Created especially to undertake commercial operations, UNECA worked in more than fifteen foreign countries.[90] It took on major projects in Iraq, Libya, and Angola. In each country it set up a subsidiary.

UNECA's ability to negotiate commercial contracts proved limited, though. UNECA worked mainly only in countries friendly to Cuba. It therefore missed out on many of the lucrative Third World construction contracts at the time, in the oil-rich Middle East. And as politically sympathetic countries became strained by foreign debt problems in the 1980s, UNECA's overseas business dried up. The construction agency then turned "inward" to generate foreign exchange for the government. Since 1985 it concentrated on construction for island hard currency tourism. Tourism was more lucrative, though not morally justified as internationalism was.

Although construction had initially been the island's main source of hard currency internationalism, a high-level Cuban official noted that Havana charged foreign countries as much as $1,100 per month for a medical doctor with eight years' experience.[91] And in the early 1990s, sports internationalism became a source of hard currency. The director of Cubadeportes, S.A., reported that in 1992 his company earned $1.4 million abroad, mainly from services provided by sports specialists.[92]

On occasion aid provided free of charge paved the way to subsequent hard currency service contracts. In the Congo, for example, a donation of a plant to build prefabricated housing subsequently led to a contract to construct a highway and several farms and towns.[93] Aid in such instances proved to be an economic investment, but one not guaranteed in advance.

Despite efforts to promote money-making internationalism, *Granma* reported in 1989 that there were 3,000 Cubans working in twenty-one African countries free of charge.[94] The newspaper noted that Angola, Ethiopia, Iran, Mozambique, Guinea-Bissau, Vietnam, Laos, North Korea, Yemen, Iraq, Mongolia, Afghanistan, Sri Lanka, and the Philippines were some of the recipients of gratis aid. *If* no internationalists in these countries worked for pay, the government by the close of the 1980s had ceased to be able to use overseas workers to generate much-needed hard currency, even in countries where it previously had. Sensitive to recipient-country fiscal constraints, the Cuban government even turned some initial hard currency contracts into donations. African countries that had been charged modest sums for cooperative programs were exempted from payments, for example, when struck hard by their own domestic economic problems.[95] And on a visit to Nicaragua Castro decided to turn a 1983 contract for building a sugar mill, for which Cuba had received "favorable financing terms," into a gift.[96]

The economic benefits of internationalism were not, however, confined to hard currency service contracts. Aid also helped pave the way to trade, even if less than the government would have liked. Exports to Africa, the main recipient of island aid, increased 560 percent in the first half of the 1970s, another 117 percent in the latter half.[97] Trade with Algeria, where Cuba sent one of its first internationalist missions, in particular picked up in the 1970s. The value of Cuban exports to the North African country rose from about 3 million pesos in 1970 to over 93 million pesos a decade later. Exports to Africa came to exceed those to the European Economic Community.[98] However, because Cuba's global export earnings rose at this time, Africa's share of total exports rose from only 2 to 6 percent.

Global export earnings improved in part because trade with Third World countries in other regions of the world picked up. The total value of exports to developing market economies increased fivefold in the course of the 1970s.[99] Less developed countries (LDCs), which had accounted for 14 percent of total exports at the start of the decade accounted for 19 percent at its end. And Cuba came to have a positive trade balance with Third World economies. Aid in itself did not account for the growth in trade, but it helped predispose the less developed world to do business with Cuba.

Unfortunately for Havana, trade gains proved short-lived. Exports to Africa dropped to 1 and 2 percent of total trade in 1985 and 1989, respectively. Exports to Angola dropped precipitously, from 38 million pesos in 1980 to 6 million pesos at the decade's end. While exports to Algeria also dropped, to 37 million pesos, the North African country remained one of the top ten market economies to which Cuba exported in the latter 1980s.[100]

Although trade to Central American and Caribbean countries remained minor, accounting for less than 1 percent of total island exports,[101] trade to certain countries in the region improved. Trade with Nicaragua, in particular, picked up. Exports to Nicaragua rose from 2,000 pesos in 1975 to nearly 20 million pesos a decade later. Even after the Sandinistas were voted out of office, the Nicaraguan government continued trade dealings with Cuba. In 1992 only three other Latin American countries purchased more goods from Cuba, and the others were much larger (Mexico, Brazil, and Venezuela).[102] That year Cuba agreed to send the Central American country medical equipment, medicine, and specialized personnel in exchange for Nicaraguan farm goods.[103] And Belize, a recipient of island medical aid for twenty years, in the early 1990s sent officials to Cuba to negotiate commercial ties (including sugar industry assistance);[104] earlier aid undoubtedly predisposed this Central American country, as well as Nicaragua, to do business with Cuba.

Middle Eastern aid recipients also turned to Cuba for imports. This was true both of Iraq and Iran. In the early 1990s Iran, which according to a previously cited *Granma* article had in 1989 been a recipient of gratis aid, made plans to buy island sugar harvesters and medical products, and it contracted Cuba for medical care and medical training (in exchange for oil).[105]

While aid often was an investment, with payoffs in trade unknown at the time contracted, export deals on occasion were directly linked to aid missions. Construction contracts, for example, at times had cement exports as part of the package. The contracts help explain why cement exports rose to an average of 200,000 to 400,000 tons a year in the early 1980s. Cuba began to export significant quantities of cement in 1977, when construction internationalism expanded and became a money-making venture. In that year nearly 8 percent of cement output was exported, and in 1980 over 12 percent was. Domestic demand for cement for housing construction was sacrificed for hard currency "solidarity," especially during the years when UNECA worked abroad.

Educational assistance also opened markets. In 1985 about half of Cuba's paper production was earmarked for export, and the island exported textbooks to countries where it had educational and technical assistance missions—for example, to Angola and Nicaragua. In 1986 Cuba planned to export 14 million textbooks.[106]

The government sometimes even managed to use internationalism to negotiate more favorable trade agreements than otherwise would have been likely. This seems at least to have been true with sugar dealings. Several countries that received Cuban aid paid, beginning in the latter 1970s, above prevailing world market prices for the sweet.[107] Until 1977 Cuba typically sold sugar to Angola, Iraq, Algeria, Morocco, Egypt, and Vietnam at prices below the prevailing world market price, but afterwards at above the world market price. Communist Vietnam was charged the most! Since sugar importers have a vested interest in buying the commodity as cheaply as possible, there is reason to believe that Cuba provided "tied aid." The Cubans, however, never publicly acknowledged conditionality to their aid.

In addition to charging for bilateral service contracts and promoting trade with aid, the national leadership initiated some other creative money-making internationalist strategies. For one, it formed joint ventures with Western market firms specifically with this end in view. In 1985, for instance, Cuba proposed to form joint companies with Brazil to carry out civilian construction projects in Africa and Latin America.[108] The island's leadership sought to benefit from Brazilian overseas contacts and to make Cuban services attractive to countries ideologically opposed to communism. Two years later Cuba and Brazil talked of setting up joint enterprises to develop and market products based on Cuban genetic engineering research and cooperative projects for the production of medicines, and in 1993 they agreed to produce sugarcane harvesters in Brazil for export to third countries;[109] here too the Cubans hoped to benefit from Brazil's marketing networks. Back in 1987 Cuba also sought to have its technical personnel included in a British company's bids for third-country engineering, construction, and health projects.[110] Meanwhile, in the early 1990s Cuba negotiated medical assistance contracts for hard currency debt repayments. In 1993, for example, Colombia agreed to allow Cuba to pay off its $40 million debt to the South American country in medicines.[111] The island's leadership, moreover, sought Western industrial country capital and expertise to help develop export markets opened up by island aid programs. The French firm, Creusot-Loire, for example, provided 40 percent of the investment capital, plus knowhow and equipment, for a Cuban paper factory that was to earmark 40 percent of its production for export (initially to repay the French firm).[112] Paper products included materials used in island overseas educational programs.

While negotiating with Western firms to market products and services abroad, Cuba also became a marketing agent for Eastern European Communist country firms in the capitalist countries of Latin America. In particular, Cuba's *sociedad anónima*, Tractoimports, became the regional representative for an East German company in 1988, before German reunification.[113] The East European enterprise valued Cuba's Western hemisphere contacts. Tractoimports (described in greater detail below) capitalized on markets opened up by aid, though it sought markets in other countries as well.

In the 1980s Cuba's medical internationalism became especially commercialized, in the process of being transformed. A fine line evolved between medical aid provided in a disinterested manner and profiteering from sales of Cuban medicines.[114] The island came to export some 12 percent of its pharmaceutical production, partly in conjunction with medical missions abroad.

High-tech biotechnology and medical equipment, as well as pharmaceuticals, that Cuba began manufacturing in the latter 1980s were designed, as noted in chapter 3, with exports and not merely the domestic market in mind. In some cases aid helped open up export markets to medical manufacturers; in other countries, though, deals were negotiated in the absence of aid. Ghana, for example, a recipient of island medical brigades, agreed in 1992 to buy Cuban medicine and medical equipment, along with other manufactured goods. Yet Brazil, which in 1992 purchased $210 million in meningitis B vaccine, was not an aid beneficiary.[115]

In 1991 Castro expressed optimism about the prospects of what might be called the "new medical internationalism," based on a new specialty, "technomedicine." On one occasion he noted that "I am sure . . . that we are going to be exporters of health and we're not only going to export years of life, but healthy years of life."[116] "Technomedicine" was developed to the point that it was one of the only exports to the Commonwealth of Independent States, the former Soviet Union, that increased in 1991; that same year the vestige of the once superpower also paid Cuba for physician and dental services in hard currency.[117]

The Cubans made a concerted effort to promote medical exports independently of aid. Beginning in 1985 the island hosted "Health for All Medical Technology International Fairs." At the fairs island enterprises and hospitals exhibited domestically produced equipment with export potential. Furthermore, enterprises were set up specifically to produce and market health products overseas,[118] and established medical-related government and semiautonomous agencies became trade-oriented.[119] The prestigious Center of Genetic Engineering and Biotechnology formed HeberBiotec to market its products overseas for hard currency, and MediCuba, the export-import division of the Ministry of Public Health, began to promote medical exports while COPEXTEL, CECE, and CenterSoft exported and marketed SUMA equipment (a microcomputer-based laboratory system used in diagnosing malignant blood-based diseases, including AIDS).[120]

Deals were not confined to the medical field. Imexin, an import-export and consultancy enterprise associated with CECE, for example, offered software for the sugar as well as the public health sectors in the latter 1980s.[121] Meanwhile, Tractoimports, which began as an importer of agricultural machinery equipment, subsequently took on the role of an export corporation.[122] Its most important export products initially were harrows, plows, and hand pumps, sold primarily to Nicaragua, Uruguay, Mexico, Angola, Vietnam, and Ethiopia, but in 1988 steps were taken to develop export markets for island sugar harvesters as well, in Panama, Nicaragua, and the Dominican Republic.[123] Aid programs in the poorer of the countries—in Nicaragua, Angola, Vietnam, and Ethiopia—probably helped predispose the governments to do business with Cuba. However, here too Cuba's overseas deals were not confined to aid recipients.

Since the "new internationalism" occurred when other debt-ridden countries lacked cash, for trade as well as service deals, Cuba negotiated a variety of barter arrangements that reflected efforts to commercialize "aid."[124] Cubans, for example, offered Spanish specialists training in tropical medicine, epidemiology, public health, and advanced nursing, in exchange for Spanish technical assistance, training and research, and urban redevelopment and housing construction aid. Similarly, Brazil paid Cuba in kind for meningitis B vaccine. Brazil agreed to purchase about 100 million doses of the vaccine at seven dollars a dose (though initially agreeing to pay ten dollars a dose) in exchange for buses, consumer goods, and refinery technology.[125] Some other barter agreements involved Cuban assistance in setting up a family doctor program and fighting a dengue fever epidemic, plus developing cane by-products in Ecuador, in exchange for assistance in building up the Cuban oil industry and in banana growing; island cement, pharmaceuticals, medical equipment, detergent, and car battery exports for Guyanese rice, timber, and kaolin; island sugar, medicine, paper, building materials, and spare parts in exchange for Ugandan coffee, beans, and timber; and Cuban medicines and medical equipment, sugar industry equipment, scrap iron, and cattle for Peruvian capital goods, especially for the mining sector. Cuba—as noted above—had previously provided Peru with earthquake relief, and it had donated trawlers to the South American country for the fishing industry. It also had sent medical, technical, and teacher internationalists to the Burnham government in Guyana. Meanwhile, Cuba signed a cooperative agreement with Iran to provide the Middle Eastern country with sugar, and sugar industry technology and expertise, along with pharmaceutical products and other services, in exchange for oil and industrial goods. Previous aid probably helped pave the way for this as well as the other accords.

With income-generating internationalist opportunities limited, the government also creatively sought to encourage medical tourism, a form of "commercial solidarity": hard currency tourism involving low-cost medical care.[126] Advertising "sun and surgery," Cuba encouraged foreigners to take advantage of its advanced medical technology and special cures.[127] It offered treatments for vitiligo, retinitis pigmentosis (an eye disease considered incurable in many other countries), varicose veins, hip replacements, obesity, cosmetic, dental, and cardiology surgery, and organ transplants.[128] In 1992 Cuban medical thermal springs and medical and psychiatric sanitoria, including centers that treated what the government referred to as the "sicknesses of civilization" (stress, drugs, and alcoholism), were added to the menu of health tourism offerings. That same year a twelve-story 250-bed hotel for foreign patients and their families opened, linked to an orthopedic hospital; Cuba offered an exclusively dollar hospital in the Havana suburb of Miramar; a section was reserved for foreigners in Havana's largest, most modern medical complex, and an international clinic in Varadero offered treatment for skin disorders, cancers, cardiovascular illnesses, and dental care. The Varadero clinic alone reportedly earned $385,000 in 1992, a Cubanacán clinic about $14 million.[129]

Sociedades anónimas established to promote tourism and foreign investment in tourism added health tourism to their repertoire of offerings: this was true both of Cubanacán and of Gaviota. A Cubanacán-linked Havana clinic, for example, offered treatment for dengue, conjunctivitis, meningitis, hepatitis, shingles, warts, leukemia, cancer, and schizophrenia.[130]

The vitiligo treatment program attracted patients from over seventy countries for a seven-day cure. Cuba even set up vitiligo promotional and support groups abroad, both to treat patients with medication imported from the island and to organize charter flights for patients to come to Cuba for care. Venezuela was the first country to set up a National Vitiligo Group. The Venezuelan group had 4,000 members in 1993.[131] Vitiligo treatment makes use of the human placenta-based drug melagenin.

Cuba's major competitive advantage in the health-tourist sector, as in other technical assistance fields, was the low cost of services. A ten-day trip for vitiligo treatment, including sightseeing, in 1986 cost $750 (doctor fees an additional thirty-five dollars, and a week's worth of medicine only three dollars).[132] And in 1993 a CAT scan cost $292, one-third the amount charged at the time in the United States.[133] Cuban officials claimed to be making capitalist use of one of their most notable achievements—universal health care. "We are competing on a capitalist footing with the best hospitals in the world," the 1993 head of Cubanacán, Abraham Maciques, told a foreign reporter.[134]

The government's efforts to commercialize internationalism in no small part was rooted initially in *Soviet-bloc deficiencies.* The Soviet bloc, as delineated in earlier chapters, never provided all the goods and services islanders wanted. Island expansion and diversification of overseas programs and trade, and the promotion of training and treatment domestically, for hard currency represented creative initiatives to turn the human capital successes of the revolution into money-making endeavors. Accordingly, *the economic limitations—and not merely the political-military strength—of the Soviet bloc gave Cuba reason to "go international."* With the collapse of the Soviet bloc, the need to commercialize internationalism became all the greater. Fortunately for Cuba the health sector had been developed to the point that Cuba could market some of its products and services for hard currency, as gratis aid became a luxury Cuba could no longer readily afford. In addition to money earned from service contracts and health tourism, medical and pharmaceutical products may have brought in about 10 percent of Cuba's hard currency export revenue in 1992.

And during the Special Period Cuba benefited from internationalism in yet another way. Former island aid recipients began to assist Cuba in its hour of need. For example, Guyana and Vietnam sent rice, Nicaragua sent powdered milk, Peru sent food and medicines. While assistance was not confined to former aid recipients and not all earlier aid recipients offered Cuba a helping hand, previous Cuban generosity undoubtedly inclined other poverty-stricken countries to provide islanders with some relief.

Domestic Opportunity Costs

All countries experience domestic opportunity costs when they export goods, capital, and personnel, and Cuba was no exception. The island unquestionably could have benefited from use of all possible resources to improve its economy. But in what ways specifically did the overseas activities drain the economy, and did the economic costs of overseas ventures outweigh the gains?

The government, unfortunately, never released information on actual expenditures incurred. A Cuban economist, Edith Felipe, estimates the dollar value of island aid given between 1963 and 1989 at $1,537.2 million (including the scholarship program), the equivalent of about .7 percent of the national product:[135] a percentage of the national product comparable to the aid offerings of the much richer United States! Felipe calculates that construction, medical, and educational programs accounted for 80 to 90 percent of all civilian assistance, and donations of goods for a small fraction of aid.[136] The dollar value of total assistance peaked in the early 1980s. By 1989 aid allotments were back to levels of the latter 1970s. The cutback in internationalist expenditures was consistent with "rectification" austerity, if not with the "rediscovery" then of Ché and official reemphasis on the values he stood for.

Military internationalism also weighed on the economy. In the 1970s, when Cuba sent tens of thousands of Cubans on military missions, no other Latin American country allocated as high a percentage of its gross product to military expenditures as Cuba.[137] Moreover, at the time the military budget increased at a faster rate than the economy expanded.[138] Since domestic security was not then a major concern, the growth in military expenditures undoubtedly stemmed partly from the mounting fiscal burden of overseas activity. Cuba's military assistance to Angola was especially costly.

The internationalism programs, meanwhile, utilized labor that might otherwise have been employed domestically. Since Cuba "went international" on a large scale during a period of rising unemployment (in the latter 1970s), the labor drain on the economy was not as great as it would have been at a time when labor was in high demand. By the early 1990s, when the number of islanders on international missions dropped precipitously, Cuba had a surplus of people that could have been sent abroad with minimal if any domestic labor cost. The size of internationalist missions dwindled for reasons other than costs to the domestic labor pool.

When economic benefits outweighed costs to the government, the same was not necessarily true for individual enterprises, including state-owned enterprises. In the latter 1970s some firms expressed reluctance to release employees for international assignments because they believed their production would suffer as a consequence;[139] concern with their own profitability picked up with the implementation of the SDPE. And when the government in the early 1990s encouraged enterprises to negotiate hard currency deals on their own, including in conjunction with the "new internationalism," enterprises had an incentive to "go international" while the government ran the risk of appropriating little of the hard currency enterprises generated and having to absorb hard currency and other costs enterprises incurred (e.g., import costs). In the foreign as well as the domestic arena, what was good for the government and for enterprises was not necessarily one and the same.

In terms of island shortages, Cuba could least afford to send construction workers abroad.[140] The government sent builders overseas despite unmet domestic housing needs. Minibrigade construction tapered off in the latter 1970s, just when participation in overseas building brigades increased; supplies went to projects abroad. Moreover, the government made its best construction workers internationalists, so as to better compete for foreign contracts.[141] The JUCEPLAN (planning) chief, in an unusually candid interview, admitted that consumer needs for cement were being sacrificed to obtain foreign exchange.[142] And in 1980 the government announced that the *only* restriction on use of work center profit funds—established in conjunction with the SDPE—would be housing construction. The reason given was insufficient building supplies, a problem compounded by the allotment of materials to international construction brigades.

Cuba was in a much better position to send medical cadre and teachers abroad than construction workers. In 1980 it had the third highest doctor, second highest nurse, and one of the best if not the best student/teacher and enrollment ratios in Latin America (see Appendix, Tables 4.1 and 5.1), and its per capita regional rankings on each measure rose in the course of the 1980s. Thus, the domestic costs of sending teachers and medical cadre abroad, from a regional perspective, were low.

If the social costs were low, the economic costs, to the country's overall growth capacity, have been alleged to be high.[143] The economic growth rate, which reached a record high under Castro in the mid-1970s, declined around the time that overseas missions became large in scale. But the economic slowdown had less to do with the expansion of overseas programs than with the ramifications of the dramatic plunge in export earnings with the plunge in world sugar prices. Moreover, in most years between the mid-1970s and mid-1980s, and especially in the early 1980s, the island's growth rate (according to available information) compared favorably with that of other Latin American countries with no comparable internationalist missions. Thus, from a regional as well as a domestic vantage point, internationalism did not jeopardize the island's growth capacity. Meanwhile, whatever the direct costs of sending teachers and medical cadre abroad rather than keeping them at home, they were not even reflected in statistics on the island's macro economic performance. Such service activity is considered, in Marxist calculations, to be "nonproductive," and therefore excluded from national product estimates.

The island's growth rate, of course, might have been higher had the human and material resources been reserved for domestic use. However, it must be remembered that overseas missions absorbed men (and, to a limited extent, women) who might otherwise have been unemployed, and more importantly, some of the missions, directly and indirectly, benefited the economy by generating much-needed foreign exchange, a top state institutional concern since the latter 1970s.

A complete assessment of the costs of internationalism must also consider third-country responses to island overseas missions. Although internationalism paved the way to some LDC commercial service and trade contracts, and some aid reciprocity during the Special Period, Cuba would have benefited much more from an end to the U.S. embargo. Under President Carter relations between Washington and Havana, as noted, had taken a turn for the better, only to deteriorate when Cuba sent tens of thousands of troops to Ethiopia and Angola.[144] Cuba's military involvements in Africa, moreover, contributed to the suspension, reduction, and nonrenewal of island aid from Sweden, Holland, Norway, West Germany, and Canada between 1976 and 1978.[145] Thus, the very internationalism that won Cuba Third World allies and helped Castro be elected head of the Non-Aligned Movement, was hostilely received by the industrial West.

Nonetheless, except for under President Carter, internationalism did not cost Havana a "normalization" of relations with Washington. When Castro brought his troops home in the latter 1980s, President Bush merely changed the criterion for terminating the embargo: he insisted (as described in chapter 4), on competitive multiparty elections.

Finally, internationalism became a source of corruption. The thousands of foreign scholarship students in Cuba had access to *diplotiendas*, well-stocked stores for diplomats, tourists, and other foreign visitors. Foreign students took advantage of the stores. They would supplement their monthly stipends with money earned from black-market sales of goods attained at *diplotiendas*.[146] And at the highest level corrupting effects of internationalism came to the fore with the conviction and execution of General Ochoa in 1989 (see chapter 3). Ochoa had conducted off-the-books transactions both to help finance his war activities and to improve his troops' living conditions, to keep their morale up. His predecessors in Angola also supplemented their budgets with exports of diamonds, ivory, quartz, and other materials to Western Europe. When taking over, Ochoa continued these shipments and added others. Allegedly because Havana had not provided sufficient money to build an airport in southern Angola, considered essential for winning the war there, Ochoa used his global military contacts to broker lucrative arms deals and he sold Cuban sugar, cement, and other goods in the Angolan black market.[147] Such illicit deals were tolerated since they addressed official internationalist objectives that the Cuban government on its own could ill afford, but the tacit rule was that Fidel, with his almost religious disdain for money, was not to know of them. This would suggest that Castro's global ambitions induced his trusted cadre to engage in illicit activity and that Ochoa's undoing was rooted in macro dynamics.

FUTURE PROSPECTS OF INTERNATIONALISM

Is internationalism a viable future strategy? Both global and domestic conditions do not bode well.

Politically sympathetic Third World governments would be most inclined to contract Cuban internationalists. Industrial countries have little use for Cuban services since they have their own trained labor force, and non-Left-leaning Third World governments are wary that resident island internationalists would be politically destabilizing. But the collapse of the Soviet Union reduced the number of politically sympathetic countries. Without prospects of Soviet assistance LDC governments took a "rightward" turn. They recognized that they had more to gain from U.S. and Western multilateral ties than from any Cuban connection. The 1992 U.S. Cuban Democracy Act (see chapter 4) gave LDCs an added disincentive to have dealings with Cuba, for they would thereby be disqualified for aid from Washington.

Third World fiscal problems further limit Cuba's prospects. Already in the 1980s Havana's decision to withdraw troops both from Ethiopia and from Angola was partly rooted in the growing inability of the two African countries to meet payments.[148]

Cultural barriers are an additional obstacle, especially in the field of education. While cultural barriers remained least problematical in Spanish Latin America, African governments increasingly wanted aid providers who were conversant in English if not their native languages.

The Soviet global withdrawal, in turn, made large-scale Cuban military missions improbable. Even though Cuba typically "went international" at its own volition, large-scale military missions, as noted, relied on matériels provided by Moscow. Since overseas military missions helped pave the way for civilian aid and trade, prospects for the latter were thereby also affected.

Castro faced domestic contraints as well. In the 1980s Cuban sources had reported on hundreds of thousands of islanders volunteering for overseas assignments.[149] The government attracted volunteers with material and moral incentives. The government promised internationalists, upon their return, a 20 percent pay raise, special pension benefits, priority access to housing, and coveted consumer goods.[150] It also promised them jobs and representation at major Party events, and special consideration in university admissions.[151] However, during the Special Period returnees did not get promised jobs, as opportunities outside of agriculture collapsed, and there was little housing and few consumer goods to allocate. Overseas service must have been viewed as less attractive under the circumstances.

The Special Period crisis, moreover, made islanders resentful of material assistance to other LDCs. Ordinary Cubans came to see internationalism as conflicting with their own basic needs. Indicative of the changed domestic mood, in 1991 in Cienfuegos dock workers refused to load food that was to be shipped to Iraq. The dock workers were arrested and troops were brought in to load the supplies.[152] Dock workers were also rumored to have refused to load chicken for Nicaragua and condensed milk for Haiti. The workers may not have refused, but such rumors that circulated among the populace reveal how the government's commitment to internationalism came to be sabotaged, in words as well as deeds, by islanders who had been encouraged for decades to identify with the plight of others abroad. Resentment mounted to the point that an island journalist with whom I spoke about internationalism asserted that "it's dead."

Some 2,300 islanders, by the government's admission, lost their lives on international missions (2,016 in Angola).[153] Yet by the early 1990s the government had little to show for the fatalities. True, Cuban cadre had paved the way to negotiated Angolan and Namibian settlements and in helping to defeat South African forces they contributed to the demise of apartheid (by weakening the political power of conservatives in the white government). But the Angolan government after the demise of the Soviet Union dissociated itself from Cuba, at the same time that the Cuban government promoted collective amnesia about its former Angolan involvement. Official media coverage of civil strife in the African country made no mention of former ties to the MPLA. Under the circumstances Cubans could not be expected to easily accept risking their lives for new missions abroad.

And during the Special Period the government, for its own fiscal reasons, found gratis programs a luxury it could no longer afford. Its ambitious island-based scholarship program, for example, drew to a sudden halt. As of mid-1993 no new students were expected (at least not from Africa and the Caribbean).[154] The government had enough difficulties feeding its own people, let alone foreigners.

In sum, internationalism, a creative extension of the social welfare accomplishments of the revolution described in chapters 5 and 6, by the early 1990s had largely run its course, economically and politically. The government's main prospects for commercializing internationalism, to meet its growing hard currency needs, centered on exports of competitively priced pharmaceuticals, biotechnology products, and medical equipment, plus health tourism in Cuba: deals premised more on market competition than socialist ideals.

Dwindling prospects notwithstanding, the government remained officially committed to internationalism. The 1991 Party Congress reaffirmed the country's commitment to solidarity with revolutionary, progressive, and democratic forces abroad. Castro used the occasion, though, to add a new twist to internationalism. Said he, "Now our internationalist efforts should be focused on defending and preserving the Cuban revolution. Our greatest internationalist duty . . . [is] to defend this trench, this bastion of socialism."[155] This defensive rationale stood in marked contrast to the offensive call of the 1960s, when Castro asserted that the duty of every revolutionary was to make revolution and when Ché called for "one, two, many Vietnams."

The crisis of the 1990s, in essence, led Castro to attempt to redefine the meaning and purpose of internationalism. Both conditions at home and abroad made his earlier efforts to take on a global role unprecedented for a Third World country, and a utopian ideal no longer imaginable.

Chapter Eight

THE RELEVANCE OF THE REVOLUTION

C ALLING FOR SOCIAL REFORM, diversified economic development, and democracy, Castro came to power with widespread political support. But even as powerful, autocratic, and charismatic a leader as Castro, after centralizing control of the economy and polity, could not remake society as he so chose. Over the years his efforts to remake society met with constraints, as well as with opportunities, that were not of his choosing. On numerous occasions he was shown to have modified economic and social strategies because of unforeseen circumstances and unintended consequences of policies in effect. Constraining forces became so overwhelming by the 1990s that the revolution's accomplishments began to erode.

What Occurred? The Cuban Experience Summarized in Historical and Comparative Perspectives

Comparisons between Cuba before and after the revolution and between socialist Cuba and other countries in Latin America during the years of Castro's rule permit an objective assessment of the ways that the island's social transformation was and was not of consequence. Table 8.1 (see Appendix) provides a summary of how Cuba fared on social and economic indicators three decades after the revolution.

Viewed historically, the socialist transformation made a difference. Between 1959 and 1989, Cuba's national product improved, in general and on a per capita basis. Moreover, Cuba reduced its dependence on a single commodity for trade, and it reduced the importance of exports in the national economy. Many of the problems of the Old Order had been attributed to the economy's dependence on sugar.

The social accomplishments of Castro's Cuba were even more impressive. Life expectancy rose, infant mortality declined, medical and educational facilities and services expanded, nutritional standards improved, and rural/urban inequities diminished considerably. And the accomplishments, as this book demonstrates, resulted from deliberate government efforts. Castro created a cradle-to-grave welfare state for all Cubans, including for rural and urban poor previously excluded from social programs.

Although not shown in the table for this chapter, chapter 7 illuminated ways that Castro even tried to extend benefits of the revolution to other Third World countries. Cuban internationalists provided economic and social as well as military aid to other countries in need. The extent of Cuba's overseas commitments, especially between the mid-1970s and latter 1980s, was unprecedented for a Third World country with limited resources.

But the improvements were not without fiscal costs, and they proved by the 1990s to be contingent on a set of historical conditions that by then no longer existed. The government accumulated a large foreign debt in the process of attempting to develop the economy, raise social welfare standards, and offer international assistance. Not only did the government become increasingly indebted to foreign creditors (to the Soviet Union as well as to the Western sources summarized in the Appendix, Table 8.1); also, the government's domestic deficit mounted, despite efforts (such as through the Rectification Process of the latter 1980s) to increase state revenue and reduce expenditures.

Viewed from a comparative perspective the accomplishments of the revolution proved more mixed. In certain domains other countries accomplished more in the absence of revolution. Relative to other countries in the region, Cuba did best on aspects of development that did not involve dealings with the external world. Despite Castro's efforts to reduce the island's dependence on sugar, other countries in the region became less monoproduct export-dependent. To make matters worse, Cuba depended, for historical reasons, on one of the least desirable commodities. Sugar is exceptionally price volatile and vulnerable to declining world market value because of its easy substitutability. The way the Spanish colonists developed and integrated the island into the world economy set parameters for Cuban socialism.

Cuba's comparative trade disadvantage contributed, in turn, to greater foreign indebtedness over the years, relative to the other countries. Cuba became more indebted to Western creditors than most of the capitalist countries of Latin America (and the rest of the Third World), not in absolute dollars but in its repayment capacity, reflected in the hard currency debt/hard currency export ratio. Global geopolitical, political, and economic dynamics, as well as domestic inefficiencies and problems, contributed to the island's regional marginalization in externally linked aspects of the economy.

From a regional as well as national historical vantage point the revolution fared better in the social domain. On all measures Cuba's regional ranking either improved or remained the same (only its ranking in the primary school enrollment rate dropped, which at 106 percent reflected the rate of grade repeaters, not dropouts). And on indicators where its ranking did not change, Cuba typically ranked the highest in the region all along.

Yet the collapse of the Soviet bloc and the Soviet Union altogether threatened the very accomplishments of the revolution and exacerbated its failures. Castro's government creatively tried to adapt to the "new world (dis)order," by promoting market reforms and even precapitalist survival strategies, along with policies more consistent with ideal-typical socialism. But its success at implementing reforms was not immediately apparent. By 1993 Cuba could no longer even count on sugar to generate essential export earnings to finance imports and service its foreign debt.

The crisis compelled Castro to concede many of the principles the revolution had stood for. Promotion of foreign investment and tourism, a dollarization of the economy, and a welcoming of Cuban-American remittances were unimaginable in the early years of Castro's rule but considered essential to survival during the Special Period. Indeed, islanders' best hope of survival as the official economy ceased to satisfy their needs was through reliance on kin who previously rejected the revolution or on hard currency earned through tourism, both once considered "politically incorrect." During the Special Period political loyalty to Fidel and the "party of disciples" for ordinary cadre promised less material reward, and less hope of meeting basic subsistence needs.

The crisis caused by the "new world (dis)order" also caused the state's hold over society to wither away, de facto though not de jure, and more so, paradoxically, than in many societies where state power was less centralized economically and politically. It withered not because Marx's utopian communist stage had been attained but because its legitimacy eroded as Castro's ability to prove his and his government's worth, central to charismatic authority, collapsed with the demise of Soviet aid and trade. Moreover, the government was driven to the brink of bankruptcy as it tried to maintain its welfare projects despite the fall in revenue that came with the collapse of Soviet aid and trade. A trade-dependent economy was in an especially poor position to absorb a drastic cut in trade and a drastic deterioration in terms of trade.

WHAT IS TO BE LEARNED? THEORETICAL IMPLICATIONS

Cuba's experience under Castro reveals how misleading and inaccurate Cold War conceptions of Communist states were. Such states are not intrinsically strong and powerful. Centralization of formal political and economic power allowed for autocratic decision-making, but not necessarily for automatic implementation of elite-determined policies. It allowed for greater influence over social than economic policy and, within the economic domain, over "inwardly" more than "outwardly" oriented policy: but only under historically contingent conditions that no longer existed in the 1990s.

Nationalization of economic ownership did not make Castro's commitment to a social welfare state inevitable, but it helped make it possible. With the economy in state hands Castro faced no opposition from a business community that in most of the rest of Latin America resisted taxation to finance social programs for the rural and urban poor.

The Cuban experience highlights, however, how the very social successes of socialism can exacerbate state problems. Castro's social project contributed to the government's continued legitimacy when other authoritarian governments in the region—both the long-standing autocratic rulers, such as Gen. Alfredo Stroessner in Paraguay and François Duvalier in Haiti, and the more modern military regimes of the 1960s through 1980s—fell from grace. Yet as illustrated in chapter 5, the welfare state contributed to a "demographic revolution" that led social welfare expenditures with time to outpace social welfare revenue, and its contribution to regime legitimacy began to crumble in the 1990s when programs had to be cut back.

The Cuban case also showed how problems of state socialism are apt to be compounded by tensions embedded in government efforts to maximize control over production and distribution and appropriation of the monies thereby generated, and individual and enterprise market-linked efforts to maximize their own profits. When the government reined in private individual and enterprise economic activity to address its institutional concerns, it justified its initiatives ideologically: Guevarism and Marxism-Leninism offered a rationale for a state-centered economy, and the discourse helped legitimate policies that involved material sacrifices and diminution of economic autonomy. But because both the statist and the market emphasis left government problems unresolved, the government periodically shifted its state-market mix. The marked shifts—associated with the "push for communism" and the "maximum of ruralism" in the late 1960s, with the "retreat to socialism" and the "market opening" of the 1970s through mid-1980s, with "rectification" in the latter 1980s, and with the Special Period of the early 1990s—reflect different strategies attempted by the state to deal with economic and political concerns that policies in effect failed to resolve.

The government relied on different state-market mixes over the years in both the internally and the externally oriented sectors of the economy. But Castro increasingly was pressed to subordinate "inwardly" oriented development to hard currency export promotion. Hard currency debt and hard currency trade-based exigencies compelled the government to sacrifice islander needs and wants while still officially committed to socialism. The external market constraints also compelled the state to sacrifice its moral and nationalist principles, and to relinquish control over investment and trade, and profits thereby generated, to new quasi-autonomous capitalist-like enterprises and foreign capital. At the same time, moreover, it ran the risk of having to absorb losses the enterprises incurred.

Chapters 2 through 4 highlighted forces influencing government economic strategies over the years and their impact. I showed how developments in Cuba were, first and foremost, shaped by global economic and political dynamics. Global forces did not predetermine what Castro did and did not do, but they set limits and created opportunities. The course of the revolution was particularly affected by the Cold War and both U.S. and Soviet policy within that context. The United States' early anti-Castro and the Soviets' pro-Castro policies set the parameters for subsequent Cuban development options. Soviet willingness to trade with Cuba, when the United States refused to, and its willingness to subsidize the revolution, economically and militarily, created the conditions under which Castro had the means to promote industrialization and internationalism, and develop a social welfare state. Soviet support also induced Castro to adopt a "vanguard party" political system that was well suited to efforts to institutionalize charismatic rule, allowing as it did for a "party of disciples."

Soviet willingness to "take on" Cuba proved a mixed blessing, entailing costs as well as benefits: costs concealed for decades in light of gains, but costs that came to haunt Castro's government once Soviet aid ended, trade plunged, and terms of trade turned against the island. Because the Soviets had refused over the years to buy little besides sugar from Cuba and because they agreed to buy the sweet at a highly subsidized price, Cuba had little incentive to develop other goods for export: the Soviets guaranteed no other markets (except for nickel), and Cuba could produce nothing else as profitably. When sales to the once superpower collapsed with the dissolution of the Soviet Union, Cuba was left with a relatively limited range of products to market internationally. And the volume of the goods it had to sell dropped dramatically once essential Soviet-imported inputs no longer arrived.

Compounding the island's problems, the Soviet Union had developed Cuba in its own image: with fuel-inefficient heavy industry, large in scale. This mode of development was not inherent to socialism but to the historical form it took in the once superpower. Castro had no alternative industrial model on which to build, given Cold War dynamics. The scale of operations made bad investments costly. Cuba sank large capital of its own in jointly sponsored projects that threatened to lay idle when the Soviets pulled out. Because projects were costly to run and internationally uncompetitive, they were unattractive to potential alternative investors. Moreover, with Moscow favoring heavy over light industry, islander yearnings for material goods went unsatisfied. In principle, the Soviets helped lay the basis for "upstream" light industry, but over a thirty-year period Cuba produced only a paltry number of consumer goods and their quality did not compare to their Western equivalents.

The adverse effects of Soviet trade and aid will weigh on the Cuban economy for the foreseeable future, at the same time that the benefits have been relegated to history. Cuba must bear the consequences of the Soviet-inspired development model even after global geopolitics changed and Cuba's economic dependence on Moscow ended.

Analyses of Cuba that took Cold War politics and ideology at face value assumed there to be two worlds of development and that under Castro Cuba shifted from one bloc and one mode of dependence to another. This conceptualization blinded observers from recognizing analytically and often even empirically the continued impact of world market dynamics and Western government policies. Developments in Castro's Cuba proved to be affected over the years by world market commodity prices, access to Western financing, Western interest rates, and even the value of the dollar (because commodities are traded internationally in dollars), along with Soviet-bloc dynamics. Castro came to understand the importance of these factors, even when his government concealed them at the ideological level.

Global market forces were of consequence long before the collapse of the Soviet bloc. What changed in the early 1990s was the scale of their significance and how their influence was felt. Whereas in the mid-1970s Western trade and financing facilitated island industrialization, two decades later global dynamics compelled Castro to deindustrialize, to shift from a productive to a service-oriented economy, and to subordinate domestic priorities to the interests of foreign investors and hard currency opportunities. Meanwhile, hard currency–oriented joint ventures, dominated by foreign capital, became the most dynamic and in many respects the most important units in the economy. These changes occurred at the same time that Castro remained publicly committed to socialism.

Although capitalism proved itself the superior economic system, I show global market as well as Soviet-bloc dynamics to have had mixed effects on the island economy. The West had its most positive impact in the mid-1970s, when the world sugar price reached a record high, when there was an influx of Western financing (at moderate interest rates), and when the dollar was relatively strong. Cuba was most negatively affected by world market conditions when it pressed for the 1970 ten-million-ton sugar harvest at a time of low international prices, and when in the 1980s interest rates rose, sugar export/oil import terms of trade turned against Cuba, and new Western financing subsided.

Following the collapse of the Soviet bloc, Cuba was in a worse position than other Latin American countries and in a worse position than before the revolution to deal with the global market economy. Not only was Cuba dependent on internationally uncompetitive Soviet technology. Also, it no longer benefited from guaranteed export markets and from export subsidies, as it had under the Old Order as well as under the Soviets. In addition, Havana was cut off from increasingly important multinational marketing networks.

Meanwhile, politics at the international level, independent both of global geopolitical and world market dynamics, were shown to have influenced Cuban development options. Internal Soviet politics reverberated 6,000 miles away. Moscow turned gradually against Cuba under Brezhnev, and much more so under Gorbachev. In the course of the 1980s an "anti-Cuban" political coalition, with which Yeltsin was associated, gained force. And as the Soviet Union disintegrated economically and politically, Moscow's Cuban policy began to be shaped increasingly in Washington: a prerequisite for U.S. assistance.

U.S. politics affected Cuban options even in the absence of diplomatic and economic relations between the closest of neighbors. As noted, Cuban-U.S. relations improved under President Carter but deteriorated again in the Reagan-Bush years. Beginning in the 1980s, a U.S. administration–backed Cuban-American lobby became sufficiently powerful to step up anti-Castro initiatives, at the same time that Washington softened its stance first toward Chinese and then toward Soviet and Vietnamese Communism. The growing size and power of the Cuban-American community, especially its most conservative, organized segment, influenced U.S. policy independently of Cold War politics. Washington responded to the special interests represented by the CANF, the Cuban-American National Foundation. Bush stepped up his pandering to Cuban-Americans as he sought the Florida electoral vote for the 1992 election. Cuban-Americans are heavily concentrated in the state. Clinton, after winning the national election despite losing Florida, immediately continued his predecessor's anti-Castro policy to court Cuban-American support.

Changing U.S. political dynamics following the 1992 election began, however, to create the conditions for a possible shift in U.S. policy toward Cuba. For one, Clinton was less closely tied to the CANF than Reagan or Bush. Second, the Cuban-American community began to divide on what U.S. Cuban policy should be. Mariel and post-Mariel émigrés, more than their elite predecessors, had friends and relatives still in Cuba, and they were upset over islander distress caused by the blockade in the absence of Soviet aid and trade. The well-being of their island relatives carried more weight than their anti-Communist and anti-Castro sentiments. The changed circumstances gave birth, in August 1993, to a more moderate Cuban-American coalition, the Cuban Committee for Democracy, comprised of business executives, academics, and other professionals. The new group sought to undermine the Foundation's veto power over American policy toward Cuba. Also, Clinton began to have reason for concern about the U.S. ramifications of possible island violence and stepped-up illegal emigration, as life in Cuba deteriorated.[1]

But Castro never passively acquiesced to conditions imposed from abroad. For decades the skilled tactician managed to manipulate the Cold War, in certain respects, to his country's advantage, attaining more aid from Moscow than other LDC Soviet-bloc countries. Cuban internationalism, as noted, even influenced Soviet foreign policy, along with Soviet Cuban policy.

As important as global geopolitical, political, and economic forces were in shaping how the revolution evolved, so too were domestic forces. Ordinary people helped determine the course of Cuban history in ways that paradigms of Communist politics, including the totalitarian, all powerful, ideologically driven and the more nuanced bureaucratic politics variant, left largely unanalyzed and unexplained.[2] Time and again islanders did not passively march to Castro's and the Party's orders. About one-tenth of the population opted out, choosing to emigrate through legal or illegal means. While few remaining islanders took on the risks of outright rebellion, many of them defied state orders over the years in covert ways, sometimes on such a scale that the leadership was pressed, for economic and political reasons, to modify policies in significant ways. Worker demands initially contributed to the radicalization of the revolution. Subsequently, as detailed, islanders engaged in foot-dragging, absenteeism, pilfering, black marketeering, and other acts of quiet defiance that sabotaged what people in positions of authority could exact from them. Also, islanders turned to syncretic religions (and a growing minority to evangelical Protestantism), a mode of cultural resistance to a once self-proclaimed atheistic state. Covert acts of defiance permeated even the interstices of the state apparatus, as bureaucrats used and abused their positions for their own ends. People resisted conditions not to their liking in patterned ways contingent, on the one hand, on state policy, and on the other hand, on their own particular "structure of opportunities."

Periodic antibureaucratic and anticorruption campaigns, and dismissals of key alleged law violators, never stopped disobedience because the individuals targeted were a manifestation but not the source of the problem. The fundamental difficulties were chronic scarcities and the government's inability to convince people to settle for nonmaterial rewards.

By the end of 1993, when this book was completed, the government's and Party's moral authority had declined to the point that they had great difficulty imposing their will and way on the populace. Challenges from civil society were much greater and more widespread and varied than was conveyed by the minority of active dissidents on which the foreign press focused. As the state's authority eroded, civilian disobedience quietly picked up.

Only by "bringing people back in" to the analysis of state socialism can developments in Cuba (and, by implication, other states that restrict overt challenges to authority) be adequately understood. Informal social, political, and economic dynamics are the least analyzed aspect of Cuban Communism, but not because of their lack of importance. Rather, they have received little attention because the government has denied their existence and political analysts in the main have focused on the formal polity. By overlooking informal dynamics and the forces that pattern them, the state appeared much more powerful vis-à-vis civil society than actually was the case.

Government control of the mass media and the school system led analysts to exaggerate, in turn, the weight of ideology at both the leadership and mass level. Ideology did not determine government policy as much as public proclamations and most foreign commentators suggested. I showed seemingly ideologically driven and economically irrational policies to be associated with leadership efforts to legitimate material deprivations that otherwise might have provoked protest. The national leadership selectively drew on ideology, reinterpreted ideology, and promoted and demoted proponents of different Marxist-Leninist and Guevarist views, as conditions changed. Ideology was neither fixed in content nor in its implementation.

While Cold War conceptions of Communism left much of Cuban history under Castro unaccounted or misaccounted for, Marxist and neo-Marxist analyses have proved wanting for other reasons. The Cuban experience reveals that *dependentistas* incorrectly attributed Latin American underdevelopment only to the capitalist mode of production, imperialism, and dependence specifically on the United States for trade and aid, implying that a socialist mode of production and international socialist solidarity would allow for diversified development. Economically, Cuba's socialist transformation did not allow the island to overcome its monoproduct export dependence and to expand and diversify its economic base any more than other Latin American countries. Even Castro, by the 1990s, saw the United States as the best solution to the island's economic woes, not, as in years past, as the source of its problems. World systems theory, which offers an explanation for how and why global market dynamics are of consequence even when countries are ideologically committed to socialism and devoid of internal capitalist-class relations, in turn, provides no basis for understanding the import of geopolitical and political forces at the international level and of nonmarket forces domestically. And while a "mode of production" analysis helps explain how Cuba was able to develop a welfare state and reduce historically rooted injustices and inequities, the weight of the aforementioned external and domestic forces, and the discretionary ways Castro has used the powers of the state over the years, reveal that history is not mechanistically determined by property and class relations.

Thus, the Cuban experience shows how leaders and ordinary citizens alike under Soviet-bloc Communism could and did make history, but under conditions not of their making or choosing and, at times, beyond their comprehension. Their actions, affected on occasion by unforeseen circumstances, generated unintended as well as intended consequences. The factors summarized above and illustrated in earlier chapters all influenced the course of Cuban history under Castro, though none predetermined that history.

What Is to Be Done?

On January 1, 1989, the thirtieth anniversary of the revolution, hardly anyone the world over would have predicted that the Communist governments in the Soviet bloc would collapse with such speed and, with the exception of Romania, with so little violence. While the ramifications of this collapse will influence Cuba's future, how the island will evolve depends on enough contingencies, as they did in years past, that little else can be predicted. Yet, even if developments are overcome by unpredictable events, the logic of my analysis in previous chapters suggests different possible political and economic scenarios, with different effects.

Since Castro is not immortal the matter of succession necessarily arises. Fidel himself acknowledged at the time of the 1993 Cuban elections that even marathon runners can tire, and that he hoped he would not be asked by his countrymen to run for office again.[3] Whether or not he serves out his current term of office and whether he would concede to retire should he serve out the term, an understanding both of charisma and of the post-Communist experiences of other Soviet-bloc countries give little reason for political and economic optimism. It also is questionable whether the benefits of the revolution can be retained while its shortcomings are corrected.

Given the dynamics of charisma, Castro is the best hope for a smooth leadership and possibly regime transition. His opponents would welcome a change, although their support would hinge on the transition proposed, and his followers would back what their revered leader wants, as they have for over three decades. Since Castro has signaled that he is ready to resign when his current term of office expires, Washington would do well to work with and not against him, to maximize the prospects of a peaceful transition (and minimize the number of Cubans seeking refuge in the United States, in which case Cuba's problems would become the United States' problems as well).

Officially, Fidel's brother Raúl, as noted, has been designated next in line. However, the citizenry is unlikely to accept rule by Raúl, as he lacks both charisma and respect. Raúl would therefore have to rely even more on repression than Fidel did: this would be fiscally costly for an already bankrupt state and would also increase Cuba's international political and economic isolation.

A leadership change involving no regime transition might also occur without Raúl. Raúl might consider himself too advanced in age or the circumstances under which he would take office too uninviting when Fidel steps down. In chapter 4 I described how Fidel laid the groundwork for a generational if not an individual transition (other than Raúl). A new generation gained political status, political visibility, and symbolic power beginning with the 1991 Party Congress. Exceptional in the Communist world, Fidel engineered this generational transition. But he did so while stymieing individual leadership development, as the fates of General Ochoa and Carlos Aldana, among others, bear all too dramatic testimony; Carlos Lage and Roberto Robaina, at the time of writing, were the two main exceptions, and Lage's fate was contingent on the success of Special Period reforms that were not yet apparent. Moreover, with Cubans more committed to Castro than to Communism, the polity is unlikely to accept "new wine in old bottles," continued "vanguard party" rule with new faces, in the absence of Fidel. Any Communist Party–based regime will have problems of legitimation and problems therefore of exhorting citizen cooperation, especially in the absence of an "economic miracle"—rooted, for example, in a removal of the U.S. embargo and major oil discoveries—that significantly reverses the economic collapse of the early 1990s.

Even if the Party itself is transformed into a more inclusionary nationalist institution à la Mexico's PRI, the Party of the Institutionalized Revolution, as Castro attempted to do in the early 1990s, its prospects are limited. The change is too little too late, again unless accompanied by a major economic reversal.

Alternatively, there might be a military coup, in which lower-level officers break ranks with Raúl, their top officer. Although the military would not have legitimate claims to rule, they could argue that political order is impossible without them, given the dire economic situation and mounting discontent, and that they would return to the barracks when conditions allowed. A coup would help the armed forces regain institutional opportunities lost with the collapse of internationalism and the collapse of the economy. The Nicaraguan experience suggests that the military are likely to be a force that any post-Castro government will have to contend with, even if they do not formally take command of the government. The Sandinistas conceded the right to rule for the continued right to control the military, and they thereby retained considerable informal political clout. However, a military more concerned, in Raúl Castro's words, with "beans than cannons," that is, with basic subsistence, hardly holds much promise, in the absence of an economic turnaround or new external support.

A multiparty system, in turn, stands some chance. However, at the 1993 Ibero-American summit Castro made clear he still opposed such a transformation. Implementation of a multiparty system might lead Washington to end the embargo, which would help revitalize the economy. Improved living standards would be politically popular and lend support to any government, whatever its ideological leaning.

But it need be remembered that Cuba, since independence from Spain, has had little experience with multiparty democracy on which to build. The implications of this inexperience are more severe at the leadership than the rank-and-file level. While ordinary citizens have had experience with grass-roots involvements (as described in earlier chapters), there is no leadership class trained to tolerate dissent and committed to negotiation. The post-Communist experiences of other Soviet-bloc countries give particular reason for concern here. Their experiences have varied with how open to compromise Old Communist elites and their opponents have been when faced with confrontations from civil society.[4] There have been few Vaclav Havels, genuinely committed to democratic principles and willing to compromise and concede power when challenged "from below."

Might the Cuban-American community abroad be an alternative leadership source? Jorge Mas Canosa, who built up a government-in-exile of sorts and with political ambitions for himself in a post-Castro era, is no exemplar of a democrat. But no other single group or individual matches him in organization, wealth, or political connections outside Cuba—resources he can draw upon in any political contest. Indicative of the antidemocratic tendencies not only of Mas Canosa's CANF but also of other elements within the Cuban-American community, Americas Watch, which monitors human rights violations in Latin America, commissioned a Florida study.[5] If groups out of power are intolerant of basic human rights, there is little reason to believe their tolerance would pick up in power. Therefore, only if more politically open-minded forces within the Cuban-American community gain influence, and if they work with Cubans with more legitimate national political claims, does democratic pluralism stand a good chance.

Democracy also needs an organizational base on which to build. Intermediate-level institutions know best how people think, and they are best-positioned to articulate and defend those sentiments. The organizations created and controlled by Castro might gain autonomy to the point that they take on such a mediating role. By the early 1990s, though, the CDRs and the FMC, in particular, had lost (as noted) much of their earlier vitality and meaning to their respective constituencies; under the circumstances members are unlikely to view them as sufficiently credible to take on this role. The labor confederation, meanwhile, became so controlled at the higher levels, and workers, especially in industry, had taken such a beating with plant closings and efforts to make enterprises internationally competitive, that the established union movement is unlikely to take on the transformatory role its Polish counterpart, for example, did. A "Solidarity" the CTC is not.

In the absence of meaningful intermediate organizations to channel people's concerns, the brewing discontent may prompt turmoil. Angry and unconstrained, the populace, with militia training, may take history into their own hands. And the hard-core of disciples may fight back, defending the government to which they remain committed.

The significance of intermediate organizations for a democratic transition is also well illustrated by the experiences of the European post-Communist governments. The richer organizational life had been under Communist rule, the more successful the transition to democracy: Poland and Hungary at one extreme, Romania at the other. Cuba is closer to being a Romania in this respect, for at the intermediary organizational level civil society in Cuba remains weak.[6]

The absence of organizations with meaning to their constituencies has ramifications not merely for the prospects of democracy but also for the very defense of the revolution's accomplishments. This became apparent during the Special Period when the FMC played no role in defending the withering of women's revolutionary-won gains. The FMC encouraged women, as noted, to make their own clothes, their own soap, their own candles for lighting. These artisan activities were encouraged for survival purposes, but men were not exhorted to do the same. The FMC retreated from its initial role of "liberating" women to advocating activities that made women's work more onerous.

Similarly, no organization addressed the withering of social services, fought for their protection, or spoke to the issue of priorities. If Cubans do not organize, they may all too easily face the same devastating experiences as their former East European comrades and the poor in other Latin American countries following "neoliberal restructuring." Should programs need, for fiscal reasons, to be cut, there are choices to be made. Social programs involve political choices and not merely fiscal resources. Should low-cost programs that benefit large numbers be slashed, or high-cost programs that benefit more privileged and select groups—for example, public health, preventive care programs that target large numbers of low-income groups, or capital-intensive cancer and other treatments that target a select, more privileged constituency? And should costly education programs that train elites or mass education be cut back, if the school budget need be pruned?

The threat that this de facto organizational vacuum poses for the poorest stratum, in the cities and the countryside, and for women and dark-skinned islanders, is particularly great. Any government that tries to restore fiscal order and make the economy more internationally competitive is likely to turn its back on the politically weak and unorganized. The unique "mass"-oriented achievements of the revolution may erode in the process.

Economically, Cuba's prospects rest on much more than stepped-up production and production efficiency. Cuba needs access to markets, ideally under favorable trade conditions. Access to the North American market, given its proximity and the size of its economy, is essential.[7] Access to the U.S. market will, however, involve more than a lifting of the legal barrier to trade, for Cuba by the 1990s was in a poor position to compete for U.S. business. Other Third World countries had decades of experience in industrial export promotion on which to build, and the Caribbean Basin Initiative and the North American Free Trade Agreement (NAFTA) give other countries in the region preferential access to the U.S. market. Because trade within the Soviet bloc had been negotiated rather than based on competitiveness, and because Cuba (as noted) relied on internationally uncompetitive Soviet technology, the island has few products that meet world standards. Its main basis of competition therefore will, for the immediate future, rest on pricing its goods and services low, which will limit both the state's revenue-generating capacity and labor's earning power. Both the government and labor will be "squeezed" in the process, as they have to date.

Economic relations with the United States may also be hampered by lawsuits and the island's hard currency debt. U.S. firms may seek compensation for businesses Castro expropriated in his first years of rule before resuming trade and before reinvesting in Cuba. And foreign banks to which Castro's government incurred debts may insist that new export earnings linked to the lifting of the embargo be used for loan repayments, not imports (for consumption or the expansion of the island's productive capacity).

With the government effectively bankrupt and individuals and enterprises without significant investment capital, economic growth will hinge on attracting foreign capital as well as expanded trade. It also will rest on a legalization of at least contained domestic private economic activity: to make legal the illegal economy and stimulate initiative and productivity lost with Special Period demoralization. Tolerance of at least contained privatization may come to include worker-shareholding schemes, possibly drawing on the Czech and Hungarian examples.[8]

Market reforms are no automatic cure-all for an economic takeoff, and they do not in themselves guarantee that the social gains of the revolution will be preserved.[9] I have shown that the partial market reforms punctuating Cuban history under Castro left fundamental problems unresolved. And the removal of market "fetters" in post-Communist European countries did not give immediate reason for optimism either: they typically left the economy in disarray, while social conditions deteriorated.

Cuba needs to adapt to the "new world order" in a manner that strengthens its economic base, respects democratic principles, and preserves the social gains of the revolution. This is no easy task. But no anti-Communist or anti-Castro sentiment should allow Cuba's health welfare accomplishments, its reduction of rural/urban and class inequities, and the gains of women and dark-skinned islanders to become a matter of history. These are the Cuban revolution's contribution to the art of the possible, and future generations should be allowed to enjoy them.

APPENDIX

TABLES

TABLE 1.1

Role of Trade in the Cuban Economy in Select Years: Main Export as Percentage of Total Exports, Exports as Percentage of GMP, and Manufactures (MFG) as Percentage of Total Exports, and Cuba's Latin American (LA) Ranking on Each Measure

	Main export as % of all exports[j]	LA rank, dependence on one export[g]	Exports as % of GMP[f, i]	LA rank, role of exports in GDP/GMP[e, f]	MFG as % of all exports[j]	LA rank MFG/ export ratio[b]
1950	89.2	—	32	2	—	—
1955	79.6	4	27	4	—	—
1960	79.4	3	23[c]	6	—	—
1965	86.2	2	17	11	.1	13
1970	76.8	2	25	5[d]	.1	—
1975	89.1	2	33	3[d]	.1	—
1980	82.7	1[a]	28	4	5.1	17
1984–85	74.5	2	22	9	1.7	16[i]
1989	73.2	2[b]	20	7	3.4	17[i]

Sources: Susan Eckstein, "How Consequential Are Revolutions? The Latin American Experience," in *Comparative Political Dynamics,* ed. Dankwart Rustow and Kenneth Erickson (New York: HarperCollins, 1991), 326–27, and the references therein; Cuba, Comité Estatal de Estadísticas (CEE), *Anuario Estadístico de Cuba 1989* (Havana: CEE, 1991), 88, 260, 262; James Wilkie, Enrique Ochoa, and David Lorey, *Statistical Abstract of Latin America* 28 (Los Angeles: University of California, Latin American Center, 1990): 570; World Bank, *World Development Report* (New York: Oxford University Press, 1991), 208–9, 230–31, 232–33.

[a] Data for 1980–1982 for all countries except Cuba.

[b] Data for 1988 for all countries except Cuba.

[c] 1961.

[d] Tied with one other country.

[e] Information for seventeen countries for 1950, nineteen countries for 1955, thirteen countries for 1988, and all twenty countries for other years. Countries with information missing for a given year are assumed to have the same ranking as in the proximate year with available data. The higher the country rank, the higher the export/GDP ratio. The Cuban data refer exclusively to the value of commodity exports, whereas the data on the other countries refer also to the value of nonfinancial services.

[f] National product in current GDP or GNP prices for all countries except Cuba. In Cuba, national product calculations are based on GNP estimates for 1950 and 1955, on GMP estimates (gross material product) for 1960 through 1970, and on GSP (gross social product) extimates thereafter, all in current prices. GMP is a conservative estimate of GDP, and GSP, with its double counting, exaggerates the value of the national product as reflected in

TABLE 1.1 (*cont.*)

GDP/GNP. Therefore, Cuba's export/national product ratios are higher than they would be were GDP estimates used in the years when calculations are in GMP, and lower than they would be when calculations are based on GSP figures. Both because Cuba has changed its bases of national product calculation over the years and because Cuba in all years since the revolution used a different bases of calculation than the market economies in the region, Cuban export/national product figures must be viewed as rough estimates. (Export/national product figures based on national material product calculations, referred to in Table 2.1, so exaggerate the role of exports in the economy that I do not use them here.)

 g Insufficient data to rank countries in 1950; information for all twenty countries for all other years.

 h Cuban exports of cooking oil, butter, chemical products, machinery, transportation material, and other manufactures (but excluding industrial sugar processing); data defined as "manufactures" for all other countries.

 i Data for all countries except Haiti and the Dominican Republic.

 j The role of sugar in exports and the role of exports in the economy, in turn, are affected by the subsidized price the Soviet Union paid Cuba in most years.

TABLE 2.1
Cuban Gross Domestic Product and Gross Domestic Product Per Capita in Select Years: Value in 1980 Constant U.S. Dollars and Ranking among Latin American Countries

	GDP (U.S.$) millions[a]	LA rank GDP	GDP per capita[a]	LA GDP per capita rank
1955	$ 5,555	9	$ 871	10
1960	6,235	8	887	6
1965	7,190	8	921	10
1970	7,414	8	867	12
1975	10,810	8	1,158	8
1980	14,159	8	1,455	9
1985	17,113	—	1,686	—
1989[b]	17,361	—	1,641	—
1991[b]	14,538	—	1,278	—

Sources: Eckstein, "How Consequential Are Revolutions? The Latin American Experience," 316–17, and the references therein; James Wilkie and David Lorey, *Statistical Abstract of Latin America* 25 (Los Angeles: University of California, Latin American Center, 1987): 748; Economist Intelligence Unit (EIU), *Cuba Country Profile 1991–92:* 12, *Cuba Country Profile 1992–93:* 12, *Cuba Country Report* no. 4 (1990): 3, and *Cuba Country Report* no. 4 (1991): 3; Carmelo Mesa-Lago and Jorge Pérez-López, "Cuban Economic Growth in Current and Constant Prices, 1975–88: A Puzzle on the Foreign Trade Component of the Material Product System," in James Wilkie and Carlos Alberto Contreras (eds.), *Statistical Abstract of Latin America* 29, part 1 (Los Angeles: University of California, Latin American Center Publications, 1991): 602. Claes Brundenius, *Revolutionary Cuba: The Challenge of Economic Growth with Equity* (Boulder, Colo.: Westview, 1984), 39.

TABLE 2.1(*cont.*)

[a] Constant 1981 pesos converted to dollars at the 1981 year-end official exchange rate. The official exchange rate does not reflect the real value of the peso, even by the government's own admission (in 1993). Nonetheless, dollar figures are used for cross-national purposes. Calculations also are affected by changes in bases of Cuban national product calculations over the years. For the 1985–91 period I rely on conversions of GSP (from EIU sources) to net material product estimates (by Mesa-Lago and Pérez-López, "Cuban Economic Growth in Current and Constant Prices," and Mesa-Lago personal communication), in dollars based on the official peso-dollar exchange rate. For 1980 and earlier I rely on Brundenius' (in *Revolutionary Cuba*) GDP estimates. GSP estimates are larger than GDP estimates, while net material product (and gross material product) estimates are lower than GDP estimates (since they exclude the value of non-productive services). Because of these methodological problems the figures in the Table should be regarded as rough estimates.

[b] Estimate.

TABLE 2.2
Cuban Female Participation in the Labor Force

	Percent of civilian labor force	Percent of unemployed	Female unemployment rate[c]	Total unemployment rate[d]	Total activity rate[a]
1956	13	12	—	—	—
1960	13	35	32	12	—
1968	16	—	—	4[b]	—
1970	18	18	1	1	25
1974	23	58	10	4	31
1980	31	59	8	4	48
1985	37	—	—	—	—
1988–90	39	—	—	6	43

Sources: Brundenius, *Revolutionary Cuba*, 73; Carmelo Mesa-Lago, *The Economy of Socialist Cuba: A Two-Decade Appraisal* (Albuquerque: University of New Mexico Press, 1981), 111, 118, 123; CEE, *Anuario Estadístico de Cuba 1989*, 117; *Granma International*, 5 May 1991: 3; EIU, *Cuba Country Report* no. 3 (1991): 3, and no. 4 (1991): 3, and *Cuba Country Profile 1991–92*, 10, 36–38; World Bank, *World Development Report* (1991): 244–45, 250–51.

[a] Occupied labor force as a percent of available labor force; available labor force equals population of working age (17 to 54) minus full-time students.

[b] Estimated by Carmelo Mesa-Lago.

[c] Female unemployment as a percent of female participation in the labor force.

[d] Combined male and female rate.

TABLE 2.3

Cumulative Outstanding Cuban Western Debt: Amount and Amount Relative to FOB Value of Foreign Exchange–Generating Exports, and Cuba's Latin American (LA) Ranking on Both Measures

	Amount (millions $US)[a]	LA rank, amount[d]	Debt as % exports	LA rank, debt/export ratio[c, d]
1970	291.0	9	—	—
1975	1,338.0	7	117	11
1980	4,536.8	9	273	5
1985	3,566.4[b]	15	484	3
1989	7,300.0	11	649	2

Sources: Eckstein, "How Consequential Are Revolutions? The Latin American Experience," 330–31, and the references therein; EIU, *Cuba Quarterly Economic Review* no. 3 (1991): 3, no. 4 (1991), and no. 2 (1992): 3; and EIU, *Cuba Country Profile 1991–92*: 10; World Bank, *World Development Report* (1991), 244–45, 250–51, 264–65; Carmelo Mesa-Lago, "The Economic Effects on Cuba of the Downfall of Socialism in the USSR and Eastern Europe," in *Cuba After the Cold War*, ed. Mesa-Lago (Pittsburgh: University of Pittsburgh Press, 1993), Table 5.5.

[a] Disbursed hard currency public debt. Cuba's Soviet and Soviet-bloc debt (which, according to Western sources, accounted in 1989 for 71 and 79 percent, respectively, of the island's total debt) are excluded. The real value of the non-hard currency debt deteriorated after 1989, with the fall in the value of the ruble.

[b] Preliminary.

[c] Total disbursed debt data for all countries in 1980, 1985 and 1989, and for most countries in 1970 and 1975. The data for countries other than Cuba in 1975 refer only to disbursed medium and long-term debt, not to short-term debt.

[d] The higher the ranking, the larger the debt or the worse the debt/export ratio.

TABLE 3.1

Fiscal Revenue and Expenditures in the 1980s (in millions of pesos)

	1981	1982	1983	1984	1985	1986	1987	1988	1989
Budget									
Revenue	—	—	11,128	11,854	12,294	11,699	11,272	11,386	11,904
Expenditure	—	—	11,394	11,930	12,547	11,887	11,881	12,532	13,528
Balance	—	—	−266	−76	−253	−188	−609	−1,146	−1,624
Hard currency									
balance of payments									
(commodity trade)									
Exports[a] (FOB)	1,406	1,536	1,234	1,136	1,171	907	965	1,113[c]	950[d]
Imports (FOB)	1,121	734	793	1,063	1,177	1,071	1,024	1,048[c]	960[d]
Trade balance	285	802	441	73	−6	−164	−59	65[c]	−10[d]
Hard currency									
tourist receipts	44	51	59	76	87	98	112	—	250[b]
Hard currency									
current-account									
balance	—	—	—	−212	−506	−1,961	−1,318	−380[d]	−600
Hard currency									
commodity earnings									
Sugar	866	648	263	250	171	210	223	—	—
Oil reexport	151	262	498	484	527	249	286	—	—

Sources: EIU, *Cuba Annual Supplement(s)* or *Cuban Country Profile(s) 1987–88*: 21, 24, 25; *1988–89*: 21, 22; *1991–92*: 30; and *1992–93*: 26; EIU, *Cuba Quarterly Economic Review* no. 4 (1988): 14, no. 2 (1989): 2, no. 4 (1989): 2, no. 2 (1990): 3, and no. 2 (1992): 3; Carmelo Mesa-Lago, "Cuba's Economic Counter Reform (*Rectificación*): Causes, Policies, and Effects," in *Cuba After Thirty Years: Rectification and the Revolution*, ed. Richard Gillespie (London: Frank Cass, 1990), table 1; María Dolores Espino, "International Tourism in Cuba: An Economic Development Strategy?" (Paper delivered at the Association for the Study of the Cuban Economy, Florida International University, Miami, August 1991), table 12.

[a] Includes reexports.

[b] 1990 $US.

[c] Preliminary.

[d] Estimate.

TABLE 4.1

Cuban Primary and Secondary School Pupil/Teacher Ratios and the Percentage of the Relevant Age Groups Enrolled in the Two Education Levels, and Cuba's Latin American (LA) Rankings in Select Years

	Pupil/teacher ratio				Enrollment ratio			
	Primary	LA rank[b, c]	Secondary	LA rank[b, f]	Primary	LA rank[b]	Secondary	LA rank[b]
1960	36[a]	13	19	17[d]	109[a]	2[d]	14	8
1965	29	5[d]	16	11[e]	121	2	23	8
1970	25	2	12	3	—	—	—	—
1975	22	2[d]	13	3	126	1	35	9[d]
1980	17	—	13	—	112	6[d]	71	1
1985	14	—	12	—	—	—	75[g]	1
1988	12	1	11	—	104[i]	9[h]	—	—

Sources: World Bank, *World Development Report* (1988), 280–81; (1989), 232; (1990), 244; and (1992), 286.

[a] Public schools only.

[b] The higher the rank, the better the ratio.

[c] Data for nineteen countries in 1960 and 1975, for sixteen countries in 1988, and for all twenty countries in other years where data are sufficient for ranking.

[d] Tied with one other country.

[e] Tied with three other countries.

[f] Data for twenty countries in 1975, for nineteen countries in 1965, for 18 countries in 1970, and for seventeen countries in 1975; insufficient country data to rank in other years.

[g] 1984.

[h] Tied with two other countries.

[i] Cuba's primary education enrollment rate in 1990 was 103.

TABLE 5.1

Cuban Medical Delivery System and Cuba's Latin American
(LA) Ranking in Select Years

	Number	LA Ranking
Population per physician[a]		
1958	1,081	—
1960	1,038[d]	3
1965	1,252	—
1970	1,390	4
1974	1,122	4
1980	638	3
1984	524[c]	2
1989	303	—
Population per nursing population[b]		
1958	1,353[d]	—
1960	1,199[d]	5
1965	810	—
1970	724	2
1974	480	3
1980	358	2
1984	377	1[e]
1989	163	—
Population per hospital bed		
1958	237	—
1960	216	3
1965	202	—
1970	213	3
1975	218	—
1980	219	—
1985	158	—
1989	136	—

Sources: World Bank, *World Development Report* (1978), 108–109; (1979), 168–69; (1983), 194–95; (1990), 232–33; World Bank, *World Tables* (Baltimore: Johns Hopkins University Press, 1976), 518–21; Brundenius, *Revolutionary Cuba*, 39, 101; Julie Feinsilver, "Cuba as a 'World Medical Power': The Politics of Symbolism," *Latin American Research Review* 24, no. 2 (1989), 8; CEE, *Anuario Estadístico de Cuba 1989*, 353, 481.

[a] Data for eighteen countries for 1974, and for twenty countries for 1960, 1970, 1980, and 1984. The two countries lacking 1974 information were assumed to have the same ranking as in the closest year with information.

[b] Data for sixteen countries for 1960, for twenty countries for 1970, for fifteen countries for 1974, for eighteen countries for 1980, and for seventeen countries for 1984. All countries with figures missing for a given year are assumed to have the same ranking as in the closest year with information.

[c] Approximate.

[d] Estimate.

[e] No data for Uruguay, Venezuela, and Peru.

TABLE 5.2
Cuban Nutrition, Life Expectancy and Infant Mortality, and
Cuba's Latin American (LA) Rankings in Select Years

	Total	LA ranking[a]
Daily per capita caloric supply[b]		
1951–57	2,740	—
1961–65	2,430	6
1970	2,688	4
1975	2,726	4
1980	2,762	4
1983–85	3,094	3
1988–89	3,103	3
1993 (April)[e]	2,000	—
Daily per capita protein supply (total grams per day)[b]		
1961	62.8	7
1965	62.5	8
1970	63.1	9
1975	64.4	9
1980	65.7	10
1983–85	76.2	5
Life expectancy		
1950–55	59	3
1960	64	3
1965	67	2
1970	70	1
1975	71	1
1980	74	1
1985	77	1
1990	75	1
1992	76	—
Infant mortality (deaths per 1,000 live births in first year of life)[d]		
1945–49	39	1
1955–59	32	1
1960	35	1
1965	38	1
1970	36	3
1975	27	2
1980	20	1
1985	16	1
1990	11	1
1992	10	—

TABLE 5.2 (*cont.*)

Sources: Eckstein, "How Consequential Are Revolutions?" 343–43, and the references therein; James Wilkie and Enrique Ochoa, *Statistical Abstract of Latin America* 27 (Los Angeles, University of California, Latin American Center, 1989), 158; CEE, *Anuario Estadístico de Cuba 1990* (Havana: CEE, 1992), World Bank, *World Development Report* (1990), 178–79; United Nations Development Programme, *Human Development Report 1991* (New York: Oxford University Press, 1991), 126–27; Population Reference Bureau (PRB), *1991 World Population Data Sheet* (Washington, D.C.: PRB, April 1991), unnumbered page; EIU, *Cuba Country Report* no. 2 (1991), 16; "Cuba Estadísticas Sociales Seleccionadas 1989–1992" (Havana: mimeo, 1993).

[a] The higher the rank, the better the situation.

[b] Information for all twenty countries, except 1983–85 for which data are missing for El Salvador and Nicaragua.

[c] Tied in rank with one other country.

[d] Information for nineteen countries for 1945–49, for eighteen countries for 1955–59, 1965, and 1970, and for twenty countries for all other years.

[e] Estimate (personal interview, Havana 1993).

TABLE 5.3
Cuban Crude Birth Rate (CBR) and Total Fertility Rates
(TFR) and Cuba's Latin American (LA) Rankings in
Select Years

	CBR (per 1,000)		TFR	
	Cuban	LA rank[a]	Cuban	LA rank[a]
Year				
1955	27	—	3.76[c]	—
1960	30	3	4.67[d]	3
1965	34	4	4.29[e]	3
1970	28	3	3.70	3[b]
1975	21	1[b]	2.70	1
1980	14	1	1.58	1
1985	17	1	2.0	1
1990	15	1	1.7	1

Sources: Sergio Díaz Briquéts and Lisandro Pérez, "Fertility Decline in Cuba: A Socioeconomic Interpretation," *Population and Development Review* 8 (September 1982), 513; Ministerio de Salud Pública (MINSAP), *Informe Anual* (Havana: MINSAP, 1983), 29; World Bank, *World Development Report* (1987), 256–57; United Nations Population Fund (UNPF), *The State of the World Population 1990* (New York: UNPF, 1991), 36.

[a] The higher the rank, the lower the birth rate.
[b] Tied with one other country.
[c] 1955–1960.
[d] 1960–65.
[e] 1965–70.

TABLE 5.4

Cuban Population by Age Group and Cuba's Latin American (LA)
Ranking in Select Years

	Age					
	0–14		15–64		65+	
	Percent	LA rank[a]	Percent	LA rank[a]	Percent	LA rank[a]
1960	36	18	61	3	4	5
1970	38	18	57	4	6	3
1981	30	18	59	5	11	1
1989	23	20	68	1	8	3

Sources: World Bank, World Tables (1980), 438, 440, and World Tables
(1984), 50–97; Delegación Cubana Conferencia Internacional de Población
(DCCIP), Cuba y su Población (Havana: DCCIP, 1984), 16; MINSAP, Informe Anual (1989), 19; PRB, 1991 World Population Data Sheet, unnumbered page.

[a] The higher the rank, the larger the percentage of the population in a given
age bracket.

TABLE 5.5

Social Security Income and Expenditures in Select Years (in millions of pesos)

	1962	1965	1974	1980	1985	1989
Income[a]	332.4	344.5	422.7	485.1	713.9	797.1
Expenditures[b]	151.9	249.8	553.4	709.3	965.1	1282.6
Balance	170.5	94.7	−130.7	−224.2	−251.2	−485.5
Balance as percentage of income	53.0	28.0	−31.0	−46.0	−35.0	−61.0
Pensions as percentage of expenditures[c]	—	—	75.0	76.0	79.0	81.0

Sources: Carmelo Mesa-Lago, El Desarrollo de la Seguridad Social en America Latina
(Santiago, Chile: CEPAL/Naciones Unidas, 1985), 294; CEE, Anuario Estadístico de Cuba
1989, 113, 128; "Cuba Estadísticas Sociales Seleccionadas 1989–1992."

[a] Excludes income from the health system and income from the private sector.

[b] Includes pension and temporary loan expenditures (except of the armed forces and
social assistance program); excludes health and administration expenses.

[c] Includes old age, death, and invalid pensions.

TABLE 6.1

Urbanization in Cuba in Select Years and Cuba's Latin American (LA) Urban Rankings

	Cuba (percent)	LA urban ranking
Percentage of cities with population over 20,000		
1950	33	4
1960	39	5
1970	43	6
1980	48	6
Percentage of cities with population over 100,000		
1950	20	4
1960	25	8
1970	31	7
1980	33	8
1989	20	—
Largest city's share of total national population		
1950	20	4
1960	22	5
1970	20	7
1984–85	20	7[a]
1989	20	—

Sources: Wilkie and Ochoa, *Statistical Abstract of Latin America* 27 (1989): 105; *Economic Bulletin of Latin America* 18, nos. 1 and 2 (1973), 108–109; CEE, *Anuario Estadístico de Cuba 1989*, 57, 58.

[a] Tied in rank with one other country.

TABLE 6.2
Extent of Urban Bias in Elementary Education

	Student/faculty ratio		Percent of students with scholarships		Graduates as a percentage of matriculated	
	In urban areas	In rural areas	In urban areas	In rural areas	In urban areas	In rural areas
1965–66	26	34	4	1	8	3
1970–71	24	27	5	3	6	4
1975–76	22	21	2	3	15	10
1980–81	18	16	3	4	16	14
1985–86	15	13	2	5	19	17
1989–90	14	11	2	4	18	16

Sources: CEE, Anuario Estadístico de Cuba 1987 (Havana: CEE, 1988), 529, 531, and Anuario Estadístico de Cuba 1989, 311–15, 317.

TABLE 6.3
Availability and Usage of Medical Facilities: Ratio of
Rural to Urban[a]

	hospital beds	hospital admissions	outpatient consultations
1958	1:571	—	—
1965	1:10	1:12	1.3
1970	1:18	1:16	1:4
1975	1:15	1:13	1:4
1980	1:18	1:18	1:5
1985	1:20	1:15	1:5
1989	1:17	1:17	1:4

Sources: CEE, Anuario Estadístico de Cuba 1987, 581–82, 584–85, 588, and CEE, Anuario Estadístico de Cuba 1989, 358–59, 365.

[a] Ratios of rural hospital admissions, beds, and hospital outpatient consultations to urban general hospital and surgical clinic admissions, beds, and outpatient consultations.

TABLE 8.1

Summary of Economic and Social Changes Under Castro (through 1989) for which Both Comparative and Historical Data Were Available

	Within Cuba	Change in Latin American rank
Gross national product	+	+
Per capita national product	+	+
Decline in monoproduct export dependence	+	−
Decline in export's importance to national product	+	+
Manufacturing exports as percent of total exports	+	−
Total hard currency debt	−	+
Debt/export ratio	−	−
Secondary school enrollment ratio	+	+
Elementary school student/faculty ratio	+	+
Secondary school student/faculty ratio	+	+
Population per physician	+	+
Population per nursing population	+	+
Population per hospital bed	+	=
Daily per capita caloric supply	+	+
Daily per capita protein supply	+	+
Life expectancy	+	+
Infant mortality	+	=
Total fertility rate	+	+
Decline in single-city concentration	=	+

+ signifies improvement.
− signifies deterioration.
= signifies no change.

NOTES

PREFACE

1. Some standard early works on totalitarianism include Carl Friedrich, ed., *Totalitarianism* (Cambridge: Harvard University Press, 1954), and Friedrich and Zbigniew Brzezinski, *Totalitarian Dictatorship and Autocracy* (Cambridge: Harvard University Press, 1956); and Adam Ulam, *The New Face of Soviet Totalitarianism* (Cambridge: Harvard University Press, 1963). For a discussion of contrasts between totalitarian and authoritarian regimes, see Juan Linz, "Totalitarian and Authoritarian Regimes," in *Handbook of Political Science*, vol. 3, *Macropolitical Theory*, ed. Fred Greenstein and Nelson Polsby (Reading, Mass.: Addison-Wesley, 1975), 175–412.

2. The most important exposition of the interest-group approach is H. Gordon Skilling and Franklyn Griffiths, eds., *Interest Groups in Soviet Politics* (Princeton: Princeton University Press, 1964). See also J. J. Schwartz and William Keech, "Group Influence in the Policy Process in the Soviet Union," *American Political Science Review* 62, no. 2 (March 1968): 840–51. For criticism of the interest-group approach see William Odom, "A Dissenting View of the Group Approach to Soviet Politics," *World Politics* 28, no. 4 (July 1976): 542–67, and the special issue of *Studies in Comparative Communism* 8, no. 3 (August 1975). In reference to Cuba see William LeoGrande, "A Bureaucratic Approach to Civil-Military Relations in Communist Political Systems: The Case of Cuba," in *Civil-Military Relations in Communist Systems*, ed. Dale Herspring and Ivan Volgyes (Boulder, Colo.: Westview, 1978), 201–18.

3. See the essays in Mark Field, ed., *Social Consequences of Modernization in Communist Societies* (Baltimore: Johns Hopkins University Press, 1976). Although the East European and Soviet literature focused primarily on economic modernization, Jorge Domínguez in *Cuba: Order and Revolution* (Cambridge: Belknap Press of Harvard University Press, 1978) highlighted modernizing, institutional differentiating tendencies in the political domain in Cuba. He does not belittle the role of politics, as "convergence school" writings about technical developments tend to do.

4. On "modes of production," see Colin Henfrey, "Dependency, Modes of Production, and the Class Analysis of Latin America," *Latin American Perspectives* 8, nos. 3–4 (Summer/Fall 1981): 17–54; with specific reference to Cuba, see Arthur MacEwan, *Revolution and Economic Development in Cuba* (London: Macmillan, 1981).

5. On ideal-types see Max Weber, *Economy and Society*, ed. Guenther Roth and Claus Wittich (Berkeley: University of California Press, 1978). For my analytic purposes socialism is primarily associated with state ownership and control of the economy and capitalism primarily with private ownership and market coordination of economic activity. In chapter 4 I discuss the partial "retreat" to precapitalist strategies, associated with nonmechanized economic activity. Empir-

ically, contemporary societies combine a mixture of "ideal-type" features, and Cuba, as I will demonstrate, is no exception.

6. Immanuel Wallerstein, *The Modern World System* (New York: Academic Press, 1974), and *The Capitalist World-Economy* (Cambridge: Cambridge University Press, 1979).

7. Ivan Szeleny, "Social Inequalities in State Socialist Redistributive Economies: Dilemmas for Social Policy in Contemporary Socialist Societies of Eastern Europe," *International Journal of Comparative Sociology* 19, nos. 1–2 (1978): 63–87; Zsuzsa Ferge, *A Society in the Making: Hungarian Social and Societal Policy, 1945–1975* (White Plains, N.Y.: M. E. Sharpe, 1979); David Stark, "Rethinking Internal Labor Markets: New Insights from a Comparative Perspective," *American Sociological Review* 51 (1986): 492–504. See also Stark and Victor Nee, "Toward an Institutional Analysis of State Socialism," 1–32, in *Remaking the Economic Institutions of Socialism: China and Eastern Europe*, ed. Nee and Stark (Stanford, Calif.: Stanford University Press, 1989), for a brief but excellent discussion of the "institutionalist" perspective and how it contrasts with other thinking about socialism.

8. Carmelo Mesa-Lago, "Availability and Reliability of Statistics in Socialist Cuba," *Latin American Research Review* 4, no. 1 (Winter 1969): 53–91, and no. 2 (Summer 1969): 47–81. For a debate on Cuba's economic performance see Claes Brundenius and Andrew Zimbalist, "Recent Studies on Cuban Economic Growth: A Review," *Comparative Economic Studies* 27, no. 1 (Spring 1985): 21–45, and "Cuban Economic Growth One More Time: A Response to 'Imbroglios,'" *Comparative Economic Studies* 27, no. 3 (Fall 1985): 115–31, on the one hand, and Mesa-Lago and Jorge Pérez-López, "Imbroglios on the Cuban Economy: A Reply to Brundenius and Zimbalist," *Comparative Economic Studies* 27, no. 1 (Spring 1985): 21–45, and "The Endless Cuban Economy Saga: A Terminal Rebuttal," *Comparative Economic Studies* 27, no. 4 (Winter 1985): 67–82, on the other.

9. Andrés Oppenheimer, in *Castro's Final Hour* (New York: Simon and Schuster, 1992), 301–2, reports a Cuban joke that is telling. The joke concerns why the traditional Cuban staple, pork, is hard to come by. The farm manager, fearing Fidel will be disappointed by the lower-than-expected production, writes in his report that the pig delivered seven piglets, even though it delivered only six. His supervisor, the regional farm director, changes the figure to eight piglets. His boss, the national farm director, raises the number to nine. His boss, the minister of agriculture, the man who has to submit the report personally to Castro, changes the figure to ten piglets. "Great! Fantastic!" says Fidel upon seeing his prediction come true. "We'll use 60 percent of the pigs for export, and 40 percent for domestic consumption."

10. See Susan Eckstein, "Commentary: Bases of Disagreements about Cuban Economic Performance: A Sociological Perspective," in *Cuban Studies Since the Revolution*, ed. Damian Fernández (Gainesville: University Press of Florida, 1992). I discuss how and why factors other than deficient data account for differing interpretations of Cuba's economic performance. By contrast, Jorge Pérez-López, in his excellent review of the literature contained in "Thinking About the Cuban Economy in the 1990s," in the same volume, implies that differences in

assessments are attributable mainly to data deficiencies. Because data do not "speak for themselves," my work draws on empirical material of authors with whom I take issue analytically.

CHAPTER ONE
THE LIMITS AND POSSIBILITIES OF SOCIALISM

1. The contextual factors discussed in this section are not necessarily the only ones shaping policy options and outcomes but, as I argue, there are analytically grounded reasons why these are likely to be especially consequential.

2. Jean Stubbs, *Cuba: The Test of Time* (London: Latin American Bureau, 1989), 82, 87.

3. For discussions of the "Sovietization of Cuba" and Cuban-Soviet relations see, above all, Carmelo Mesa-Lago, *Cuba in the 1970s* (Albuquerque: University of New Mexico Press, 1974); Leon Goure and Julian Weinkle, "Soviet-Cuban Relations: The Growing Integration," in *Cuba, Castro and Revolution*, ed. Jaime Suchlicki (Coral Gables, Fla.: University of Miami Press, 1972); Mesa-Lago and Fernando Gil, "Soviet Economic Relations with Cuba," in *The USSR and Latin America: A Developing Relationship*, ed. Eusebio Mujal-Leon (Winchester, Mass.: Unwin Hyman, 1989), 183–232; William LeoGrande, "Cuban Dependency: A Comparison of Pre-Revolutionary and Post-Revolutionary International Economic Relations," *Cuban Studies/Estudios Cubanos* 9, no. 2 (July 1979): 1–28; José Luis Rodríguez, "Las relaciones económicas Cuba-URSS: 1960–1985," *Temas de Economía Mundial* 17 (1986): 9–33; Lawrence Theriot and Jenelle Matheson, "Soviet Economic Relations with Non-European CMEA: Cuba, Vietnam and Mongolia," in Joint Economic Commission of the U.S. Congress, *Soviet Economy in a Time of Change* (Washington, D.C.: GPO, 1979), 551–81.

4. Wayne Smith, *The Closest of Enemies* (New York: W. W. Norton, 1987).

5. For a theoretical discussion of this issue with respect to capitalist countries see James O'Connor, *The Origins of Socialism in Cuba* (Ithaca: Cornell University Press, 1970).

6. Karl Marx's discussion between leadership and social structure, in "The Eighteenth Brumaire of Luis Bonaparte," in *Marx and Engels: Basic Writings on Politics and Philosophy*, ed. Lewis Feuer (Garden City, N.Y.: Doubleday, 1959), 318–48, speaks to this point.

7. János Kornai, "Resource-Constrained versus Demand-Constrained Systems," *Economietrica* (July 1979): 801–19, and Kornai, "'Hard' and 'Soft' Budget Constraint," *Acta Oeconomica* 25 (1980): 231–46, and Kornai, "The Soft Budget Constraint," *Kylos* 39 (1986): 3–30.

8. See David Stark and Victor Nee, "Toward an Institutional Analysis of State Socialism," and other essays in *Remaking the Economic Institutions of Socialism: China and Eastern Europe*, ed. Nee and Stark (Stanford, Calif.: Stanford University Press, 1989).

9. Kornai, "The Soft Budget Constraint," 13–20.

10. Milovan Djilas, *The New Class* (New York: Praeger, 1957).

11. Robert Michels' classic sociological study *Political Parties: A Sociological Study of the Oligarchical Tendencies of Modern Democracy*, trans. Eden and

Cedar Paul (New York: Free Press, 1962), speaks to this point. Michels argued that organizational dynamics induce oligarchy even in organizations committed to socialist and egalitarian principles.

12. On the professionalization and "upgrading" of the Cuban labor force and its purported ramifications, see Frank Fitzgerald, "Cuba's New Professionals," in *Transformation and Struggle: Cuba Faces the 1990s*, ed. Sandor Halebsky and John Kirk (New York: Praeger, 1990), 189–204.

13. For excellent discussions of forms of resistance see James Scott, *Weapons of the Weak: Everyday Forms of Peasant Resistance* (New Haven: Yale University Press, 1986), and Scott, "Everyday Forms of Peasant Resistance," in *Everyday Forms of Peasant Resistance*, ed. Forrest Colburn (Armonk, N.Y.: M. E. Sharpe, 1989), 3–33.

14. On the impact of such contextual factors on defiance, see Susan Eckstein, "Power and Popular Protest in Latin America," in *Power and Popular Protest: Latin American Social Movements*, ed. Eckstein (Berkeley: University of California Press, 1989), 14.

15. Scott, "Everyday Forms of Peasant Resistance."

16. Emile Durkheim, *Division of Labor in Society* (Glencoe, Ill.: Free Press, 1947).

17. Alex Inkeles, "The Totalitarian Mystique: Some Impressions of the Dynamics of Totalitarian Society," in *Totalitarianism*, ed. Carl Friedrich (Cambridge: Harvard University Press, 1954).

18. Scott, *Weapons of the Weak*.

19. Juan Linz, "Totalitarian and Authoritarian Regimes," in *Handbook of Political Science*, vol. 3, *Macropolitical Theory*, ed. Fred Greenstein and Nelson Polsby (Reading, Mass.: Addison-Wesley, 1975), 175–412.

20. Arthur MacEwan, *Revolution and Economic Development in Cuba* (London: Macmillan, 1981), 25.

21. O'Connor, *The Origins of Socialism in Cuba*, 1.

22. Ibid., 54.

23. The Ortodoxo Party advocated honest government and socioeconomic reforms. It had a largely middle-class constituency.

24. Fidel Castro, *History Will Absolve Me* (New York: Lyle Stuart, 1961), 19.

25. Ibid., 21, 68.

26. Peasants have played a critical role in most twentieth-century revolutionary movements, although the peasant segment critical to the movements has not always been the same and scholars are not in agreement on which types of agriculturalists have been of greatest consequence to modern revolutions. On the role of peasants in modern revolutions, see Barrington Moore, *Social Origin of Dictatorship and Democracy* (Boston: Beacon Press, 1966); Eric Wolf, *Peasant Wars in the Twentieth Century* (New York: Harper and Row, 1969); Jeffery Paige, *Agrarian Revolution: Social Movements and Export Agriculture in the Underdeveloped World* (New York: Free Press, 1975); Theda Skocpol, *States and Revolution: A Comparative Analysis of France, Russia, and China* (New York: Cambridge University Press, 1979); Timothy Wickham-Crowley, "Winners, Losers, and Also-Rans: Toward a Comparative Sociology of Latin American Guerrilla Movements," in *Power and Popular Protest*, ed. Eckstein, 132–81.

27. Maurice Zeitlin, *Revolutionary Politics and the Cuban Working Class* (New York: Harper Torchbooks, 1970).

28. Prerevolutionary rural Cuba included people who combined independent farming with wage work. See Brian Pollitt, "Some Problems of Enumerating the Peasantry in Cuba," *Journal of Peasant Studies* 5, no. 2 (January 1977).

29. Georgie Anne Geyer, *Guerrilla Prince: The Untold Story of Fidel Castro* (Boston: Little, Brown, 1991), 205.

30. On the prerevolutionary bourgeoisie see Robin Blackburn, "Prologue to the Cuban Revolution," *New Left Review* 21 (October 1963): 52–91.

31. Lee Lockwood, *Castro's Cuba, Cuba's Fidel* (New York: Vintage, 1969).

32. MacEwan, *Revolution and Economic Development in Cuba*, 20.

33. See O'Connor, *The Origins of Socialism in Cuba*, 12–36, for a discussion of prerevolutionary investment patterns. The nineteen Latin American countries with which I compare Cuba in the text and tables of this book are Argentina, Bolivia, Brazil, Chile, Colombia, Costa Rica, the Dominican Republic, Ecuador, El Salvador, Guatemala, Haiti, Honduras, Mexico, Nicaragua, Panama, Paraguay, Peru, Uruguay, and Venezuela. Small island economies and the English-speaking countries in Latin America are excluded.

34. Blackburn, "Prologue to the Cuban Revolution."

35. MacEwan, *Revolution and Economic Development in Cuba*, 17.

36. On prerevolutionary rural conditions, see Lowrey Nelson, *Rural Cuba* (Minneapolis: University of Minnesota Press, 1950); International Bank for Reconstruction and Development (IBRD), *Report on Cuba* (Washington, D.C.: IBRD, 1951); Wyatt, MacGaffey and Clifford Barnett, *Twentieth-Century Cuba: The Background of the Castro Revolution* (Garden City, N.Y.: Doubleday Anchor, 1965).

37. World Bank, *Land Reform in Latin America: Bolivia, Chile, Mexico, Peru, and Venezuela*, Staff Working Paper no. 275 (Washington, D.C.: World Bank, 1978), 2.

38. Data for the prerevolutionary period through the 1960s are believed to underestimate infant mortality owing to inadequate registration of deaths. See Sarah Santana, "Some Thoughts on Vital Statistics and Health in Cuba," in *Cuban Political Economy: Controversies in Cubanology*, ed. Andrew Zimbalist (Boulder, Colo.: Westview, 1988). In comparing Cuban with other Latin American statistics, one must keep in mind that underreporting undoubtedly was a problem in other countries at the time as well.

39. Blackburn, "Prologue to the Cuban Revolution." Employment in the sugar sector affected income-earning opportunities in other sectors as well, for the income of sugar workers stimulated demand for goods and services.

40. Zeitlin, *Revolutionary Politics and the Cuban Working Class*.

41. Geyer, *Guerrilla Prince*, 6.

42. Ibid.

43. On Weber's discussion of charisma, see *Max Weber: On Charisma and Institution Building*, ed. S. N. Eisenstadt (Chicago: University of Chicago Press, 1968).

44. There is a tendency of critics of Castro's autocratic, personalistic rule to not fully appreciate the dynamics of charismatic governance and the difficulties of

its routinization; such a lack of appreciation does not deny the personal character-
istics they ascribe to Castro. Castro's personality, indeed, made him more suited
for charismatic rule than for multiparty politics. He has been described as a mega-
lomaniac. For critical psychological or partially psychological interpretations of
Fidel's tendency to dominate "everyone and everything," see Robert Quirk, *Fidel
Castro: The Full Story of His Rise to Power, His Regime, His Allies, and His
Adversaries* (New York: W. W. Norton, 1993); Geyer, *Guerrilla Prince*; and
Andrés Oppenheimer, *Castro's Final Hour* (New York: Simon and Schuster,
1992); with specific reference to the economy see Edward González, *Cuba Under
Castro: The Limits of Charisma* (Boston: Houghton Mifflin, 1974).

To Weber such meddling would be expected, by definition, of a charismatic
leader. Prerequisites of charismatic rule explain but do not excuse Castro's all-
encompassing leadership style. In turn, the intensity of commitment associated
with charismatic rule may help explain why Cubans opposed to Castro frequently
reacted with such intensity as well. Weber never explored the relationship between charisma and nonbelievers.

45. Eisenstadt, *Max Weber*, 51.

46. Geyer, *Guerrilla Prince*, 295.

47. Herbert Mathews, *Fidel Castro* (New York: Simon and Schuster, 1970),
235.

48. Castro, "On the Question of Revolutionary Charisma," in *Cuba in Revolution*, ed. Rolando Bonachea and Nelson Valdés (Garden City, N.Y.: Doubleday, 1972), 169–70.

49. On early political developments see Jorge Domínguez, *Cuba: Order and
Revolution* (Cambridge: Belknap Press of Harvard University Press, 1978); Mathews, *Fidel Castro*; Theodore Draper, *Castroism: Theory and Practice* (New York:
Praeger, 1965); Carollee Bengelsdorf, "Between Vision and Reality: Democracy
in Socialist Theory and Practice" (Ph.D. diss., Massachusetts Institute of Technology, 1985); Maurice Halperin, *The Rise and Decline of Castro* (Berkeley: University of California Press, 1972); and González, *Cuba Under Castro*; as well as the
references contained in these works.

50. Conversation with Jorge Domínguez. As a proportion of the population
eligible for membership (on the basis of age), Party-per-population figures would
be higher. The Cuban political scientists Haroldo Dilla Alfonso, Gerardo
González, and Ana Vincentelli, in "Cuba's Local Governments: An Experience
Beyond the Paradigms," *Cuban Studies/Estudios Cubanos* 22 (1992): 151–70,
estimate that about 15 percent of the population with electoral rights belonged to
the Party around 1989. According to *Granma Weekly Review*, 5 May 1991: 12,
the Party included 600,000 members and candidates, with about the same number in the UJC, the Party's youth division; the two organs of the Party would
accordingly involve about 9 percent of the population.

51. For the most detailed analysis of the organization and evolution of the
PCC through the 1970s, see Domínguez, *Cuba: Order and Revolution*, esp. 306–
40. See also William LeoGrande, "Party Development in Revolutionary Cuba,"
in *The Cuba Reader: The Making of a Revolutionary Society*, ed. Philip Brenner
et al. (New York: Grove Press, 1989), 156–71; and Nelson Valdés, "The Changing Face of Cuba's Communist Party," in *The Cuba Reader*, 172–83.

52. Alternatively, the Party has been portrayed as composed of factions rooted in the anti-Batista struggle, the direction of the revolution varying with shifts in which factional alliance dominated. See González, *Cuba Under Castro* and "Institutionalization, Political Elites, and Foreign Policy," in *Cuba in the World*, ed. Cole Blasier and Carmelo Mesa-Lago (Pittsburgh: University of Pittsburgh Press, 1979), 3–36. This "who rules" approach cannot explain policies bearing no link to the anti-Batista struggle and the early 1990s incorporation of individuals into top posts who did not partake in the anti-Batista struggle (described in chapter 4).

53. Eisenstadt, ed., *Max Weber*, 57–58.

54. There were, however, *diplotiendas* where well-connected Cubans, as well as foreigners, could with hard currency attain a variety of goods that were unavailable to the ordinary citizen until mid-1993.

55. Reflecting the selective access to Party privileges, a former diplomat and Party member told me that his material lifestyle did not change when he left the Party. He added that only the top leadership get perks of any consequence.

56. By way of illustration, the same day in 1992 that Cuban hosts of a conference I attended graciously gave a surprise birthday party for one of the foreign participants, with rum and cake, I learned from Cubans with no political connections that children rarely could get birthday cakes any more. By 1993 cakes were obtainable for ordinary citizens only in the black market, for about 50 pesos.

57. Richard Fagen, *The Transformation of Political Culture in Cuba* (Stanford, Calif.: Stanford University Press, 1969), esp. 69–103.

58. See Max Azicri, *Cuba: Politics, Economics and Society* (New York: Pinter, 1988), 114–17, and Azicri, "Women's Development Through Revolutionary Mobilization: A Study of the Federation of Cuban Women," *International Journal of Women's Studies* 2, no. 1 (1979), reprinted in *The Cuba Reader*, ed. Brenner et al.; and Vilma Espín, *La Mujer en Cuba* (Havana: Editora Política, 1990).

59. On labor and the CTC see Linda Fuller, "The State and the Unions in Cuba Since 1959," in *Labor Autonomy and the State in Latin America*, ed. Edward Epstein (Boston: Unwin Hyman, 1989), 133–71, and Fuller, *Work and Democracy in Socialist Cuba* (Philadelphia: Temple University Press, 1992); Zeitlin, *Revolutionary Politics and the Cuban Working Class*; Merifeli Pérez-Stable, "Class, Organization and Conciencia: The Cuban Working Class After 1970," in *Twenty-Five Years of Revolution, 1959–84*, ed. Sandor Halebsky and John Kirk (New York: Praeger, 1985); and Domínguez, *Cuba: Order and Revolution*, 267–71. On ANAP see Domínguez, *Cuba: Order and Revolution*, 445–60; Stubbs, *Cuba: The Test of Time*.

60. Domínguez, *Cuba: Order and Revolution*, 279–80.

61. Ibid.

62. Dilla Alfonso, González, and Vincentelli, "Cuba's Local Governments."

63. On the organization and function of sports, see Raudol Ruiz Aguilera, "The Cuban Sports Program," in *The Cuba Reader*, ed. Brenner et al., 430–34; Julie Marie Bunck, "The Politics of Sports in Revolutionary Cuba," *Cuban Studies/Estudios Cubanos* 20 (1990): 111–32; John Griffiths, "Sport: The People's Right," in *Cuba: The Second Decade*, ed. John Griffiths and Peter Griffiths (London: Writers and Readers Publishing Cooperative, 1979), 247–60; Paula Pettavino, "Novel Revolutionary Forms: The Use of Unconventional Diplomacy in

Cuba," in *Cuba: The International Dimension,* ed. Georges Fauriol and Eva Loser (New Brunswick, N.J.: Transaction Books, 1990), 373–404.

64. *New York Times,* 19 August 1991: C4.

65. *New York Times,* 4 August 1991: A2.

66. Eisenstadt, ed., *Max Weber,* 53.

67. See Roger Reed, *The Cultural Revolution in Cuba* (Geneva: Latin American Round Table, 1991), for a critical discussion of control of cultural expression; John King, "Cuban Cinema: A Reel Revolution?" in *Cuba After Thirty Years: Rectification and the Revolution,* ed. Richard Gillespie (London, Frank Cass, 1990), 140–60; John Nichols, "The Mass Media: Their Functions in Social Conflict," in *Cuba: Internal and International Affairs,* ed. Jorge Domínguez (Beverly Hills, Calif.: Sage, 1982), 71–111; Mario Benedetti, "Present Status of Cuban Culture," in *Cuba in Revolution,* ed. Bonachea and Valdés, 500–26; Azicri, *Cuba: Politics, Economics and Society,* 180–87; and essays in *The Cuba Reader,* ed. Brenner et al., 487–513.

68. Nichols, in "The Mass Media," argues that during periods when the government encouraged decentralization, press coverage was most open and comprehensive.

69. Stubbs, *Cuba: The Test of Time,* 19.

70. Ibid.

71. The government's tolerance of Afro-Cuban religious sects has a longer history. Already in 1970 the official position was to embrace the sects as part of Cuba's cultural history, and Afro-Cuban cults flourished at the time. However, membership in the Party was denied to professed sect members. See Oscar Lewis, Ruth Lewis, Susan Rigdon, *Neighbors: Living the Revolution* (Urbana: University of Illinois Press, 1978), 549–51.

72. Economist Intelligence Unit (EIU), *Cuba Country Profile 1991–92,* 4.

73. Jorge Domínguez, "Leadership Changes, Factionalism, and Organizational Politics in Cuba Since 1960," in *Leadership Change in Communist States,* ed. Raymond Taras (Boston: Unwin Hyman, 1989), 144.

74. Max Weber's discussion of the problem of succession under charismatic rule by implication provides a better understanding of efforts to establish "dynastic Communism" than do Cold War totalitarian regime-type analyses of the former Soviet-bloc states. Succession proved to be the least of Soviet and East European Communist regime problems. Fidel's other brother, Ramón, managed a cattle-breeding farm. Other family members were appointed to less important jobs. See Oppenheimer, *Castro's Final Hour,* 279–85.

75. Karl Marx, "The Civil War in France," in *Marx and Engels,* ed. Feuer, 366.

76. Bengelsdorf, "Between Vision and Reality."

77. A study of four municipalities in different regions of the country found, for example, that attendance at nomination meetings varied from 73 to 91 percent between 1979 and 1989 (though it peaked in 1984). Dilla Alfonso, González, and Vincentelli, "Cuba's Local Governments."

78. Ibid.

79. According to official data women never accounted for more than 20 percent of the elected delegates between 1976 and 1989. Ibid.

80. Bengelsdorf, "Between Vision and Reality." Similarly, Lourdes Casal, in

"Cultural Policy and Writers in Cuba," in *The Cuba Reader*, ed. Brenner et al., 483, found that at the December 1978 National Assembly session blacks and mulattos accounted for approximately 36 percent of all delegates, a fourfold increase with respect to the level of black and mulatto representation in equivalent elected structures before the revolution. The national leadership was not, however, supportive of all social minorities—for example, homosexuals.

81. Jorge Domínguez, "The Civic Soldier in Cuba," in *Political-Military Systems: Comparative Perspectives*, ed. Catherine Kelleher (Beverly Hills, Calif.: Sage, 1974).

82. William LeoGrande, "A Bureaucratic Approach to Civil-Military Relations in Communist Political Systems: The Case of Cuba," in *Civil-Military Relations in Communist Systems*, ed. Dale Herspring and Ivan Volgyes (Boulder, Colo.: Westview, 1978), 211.

83. United Nations Development Programme (UNDP), *Human Development Report 1991* (New York: Oxford University Press, 1991), 156–57.

84. EIU, *Cuba Country Profile 1991–92*, 7; Michael Mazarr, "The Cuban Security Apparatus," in *Cuba: The International Dimension*, ed. Fauriol and Loser, 257–92. Formed in 1980, the Territorial Militia involved women, students, and workers who trained for forty hours a year. The militia were to provide rearguard defense and protect factories and farms.

85. *Boston Globe*, 26 September 1991: 30.

86. On the Soviet military presence in Cuba see Suchlicki, "Cuba and the United States," in *Cuba: The International Dimension*, ed. Fauriol and Loser, 53–58.

87. Jorge Domínguez, "The Cuban Armed Forces, the Party and Society in Wartime and During Rectification (1986–1988),' in *Cuba After Thirty Years*, ed. Gillespie, 45–62.

CHAPTER TWO
THE "PUSH FOR COMMUNISM" AND THE "RETREAT TO
SOCIALISM"

1. Fidel Castro, *History Will Absolve Me* (New York: Lyle Stuart, 1961), esp. 33–38.

2. Maurice Zeitlin, *Revolutionary Politics and the Cuban Working Class* (New York: Harper Torchbooks, 1970), vii–lii.

3. Robert Scheer and Maurice Zeitlin, *Cuba: An American Tragedy* (Harmondsworth, Middlesex: Penguin, 1964).

4. Studies on the early revolutionary period are by now numerous. They include James O'Connor, *The Origins of Socialism in Cuba* (Ithaca: Cornell University Press, 1970); Carmelo Mesa-Lago, *The Economy of Socialist Cuba: A Two-Decade Appraisal* (Albuquerque: University of New Mexico Press, 1981), and Mesa-Lago, *Cuba in the 1970s* (Albuquerque: University of New Mexico Press, 1974); Archibald Ritter, *The Economic Development of Revolutionary Cuba* (New York: Praeger, 1974); José Luis Rodríguez, *Estrategia del desarrollo económico en Cuba* (Havana: Editorial de Ciencias Sociales, 1990); Leo Huberman and Paul Sweezy, *Socialism in Cuba* (New York: Monthly Review Press,

1969); Arthur MacEwan, *Revolution and Economic Development in Cuba* (London: Macmillan, 1981); Dudley Seers, ed., *Cuba: The Economic and Social Revolution* (Chapel Hill: University of North Carolina Press, 1964); Claes Brundenius, *Revolutionary Cuba: The Challenge of Economic Growth with Equity* (Boulder, Colo.: Westview, 1984).

5. O'Connor, *Origins of Socialism in Cuba*, 219.

6. Mesa-Lago, *The Economy of Socialist Cuba*, 58.

7. Susan Eckstein, "The Impact of the Cuban Revolution: A Comparative Perspective," *Comparative Studies in Society and History* 28, no. 3 (July 1986): 506. It ranked seventh in 1955 and fifth in 1960, but seventeenth in 1965. The higher the rank, the more favorable the balance of trade (namely, exports exceed imports).

8. Karl Marx, "Critique of the Gotha Program," in *Dynamics of Social Change: A Reader in Marxist Social Science*, ed. Howard Selsam, David Goldway, and Harry Martel (New York: International Publishers, 1970), 382–86. In the present book, "communism" refers to Marx's utopian societal stage of development, "Communism" to the historically specific regimes that instituted Leninist "vanguard party" rule.

9. For more detailed empirical studies of the 1959 to 1985 period see Susan Eckstein, "State and Market Dynamics in Castro's Cuba," in *State vs. Markets in the World Economy*, ed. Peter Evans, Dietrich Rueschmeyer, and Evelyne Stevens (Beverly Hills, Calif.: SAGE, 1985); Andrew Zimbalist and Susan Eckstein, "Patterns of Cuban Development: The First Twenty-five Years," in *Cuba's Socialist Economy Toward the 1990s*, ed. Zimbalist (Boulder, Colo.: Lynne Rienner, 1987); Andrew Zimbalist and Claes Brundenius, *The Cuban Economy* (Baltimore: Johns Hopkins University Press, 1989); Jorge Pérez-López, *Measuring Cuban Economic Performance* (Austin: University of Texas Press, 1987); and the references cited in note 4, above.

10. The most influential portrayer of this conception is Carmelo Mesa-Lago. For references see note 4, above.

11. Commentators have understood *specific* late 1960s policies as rooted in economic considerations but not the diversity of policies described here. With respect to specific policies, see Brian Pollitt and G. B. Hagelberg, *Labour Supply, Harvest Mechanization and the Demand for Cuban Sugar*, Occasional Paper no. 54 (Glasgow: Institute of Latin American Studies, University of Glasgow, 1992), 12; Edward Boorstein, *The Economic Transformation of Cuba* (New York: Month Review Press, 1968); MacEwan, *Revolution and Economic Development in Cuba.*

12. Marx, "Critique of the Gotha Program."

13. See especially V. I. Lenin, "What Is to Be Done?" *Lenin: Selected Works*, vol. 1 (New York: International Publishers, 1967), 97–256.

14. See *Man and Socialism in Cuba*, ed. Bertram Silverman (New York: Atheneum, 1971).

15. MacEwan, *Revolution and Economic Development in Cuba*, 73.

16. These changes are discussed in more detail in Susan Eckstein, "The Socialist Transformation of Cuban Agriculture: Domestic and International Constraints," *Social Problems* 29, no. 2 (December 1981): 178–96.

17. Mesa-Lago, *The Economy of Socialist Cuba*, 15, 23; Huberman and Sweezy, *Socialism in Cuba*, 131–40.

18. Eckstein, "The Impact of the Cuban Revolution," 521–22. On income distribution specifically in Cuba, see Brundenius, *Revolutionary Cuba*, 113, 114, 116.

19. See Ché's writings and speeches in *Ché Guevara and the Cuban Revolution*, ed. David Deutschmann (Sydney: Pathfinder, 1987).

20. Yet the government did not force workers to take salary cuts in cases where the new wage scale was lower than before the revolution. Tolerance of so-called "historical wages" reflected an accommodation to the material interests of the more privileged prerevolutionary workers.

21. Roberto Bernardo, *The Theory of Moral Incentives in Cuba* (Tuscaloosa: University of Alabama Press, 1971).

22. Bertram Silverman, "Economic Organization and Social Conscience: Some Dilemmas of Cuban Socialism," in *Cuba: The Logic of the Revolution*, ed. David Barkin and Nita Manitzas (Andover, Mass.: Warner Modular Publications, 1973), p. 21; Economist Intelligence Unit (hereafter, EIU), *Cuba: Annual Supplement* (1971), 3; and Dirección Central de Estadística (DCE), *Anuario Estadístico de Cuba, 1972* (Havana: Junta Central de Planificación, 1974), 34.

23. Cuban Communist Party, "Bureaucracy and Revolution," in *Cuba in Revolution*, ed. Rolando Bonachea and Nelson Valdés (Garden City, N.Y.: Doubleday, 1972), 185.

24. Roberto Hernández and Carmelo Mesa-Lago, "Labor Organization and Wages," in *Revolutionary Change in Cuba*, ed. Mesa-Lago (Pittsburgh: University of Pittsburgh Press, 1971), 237.

25. On internal CTC electoral procedures and dynamics, see Jorge Domínguez, *Cuba: Order and Revolution* (Cambridge: Belknap Press of Harvard University Press, 1978), 291–96.

26. On other labor participatory involvements in the latter 1960s, see Zeitlin, *Revolutionary Politics and the Cuban Working Class*, and Linda Fuller, *Work and Democracy in Socialist Cuba* (Philadelphia: Temple University Press, 1992).

27. Zeitlin, *Revolutionary Politics and the Cuban Working Class*, xxv.

28. On the Labor Councils, see Hernández and Mesa-Lago, "Labor Organization and Wages," 221–24.

29. Domínguez, *Cuba: Order and Revolution*, 297.

30. By contrast, before the revolution rich landlords dominated farm associations.

31. Andrés Bianchi, "Agriculture," in *Cuba: The Economic and Social Revolution*, ed. Seers, 133; Donald Bray and Timothy Harding, "Cuba," in *Latin America: The Struggle with Dependency and Beyond*, ed. Ronald Chilcote and Joel Edelstein (New York: John Wiley, 1974), 635; Nancy Forster, "Cuban Agricultural Productivity: A Comparison of State and Private Farm Sectors," *Cuban Studies/Estudios Cubanos* 11 (July 1981); René Dumont, *Cuba: Es Socialista?* (Caracas: Editorial Nuevo Tiempo, 1970).

32. Boorstein, *The Economic Transformation of Cuba*, 68. The more land ownership shifted to the public domain, the more the government could regulate land usage. When emphasizing agricultural import substitution and diversifica-

tion in 1962, about a quarter of former cane plantations had been replanted with other crops. The government at the time, though, had less acreage under its control than after the 1963 agrarian reform law.

33. Sergio Roca, "Cuban Economic Policy in the 1970s: The Trodden Paths," in *Cuban Communism*, ed. Irving L. Horowitz, 3d ed. (New Brunswick, N.J.: Transaction Books, 1977), 269.

34. Huberman and Sweezy, *Socialism in Cuba*, 137–38.

35. Zimbalist and Brundenius, *The Cuban Economy*, 112.

36. Susan Eckstein, "The Debourgeoisement of Cuban Cities," in *Cuban Communism*, ed. Horowitz, 4th ed. (New Brunswick, N.J.: Transaction Books, 1981), 96.

37. Mesa-Lago, *The Economy of Socialist Cuba*, 44.

38. Cuban Communist Party, "Bureaucracy and Revolution," 193, 198.

39. Huberman and Sweezy, *Socialism in Cuba*, 113.

40. Castro acknowledged that the counterrevolutionary movement in the Escambray region received some support from small farmers. Lee Lockwood, *Castro's Cuba, Cuba's Fidel* (New York: Vintage, 1969), 101–2.

41. Domínguez, *Cuba: Order and Revolution*, 441–45.

42. On the adverse economic consequences of the latter 1960s policies, see Sergio Roca, *Cuban Economic Policy and Ideology: The Ten Million Ton Sugar Harvest* (Beverly Hills, Calif.: SAGE, 1976).

43. Carmelo Mesa-Lago and Fernando Gil, "Soviet Economic Relations with Cuba," in *The USSR and Latin America: A Developing Relationship*, ed. Eusebio Mujal-Leon (Winchester, Mass.: Unwin Hyman, 1989), 184.

44. Ibid.

45. William LeoGrande, "Cuban Dependency: A Comparison of Pre-Revolutionary and Post-Revolutionary International Economic Relations," *Cuban Studies/Estudios Cubanos* 9, no. 2 (July 1979): 1–28.

46. Mesa-Lago and Gil, "Soviet Economic Relations with Cuba," 199.

47. Dumont, *Cuba: Es Socialista?*; K. S. Karol, *Guerrillas in Power* (New York: Hill and Wang, 1970).

48. Mesa-Lago, *Cuba in the 1970s*, 38.

49. Mesa-Lago, *The Economy of Socialist Cuba*, 27.

50. Domínguez, *Cuba: Order and Revolution*, 275–76.

51. Hernández and Mesa-Lago, "Labor Organization and Wages," 223, 224.

52. Huberman and Sweezy, *Socialism in Cuba*, 118.

53. Carmelo Mesa-Lago, "The Economy: Caution, Frugality, and Resilient Ideology," in *Cuba: Internal and International Affairs*, ed. Jorge Domínguez (Beverly Hills, Calif.: Sage, 1982), 126; *Granma Weekly Review*, 4 March 1984: 4, and 27 May 1984: 2.

54. Cited in Jorge Pérez-López, "Thinking About the Cuban Economy in the 1990s," in *Cuban Studies Since the Revolution*, ed. Damian Fernández (Gainesville: University Press of Florida, 1992), 156–57.

55. Mesa-Lago, *Cuba in the 1970s*, 83.

56. Domínguez, *Cuba: Order and Revolution*, 271–72.

57. See Pérez-Stable, "Class, Organization and Conciencia: The Cuban Working Class After 1970," in *Twenty-Five Years of Revolution, 1959–84*, ed. Sandor

Halebsky and John Kirk (New York: Praeger, 1985), 292; and Andrew Zimbalist, "Cuban Economic Planning: Organization and Performance," in ibid., 218.

58. Linda Fuller, "Union Autonomy at the Socialist Workplace: A Comparison of Cuba and the German Democratic Republic," *Socialism and Democracy* 11 (September 1990): 83–85. Fuller argues that worker assemblies sparked more interest, debate, and controversy in Cuba than in the German Democratic Republic and that they did so because Cuban workers perceived a greater likelihood that a real change in the workplace plan could result.

59. EIU, *Cuba Quarterly Economic Review* (third quarter, 1980): 6. In 1979 slightly less than 50 percent of all jobs were normed.

60. Zimbalist, "Cuban Economic Planning," 219.

61. The First Party Congress also issued a thesis on obstacles to women's full participation in the labor force. See *Sobre el Pleno Ejercicio de la Igualdad de la Mujer: Tesis y Resolución* (Havana: Departamento de Orientación Revolucionaria del Comité Central del Partido Comunista de Cuba, 1976). On women's rights see also Robin Morgan, *Sisterhood Is Global: The International Women's Movement Anthology* (Garden City, N.Y.: Doubleday Anchor, 1984), 166.

62. Cuba, Comité Estatal de Estadísticas (hereafter, CEE), *Anuario Estadístico de Cuba 1989* (Havana, CEE, 1991), 307.

63. Alfonso Farnos Morejón, Fernando González Quiñones, and Raúl Hernández, "Cuba," in *Working Women in Socialist Countries: The Fertility Connection*, ed. Valentina Bodrova and Richard Anker (Geneva: International Labor Organization, 1985), 229.

64. Morgan, *Sisterhood Is Global*, 171.

65. Brundenius, *Revolutionary Cuba*, 115.

66. Zimbalist and Brundenius, *The Cuban Economy*, 124.

67. See the survey cited in Domínguez, *Cuba: Order and Revolution*, 278. This reported function is especially noteworthy in that more than half the people interviewed were union leaders and four-fifths were Vanguard Workers.

68. Andrew Zimbalist, "In Search of Efficiency," *Cuba Business* (April 1991), 10.

69. EIU, *Cuba Quarterly Economic Review* (fourth quarter, 1980): 8.

70. Domínguez, *Cuba: Order and Revolution*, 454; Medea Benjamin, Joseph Collins, and Michael Scott, *No Free Lunch* (San Francisco: Institute for Food and Development Policy, 1984), 160.

71. Jean Stubbs, "Gender Issues in Contemporary Cuban Tobacco Farming," in *Cuba's Socialist Economy*, ed. Zimbalist, 51.

72. On the new emphasis on agricultural cooperatives, see Juan Valdéz, "El proceso de colectivización rural en Cuba," *Cuadernos del Tercer Mundo* 3, no. 1 (March 1980): 121–37; Cristóbal Kay, "Recent Developments in Rural Cuba: Collectivisation, Economic Reforms and Rectification," *Bulletin*, no. 1 (European Association of Development Research and Training Institute, 1988); Carmen Diana Deere, Mieke Meurs, and Niurka Pérez, "Toward a Periodization of the Cuban Collectivization Process: Changing Incentives and Peasant Response" (Paper prepared for the Latin American Studies Association, Washington, D.C., April 1991).

73. CEE, *Anuario Estadístico de Cuba 1989*, 184, 185.

74. Research Team on the Cuban Economy, *The Most Outstanding Aspects of the Cuban Economy, 1959–83* (Havana: University of Havana, Economic Sciences Area, 1984), 24.

75. Benjamin, Collins, and Scott, *No Free Lunch*, 174.

76. *Granma Weekly Review*, 11 March 1984: 3; Claes Brundenius, *Economic Growth, Basic Needs and Income Distribution in Revolutionary Cuba*, Discussion Paper no. 130 (Lund, Sweden: Research Policy Institute, Lund University, 1981), 116.

77. For Cuba's Western relations during this period see Susan Eckstein, "Capitalist Constraints on Cuban Socialist Development," *Comparative Politics* (April 1980): 263–68.

78. Moscow provided credits to cover Cuba's 1973–1975 Soviet trade deficit, and it extended a $362 million credit to be paid over twenty-five years for the development of nickel, textiles, energy, transportation, sugar mechanization, geological exploration, and irrigation. See Mesa-Lago and Gil, "Soviet Economic Relations with Cuba," 185, 219.

79. Fidel Castro, "The Struggle for Women's Equality," in *Women and the Cuban Revolution*, ed. Elizabeth Stone (New York: Pathfinder Press, 1981), 65.

80. Max Azicri, "Women's Development Through Revolutionary Mobilization," in *The Cuba Reader*, ed. Philip Brenner et al. (New York: Grove Press, 1989), 466. The 1973 CTC Congress had opposed earlier efforts to restrict women from certain jobs.

81. Mesa-Lago, *The Economy of Socialist Cuba*, 120.

82. The cost for day care varied between three and forty pesos per child per month, depending on family income. The fee scale reflects the state's continued commitment to the nation's poor.

83. Data on usage are based on average yearly matriculation, not on the number of children who attend some or all of the year.

84. For further discussion see Susan Eckstein, "On Socialist Fiscal Crises: Lessons from Cuba," *Theory and Society* 17 (1988): 238–42.

85. EIU, *Cuba Quarterly Economic Review* (second quarter, 1980): 11.

86. Marta Harnecker, *Cuba: Dictatorship or Democracy?* (Westport, Conn.: Lawrence Hill, 1979); Carollee Bengelsdorf, "Between Vision and Reality: Democracy in Socialist Theory and Practice" (Ph.D. diss., Massachusetts Institute of Technology, 1985), chap. 5.

87. Domínguez, *Cuba: Order and Revolution*, 459–61.

88. People tended to buy their full quotas even though they did not need or want everything. They would then engage in informal swapping with friends and relatives until they wound up with preferred items. Since trade in rationed goods was technically illegal, such exchanges were viewed as a "gray market."

89. *Granma Weekly Review*, 12 October 1986: 3–4.

90. The Soviets paid for only a fraction of Cuban goods in hard currency. However, prior to the revolution the Soviets' much more limited purchases were paid for in hard currency.

91. Western bank borrowing was linked at the time to increased bank liquidity (namely, petrodollars) on the one hand, and to high sugar prices on the other, the latter implying that Cuba was well positioned to repay the loans.

92. Castro took advantage of President Carter's lifting of travel restrictions.

93. Brundenius, *Revolutionary Cuba*, 76.

94. Mesa-Lago, *The Economy of Socialist Cuba*, 188–89.

95. U.S. Department of Commerce, "U.S. Commercial Relations with Cuba: A Survey" (Washington, D.C.: Domestic and International Business Administration, Bureau of East-West Trade, August 1975), 41.

96. United Nations (UN), *Balance Preliminar de la Economía Latinoamericana en 1983* (New York: Comisión Económica Para America Latina, 1983), 11.

97. Eckstein, "The Impact of the Cuban Revolution," 506.

98. Eckstein, "Income Distribution and Consumption in Postrevolutionary Cuba: An Addendum to Brundenius," *Cuban Studies/Estudios Cubanos* 10 (January 1980): 257; Forster, "Cuban Agricultural Productivity," 107–9, and Eckstein, "How Consequential Are Revolutions," in *Comparative Political Dynamics*, ed. Dankwart Rustow and Kenneth Erickson (New York: HarperCollins, 1991), 319 and references in the tables.

99. *Latin American Economic Report* (20 January 1978): 20.

100. Lawrence Theriot and Carol Callahan, *Cuba Trade with the Industrialized West, 1973–1978* (Washington, D.C.: U.S. Department of Commerce, International Trade Administration, Office of East-West Policy and Planning, April 1980), table 9.

101. Eckstein, "The Impact of the Cuban Revolution," 506.

102. Ibid., 515.

103. *Latin American Economic Report* (24 September 1976): 146, 148.

104. Eckstein, "The Impact of the Cuban Revolution," 515.

105. *Granma Weekly Review*, 27 August 1989: 12; UN, *Balance Preliminar de la Economía Latinoamericana en 1983*, 11. (See also Appendix, Table 2.2.) On the reliability of these figures, see Jorge Pérez-López, "Bringing the Cuban Economy into Focus: Conceptual and Empirical Challenges," *Latin American Research Review* 26, no. 3 (1991): 16.

106. Calculated from data presented in Claes Brundenius, "The Role of Capital Goods Production in the Economic Development of Cuba" (Paper presented at workshop on "Technology Policies for Development," Research Policy Institute, University of Lund, Sweden, 29–31 May 1985), 11, 20, 21. Also see Miguel Figueras, *La Producción de Maquinaria y Equipos en Cuba* (Havana: JUCEPLAN, 1982); Claes Brundenius, "Development and Prospects of Capital Goods Production in Revolutionary Cuba," *World Development* 15, no. 1 (January 1987): 95–112; and Arturo Bas Fernández et al., "Desarrollo de la industria de bienes de capital en la Republica de Cuba," *Economía y Desarrollo* 82 (September–October 1984): 10–24.

107. CEE, *Anuario Estadístico de Cuba 1989*, 201–2.

108. Benjamin, Collins, and Scott, *No Free Lunch*, 67, 68.

109. Ibid., 78.

110. Stubbs, "Gender Issues in Contemporary Cuban Tobacco Farming," 54.

111. A study of 138 cooperatives in the tobacco sector in 1985 found 37 percent to operate at a loss. Stubbs, "Gender Issues in Contemporary Cuban Tobacco Farming," 55.

112. When the government initiated the "Rectification Process" (see chapter

3), *Granma Weekly Review* contained frequent articles about such worker abuses.

113. Women were hit by the economic downturn very soon after the state implemented its policies facilitating women's participation in the labor force. The economic downturn followed an unanticipated sudden and dramatic plunge in world sugar prices. Some of the prowomen's policies (e.g., the Family Code) were conceived at least a year before implementation because they first were discussed at work centers and at mass organization meetings.

114. It is difficult to compare women's participation in the labor force cross-nationally because countries do not use a uniform enumeration system. Women's participation rates are probably most underrepresented in countries where women contribute considerable unpaid family labor.

115. Morgan, *Sisterhood Is Global*, 166.

116. Although the economic activity rate is higher among divorced than married (legally or consensually) women, the activity rate increased more, in the 1970s, among legally and consensually married women than among divorcées. Farnos Morejón, González Quiñones, and Hernández, "Cuba," 223. Consequently, women entered the labor force in record numbers not merely because of their changed marital status. On divorce rates and problems of interpreting divorce statistics, see National Research Council (NRC), *Fertility Determinants in Cuba* (Washington, D.C.: National Academy Press, 1983), 79.

117. Farnos Morejón, González Quiñones, and Hernández, "Cuba," 228. Studies of women in Third World market economies show that women participate in the paid labor force when material benefits outweigh costs. Nancy Birdsall and William McGreevey, "Women, Poverty, and Development," in *Women and Poverty in the Third World*, ed. Mayra Buvinić. Margaret Lysette, and William McGreevey (Baltimore: Johns Hopkins University Press, 1983), 8.

118. Eckstein, "On Socialist Fiscal Crises," 242.

119. Sergio Roca, "State Enterprises in Cuba Under the New System of Planning and Management," *Cuban Studies/Estudios Cubanos* 16 (1986): 153–79; see also Zimbalist and Eckstein, "Patterns of Cuban Development," 21 nn. 36 and 37.

120. *Cuba Business* (February 1990): 11.

121. EIU, *Cuba Quarterly Economic Review* (fourth quarter, 1980): 8.

122. EIU, *Cuba Quarterly Economic Review* (third quarter, 1979): 6.

123. EIU, *Cuba Quarterly Economic Review* (first quarter, 1980): 8.

124. Zimbalist and Eckstein, "Patterns of Cuban Development," 16.

125. Pérez-Stable, "Institutionalization and Workers' Response," *Cuban Studies/Estudios Cubanos* 6 (1976): 31–54. Pérez-Stable's sample of fifty-seven workers was not selected randomly. Highly educated and politically involved workers are "overrepresented."

126. A. Herrera and H. Rosenkranz, "Political Consciousness in Cuba," in *Cuba: The Second Decade*, ed. John Griffiths and Peter Griffiths (London: Britain-Cuba Scientific Liaison Committee, 1979), 48.

127. Alejandro Armengol Ríos and Ovidio D'Angelo Hernández, "Aspectos de los procesos de comunicación y participación de los trabajadores en la gestión de las empresas," *Economía y Desarrollo* 42 (July–August 1977): 156–79.

128. Fuller, *Work and Democracy in Socialist Cuba*, 47–56.

129. EIU, *Cuba Quarterly Economic Review* (first quarter, 1980): 5, and *Cuba: Annual Supplement* (1980): 5.

CHAPTER THREE
THE LATE 1980s CAMPAIGN TO "RECTIFY ERRORS AND
NEGATIVE TENDENCIES"

1. José Luis Rodríguez, "Aspectos económicos del proceso de rectificación," *Cuba Socialista* 44 (April–June 1990): 86–101. In a book that covered developments between 1959 and 1986, Rodríguez, by contrast, emphasized the accomplishments of the revolution, consistent with the then official view: see his *Estrategia del Desarrollo Económico en Cuba* (Havana: Editorial de Ciencias Sociales, 1990).

2. See Carmelo Mesa-Lago, "Cuba's Economic Counter Reform (*Rectificación*): Causes, Policies and Effects," in *Cuba After Thirty Years: Rectification and the Revolution*, ed. Richard Gillespie (London: Frank Cass, 1990), and Mesa-Lago, "On Rectifying Errors of a Courteous Dissenter," *Cuban Studies/Estudios Cubanos* 20 (1990): 87–110. I take issue with his interpretation in my essay "The Rectification of Errors or the Errors of the Rectification Process in Cuba?" *Cuban Studies/Estudios Cubanos* 20 (1990): 67–86. A subsequent exchange between us appears in *Cuban Studies/Estudios Cubanos* 21 (1991).

3. *Granma Weekly Review* (hereafter, GWR), 13 December 1987: 10.

4. GWR 22 January 1989: 4 (supplement).

5. GWR 15 June 1986: 3.

6. GWR 12 October 1986: 3.

7. GWR 13 December 1987: 10.

8. GWR 18 October 1987: 6.

9. GWR 27 April 1986: 9.

10. For an anthology in English that includes key essays on Ché from the late 1980s see *New International* 8 (1991). See also Carlos Tablada, *The Economic Thought of Ché Guevara: Economics and Politics in the Transition to Socialism* (New York: Pathfinder, 1990).

11. GWR 18 October 1987: 4.

12. GWR 8 October 1987: 4–6.

13. Rodríguez, "Aspectos económicos del proceso de rectificación," 92.

14. GWR 7 February 1988: 9.

15. Economist Intelligence Unit (hereafter, EIU), *Cuba Country Report* no. 1 (1990): 14.

16. GWR 10 January 1988: 3.

17. Cuba, Comité Estatal de Estadísticas (hereafter, CEE), *Anuario Estadístico de Cuba 1989* (Havana: CEE, 1991), 195.

18. Mesa-Lago, "Cuba's Economic Counter Reform," 107.

19. As of the mid-1980s, around the time of the launching of the RP, there were over two thousand brigades in agriculture, industry, and construction. *Trabajadores*, 9 May 1986: 4.

20. *Cuba Business* (hereafter, CB), October 1989: 8.

21. Rodríguez, "Aspectos económicos del proceso de rectificación," 97.

22. GWR 10 December 1989: 4.

23. GWR 11 June 1989: 5.

24. GWR 3 August 1986: 5.

25. *Normas*, income paid for overfulfillment of work expectations (piece-rate payments), accounted for 6 percent of worker income in 1985. Other material incentives at the time included *primas*, bonuses given to groups of workers for increasing exports, saving raw materials, overfulfilling targets, or developing new products, and *premios*, profit-sharing. The RP resulted in the reduction of all three incentives. Andrew Zimbalist, "In Search of Efficiency," CB April 1991: 11.

26. GWR 12 October 1986: 4.

27. Labor strategies to increase earnings independently of productivity undermined enterprise interests, when enterprises were responsible for their own cost accounting and expenditures reduced retainable profits; when enterprises were not allotted a profit fund, the state bore the labor costs. Labor pushed for continued material incentives. See the May 1987 issue of *Trabajadores*; by contrast, the Union of Young Communists (UJC), in their publication *Juventud Rebelde*, argued in favor of moral incentives.

28. Andrew Zimbalist and Claes Brundenius, *The Cuban Economy* (Baltimore: Johns Hopkins University Press, 1989), 131, 133.

29. EIU, *Cuba: Country Profile 1986–87*, 8.

30. GWR 27 April 1986: 10 (supplement).

31. GWR 23 September 1990: 8.

32. GWR 8 July 1990: 9. For a discussion of the appropriate role of planning, enterprise self-financing, and pricing, see the articles in *Economía y Desarrollo* 18 (1988).

33. GWR 12 February 1989: 3. However, while toothpaste was put on the ration system, it remained available at a higher price on the "parallel market" as well.

34. Rationed goods are marketed through *acopio* (state procurement) stores.

35. CB August 1988: 6.

36. *Granma International* (hereafter, GI), 5 May 1991: 7.

37. GWR 3 August 1986: 5.

38. GWR 21 February 1988: 3, and 25 December 1988: 9.

39. EIU, *Cuba Country Report* no. 2 (1989): 12.

40. EIU, *Cuba Country Report* no. 3 (1988): 11.

41. GWR 12 February 1989: 3.

42. GWR 21 February 1988: 3.

43. CEE, *Anuario Estadístico de Cuba 1989*, 116.

44. *The Economist*, 28 July 1990: 32.

45. CB August 1989: 16.

46. EIU, *Cuba Country Report* no. 2 (1990): 19.

47. CB February 1990: 14.

48. EIU, *Cuba Country Report* no. 2 (1990): 20. Cubatabaco claimed the dispute centered on ownership of the brand name, while Davidoff claimed it centered on the declining quality of the Cuban cigars. Both the Cuban and the British company planned to continue to market cigars under the Davidoff name. Da-

vidoff made plans to get its future supplies from the Dominican Republic. Cuba-tabaco's international cigar war continued well into the 1990s. See CB May 1993: 8.

49. The discussion of *sociedades anónimas* (SAs) draws heavily on CB October 1989: 12.

50. On Cubanacán and tourism, see CB April 1991: 3.

51. CB April 1991: 3.

52. CB April 1991: 12; GWR 2 September 1990: 4; EIU, *Cuba Country Report* no. 3 (1991): 21.

53. The government, through the National Tourism Institute (INTUR), directly promoted tourism.

54. CB April 1990: 15.

55. *New York Times*, 26 July 1990: 8.

56. CB April 1990: 15.

57. Brazil insisted on a renegotiation of their original contract. The Brazilians complained that Cuba failed to hand over relevant scientific and technical documentation, that there were problems with delivery delays, and that some 90,000 doses were contaminated. A spokesperson for Cubanacán admitted that a small quantity might have been contaminated.

58. CB February 1990: 16.

59. GWR 16 September 1990: 3.

60. Cited in Jorge Pérez-López, "Cuba's Foreign Economic Relationships," in *Cuba: The International Dimension*, ed. Georges Fauriol and Eva Loser (New Brunswick, N.J.: Transaction Books, 1990), 313.

61. EIU, *Cuba Country Report* no. 3 (1989): 14.

62. María Dolores Espino, "International Tourism in Cuba: An Economic Development Strategy?" (Paper delivered at the first annual meeting of the Association for the Study of the Cuban Economy, Florida International University, August 1991), table 8 (page unnumbered).

63. Net, as opposed to gross, hard currency earnings are not publicly available. The import component of tourist receipts probably is about one-third, the typical range of Caribbean countries. Espino, "International Tourism in Cuba," 14.

64. Ibid.

65. Ibid., table 10.

66. On debates over the role "parallel markets" were to assume, see Medea Benjamin, Joseph Collins, and Michael Scott, *No Free Lunch* (San Francisco: Institute for Food and Development Policy, 1985), 84–86.

67. Ibid.

68. GWR 12 October 1986: 3.

69. Cited in Mesa-Lago, "Cuba's Economic Counter Reform," 108.

70. See János Kornai, "The Soft Budget Constraint," *Kylos* 39 (1986): 3–30.

71. GWR 27 April 1986: 10 (supplement).

72. Zimbalist and Brundenius, *The Cuban Economy*, 12.

73. GWR 18 October 1987: 6.

74. Ibid.

75. GWR 3 August 1986: 5.

76. GWR 27 April 1986: 10 (supplement).

77. GWR 13 December 1987: 9.

78. GWR 15 February 1987: 4–5.

79. GWR 1 February 1987: 2.

80. GWR 12 October 1986: 4.

81. CB August 1988: 14; EIU, *Cuba Country Report* no. 1 (1988): 12.

82. CB October 1989: 8.

83. EIU, *Cuba Country Report* no. 3 (1988): 11, and no. 4 (1988): 9.

84. CB October 1989: 8.

85. GWR 22 January 1989: 5.

86. Low agricultural output frequently was attributed to insufficient labor. Because of a labor scarcity in the sector, soldiers were called upon to help out in periods when demand for workhands peaked. In 1990 four thousand soldiers extended their military service by two months to help with harvesting. CB April 1990: 12.

87. Although the government encouraged manufacturing exports, I am unaware of any evidence suggesting that farm machinery sold domestically impaired foreign sales. Cuba had the largest cane combine harvester plant in the world; it produced 650 machines a year. According to *Cuba Business* (April 1988: 6), Cuba needed to develop its exports to substantially expand its production of capital goods.

88. GWR 22 January 1989: 3.

89. GWR 6 July 1986: 2.

90. GWR 13 July 1986: 9.

91. GWR 18 October 1987: 5.

92. GWR 27 April 1986: 10 (supplement).

93. EIU, *Cuba Country Report* no. 4 (1986): 9.

94. GWR 12 February 1986: 7.

95. Mesa-Lago speaks of the "errors of rectification," as opposed to the "rectification of errors." See his "Cuba's Economic Counter Reform," 98–138.

96. EIU, *Cuba Country Report* no. 2 (1990): 3; Elena Alvarez, *The External Sector of the Cuban Economy in the 80's* (Havana: Instituto de Investigaciones Económicas, JUCEPLAN, n.d.), 13.

97. CB December 1988: 11.

98. EIU, *Cuba Country Profile 1991–92*, 38.

99. GWR 12 March 1989: 2.

100. CEE, *Anuario Estadístico de Cuba 1989*, 82.

101. EIU, *Cuba Country Report* no. 2 (1988): 9–10.

102. GWR 23 April 1989: 3; CB October 1988: 1.

103. CB December 1988: 12.

104. EIU, *Cuba Country Profile 1991–92*, 27.

105. CB February 1990: 7.

106. Ibid.

107. CEE, *Anuario Estadístico de Cuba 1989*, 201–3. Factors other than "rectification," such as climatic conditions, can have contributed to procurement decreases.

108. CEE, *Anuario Estadístico de Cuba 1989*, 111.

109. Ibid., 184.

110. CEE, *Anuario Estadístico de Cuba 1989*, 238, 239.

111. Disparities between wholesale and retail sales in all periods may be attributable also to state channeling of goods to work centers and schools, to the state's withholding of inventory, to theft, and to diversion of goods to private market channels, legally or illegally.

112. CEE, *Anuario Estadístico de Cuba 1989*, 240–41.

113. Ibid., 100–1. Personal consumption includes goods and services acquired directly by the population—not only goods purchased through retail outlets but also agricultural autoconsumption, private use of electricity, housing, transportation, and communications. Social consumption refers to goods and services collectively consumed by the populace.

114. CEE, *Anuario Estadístico de Cuba 1989*, 321.

115. Ibid., 87. By contrast, Tony Cliff, in *State Capitalism in Russia* (London: Pluto Press, 1974), noted that the Soviet state became increasingly preoccupied with investment over consumption, an indication, in his view, of a transformation from a workers' to a bureaucratic state capitalist regime.

116. GWR 1 October 1989: 4.

117. EIU, *Cuba Country Report* no. 3 (1988): 10.

118. EIU, *Cuba Country Report* no. 1 (1990): 21.

119. EIU, *Cuba Country Report* no. 2 (1989): 12.

120. EIU, *Cuba Country Report* no. 4 (1988): 9.

121. Whether there were other motives for the highly publicized arrests, trials, and convictions remains publicly unknown. For a discussion of the scandal see *Cuba: Situation Report* (Washington, D.C.: Office of Research for the Staff of the Radio Martí Program, February 1990).

122. He subsequently died in prison.

123. CB August 1989: 1.

124. EIU, *Cuba Country Profile 1991–92*, 39.

125. The illicit activity may have been prompted by an effort of high-ranking functionaries to address institutional and not merely personal interests. Ochoa, a man of modest lifestyle, for example, said he was looking out for his country's interests when breaking the law. *Cuba: Situation Report*, 12.

126. GWR 22 July 1990: 9.

127. John Walton, "Debt, Protest, and the State in Latin America," in *Power and Popular Protest: Latin American Social Movements*, ed. Susan Eckstein (Berkeley: University of California Press, 1989), 299–328.

CHAPTER FOUR
FROM COMMUNIST SOLIDARITY TO COMMUNIST SOLITARY

1. Economist Intelligence Unit (hereafter, EIU), *Cuba Country Profile 1990–91*, 5.

2. EIU, *Cuba Country Report* no. 1 (1991): 20.

3. *Cuba Business* (hereafter, CB), October 1989: 1; *Granma International* (hereafter, GI), 5 May 1991: 14.

4. *Granma Weekly Review* (hereafter, GWR), 30 December 1990: 2.

5. CB April 1990: 17; GWR 28 July 1990: 32.

6. EIU, *Cuba Country Report* no. 2 (1990): 17.

7. GWR 30 December 1990: 2.

8. EIU, *Cuba Country Profile 1990–91*, 5.

9. CB February 1991: 14.

10. *The Economist*, 28 January 1990: 51.

11. EIU, *Cuba Country Report* no. 1 (1990): 2; personal interview, Havana, 1993.

12. EIU, *Cuba Country Report* no. 4 (1991): 22.

13. CB August 1990: 15.

14. GI 5 May 1991: 12.

15. Ibid.

16. EIU, *Cuba Country Profile 1991–92*, 33.

17. EIU, *Cuba Country Report* no. 4 (1992): 5.

18. GI 8 December 1991: 2.

19. EIU, *Cuba Country Report* no. 2 (1991): 17; CB April 1990: 8.

20. EIU, *Cuba Country Report* no. 2 (1992): 19.

21. EIU, *Cuba Country Report* no. 2 (1990): 8.

22. GWR 3 February 1991: 1.

23. CB June 1990: 14; EIU, *Cuba Country Report* no. 2 (1990): 20, and *Cuba Country Profile 1990–91*, 23.

24. CB February 1991: 2.

25. CB December 1990: 2. Aware of the likely "Balkanization" of the Soviet Union, Havana began to develop contacts with individual Soviet republics already prior to the USSR's demise.

26. GI 20 September 1992: 5. The deterioration in terms of trade accounted for 60 percent of the increase in Cuba's Soviet debt in the 1980s.

27. *The Economist*, 16 May 1992: 51.

28. GI 5 May 1993: 4.

29. EIU, *Cuba Country Report* no. 4 (1992): 16; GI 20 September 1992: 5.

30. GWR 27 January 1991: 9, and 17 February 1991: 10; EIU, *Cuba Country Report* no. 2 (1991): 21.

31. GI 19 July 1992: 5.

32. EIU, *Cuba Country Report* no. 3 (1991): 14.

33. EIU, *Cuba Country Report* no. 3 (1990): 16.

34. EIU, *Cuba Country Report* no. 2 (1992): 13, and no. 4 (1992): 13; GI 30 June 1993: 15.

35. GWR 27 January 1991: 8. The Capital Cities/ABC television network initially offered to pay Cuba $8.7 million for broadcast rights, but the U.S. Treasury Department said the contract violated the U.S. trade embargo. Subsequently, ABC struck a deal with the Treasury Department, but one much less favorable to Cuba than the original offer. Cuba was to receive only $1.2 to $1.3 million from the network. *Christian Science Monitor*, 6 February 1991: 10.

36. GI 7 July 1991: 2.

37. Gillian Gunn, "Cuba's Search for Alternatives," *Current History* (February 1992): 62.

38. EIU, *Cuba Country Report* no. 3 (1990): 21.

39. President Bush urged other countries to make their aid to the Soviet Union also conditional on Moscow's cutting off assistance to Cuba. The government of reunified Germany complied with Bush's request. CB August 1990: 15.

40. EIU, Cuba Country Report no. 3 (1990): 16, and no. 3 (1991): 15.

41. GI 12 April 1992: 4.

42. *Latin American Weekly Report* (hereafter, LAWR), 15 April 1993: 177.

43. EIU, *Cuba Country Report* no. 3 (1991): 14; Gunn, "Will Castro Fall?" 64. The Spanish government was not, however, merely responding to U.S. pressure. The measures were partly a response to anger over Havana's handling of asylum-seekers. Yet Spanish aid picked up again in 1992 when the European country donated powdered milk valued at $1.2 million. GI 5 July 1992: 5.

44. EIU, *Cuba Country Report* no. 3 (1992): 12. However, in 1993 the EEC provided Cuba with humanitarian assistance to combat optic neuritis, the illness that caused some 40,000 islanders to experience sudden blindness (see chapter 5). GI 18 August 1993: 13.

45. GWR 30 December 1990: 9.

46. Carmen Diana Deere, *Socialism on One Island? Cuba's National Food Program and Its Prospects for Food Security*, Working Paper no. 124 (The Hague: Institute of Social Studies, June 1992).

47. Between 1986 and 1989, Cuba imported all grains and 90 percent or more of all oils, fats, and beans consumed domestically. Elena Alvarez González, *Algunos Efectos en la Economía Cubana de los Cambios en la Conyuntura Internacional* (Havana: Instituto de Investigaciones Económicas, mimeo, 1991), 3. Between 1989 and 1991 food imports fell 30 percent. CB January–February 1993: 5.

48. EIU, *Cuba Country Profile 1990–91*, 19; CB October 1990: 3; GWR 14 October 1990: 3. Poultry was to replace beef in islanders' diet so that cattle could be used as beasts of burden for fuel-saving purposes. However, the poultry stock also diminished with cutbacks in imported feed.

49. GI 8 December 1991: 2.

50. GI 5 May 1991: 13.

51. In September 1991 only one-half of all consumers, according to official sources, maintained the required 10 percent reduction. GI 22 September 1991: 4.

52. *Boston Globe*, 31 December 1990: 6.

53. Although *Granma* printed less, it expanded coverage to include information on solidarity groups around the world—groups that sympathized with Cuba and that sent material aid, however minimal.

54. *The Economist*, 9 February 1991: 98.

55. Goods were sold in two ways: *normada*, where prices were subsidized, and *liberado*, at official but nonsubsidized prices.

56. GWR 10 February 1991: 1.

57. CB April 1990: 1, or EIU, *Cuba Country Report* no. 2 (1990): 16. The 20,000 to 30,000 housing units under construction at the eve of the Special Period were, however, to be completed (GWR 10 February 1991: 1). Also, as noted in chapter 6, some social minibrigades, formed on a community rather than work-centered basis, continued to build housing.

58. GI 26 May 1991: 8.

59. Cuba, Comité Estatal de Estadísticas (CEE), *Anuario Estadístico de Cuba 1989* (Havana: CEE, 1991), 324.

60. GI 26 May 1991: 8.

61. GWR 7 October 1990: 9.

62. EIU, *Cuba Country Report* no. 4 (1990): 17.

63. GI 28 April 1991: 2.

64. Ibid.

65. GI 17 November 1991: 4.

66. Personal interview, Havana, June 1993.

67. CB December 1990: 6, 7. According to another source, as of mid-1990 there were seventy contingents, with the Blas Roca construction contingent alone involving four thousand workers. GWR 10 June 1990: 9. On *contingentes* see also Julio Carranza Valdés, "Cuba: Los retos de la economía," *Cuadernos de Nuestra America* 9, no. 19 (July–December 1992), 150. *Contingentes* involved less than 6 percent of the labor force as of mid-1992.

68. Castro reported that one permanent brigade worker did the same work as eight to ten workers who worked in agriculture twice a year for two to three weeks. GWR 14 October 1990: 8.

69. EIU, *Cuba Country Report* no. 4 (1992): 19, and no. 3 (1993): 3.

70. GI 5 May 1991: 15.

71. *New York Times*, 5 December 1990: 18.

72. Carranza Valdés, "Cuba."

73. GI 7 July 1993: 13. Also, personal interviews, Havana, June 1993.

74. EIU, *Cuba Country Report* no. 4 (1992): 20.

75. GI 27 December 1992: 11.

76. LAWR 25 October 1990: postscript.

77. *The Economist*, 16 May 1992: 51; Gillian Gunn, "Cuba's Search for Alternatives," 60; María Dolores Espino, "International Tourism in Cuba: An Economic Development Strategy?" (Paper delivered at the first annual meeting of the Association for the Study of the Cuban Economy, Florida International University, August 1991); CB June 1992: 4, 9; GI 14 June 1992: 13; GI 15 November 1992: 11; GI 7 July 1993: 3, and 28 July 1993: 5; EIU, *Cuba Country Report* no. 1 (1993): 13.

78. GI 7 July 1993: 3.

79. EIU, *Cuba Country Profile 1991–92*, 37.

80. LAWR 12 October 1992: 8. The Mexicans reportedly were attracted by the low cost of Cuban labor and preferential tariff treatment. Given how low Mexican wages are, it is striking that they found the Cuban wage structure a drawing card.

81. CB April 1991: 11; GI 31 January 1993: 5.

82. CB February 1991: 12.

83. GWR 31 March 1991: 12.

84. GI 9 August 1992: 4.

85. CB February 1991: 14.

86. Julie Feinsilver, *Healing the Masses: Cuban Health Politics at Home and Abroad* (Berkeley: University of California Press, 1993), 123.

87. CB October 1990: 3.

88. José Luis Rodríguez, "La Economía Cubana ante un Mundo Cambiante" (Havana: Centro de Investigaciones de la Economía Mundial, n.d.), 20. The Soviet Union was the principal buyer.

89. GI 8 December 1991: 2.

90. *The Economist*, 16 May 1992: 51; EIU, *Cuba Country Report* no. 4 (1992): 16.

91. EIU, *Cuba Country Report* no. 4 (1992): 20; GI 27 December 1992: 12, and 14 July 1993: 4.

92. John Attfield, "Accentuating the Positive," CB December 1991: 12.

93. GI 28 March 1993: 6.

94. CB November 1992: 7; EIU, *Cuba Country Report* no. 1 (1993): 13.

95. GWR 13 January 1991: 3. Already in 1989 four sectors paid, on average, lower salaries than agriculture: forestry, commerce, communications, and personal and community services. CEE, *Anuario Estadístico de Cuba 1989*, 114.

96. CB October 1990: 3.

97. LAWR February 1993: 75; *Boston Globe*, 30 December 1993: 52.

98. *Boston Globe*, 31 December 1990: 6.

99. EIU, *Cuba Country Report* no. 1 (1990): 18.

100. GI 15 September 1991: 3.

101. CB October 1992: 4.

102. GI 5 May 1991: 14.

103. Ibid.

104. Ibid., 15.

105. GI 20 September 1992: 5.

106. GI 7 February 1993: 1.

107. GI 5 May 1991: 15.

108. CB October 1992: 7.

109. GI 28 June 1992: 8 (supplement).

110. GI 28 March 1993: 7.

111. Andrés Oppenheimer, *Castro's Final Hour* (New York: Simon and Schuster, 1992), 226–27.

112. GI 5 May 1993: 4.

113. GI 10 January 1993: 5.

114. Ibid.

115. Ibid.

116. GWR 10 February 1991: 1.

117. GI 10 January 1993: 5.

118. GI 31 January 1993: 4.

119. GI 21 April 1992: 3.

120. Ibid., 2.

121. GI 23 June 1991: 4; GI 14 March 1993: 8, and 28 March 1993: 7.

122. GI 31 March 1991: 15.

123. EIU, *Cuba Country Report* no. 3 (1990): 10. The streamlining of the Party probably was designed, at least in part, to remove membership that disagreed with the "Party line" from positions of leadership and to win popular support by reducing the number of cadre enjoying a life of indolence.

124. Though not a formal group, "reformists" emphasized the national char-

acter of the revolution, and they sought an end to the atheistic conception of the state, single-party rule (wanting to ban only antirevolutionary parties), and Party-controlled media (wanting to bar only that which was "antirevolutionary"). They wanted the state to continue to dominate but not monopolize the economy, and they advocated a rapid integration into world markets. They blamed Soviet influence for the rigidities of the Cuban system. The reforms they espoused were to allow a "return to the sources" of the Cuban revolution. Opponents of reforms argued that the proposed changes would lead Cuba down a path of disintegration and chaos, as had happened in the Soviet Union.

125. GI 27 December 1992: 5.

126. GI 15 May 1991: 15.

127. GI 21 July 1991: 3.

128. GI 5 May 1991: 15.

129. GI 26 May 1991: 8.

130. GI 7 July 1993: 15. Armando Hart, Minister of Culture, Vilma Espín, head of the women's federation, and two political leaders, Jorge Risquét and Julio Camacho, were dropped from the Political Bureau to make way for newcomers.

131. There were at the time 88 independently functioning Cuban companies and about 240 foreign companies operating in Cuba, either on their own or jointly with the Cuban government. EIU, *Cuba Country Report* no. 3 (1992): 14.

132. GI 14 March 1993: 3, 8–9.

133. LAWR 11 March 1993: 118.

134. GI 27 December 1992: 1. Women constituted 14 percent and individuals under thirty years of age constituted 16 percent of the municipal delegates elected.

135. GI 28 March 1993: 8.

136. GI 27 December 1992: 12, and 7 July 1993: 15.

137. GI 7 February 1993: 1, 7. Yet at the same time, Castro named the respected Ricardo Alarcón head of the National Assembly, possibly to lend new life to the political organ. Indicative of an early effort under his leadership to give new meaning to the Popular Power system, elected officers were charged to check on damage caused by the March 1993 "storm of the century" in their districts.

138. GWR 10 February 1991: 1.

139. Ibid.

140. *EIU, Cuba Country Report* no. 2 (1991): 15.

141. CB April 1991: 1; EIU, *Cuba Country Report* no. 1 (1993): 11.

142. In addition to serving as first secretary of the UJC, Robaina was appointed to the Central Committee, the Council of State, the Political Bureau, and, then, the Minister of Foreign Relations.

143. EIU, *Cuba Country Profile 1992–93*, 7; and GI 5 May 1993: 4.

144. EIU, *Cuba Country Report* no. 4 (1991): 14.

145. They were criticized, for example, at the 1992 UJC Congress.

146. Jo Thomas, "The Last Days of Castro's Cuba," *New York Times Magazine*, 14 March 1993: 68.

147. In *Granma* Alberto Montaner, exiled in Spain, was accused of masterminding the declaration released in Miami in 1991. LAWR 4 July 1991: postscript.

148. EIU, *Cuba Country Report* no. 2 (1992): 14.

149. LAWR 8 October 1992: 8.

150. Darío Machado Rodríguez, *Cuba: Participación Social en los Años 90* (Havana: Centro de Estudios Sociopolíticos y de Opinión Adjunto al Comité del PCC, May 1990), 54.

151. Ibid., 40.

152. Ibid., 28, 29.

153. Ibid., 28, 47.

154. Ibid., 58.

155. Ibid., 57.

156. EIU, *Cuba Country Report* no. 4 (1990): 15.

157. A. R. M. Ritter, "Prospects for Economic and Political Change in Cuba in the 1990s" (Paper presented at the Latin American Studies Association, Washington, D.C., April 1991), 24.

158. Personal interview, Havana, July 1992. On the Mariel émigrés and the increased number of islander visits to the United States, see Ernesto Rodríguez Chávez, "El patrón migratorio cubano: Cambio y continuidad," *Cuadernos de Nuestra America* 19, no. 18 (January–June 1992).

159. *Christian Science Monitor*, 6 February 1991: 11; *Boston Globe*, 2 January 1994: 9.

160. In early 1992 the Bush administration even deported Haitians to the U.S. Guantanamo Air Base in Cuba!

161. *New York Times*, 2 June 1991: 24.

162. LAWR 28 March 1991: postscript, and 16 January 1992: postscript.

163. *New York Times*, 6 August 1991: 7; *Boston Globe*, 1 December 1993: 1.

164. GWR 8 March 1990: 1; GI 19 January 1992: 4.

165. EIU, *Cuba Country Report* no. 3 (1990): 18.

166. Protestantism in general gained in popularity during the Special Period, though Pentecostal groups most of all. Pentecostalism, like Afro-Cuban cults, involved subtle collectively shared and articulated resistance to the established order and hope for better times. In response to the growing appeal of Protestantism, two of the candidates for the National Assembly in February 1993 were ministers and both were elected. Although Cuba is still a nominally Catholic country, the leadership of Protestant denominations developed a closer working relationship with the government beginning in the 1980s than did the Catholic hierarchy and was rewarded accordingly politically. (C. Michael Hawn of Southern Methodist University informed me about these recent trends in Cuban Protestantism.)

167. Oppenheimer, *Castro's Final Hour*, 267–82.

168. CB October 1990: 3.

169. GI 28 March 1993: 8, and 7 July 1993: 15. About thirty U.S.-based radio stations broadcast an appeal to voters to either cast blank votes or spoil their ballot. According to some accounts, 20 percent of voters protested in this way in the municipal elections, 30 to 35 percent in Havana and Santiago. EIU, *Cuba Country Report* no. 1 (1993): 11, and LAWR 4 March 1993: 6.

170. Crimes against property included petty theft. Sixty percent of reported crimes against property were valued at 100 pesos or less. GI 22 July 1990: 9.

171. GI 26 April 1992: 13, and 17 May 1992: 6.

172. EIU, *Cuba Country Report* no. 1 (1991): 17.

173. CB February 1991: 12; GWR 20 January 1991: 3.

174. EIU, *Cuba Country Report* no. 3 (1991): 8.

175. EIU, *Cuba Country Report* no. 4 (1991): 18.

176. In small cities about 60 percent reported having bicycles stolen. GI 24 February 1991: 4.

177. GI 17 May 1992: 6.

178. Personal interview, Havana, June 1993; Carranza Valdés, "Cuba," 153.

179. Oppenheimer, *Castro's Final Hour*, 147.

180. Personal interview, Havana, June 1993.

181. EIU, *Cuba Country Report* no. 2 (1992): 16.

182. CB June 1992: 6.

183. Personal interview, Havana, June 1993. According to *The Economist* (24 July 1993: 46), exiles in Miami sent an estimated $300 million yearly to their families in Cuba, and decriminalization of possession of dollars might result in a doubling or tripling of that amount. If so, by the latter half of 1993 such remittances might have exceeded net earnings from tourism (see p. 104).

184. GI 26 May 1991: 9.

185. Ibid., 8.

186. LAWR 15 April 1993: 177.

CHAPTER 5
THE IRONY OF SUCCESS

1. On the Cuban medical system under Castro see Julie Feinsilver, "Cuba as a 'World Medical Power': The Politics of Symbolism," *Latin American Research Review* 24, no. 2 (1989): 1–34, and *Healing the Masses: Cuban Health Politics at Home and Abroad* (Berkeley: University of California Press, 1993). Other useful sources are cited below.

2. Before the revolution there were, however, mutualist health associations. A variant of what are now known as health maintenance organizations (HMOs), they were first established in the late nineteenth century to serve poor Spanish immigrants. They subsequently provided, for a modest fee, a range of medical services, including hospital care, to a broader cross-section of the population. See Ross Danielson, *Cuban Medicine* (New Brunswick, N.J.: Transaction Books, 1979), esp. 127–63.

3. Danielson, *Cuban Medicine*, 127–63.

4. Vicente Navarro, "Health, Health Services, and Health Planning in Cuba," *International Journal of Health Services* (1972): 413.

5. Barent Landstreet, Jr., "Cuban Population Issues in Historical and Comparative Perspective" (Ph.D. diss., Cornell University, 1976), 135.

6. *Granma International* (hereafter, GI), 14 July 1991: 8.

7. Robert Ubell, "Twenty-five Years of Cuban Health Care," in *The Cuba Reader*, ed. Philip Brenner et al. (New York: Grove Press, 1989), 441.

8. By the latter 1980s, Cuba had the highest immunization rate in Latin America. Feinsilver, *Healing the Masses*, 56.

9. Initially, patients were to see whatever doctor happened to be on duty, but the system was changed in response to patient dissatisfaction. Ubell, "Twenty-five Years of Cuban Health Care," 436.

10. GI 12 April 1992: 3.

11. Feinsilver, "Cuba as a 'World Medical Power,' " 9.

12. Ibid., 10.

13. Ibid.

14. Cuba, Comité Estatal de Estadísticas (CEE), *Anuario Estadístico de Cuba 1989* (Havana: CEE, 1991), 360.

15. Carmelo Mesa-Lago, "Alternative Strategies to the Social Security Crisis: Socialist, Market and Mixed Approaches," in *The Crisis of Social Security and Health Care*, ed. Mesa-Lago (Pittsburgh: Center for Latin American Studies, University of Pittsburgh, 1985), 324, 359 n. 13.

16. GI 5 July 1992: 3, and 15 November 1992: 11.

17. GI 15 May 1991: 13.

18. Mesa-Lago, "Alternative Strategies to the Social Security Crisis," 270.

19. Brazil, for example, ranked thirteenth among Latin American countries in life expectancy, and it had the seventh worst infant mortality in 1990. Cuba, as detailed in the Appendix, Table 5.2, ranked first in the region on both measures. United Nations Population Fund (UNPF), *The State of the World Population 1990* (New York: UNPF, 1991), 35.

20. Darío Machado Rodríguez, *Cuba: Participación Social en los Años 90* (Havana: Centro de Estudios Sociopolíticos y de Opinión Adjunto al Comité del PCC, May 1990), 19–21.

21. *Granma Weekly Review* (hereafter, GWR), 10 March 1991: 3.

22. *New York Times*, 16 July 1993: 3.

23. In the mid-1950s daily per capita intake was higher than the estimated requirement (2,460), but the diet was not well balanced. Cubans of all socioeconomic strata, including high-income groups, preferred a diet high in carbohydrates. Rice and sugar accounted for some 40 percent of caloric consumption. Sergio Díaz-Briquéts, *The Health Revolution in Cuba* (Austin: University of Texas Press, 1983), 47.

24. Personal interviews, Havana, July 1992 and June 1993.

25. The illness affecting eyesight and the nervous system was attributed to nutritional deficiencies but also to toxics (partly associated with home-brewed alcohol). *New York Times*, 16 July 1993: 3.

26. Around the turn of the century the government had invested in environmental sanitation and disease control, which helps explain why Cuban health standards were already high, relative to other countries in the region, prior to the revolution. The United States was behind the earlier health campaign because of believed benefits to its own people, given the close ties between the two countries. The Platt Amendment granted the U.S. government the right to intervene in matters of public health, as well as in other matters. Díaz-Briquéts, *The Health Revolution in Cuba*, 33, 35–36.

27. *New York Times*, 26 April 1992: 11.

28. It should be kept in mind that falling mortality rates among children contribute, statistically, to the rise in the average number of years people live.

29. Navarro, "Health, Services, and Health Planning in Cuba," 424, 430; and Díaz-Briquéts, *The Health Revolution in Cuba*, 11.

30. It seems surprising that the infant mortality rate could continue to drop when medical care and nutritional standards deteriorated with the Special Period

crisis. Cubans who believe the statistics note that the government in the early 1990s continued to assign priority to perinatal and early infant care. However, the incidence of low birthrate rose from 7.6 to 8.1 percent of all live births between 1991 and 1992. *New York Times*, 16 July 1993: 3.

31. Sarah Santana, "Whither Cuban Medicine? Challenges for the Next Generation," in *Transformation and Struggle: Cuba Faces the 1990s*, ed. Sandor Halebsky and John Kirk (New York: Praeger, 1990).

32. Cuba, Ministerio de Salud Pública (MINSAP), *Informe Anual* (Havana: MINSAP, 1989), 136.

33. Ubell, "Twenty-five Years of Cuban Health Care," 437. Less frequent but routine visits to doctors are scheduled for older children, and doctors see children at day-care centers and schools.

34. GWR 20 January 1991: 4, and 24 March 1991: 5.

35. GI 24 March 1991: 5, and the *New York Times*, 8 March 1991: 12. GI presents inaccurate figures for the Washington, D.C., rate. By the close of 1992, however, the Cuban-U.S. infant mortality differential increased: the rate during the two-year period declined more in the United States than in Cuba.

36. Alfonso Farnos Morejón, Fernando González Quiñones, and Raúl Hernández, "Cuba," in *Working Women in Socialist Countries: The Fertility Connection*, ed. Valentina Bodrova and Richard Anker (Geneva: International Labor Organization, 1985), 218.

37. Urbanization, the European background of emigrants, and a small peasantry contributed to the low prerevolutionary fertility rate. Landstreet, "Cuban Population Issues," 88.

38. A baby boomlet during Castro's first years of rule is linked to the emigration of doctors, which made abortions more difficult, and the embargo, which cut off contraceptive supplies. Optimism sparked by the revolution may also have been of consequence (Landstreet, "Cuban Population Issues," 195–200). The monograph contains an interesting discussion of demographic trends and policy under Castro, through the mid-1970s. Landstreet argues that the fertility rate declined even though the government was concerned with expanding the potential labor force pool.

39. Hernández Castellón and Catasus Cervera, *La Evolución de la Fecundidad en America Latina* (Havana: Centro de Estudios Demográficos, Centro de Investigaciones de la Economía Internacional, Universidad de la Habana, July 1984), 40–41. Cuba's teenage pregnancy rate was higher than East European Communist countries as well. See Richard Anker, "Comparative Survey," in *Working Women in Socialist Countries*, ed. Bodrova and Anker, 13. Cuban demographers recognized the need to address the problem of teenage pregnancy. In the early 1990s the government sponsored a wide-ranging program of sex education and contraceptive provisioning. As a pregnancy disincentive, teenage mothers were told that they would have to give up their studies (GI 19 May 1991: 2). As of 1989 over 60 percent of the children born to fifteen- to nineteen-year-old women were born out of wedlock (GI 17 November 1991: 3).

40. Alvarez Vásquez and Farnos Morejón, *Factores Determinantes y Características del la Fecundidad Cubana* (Havana: April 1985), 10; National Research Council (NRC), *Fertility Determinants in Cuba* (Washington, D.C.: Na-

tional Academy Press, 1983), 55. The expressed low desire for children may reflect a misinterpretation of the question. Interviewers were instructed to inquire about the number of children desired in the near future. Consequently, some women may have interpreted the question to refer to the number wanted in the immediate future rather than to the ideal completed family size.

41. UNPF, *The State of World Population 1990*, 35, 36; Population Reference Bureau (PRB), *1991 World Population Data Sheet of the Population Reference Bureau* (Washington, D.C.: PRB, April 1991), unnumbered page; World Bank, *World Development Report* (New York: Oxford University Press, 1984), 256–57, 262–63.

42. UNPF, *The State of World Population 1992* (New York: UNPF, 1992), 44. A similar percentage is reported to engage in family planning in Costa Rica.

43. NRC, *Fertility Determinants in Cuba*, 115.

44. With help from the United Nations Population Fund, Cuba built an oral contraceptive factory in the early 1990s. Economist Intelligence Unit (EIU), *Cuba Country Report* no. 2 (1991): 25.

45. Hernández Castellón, *Las Mujeres Trabajadoras y los Cambios Demográficos en Cuba* (Havana: Centro de Estudios Demográficos, Facultad de Economía, May 1982), 7.

46. Castellón and Cervera, *La Evolución de la Fecundidad en America Latina*, 38–39. The emigration of some 125,000 islanders in 1980, most of whom were in their reproductive years, contributed to the drop in the fertility rate at the time. Although not one of the twenty principal countries in Latin America, Barbados had a comparably low reproductive rate; it too had a large out-migration population.

47. CEE, *Anuario Estadístico de Cuba 1989*, 111.

48. In Chile women and men must be five years older and they must work ten years more than in Cuba to qualify for full pension benefits. GWR 22 July 1990: 6.

49. As of 1980 only private farmers not integrated into cooperatives, the unemployed, unpaid family workers, and a very small number of domestic servants were excluded from pension coverage. Moreover, farmers who were old, sick, or disabled could sell their land to the state in exchange for a "rent for life."

50. Mesa-Lago, "Alternative Strategies to the Social Security Crisis," 344.

51. NRC, *Fertility Determinants in Cuba*, 139.

52. Monthly pensions depend, primarily, on years of service and salary when economically active. Workers with twenty-five years of service were entitled, until 1979, to a pension of 50 percent of their previous average yearly salary. Between 1968 and 1973 pensions for workers in meritorious work centers were raised to 100 percent of the base salary; the benefits were subsequently cut back because they were too costly to the state.

53. According to available data, *per capita* pension outlays, in current pesos, declined between 1959 and 1969. They peaked in 1974–75 and dropped again in the latter 1970s. However, at the end of the 1970s they were still slightly higher than in 1959 (in current, though probably not in constant, pesos). NRC, *Fertility Determinants in Cuba*, 139; Mesa-Lago, "Alternative Strategies to the Social Security Crisis," 357.

54. Mesa-Lago, "Alternative Strategies to the Social Security Crisis," 323–24.

55. The low rate charged cooperative members was designed to induce independent farmers to pool their resources to form production units that, in theory, both benefited from economies of scale and advanced socialist organizing principles.

56. Cited in Max Azicri, *Cuba: Politics, Economics and Society* (New York: Pinter, 1988), 153.

57. GWR 24 June 1990: 3.

58. Carmelo Mesa-Lago, *El Desarrollo de la Seguridad Social en America Latina* (Santiago, Chile: CEPAL/Naciones Unidas, 1984), 91.

59. MINSAP, *Informe Anual*, 130; CEE, *Anuario Estadístico de Cuba 1989*, 576.

60. Exceptions include Chile and Costa Rica, as well as most of the English-speaking Caribbean, which offer universal coverage. Carmelo Mesa-Lago, "Cradle-to-Grave Crisis," *Hemisfile* 3, no. 2 (March 1992): 2. This article contains an excellent succinct summary of social security crises in Latin America.

61. United Nations Development Programme, *Human Development Report 1991* (New York: Oxford University Press, 1991), 142–43, 150–51. Panama, Costa Rica, and Nicaragua under the Sandinistas spent a higher percentage of their national product on public health.

62. Carmelo Mesa-Lago, *The Economy of Socialist Cuba* (Albuquerque: University of New Mexico Press, 1981), 34, and "Cradle-to-Grave Crisis," 12; CEE, *Anuario Estadístico de Cuba 1989*, 82. Because I know only of social security expenditure estimates in current pesos, I compare social security outlays (see Appendix, Table 5.5) with national (gross social) product data in current pesos.

63. Between 1960 and 1973, for example, only 8 percent of Soviet development aid went to health, together with education. Azicri, *Cuba: Politics, Economics and Society*, 153.

64. Machado Rodríguez, *Cuba: Participación Social en los Años 90*, 49.

65. UNPF, *The State of World Population 1992*, 41.

66. Evidence from other Communist countries also indicates that women's participation in the labor force contributed to a drop in the fertility rate. Because the birthrate fell so dramatically in the urban European regions of the USSR, the Soviet government called for cutbacks in women's participation in the labor force and in abortion options. Gail Lapidus, "The Soviet Union," in *Women Workers in Fifteen Countries*, ed. Jennie Farly (Ithaca, N.Y.: ILR Press, New York State School of Industrial Relations, Cornell University, 1985), 24. Of course, factors other than women's participation in the labor force contribute to Cuba's low and declining fertility rate, some of which were influential already before the revolution (e.g., urbanization, a weak Catholic tradition, and education). Additional factors became consequential under Castro: housing scarcity and the availability of inexpensive birth control measures (first abortion, then IUDs and "the pill"). See Sergio Díaz-Briquéts and Lisandro Pérez, "Fertility Decline in Cuba: A Socioeconomic Interpretation," *Population and Development Review* 8 (September 1982): 513–37.

67. Family size had already begun to decline in the late 1960s, before the rate of women's paid participation in the labor force rose markedly. The fertility drop then may also be traced to employment, but to the peculiarities of men's as well as women's employment. In the late 1960s men were mobilized in record numbers nationwide to help in the sugar harvest; this was the period when the island most emphasized labor-intensive sugar production. The massive labor mobilizations might explain why the birthrate dropped more between 1969 and 1970 than in any preceding year, and why the birthrate increased (for one year only) between 1970 and 1971, as the population restabilized after the "big sugar push" of 1970. The 1969–70 drop may also have been a by-product of women's work activity, for they too were mobilized for the record sugar harvest. However, they worked as "volunteers," and nonremunerated work is not recorded in official labor statistics.

68. Women's participation in the labor force, along with other factors, had a more dramatic effect on the fertility rate in Cuba than in Eastern European Communist countries. While the island's rate of women's participation in the labor force was lower than Bulgaria's, Hungary's, Poland's, the then Czechoslovakia, and the USSR (at least certain sections), where it ranged between 43 and 49 percent in 1979–80, the Eastern European countries had higher total fertility rates, ranging between 1.92 and 4.80. Anker, "Comparative Survey," 3, 13.

69. Similarly, in Eastern European Communist countries, where most women of productive age worked, female economic activity accounted for the overall fertility decline but increasingly less over the years for differential fertility rates. Anker, "Comparative Survey," 17.

70. Farnos Morejón, González Quiñones, and Hernández, "Cuba," 38. The table appears in Susan Eckstein, "On Socialist Fiscal Crises," *Theory and Society* 17 (1988): 236.

71. González Quiñones, "Fecundidad y empleo feminino en Cuba," in Raúl Hernández Castellón, Alfonso Farnos Morejón, and Fernando González Quiñones, *Algunas Características de la Reciente Evolución de la Fecundidad en Cuba* (Havana, April 1985), 42–44. Studies of Third World capitalist economies find that women minimize the costs of combining market work with child care by choosing occupations that either allow flexible hours or permit them to bring children along. Nancy Birdsall and William McGreevey, "Women, Poverty, and Development," in *Women and Poverty in the Third World*, ed. Mayra Buvinić. Margaret Lysette, and William McGreevey (Baltimore: Johns Hopkins University Press, 1983), 8.

72. Women, for example, accounted for 18 percent of all persons in management positions in 1978 and for 26 percent in 1988. CEE, *Anuario Estadístico de Cuba 1989*, 117.

73. For a further discussion of divorce see chapter 2.

74. GI 17 November 1991: 2.

75. NRC, *Fertility Determinants in Cuba*, 67. Farnos Morejón, González Quiñones, and Hernández, "Cuba," 223; CEE, *Anuario Estadístico de Cuba* (Havana: CEE, 1982), 83.

76. Housing scarcity as well was not conducive to large families. However,

intergenerational cohabitation often enables working women to have elderly family at home to tend to their children, and the housing stock expanded in the 1970s just when the fertility rate dropped.

77. Castellón and Cervera, *La Evolución de la Fecundidad en America Latina*, 34.

78. Luisa Alvarez Vásquez, *La Fecundidad en Cuba* (Havana: Editorial de Ciencias Sociales, 1985), 78–79.

79. James O'Connor attributed a fiscal crisis in highly industrial capitalist societies to the relationship between big business and the state. See his *The Fiscal Crisis of the State* (New York: St. Martin's, 1973). The Cuban experience shows that socialism may generate its own fiscal problems, albeit for somewhat different reasons.

80. Anker, "Comparative Survey," 17, 19.

81. Alvarez Vásquez, *La Fecundidad en Cuba*, 122.

82. In the Soviet Union the burdens of the "double duty" also worsened for women beginning under Brezhnev. See Francine du Plessix Gray, *Soviet Women: Walking the Tightrope* (New York: Doubleday Anchor, 1990).

CHAPTER SIX
"A MAXIMUM OF RURALISM, A MINIMUM OF URBANISM"

1. Alejandro Portes and John Walton, *Urban Latin America: The Political Condition from Above and Below* (Austin: University of Texas Press, 1976), chap. 2.

2. In East Asia, by contrast, agrarian reforms and support to small farmers resulted in slower urbanization rates than in Latin America.

3. I am concerned in this chapter with rural/urban comparisons. However, policies affecting rural and urban developments are not necessarily directed at specific geographically delineated areas but at groups of people within areas. For the differential impact of rural policies on different types of agriculturists, see Carmen Diana Deere, Ernel González, Niurka Pérez Rojas, and Gustavo Rodríguez, "Household Incomes in Cuban Agriculture: A Comparison of the State, Cooperative, and Peasant Sectors" (Amherst: Department of Economics, University of Massachusetts, unpublished paper, December 1992). On differences between rural and urban women and among women differently employed in agriculture, see Mariana Ravenet Ramírez, Pérez Rojas, and Marta Toledo Fraga, *La Mujer Rural y Urbana* (Havana: Editorial de Ciencias Sociales, 1989).

4. On the formal structure of national and regional planning, see Maruja Acosta and Jorge Hardoy, *Urban Reform in Revolutionary Cuba*, Occasional Paper no. 1 (New Haven: Yale Antilles Research Program, 1973), a translation of *Reforma Urbana en Cuba Revolucionaria* (Caracas: Síntesis Dosmil, 1971).

5. Acosta and Hardoy, *Urban Reform in Revolutionary Cuba*.

6. Claes Brundenius, *Revolutionary Cuba: The Challenge of Economic Growth with Equity* (Boulder, Colo.: Westview, 1984), 86.

7. Jill Hamberg, "Cuba," in *International Handbook of Housing Policies and Practices*, ed. Willem van Vliet (New York: Greenwood Press, 1990), 394–95.

8. On government urban policy and its demographic impact, see also Joseph Gugler, "A Minimum of Urbanism and a Maximum of Ruralism: The Cuban Experience," *International Journal of Urban and Regional Research* 4: 516–35; J. P. Garnier, *Une Ville, une Revolution: La Havane* (Paris: Editions Anthropos, 1973).

9. Little is known about government enforcement of these measures.

10. Fidel Castro, *History Will Absolve Me* (New York: Lyle Stuart, 1961), 42.

11. Ibid., 39.

12. These indicators provide only approximate evidence of the urban or rural bias of the medical system, for urban clinics and hospitals may receive rural referrals; there are national and regional hospitals that have beds set aside for rural patients and others not living in the particular city; and urban dwellers are more likely than rural folk to undergo unnecessary procedures because of easy access to facilities and services. I am grateful to Julie Feinsilver for these observations.

13. With the shift to industrial export promotion in the 1970s and especially in the 1980s, business in Latin American market economies became less concerned with locating in large cities as well. They had no need to locate near the main domestic consumer market since they produced for overseas markets, no need to locate near the main market for skilled labor since their production relied heavily on unskilled labor, and they had fiscal incentives to locate wherever governments established tax-free zones.

14. David Slater, "State and Territory in Postrevolutionary Cuba: Some Critical Reflections on the Development of Spatial Policy," *International Journal of Urban and Regional Research* 6, no. 1 (March 1982): 19.

15. Acosta and Hardoy, *Reforma Urbana en Cuba Revolucionaria*, 81.

16. For a discussion of the history of architecture and the architectural profession see Roberto Segre, *Cuba, Arquitectura de la Revolución* (Barcelona: Editorial Gustavo Gili, 1970).

17. Hamberg, "Cuba," in *Housing Policies in the Socialist Third World*, ed. Kosta Mathéy (London: Mansell, 1990), 10.

18. Segre, *Cuba, Arquitectura de la Revolución*, 111.

19. Tony Schuman, "Housing: A Challenge Met," *Cuba Review* 5 (March 1975): 6.

20. Inheritance rights changed. Upon the death of an owner, whoever lived in the domicile at the time had rights to occupancy, whatever their relation to the original owner. If the owner lived alone, ownership passed to the state.

21. Castro, *History Will Absolve Me*, 41–42.

22. Hamberg, "Cuba," in *International Handbook of Housing Policies and Practices*, 380.

23. Since rents were rarely adjusted upward when incomes increased or additional household members took jobs, over the years renters spent, on average, only 3 to 7 percent of their family income on housing. Hamberg, "Cuba," in *International Handbook of Housing Policies and Practices*, 387–88.

24. Hamberg, "Cuba," in *International Handbook of Housing Policies and Practices*, 396.

25. Hamberg, "Cuba," in *Housing Policies in the Socialist Third World*, 10.

26. *Granma Weekly Review* (hereafter, GWR), 24 January 1971: 5.

27. GWR 17 February 1975: 7.

28. Rodney Mace, "Housing," in *Cuba: The Second Decade*, ed. John Griffiths and Peter Griffiths (London: Writers and Readers Publishing Cooperative, 1979), 127, 129.

29. Mace, "Housing," 127.

30. GWR 25 April 1971: 2–3.

31. Only in new industrial areas, and existing cities and towns in underdeveloped regions, were managers, skilled workers, technicians, and professionals explicitly favored. That bias was designed to attract skilled labor to provincial areas the government developed to reduce rural/urban and other regional imbalances. Yet the minibrigade strategy excluded some of the city people with the greatest housing need, those without employment.

32. Schuman, "Housing: A Challenge Met," 14.

33. By the 1980s other Latin American governments became somewhat more proactive, through "sites and services" projects.

34. While homes contained water pipes, supply shutdowns were frequent.

35. James Wilkie and Enrique Ochoa, *Statistical Abstract of Latin America* 27 (Los Angeles: University of California, Latin American Center, 1989), 380. Hamberg, "Cuba," in *Housing Policies in the Socialist Third World*, 6.

36. For a more favorable depiction of the quality of rural housing, see Hamberg, "Cuba," in *Housing Policies in the Socialist Third World*, 6. The different depiction probably reflects a different definition of "rural."

37. Ernesto Rodríguez Chávez, "El patrón migratorio cubano: Cambio y continuidad," *Cuadernos de Nuestra America* 9, no. 18 (January–June 1992), 84.

38. Carmelo Mesa-Lago, "Cuba's Economic Counter Reform (*Rectificación*)," in *Cuba After Thirty Years*, ed. Richard Gillespie (London: Frank Cass, 1990), 108; GWR 11 March 1984: 43; Brundenius, *Revolutionary Cuba*, 95.

39. The 1984 law allowed for cooperative as well as individual self-help housing construction. Agricultural cooperatives, for one, often built housing. Second, several individual self-builders, brought together by a union or professional association, could form a team that built housing collectively. Together they could share skills, and by building multifamily units land and infrastructure costs could be minimized. See Kosta Mathéy, "Self-Help Housing Policies and Practices in Cuba," in *Beyond Self-Help Housing*, ed. Mathéy (London: Profil Verlag, 1990), 185.

40. Hamberg, "Cuba," in *International Handbook of Housing Policies and Practices*, 385.

41. With the implementation of Popular Power, local authorities increased their role in different phases of housing construction, including establishing local materials industries, assigning land, and building urban infrastructure. Local governments typically offered technical assistance, materials, and equipment for auto-construction; they less typically directly built housing. Hamberg, "Cuba," in *International Handbook of Housing Policies and Practices*, 387.

42. Cuba, Comité Estatal de Estadísticas (CEE), *Anuario Estadístico de Cuba* (Havana: CEE, 1982), 313.

43. Enrollments in Schools in the Countryside peaked in the 1979–80 school year. Over the years children enrolled in urban schools also helped out in agriculture, but on a seasonal, not daily, basis.

44. José Luis Rodríguez, "Aspectos económicos del proceso de rectificación," *Cuba Socialista* 44 (April–June 1990).

45. CEE, *Anuario Estadístico de Cuba*, 114.

46. The 11,000 families is equivalent to some 2 percent of all families in the capital. Hamberg, "Cuba," in *International Handbook of Housing Policies and Practices*, 399.

47. Hamberg, "Cuba," in *Housing Policies in the Socialist Third World*, 21.

48. Hamberg, "Cuba," in *International Handbook of Housing Policies and Practices*, 389.

49. Hamberg, "Cuba," in *Housing Policies in the Socialist Third World*, 21.

50. GWR 22 January 1989: 5 (supplement).

51. GWR 20 December 1987: 12; *Cuba Business* (hereafter, CB), June 1988: 8.

52. GWR 22 January 1989: 1, 5. The Five Year Plan for the latter 1980s had stipulated only five day-care centers.

53. Economist Intelligence Unit (hereafter, EIU), *Cuba Country Report* no. 2 (1989): 15.

54. The remainder were reserved for employees of workplaces without minibrigades and for households living in buildings that were uninhabitable or slated for demolition.

55. EIU, *Cuba Country Report* no. 1 (1990): 17; GWR 5 November 1989: 12, and 19 November 1989: 2.

56. Hamberg, "Cuba," in *Housing Policies in the Socialist Third World*, 22.

57. CB May 1993: 6–7.

58. *Granma International* (hereafter, GI), 5 May 1991: 2, and 20 September 1992: 5.

59. GI 5 May 1991: 15.

60. EIU, *Cuba Country Report* no. 4 (1990): 22.

61. GWR 21 October 1990: 9.

CHAPTER SEVEN
INTERNATIONALISM

1. Ernesto Betancourt, "Exporting the Revolution to Latin America," in *Revolutionary Change in Cuba*, ed. Carmelo Mesa-Lago (Pittsburgh: University of Pittsburgh Press, 1971), 105–26.

2. Regis Debray, *Revolution in the Revolution?* (New York: Grove Press, 1967); Ché Guevara, *Guerrilla Warfare* (New York: Grove Press, 1961).

3. H. Michael Erisman, *Cuba's International Relations: The Anatomy of a Nationalistic Foreign Policy* (Boulder, Colo.: Westview, 1985), 75; William Leo-Grande, "Cuban-Soviet Relations and Cuban Policy in Africa," *Cuban Studies/Estudios Cubanos* 10 (January 1980): 30.

4. *Granma International* (hereafter, GI), 9 June 1991: 3; Economist Intelligence Unit (hereafter, EIU), *Cuba Country Report* no. 3 (1991): 18.

5. Andrés Oppenheimer, *Castro's Final Hour* (New York: Simon and Schuster, 1992), 83.

6. EIU, *Cuba Quarterly Economic Review* no. 1 (1984): 8; *Granma Weekly Review* (hereafter, GWR), 15 October 1989: 1; *Cuba Business* (hereafter, CB), October 1989: 15.

7. EIU, *Cuba Quarterly Economic Review* no. 1 (1984): 7.

8. *Boston Globe*, 1 July 1984: 9; GWR 24 May 1986: 4.

9. EIU, *Cuba Quarterly Economic Review* no. 3 (1983): 9, William Ratliff, "Fidel Castro's Crusade in the Caribbean Basin," in *Cuba: The International Dimension*, ed. Georges Fauriol and Eva Loser (New Brunswick, N.J.: Transaction Books, 1990), 80. Between 1983 and 1986 General Ochoa oversaw island military advisers in Nicaragua, after his successful African tour of duty. Ochoa, as previously noted, was executed in 1989 for alleged illicit dealings associated with his overseas missions.

10. Ernest Evans, "Cuban Foreign Policy Toward Latin America," in *Cuba: The International Dimension*, ed. Fauriol and Loser, 11.

11. Oppenheimer, *Castro's Final Hour*, 198.

12. John Walton Cotman, *The Gorrión Tree: Cuba and the Grenada Revolution* (New York: Peter Lang, 1993).

13. Cotman, *The Gorrión Tree*.

14. Oppenheimer, *Castro's Final Hour*, 170–74.

15. Erisman, *Cuba's International Relations*, 141.

16. For a discussion of Cuba's stance, see Juan Valdés Paz, "Cuba y la crisis centroamericana," *Cuadernos de Nuestra América* 2 (July–December 1984): 120–52.

17. Michael Mazarr, "The Cuban Security Apparatus," in *Cuba: The International Dimension*, ed. Fauriol and Loser, 282.

18. Julie Feinsilver, "Cuba as a 'World Medical Power,'" *Latin American Research Review* 24, no. 2 (1989): 12.

19. GWR 30 November 1980: 3 (supplement).

20. Sergio Roca, "Economic Aspects of Cuban Involvement in Africa," *Cuban Studies/Estudios Cubanos* 10, no. 2 (July 1980): 81; Jorge Domínguez, "Armed Forces and Foreign Relations," in *Cuba in the World*, ed. Cole Blasier and Carmelo Mesa-Lago (Pittsburgh: University of Pittsburgh Press, 1979), 65–66.

21. Edith Felipe, "La ayuda económica de Cuba al Tercer Mundo: Evaluación preliminar (1963–1989)," *Boletín de Información sobre la Economía Cubana* 1, no. 2 (February 1992): 13–19; EIU, *Cuba Quarterly Economic Review* no. 1 (1981): 12.

22. EIU, *Cuba Quarterly Economic Review* no. 3 (1979): 7.

23. Cotman, *The Gorrión Tree*.

24. See Julie Feinsilver, *Healing the Masses: Cuban Health Politics at Home and Abroad* (Berkeley: University of California Press, 1993).

25. Roca, "Economic Aspects of Cuban Involvement in Africa," 58; GWR 21 September 1980: 2; Jean Stubbs, *Cuba: The Test of Time* (London: Latin American Bureau, 1989), 95.

26. Felipe, "La ayuda económica de Cuba al Tercer Mundo," 15.

27. GWR 11 November 1990: 2.

28. Cotman, "Cuba and the CARICOM States: The Last Decade," in *Cuba's Ties to a Changing World*, ed. Donna Rich Kaplowitz (Boulder, Colo.: Lynne Rienner, 1993).

29. GWR 22 September 1991: 3.

30. According to one report, up to 30,000 victims were to come in one year (GWR 15 July 1990: 1). By mid-1991 over 5,000 youth victims came for medical and dental care (GI 6 October 1991: 4). Not all Chernobyl victims received medical treatment, however. Cuban doctors claimed that a change in mental and physical climate often was as important as medical treatment (*Christian Science Monitor*, 6 February 1991: 10). Soviet children were treated for cancer, skin diseases, and other reactions (GI 26 July 1992: 3; see also GWR 24 January 1991: 11).

31. GWR 29 January 1989: 6.

32. GWR 2 September 1990: 9.

33. GI 18 August 1993: 3.

34. GI 5 July 1992: 3.

35. Felipe, "La ayuda económica de Cuba al Tercer Mundo," 18.

36. Ibid., 15.

37. GWR 11 November 1990: 2.

38. *EIU, Cuba Quarterly Economic Review no. 4* (1979): 7.

39. GWR 13 February 1983: 3.

40. Educational aid to Nicaragua ended at the same time that medical aid continued. The different sectoral receptivity to foreign aid under the Violeta Barrios de Chamorro government was a by-product of Nicaraguan domestic politics, not Cuban overseas assistance policy. Until 1993 the ministers of education and health in the Central American country differed in their political leanings. The education minister was especially conservative.

41. Felipe, "La ayuda económica de Cuba al Tercer Mundo," 15. As of 1989 over 5,000 foreign students attained university degrees in Cuba; the other students attended lower levels of the education system.

42. GI 21 August 1992: 3.

43. GWR 22 January 1989: 7.

44. Feinsilver, "Cuba as a 'World Medical Power,'" 15 n. 84.

45. GWR 7 May 1989: 3.

46. Roca, "Economic Aspects of Cuban Involvement in Africa," 60.

47. GWR 16 November 1980: 12; GWR 23 November 1980: 8, and 21 December 1980: 12.

48. Stubbs, *Cuba: The Test of Time*, 105.

49. Ratliff, "Fidel Castro's Crusade in the Caribbean Basin," 80.

50. GWR 22 July 1990: 4.

51. GWR 7 May 1989: 3.

52. GI 12 March 1992: 11. On early 1990s sports internationalism see CB October 1992: 7, and EIU, *Cuba Country Report* no. 4 (1992): 14.

53. GWR 20 July 1986: 9.

54. Ibid.

55. GWR 3 August 1986: 7.

56. Castro sent Chamorro's anti-Sandinista government a medical brigade to help stave off an epidemic after heavy rains in 1990, and the following year

Cuban specialists conducted more than 375,000 medical exams. GWR 9 September 1990: 9; GI 2 February 1992: 3.

57. EIU, *Cuba Quarterly Economic Report* no. 1 (1985): 16 and 9; Ratliff, "Fidel Castro's Crusade in the Caribbean Basin," 80.

58. Erisman, *Cuba's International Relations*, 146.

59. EIU, *Cuba Quarterly Economic Report* no. 1 (1985): 9; GWR 4 November 1990: 3.

60. Cited in Erisman, *Cuba's International Relations*, 3.

61. Wayne Smith, "U.S.-Cuba Relations: Twenty-Five years of Hostility," in *Twenty-Five Years of Revolution, 1959–84*, ed. Sandor Halebsky and John Kirk (New York: Praeger, 1985), 338.

62. Juan del Aguila, *Cuba: Dilemmas of a Revolution* (Boulder, Colo.: Westview, 1984), 111.

63. Fidel Castro, "Cuba's Internationalist Volunteers in Angola," *New International* 2, no. 2 (Fall 1985): 121, 173.

64. See, for example, LeoGrande, "Cuban-Soviet Relations and Cuban Policy in Africa," 80; William Durch, "The Cuban Military in Africa and the Middle East," Occasional Paper no. 201 (Arlington, Va.: Center for Naval Analysis, 1977); Jorge Domínguez, "The Cuban Operation in Angola: Costs and Benefits for the Armed Forces," *Cuban Studies/Estudios Cubanos* (January 1978): 10–20; Cole Blasier, "The Soviet Union in the Cuban-American Conflict," in *Cuba in the World*, ed. Blasier and Mesa-Lago, 40; Edward González, "Comment: Operational Goals of Cuban Policy in Africa," *Cuban Studies/Estudios Cubanos* 10 (January 1980): 43–48; Gordon Adams, "Cuba and Africa: The International Politics of Liberation Struggle—A Documentary Essay," *Latin American Perspectives* (Winter 1981): 109–12.

65. LeoGrande, "Cuban-Soviet Relations and Cuban Policy in Africa," 172; and Durch, "The Cuban Military in Africa and the Middle East," 46–47.

66. Erisman, *Cuba's International Relations*, 4.

67. Personal interview, Havana, July 1992.

68. EIU *Cuba Quarterly Economic Report* no. 1 (1986): 9.

69. Carlos Moore, *Castro, the Blacks, and Africa* (Los Angeles: Center for Afro-American Studies, University of California, 1988).

70. Personal communication, Christopher C. Wren (of the *New York Times*, then in Johannesburg). The government tested all high-risk subpopulations for AIDS. Twenty-five percent of all known cases were contracted abroad as of May 1992, most probably in Africa (Julie Feinsilver, personal communication, June 1992).

71. Sergei Tagor, *"Perestroika" and Soviet–Latin American Relations*, Working Paper no. 190 (Washington, D.C.: Woodrow Wilson Center for Scholars, Latin American Program, 1991).

72. Fidel Castro, *History Will Absolve Me* (New York: Lyle Stuart, 1961), 36.

73. Del Aguila, *Cuba: Dilemmas of a Revolution*, 103, 126.

74. Ibid., 103

75. See *Statutes of the Communist Party of Cuba* (Havana: Political Publishing House, 1981).

76. GI 19 July 1992: 4.

77. Castro, "Cuba's Internationalist Volunteers in Angola," 119.

78. GI 9 June 1991: 3.

79. LeoGrande, "Cuban-Soviet Relations and Cuban Policy in Africa," 23.

80. González, "Comment," 44; Roca, "Economic Aspects of Cuban Involvement in Africa," 60–63; LeoGrande, "Cuban-Soviet Relations and Cuban Policy in Africa," 9.

81. The Soviet Union raised the price when the value of sugar in the world market spiraled, as noted in chapter 2.

82. For an earlier discussion of mine on Cuba's hard currency internationalism see Susan Eckstein, "Structural and Ideological Bases of Cuba's Overseas Programs," *Politics and Society* 11, no. 1 (1982): 95–121.

83. Lawrence Theriot and Jenelle Matheson, "Soviet Economic Relations with Non-European CMEA: Cuba, Vietnam, and Mongolia," in Joint Economic Committee, *Soviet Economy in a Time of Change* (Washington, D.C.: GPO, 1979), 556, 567; Roca, "Economic Aspects of Cuban Involvement in Africa," 66.

84. Lawrence Theriot, "1980 Estimated Cuban Hard Currency Income" (U.S. Department of Commerce, International Trade Administration, Department of East-West Trade, typescript, 1981).

85. Theriot, "1980 Estimated Cuban Hard Currency Income," and Theriot, personal communication.

86. *New York Times*, 3 October 1981: 20; Carmelo Mesa-Lago, "Cuba's Centrally Planned Economy: An Equity Trade-Off for Growth," in *Latin American Political Economy: Financial Crisis and Political Change*, ed. Jonathan Hartlyn and Samuel Morley (Boulder, Colo.: Westview, 1986), 303.

87. EIU, *Cuba Country Report* no. 2 (1988): 9, and no. 3 (1988): 2; and *Cuba Country Profile 1987–88*, 19. Without presenting figures, Juan Benemelis, in "Cuba's African Policy," in *Cuba: The International Dimension*, ed. Fauriol and Loser, 149, also claims that Cuba earned currency for its military operations in Angola.

88. Some sources claim, however, that Cuba received little if any compensation in the mid-1980s. See Gillian Gunn, "Cuba and Angola," in *Cuba: The International Dimension*, ed. Fauriol and Loser, 166–67, and the references therein.

89. Felipe, "La ayuda económica de Cuba al Tercer Mundo," 15.

90. Personal interview, Havana, June 1993. UNECA also built projects free of charge, such as the Grenadian airport.

91. Feinsilver, "Cuba as a 'World Medical Power,'" 19.

92. GI 25 April 1993: 10.

93. GWR 27 February 1983: 9.

94. GWR 23 April 1989: 3.

95. Armando Entralgo and David González López, "Cuban Policy for Africa," in *U.S.-Cuban Relations in the 1990s*, ed. Jorge Domínguez and Rafael Hernández (Boulder, Colo.: Westview, 1989), 145.

96. GWR 3 April 1983: 12; EIU, *Cuba Quarterly Economic Report* no. 1 (1985): 16.

97. Cuba, Comité Estatal de Estadísticas (CEE), *Anuario Estadístico de Cuba 1989* (Havana: CEE, 1991), 254.

98. Jorge Domínguez, *To Make a World Safe for Revolution* (Cambridge: Harvard University Press, 1989), 234.

99. CEE, *Anuario Estadístico de Cuba 1989*, 254.

100. Ibid., 252–55.
101. Ratliff, "Fidel Castro's Crusade in the Caribbean Basin," 83–84.
102. CB December 1992: 2.
103. GI 10 May 1992: 4.
104. GI 23 February 1992: 12.
105. EIU, *Cuba Country Report* no. 2 (1991): 15.
106. Some of the exports, though, were donations.
107. Domínguez, *To Make a World Safe for Revolution*, 234.
108. EIU, *Cuba Quarterly Economic Report* no. 1 (1985): 14.
109. CB October 1987: 7; EIU, *Cuba Country Report* no. 2 (1993): 18.
110. CB October 1987: 7.
111. EIU, *Cuba Country Report* no. 2 (1993): 18.
112. EIU, *Cuba Quarterly Economic Report* no. 2 (1984): 11.
113. CB April 1988: 6.
114. See Feinsilver, *Healing the Masses*, 182–95.
115. GI 17 May 1992: 6. The vaccine sold to Brazil was found to be ineffective in children less than four years old and only 75 percent effective in older children (CB March 1993: 7).
116. GI 15 May 1991: 13.
117. EIU, *Cuba Country Report* no. 4 (1992): 18.
118. CB December 1987: 3, 15.
119. GI 12 May 1991: 12.
120. GWR 23 April 1989: 3. CenterSoft negotiated contracts with both Western and Eastern European countries.
121. CB December 1987: 3.
122. CB April 1988: 6.
123. Ibid., 5, 6.
124. GWR 23 April 1989: 3; GWR 10 May 1987: 9; GWR 27 August 1989: 1, and 6 August 1989: 1; CB October 1987: 15, and October 1988: 2.
125. CB October 1989: 14.
126. Patients came from South America and Europe. On health tourism see Oppenheimer, *Castro's Final Hour*, 298, and Feinsilver, *Healing the Masses*, esp. 213–14.
127. EIU, *Cuba Country Report* no. 2 (1988): 12.
128. GWR 25 May 1986: 5. See also GWR 21 May 1989: 4.
129. GI 30 June 1993: 12, and 7 July 1993: 3; EIU, *Cuba Country Report* no. 2 (1993): 13; and CB March 1993: 7.
130. GWR 11 June 1989: 4.
131. GWR 16 December 1990: 3, and 30 June 1993: 7.
132. GWR 11 June 1986: 1.
133. *Boston Globe*, 21 February 1993: 75.
134. Ibid.
135. Felipe, "La ayuda económica de Cuba al Tercer Mundo," 16, 18.
136. Ibid., 16.
137. James Wilkie, *Statistical Abstract of Latin America* 19 (Los Angeles: University of California, Latin American Center, 1978), 144.
138. Jorge Domínguez, "Political and Military Limitations and Consequences," *Cuban Studies/Estudios Cubanos* 10, no. 2 (July 1980): 23.

139. Domínguez, "The Cuban Operation in Angola," 14.

140. See Roca, "Economic Aspects of Cuban Involvement in Africa."

141. Pérez-López, "Comment," 83.

142. Jorge Pérez-López, "Cuba's Foreign Economic Relationships,"in *Cuba: The International Dimension*, ed. Fauriol and Loser, 338.

143. See Roca, "Economic Aspects of Cuban Involvement in Africa," 75; Carmelo Mesa-Lago, "The Economy and International Relations," in *Cuba in the World*, ed. Blasier and Mesa-Lago, 178; Cole Blasier, "Comment: The Consequences of Military Initiatives," *Cuban Studies/Estudios Cubanos* 10 (January 1980): 38; Domínguez, "Political and Military Limitations and Consequences of Cuban Policies in Africa," 25.

144. U.S. disinterest in normalizing relations with Cuba picked up also because a plunge in world sugar prices caused Cuba's hard currency import capacity, including of U.S. goods through third countries, to contract and because Carter tried to appease the Right as the 1980 election neared (and Reagan was his Republican opponent).

145. Carmelo Mesa-Lago, "The Economy: Caution, Frugality, and Resilient Ideology," in *Cuba: Internal and International Affairs*, ed. Jorge Domínguez, 140; EIU, *Cuba Quarterly Economic Report* no. 3 (1978): 4, 5.

146. Oppenheimer, *Castro's Final Hour*, 141.

147. Ibid., 77–79.

148. *Boston Globe*, 13 March 1984: 1, 6.

149. *Granma*, for example, reported that 300,000 persons had expressed willingness to go to Angola and Ethiopia, that some 30,000 teachers had offered to go to Nicaragua when Castro called for volunteers, that nearly all primary school teachers under thirty-five years of age volunteered to work in Nicaragua when several island teachers there were murdered by anti-Sandinistas, and that thousands of Cubans volunteered for construction projects in the Central American country when the Bluefields region was hit by Hurricane Joan in 1987. CB August 1989: 2.

150. GI 10 November 1991: 4.

151. Domínguez, *To Make a World Safe for Revolution*, 281.

152. Jorge Domínguez, colloquium on Cuba, Center for International Affairs, Harvard University, Cambridge, Mass., October 1991.

153. GWR 17 December 1989: 1.

154. CB June 1993: 6, 7.

155. GI 11 August 1991: 14.

CHAPTER EIGHT
THE RELEVANCE OF THE REVOLUTION

1. *Philadelphia Inquirer*, 13 August 1993: 21.

2. A conference at Florida International University in the spring of 1993 on *lo informal* began to give recognition to this important underanalyzed aspect of Cuban society. A paper related to this project was presented by Damián Fernández ("Formality and Informality in Cuban Politics") at the Latin American Studies Association meeting, Los Angeles, September 1993. Also, Carollee Bengelsdorf, in *The Problem of Democracy in Cuba: Between Vision and Reality*

(New York: Oxford University Press, 1994), examines the tension between political, ideological, and social dynamics during different periods under Castro.

3. *Granma International* (hereafter, GI), 28 March 1993: 8.

4. László Bruszt and David Stark, "Remaking the Political Field in Hungary: From the Politics of Confrontation to the Politics of Competition," *Journal of International Affairs* 45, no. 1 (Summer 1991): 201–45.

5. Americas Watch, *Dangerous Dialogue: Attacks on Freedom of Expression in Miami's Cuban Exile Community* (Washington, D.C.: Americas Watch, August 1992).

6. The violent interethnic conflicts in post-Communist Yugoslavia suggest that organizational vitality in civil society may be necessary but not sufficient for a peaceful democratic transition. If organizational ties reinforce ethnic divisions, they may be divisive for democracy.

7. A negotiation of the lifting of the embargo might include insistence on Cuba releasing political prisoners, termination of other human rights abuses, and settlement of claims of businesses nationalized in Castro's first years of rule. While a multiparty system could give political voice to groups and constituencies unrepresented in Castro's Cuba, U.S. insistence on it may serve to entangle the United States in Cuban domestic politics.

8. On Eastern European strategies see Oliver Blanchard et al., *Reform in Eastern Europe* (Cambridge: MIT Press, 1991).

9. For a discussion of Cuban economic alternatives and likely outcomes, see Eliana Cardoso and Ann Helwege, *Cuba After Communism* (Cambridge: MIT Press, 1992).

INDEX

abortions, 139
Abrantes, José, 84–85
absenteeism, xii, 10, 11, 36, 40, 44, 48, 57, 65, 74, 83, 87, 126, 211
Academy of Sciences, 26
accommodationist policy, 14
acopio (subsidized) outlets, 66
acquired immune deficiency syndrome (AIDS), 185, 194
actos de repudio, 118
Afghanistan, 191
Afinco, 70
Africa: Cuban civilian assistance in, 176, 179, 180, 181; Cuban military in, 93, 172–73, 181, 183, 200, 202
African and Carribean Studies Centers, 25
Afro-Cuban culture, 4, 16, 25, 122, 211
Agency for International Development (AID), U.S., 175
agrarian reform, 15, 31, 33–34, 36, 38, 152
agricultural brigades. See *contingentes*
agricultural productivity, 81, 96–97
agro-industrial complexes, 45, 162
agromercados (produce markets), 66
Alamar, 159
Aldana, Carlos, 119, 121, 214
Algeria, 172, 176, 190–93
Alice in Wondertown (film), 119
Allende, Salvador, 173
Alvardo, Gen. Juan Velasco, 173
Americas Watch, 215
ANAP. See National Small Peasants Association (ANAP)
Angola, 172–73, 176, 177, 179–81, 183–85, 187, 189–93, 195, 198, 200–202
antiloafing law (1971), 44, 48
architecture, 154
Argentina, 173
arson, 10
Artex, 69
athletes, as role models, 24

bagasse, 81
balseros (rafters), 121
Banco Financiero, 70, 71, 104
Baraguá Protest, 110, 114
Barbara (saint), 4

bateyes (mobile populations), 152
Batista y Zaldívar, Fulgencio, 14–19, 130
Bay of Pigs invasion, 22, 29, 110, 187
Beatles, 25
Belize, 192
Benetton, 104
bicycles, 112, 123, 135
biotechnology, 106–7, 132, 194
birth control, 139
Bishop, Maurice, 174, 176, 177, 180, 184
black-market activities, xii, 10, 12, 40–41, 50, 54, 78, 84, 109, 122, 124–25, 200, 211
blacks: and black separatism, 25; political participation of, 28, 187
Blas Roca construction contingent, 64, 101
boat people, 121. *See also* Mariel mass emigration (1980)
Bohemia (magazine), 113, 120
bolas (rumors), 120
Bolivia, 172, 177
Boorstein, Edward, 37
bourgeoisie. *See* petty bourgeoisie
Brazil, 132, 192–95
Brezhnev, Leonid, 91, 210
Bulgaria, 89
bureaucracy: control of, 9, 21, 27; dissatisfaction with, 120; postrevolutionary reform of, 34–35, 38, 40; rectification of errors in, 65–66, 67, 84–86; during "retreat to socialism," 44; during Special Period in Peacetime, 114
Burnham, Forbes, 177, 180, 195
Bush, George, 6, 93–94, 106, 200, 210
businesses, nationalization of, 34, 38, 153

Camaguey, 165, 167
campaign to rectify errors and negative tendencies, xvi, 12, 13, 60–87, 163–65
Canada, 94, 200
cancer, 142
Candidacy Commissions, 116–17
candles, 113
CANF. *See* Cuban-American National Foundation (CANF)
Cape Verde, 177
capitalism, 7, 102–3, 127